Electronic Discourse in Language Learning and Language Teaching

Language Learning & Language Teaching (LL<)

The LL< monograph series publishes monographs, edited volumes and text books on applied and methodological issues in the field of language pedagogy. The focus of the series is on subjects such as classroom discourse and interaction; language diversity in educational settings; bilingual education; language testing and language assessment; teaching methods and teaching performance; learning trajectories in second language acquisition; and written language learning in educational settings.

Editors

Nina Spada
Ontario Institute for Studies in Education,
University of Toronto

Nelleke Van Deusen-Scholl
Center for Language Study
Yale University

Volume 25

Electronic Discourse in Language Learning and Language Teaching
Edited by Lee B. Abraham and Lawrence Williams

Electronic Discourse in Language Learning and Language Teaching

Edited by

Lee B. Abraham
Villanova University

Lawrence Williams
University of North Texas

John Benjamins Publishing Company
Amsterdam / Philadelphia

Library of Congress Cataloging-in-Publication Data

Electronic discourse in language learning and language teaching / edited by Lee B. Abraham, Lawrence Williams.

p.   cm. (Language Learning & Language Teaching, ISSN 1569-9471 ; v. 25)

Includes bibliographical references and index.

1. Language and languages--Study and teaching--Computer network resources. 2. Language and languages--Computer-assisted instruction. 3. Second language acquisition. 4. Human-computer interaction. I. Abraham, Lee B. II. Williams, Lawrence.

P53.285.E44   2009

418'.002854678--dc22   2009025636

ISBN 978 90 272 1988 6 (HB; alk. paper) / ISBN 978 90 272 1300 6 (PB; alk. paper)

ISBN 978 90 272 9055 7 (EB)

John Benjamins Publishing Co. · P.O. Box 36224 · 1020 ME Amsterdam · The Netherlands

John Benjamins North America · P.O. Box 27519 · Philadelphia PA 19118-0519 · USA

Table of contents

About the contributors

Lee B. Abraham is Assistant Professor of Spanish in the Department of Romance Languages and Literatures at Villanova University, where he teaches courses in applied linguistics and Spanish. His research interests include the use of new technologies in language learning and teaching, language variation in Spanish, and sociolinguistic approaches to second language acquisition.
E-mail: lee.abraham@villanova.edu

Géraldine Blattner is Assistant Professor of French and Linguistics in the Department of Languages, Linguistics and Comparative Literature at Florida Atlantic University. Her research focuses on technology-enhanced foreign language learning and sociolinguistic and pragmatic variation in French-language computer-mediated discourse.
E-mail: gblattne@fau.edu

Kate Douglass is Assistant Professor of French and Language Acquisition in the Department of Modern Languages and Literatures at the State University of New York at Fredonia. She is the Program Coordinator for Adolescence Education in French and Spanish, and she teaches courses in French, language acquisition, applied linguistics, and pedagogy. Her research focuses on study abroad, the development of language learning motives, and new technologies in foreign language education.
E-mail: kate.douglass@fredonia.edu

Kathleen Farrell Whitworth is Lecturer in the Department of French, Italian, and Comparative Literature at the University of Wisconsin-Milwaukee, where she teaches courses in applied linguistics and French. Her research interests include second language acquisition, language development during study abroad, and language socialization.
E-mail: ktfw@uwm.edu

Lina Lee is Associate Professor of Spanish at the University of New Hampshire where she teaches courses in second language acquisition, applied linguistics and foreign language methodology. She has conducted research and published articles on language pedagogy, oral assessment, computer-mediated communication and discourse analysis in *Foreign Language Annals*, *Hispania*, *CALICO*, *Language Learning & Technology*, *ReCALL*, *System* and *NECTFL Review*.
E-mail: lina.lee@unh.edu

Heather Lotherington is Professor of Multilingual Education at York University in Toronto (Ontario, Canada), where she teaches multimodal, linguistically inclusive language and literacy education in the Faculty of Education and the Department of Linguistics. Her research focus is on multimodal literacies in urban, multicultural settings, and her research includes numerous collaborations in varied educational contexts, investigating and designing socially appropriate, culturally relevant and linguistically responsive language and literacy education.
E-mail: hlotherington@edu.yorku.ca

Kara McBride is a teacher trainer and Assistant Professor of Spanish at Saint Louis University. Her research interests include computer-assisted language learning (CALL), the belief systems of foreign language students and new teachers, grammar teaching in a communicative context, and speech production and comprehension.
E-mail: kmcbrid8@slu.edu

Eduardo Negueruela-Azarola is Assistant Professor of Spanish Second Language Acquisition and Director of the Spanish Basic Language Program in the Department of Modern Languages and Literatures at the University of Miami, where he teaches courses in foreign language teaching methodology, Spanish second language acquisition, Sociocultural Theory and second language learning, and advanced writing, reading, and grammar courses in Spanish. His research program explores the connection between mind, language, and culture through the creation of semiotic artifacts that mediate first and second language development.
E-mail: enegueruela@miami.edu

Deanna Neville-Verardi is a high school teacher of technology with the Simcoe-Muskoka Catholic District School Board in Central Ontario (Canada), which borders the Greater Toronto Area to the north. She is a graduate of the Master of Education program at York University, where she studied digital epistemologies. She continues to implement emerging technologies in her teaching practice and contributes to a variety of research projects in multimodal literacies.
E-mail: dneville@smcdsb.on.ca

Janel Pettes Guikema is Associate Professor of French at Grand Valley State University in Allendale, Michigan. She teaches French at all levels of the undergraduate curriculum as well as methodology of foreign language teaching. Her research interests focus on technology-enhanced language learning, literacy development, and foreign language teacher preparation.
E-mail: pettesj@gvsu.edu

Isabelle Pierozak is maître de conférences in Language Sciences at the Université François Rabelais – Tours, where she teaches courses in sociolinguistics and didactics in the Department Sodilang (SOciolinguistique et DIdactique des LANGues). Her research takes place in EA 4246 DYNADIV (DYNAmiques et enjeux de la DIVersité). She focuses on the use of electronic community spaces in various contexts (particularly in didactics) and within a qualitative approach.
E-mail: isabelle.pierozak@univ-tours.fr

Natalia Sinitskaya Ronda is a PhD candidate at the Faculty of Education at York University (Ontario, Canada). In her research, Natalia investigates emergent digital literacies. Her dissertation focuses on the informal literacy practices that are forming within online social networks such as Facebook, and on the conceptualization of these networks as digital spaces for literacy development. Her other research interests include research ethics in online environments, language change on the Internet, online cultures, and gaming in education.
E-mail: natalia_sinitskaya@edu.yorku.ca

Susana M. Sotillo is Associate Professor of Linguistics at Montclair State University in Northern New Jersey. Her research interests include the language of SMS text messages, computer-mediated communication and second language acquisition, and the use of hybrid approaches to content and language teaching. Currently she is examining the linguistic features of a large SMS corpus and exploring the use of text messaging as a mode of communication in local communities for educational and crime-prevention purposes.
E-mail: sotillos@mail.montclair.edu

Rémi A. van Compernolle is a PhD student in the Department of Applied Linguistics at The Pennsylvania State University, where he works as a research assistant for the Center for Language Acquisition. His research focuses on language variation in computer-mediated French discourse, sociocultural and sociolinguistic approaches to language learning, and the use of technology as a tool for communication in second language education.
E-mail: rav137@psu.edu

Lawrence Williams is Associate Professor of French and a Faculty Fellow in the Transformative Instruction Initiative at the University of North Texas, where he teaches courses in applied linguistics and French in the Department of Foreign Languages and Literatures. His research focuses on the use of new technologies as tools for communication and language learning in both educational and non-educational contexts.
E-mail: lawrence.williams@unt.edu

Introduction

Analyzing and exploring electronic discourse

Lee B. Abraham and Lawrence Williams

1.   Aims and scope of the volume

This volume addresses some of the fundamental issues recently identified as essential for language learning and teaching with computer-mediated communication (CMC) technologies. Over the last two decades, the growth of the Internet and the evolution of CMC technologies have expanded opportunities for communicating in other languages beyond the traditional educational setting to communities comprised of participants living all around the world. However, researchers have only begun to identify and analyze the communicative practices and literacies involved in using new and ever-changing CMC tools and participating in global communication spaces. Kern (2006) has recently identified three areas of research that deserve greater attention:

a.   … what successful participation means in different contexts (e.g., different CMC contexts, different cross-cultural contexts, different pedagogical contexts),
b.   the importance of the personal in intercultural projects – learners' sensitivity to one another's cultural identities and communicative styles, and
c.   the importance of teacher involvement in discerning, explaining, and reflecting on culturally contingent patterns of interaction with their students (p. 200).

These suggested areas of inquiry, along with our own experiences using new technologies in both educational and non-educational contexts, have provided our project with a great deal of direction at various stages of the process of developing, organizing, and preparing this volume.

The importance placed on understanding both the contexts and the patterns of communication mentioned by Kern has also been emphasized by Chapelle (2003), who suggests that research in CMC should also carefully analyze the contexts of communication, registers, pragmatic knowledge, and knowledge of the discursive and interactional features of communication in technology-mediated environments (p. 18). It is also important to point out that the social and linguistic practices of online communities (i.e., environments) are shaped by users for particular purposes with specific participants in different contexts (Lam, 2004; Thorne, 2003, 2008). As such, understanding how participants shape the discourse of these communities (e.g., chat, discussion forums, blogs, and so forth) is also of fundamental interest for research on existing, emerging, and future CMC tools.

2.   Organization of the volume

The studies presented in this volume offer insights and analyses into new types of literacies as well as a range of interactional and linguistic features of computer-mediated communication and discourse in English, French, and Spanish. However, the approaches to analyzing online communication and discourse in these languages will, in many cases, be adaptable to other languages. Although the volume is organized by type of technology and includes analyses of English, French, and Spanish, each chapter presents a different approach to understanding selected features that characterize, to varying degrees, each particular communication space. As such, the reader may find that an approach used in one chapter for a particular CMC tool or in one specific language may be readily applicable to another technology or even future CMC tools.

2.1   Part I: New literacies

This part of the volume includes three chapters that examine new types of literacies. We had originally labeled this section as electronic literacy after many discussions about the volume during which we had considered terms such as digital, information, computer, and Internet to describe the types of literacies involved in using new technologies for language teaching, language learning, communication, information retrieval, and so forth. However, it eventually became obvious that all these labels could be used to describe the various literacies that are involved in both instructional and non-instructional activities and contexts.[1] Our use of literacies follows the reasoning outlined by Lankshear and Knobel (2008):

---

1.   For treatments of the terminology and concepts associated with different types of literacies, see Bawden (2008), Lankshear and Knobel (2008, pp. 2–4), Lotherington et al. (this volume), and Murray (2005, pp. 188–191).

We believe it is important to emphasize the plurality of digital literacies because of:
- the sheer diversity of specific accounts of "digital literacy" that exist, and consequent implications of that for digital literacy policies;
- the strength and usefulness of a sociocultural perspective on literacy as practice, according to which literacy is best understood as literacies (Street, 1984; Lankshear, 1987; Gee, 1996). By extension, then, digital literacy can usefully be understood as digital *literacies* – in the plural;
- the benefits that may accrue from adopting an expansive view of digital literacies and their significance for educational learning. (p. 2)

From a sociocultural perspective on literacies, then, it is possible that a single activity might require the knowledge, skills, and framing associated with traditional notions of literacy as well as those that are associated with computer literacy or information literacy. "Engaging in these situated practices where we make meanings by relating texts to larger ways of doing and being is engaging in literacy – or, more accurately, *literacies*, since we are all apprenticed to more than one" (Lankshear & Knobel, p. 7).

In the title of this section of the volume, we have used *new* to describe or qualify the types of literacies treated in these three chapters; however, we recognize that focusing on the learning, teaching, and fostering of new literacies does not imply that *old* (i.e., offline) literacies no longer have a role in (foreign language) education. Likewise, we realize that although *literacies* in the plural might be the preferred form for many reasons, the mere use of *literacy* in the singular – by educators, learners, or researchers – should not be taken to imply that those who use the singular form do not acknowledge or understand the multiple dimensions of (any type of) literacy or literacies. Nonetheless, it seems reasonable to suggest that using *digital literacies* "allows for the kinds of analysis of social practices that identify key points at which effective learning is triggered within efficient socio-technical learning systems as well as key learning principles that can be adapted and leveraged for equitable educational learning" (Lankshear & Knobel, 2008, p. 14).

In the first chapter of this volume, Lotherington, Neville-Verardi, and Ronda address the divergences of literacy assessment and new literacy practices of teenagers in the greater Toronto area (Ontario, Canada). The authors compare the Ontario Secondary School Literacy Test (OSSLT) and a mock version of the test including multimodal activities that reflect many new literacy practices of the students in order to demonstrate the rather limited scope of the OSSLT and the discrimination created by this high-stakes assessment tool. Focus group interviews with students who had taken the OSSLT revealed that they were all highly proficient and critical users of new technologies, even those who had failed the OSSLT. This chapter serves as a stark reminder that stakeholders (i.e., students, parents, educators, politicians) need to (re)examine assessment practices continually, especially when the results have such important consequences in students' lives.

The next chapter in this section examines the navigation and interpretation of French-language hypertext in order to show the complexities of finding one's way around the Web. Although hypertext was originally mainly text, it now includes text as well as images, and the notion of the "page" has evolved to include pop-up windows, dynamic areas of pages created with Adobe Flash, and embedded advertisements. Moreover, new types of discourse and communication environments (e.g., podcasts, blogs, discussion forums, etc.) are housed on and integrated into hypertext-based webpages, which has increased the levels and paths available for navigation. The analysis of conflicting, contradictory uses of the French second-person pronouns *tu* and *vous* within and among webpages reveals some challenges associated with navigating and interpreting hypertext, and the study also reveals the challenges faced by designers of websites and those who prepare content for them.

The final chapter in this section explores the quality of translated sentences produced by some online translation sites that seem to be popular among (U.S.) students. Students worked in dyads to identify problems in the translated sentences and then improve the sentences. This task could have been designed, for example, as peer-editing of a writing assignment; however, the use of software-produced translated sentences provided students with opportunities to evaluate the advantages and weaknesses of machine-translated text. Therefore, while the students were focusing on both form and meaning for one part of the task, they were also shown how to evaluate the quality of any online software site they may consider using in the future.

2.2   Part II: Chat

In the next section of this volume, there are three studies of synchronous chat in public and private (i.e., instant messaging) environments. Sotillo's study extends learning beyond a formal instructional context by pairing up tutors and learners of English who communicate through an instant messaging application that allows both text- and voice-based chat. The results of Sotillo's analysis focusing on noticing, negative feedback, and uptake suggest, among other things, that having the capability of using both text- and voice-based chat (in addition to the occasional use of a webcam) provides students with additional opportunities and means for negotiation work and noticing linguistic forms or unknown lexical items.

The next chapter in this section analyzes language variation in two different types of public French-language chat, namely moderated and non-moderated. van Compernolle and Pierozak focus on features that manifest themselves in different forms and structures (i.e., spelling, pronouns, and the negative particle *ne*) depending on socio-contextual factors. In addition to demonstrating stark contrasts between moderated and non-moderated chat, the authors provide guidelines for introducing the analysis of chat discourse in a pedagogical context.

In the final chapter of this part of the volume, Lee presents a study of non-native speakers of Spanish paired with native speakers for synchronous chat meetings. The analysis highlights additional dimensions of communication that would not normally emerge in learner-to-learner interaction. The results suggest that students had opportunities to engage in negotiation of meaning in different ways, and at the same time, these interactions amplified their awareness and lack of awareness of certain pragmatic features of communication. This chapter also offers practical insights on implementing telecollaboration projects.

2.3   Part III: Podcasts

As the heading of this section indicates, the chapters in this part of the volume focus on podcasts and podcasting. In these chapters, listening comprehension is an obvious link that provides the overarching theme, yet each author focuses on different aspects of podcasts and the potential for integrating them into the foreign language curriculum. These chapters provide analyses of podcasts that were not created for pedagogical purposes. As such, the goal of these studies is to provide learners (and teachers) with analytical tools that they could use and develop when they explore podcasts on their own even after they are no longer students in the formal sense (i.e., enrolled in a language course).

The first chapter of this part of the volume explores English-language podcasts and podcasting. McBride defines and provides an overview of podcasts and the development of podcasting over the past few years. This chapter also provides numerous resources for teachers and students as well as recommendations for designing and implementing listening comprehension tasks based on authentic podcasts. McBride offers a flexible model for incorporating podcasts into the curriculum, depending on whether the teacher and/or the students will be responsible for finding and analyzing podcasts. Such flexibility allows the ideas in the chapter to be adaptable to any level of learning or any particular institutional context.

In the other chapter of this section, the focus shifts toward a closer analysis of selected aspects of the discourse of podcasts in French. This chapter by Guikema examines the discourse of the news archive podcast in order to demonstrate features commonly associated with scripted vs. non-scripted speech. Learners who analyze this genre of podcast – initially, perhaps, with the guidance of a teacher – will eventually discover that even though the news flash (or an excerpt of it) is a relatively short audio text, it can be very difficult to understand because of the wide range of registers or levels of speech in addition to the frequent use of both embedded and overt social and cultural references.

2.4   Part IV: Blogs and blogging

This first chapter in this part of the volume provides an analysis of interactional and discursive features of English-language blogs that were not created for pedagogical purposes. Some of the blogs selected for this corpus-driven study are personal (i.e., individual), and others are for commercial purposes. After presenting a comparison of these two types of blogs, van Compernolle and Abraham outline Herring's (2007) faceted classification scheme as a first level of analysis that can be used by learners. Additional pedagogical recommendations are provided based on the pedagogical framework of multiliteracies proposed by the New London Group (1996).

In the next chapter, Douglass examines blogs on a wide variety of topics in francophone cyberspace. This analysis is based on the dubious supposition by a popular French blogger that members of the blogging community (if such a thing exists as a singular, monolithic group) all use *tu* (the singular, informal French second-person pronoun) when addressing each other. Therefore, the analysis by Douglass focuses on the use of *tu* and the other French second-person pronoun, *vous*, which can be used for plural or singular-formal address. The findings reveal great diversity of French second-person pronoun use. This confirms the complexity of the pronoun paradigm and indicates that learners who memorize rules (e.g., *tu* for people you know and *vous* for people you do not know) will remain largely ignorant of sociopragmatic features of French that are important for interpersonal communication.

In the final chapter of this part of the volume, Negueruela-Azarola explores the rich variety and multidimensionality of Spanish-language blogs. This analysis posits the metaphors of expansion (or amplification; see Pea, 1985) and reorganization for understanding blogs, and the author proposes three types of pedagogical opportunities for L2 learners: (1) blogs as texts (i.e., artifacts); (2) blogs as psychological tools; and (3) blogs as communication. The analysis in this chapter is based on a view that recognizes blogs and blogging as components of sociocultural human activity.

2.5   Part V: Discussion forums

The first two chapters in this part of the volume include analyses of the social dimensions, structure, and discourse of online discussion forums in English (Whitworth) and French (Blattner & Williams). The chapter on English-language forums reveals some important differences between the traditional, offline notion of the Community of Practice (CoP) (Lave & Wenger, 1991) and the online CoP. It becomes clear through this chapter that the lack of a formal gatekeeping device in discussion forums leads to confusion and conflict among participants who seem to have differing views of what it means to be accepted as a "full" member of the community, which implies no longer being treated like a so-called newbie (i.e., a newcomer). Unlike the traditional CoP, which is based on an apprenticeship model of socially situated learning, the online CoP (in the case of the discussion forum) often provides rules for members, but the rules for all forums are not the same. Moreover, in the online CoP it is impossible to distinguish between members who have read and understood the rules vs. those who forget or choose to ignore them. Blattner and Williams demonstrate that there is also a great deal of variation among French-language forums; however, one main overarching concern in these forums is a preoccupation with "correct" spelling. They trace the lasting importance of this issue to the establishment of an e-roots (i.e., online or electronic grassroots) organization that was founded for the specific purpose of eradicating "voluntary" spelling mistakes (i.e., variation) on the Internet. These two chapters highlight, among other things, the importance of social aspects of communication and communities, even in online environments that have often been characterized as dehumanizing (Oberdiek & Tiles, 1995, pp. 21–28).

The final chapter in this section provides a model for using the discussion forum as a component of an Integrated Performance Assessment (IPA) (Glisan et al., 2003). Abraham and Williams highlight the flexibility of the discussion forum as a tool and environment for communication and language learning. They propose incorporating the discussion forum into the IPA either for the Interpretive Task or the Interpersonal Task. Such a technology-enhanced model of the IPA actually has great potential for extending any of its components beyond traditional classroom-based communicative activity.

3.   Acknowledgments

We are extremely grateful to the authors of the studies included in this volume who worked diligently through the proposal stage and the revision process. We truly appreciate Nina Spada and Nelleke Van Deusen-Scholl, the series editors, for their very insightful comments and suggestions. We also would like to extend our sincere appreciation to former series editor Jan Hulstijn, who reviewed the proposal and also served as an external reviewer of the entire manuscript. We would like to thank Kees Vaes, Acquisitions Editor, for his guidance and support as well as the entire John Benjamins staff. Lee Abraham would like to express his sincere gratitude to the Rev. Dr. Kail C. Ellis, O.S.A., Dean of the College of Liberal Arts and Sciences, and Dr. John R. Johannes, Vice President for Academic Affairs at Villanova University for awarding a semester leave to work on this volume.

References

Bawden, D. (2008). Origins and concepts of digital of digital literacy. In C. Lankshear & M. Knobel (Eds.), *Digital literacies: Concepts, policies and practices* (17–32). New York: Peter Lang.

Chapelle, C. A. (2003). *English language learning and technology*. Amsterdam: John Benjamins.

Glisan, E., Adair-Hauck, B., Koda, K., Sandrock, S. P., & Swender, E. (2003). *ACTFL Integrated Performance Assessment*. Yonkers, NY: ACTFL.

Kern, R. (2006). Perspectives on technology in learning and teaching languages. *TESOL Quarterly 40*, 183–210.

Lam, W. S. E. (2004). Second language socialization in a bilingual chat room: Global and local considerations. *Language Learning & Technology, 8*, 44–65. Available from http://llt.msu.edu/vol8num3/lam/default.html

Lankshear, C., & Knobel, M. (2008). Introduction: Digital literacies – concepts, policies and practicies. In C. Lankshear & M. Knobel (Eds.), *Digital literacies: Concepts, policies and practices* (pp. 1–16). New York: Peter Lang.

Murray, D. E. (2005). Technologies for second language literacy. *Annual Review of Applied Linguistics, 25*, 188–201.

Oberdiek, H., & Tiles, M. (1995). *Living in a technological culture: Human tools and human values*. London: Routledge.

Thorne, S. (2003). Artifacts and cultures-of-use in intercultural communication. *Language Learning & Technology, 7*, 38–67. Available from http://llt.msu.edu/vol7num2/thorne/

Thorne, S. (2008). Transcultural communication in open Internet environments and massively multiplayer online games. In S. Magnan (Ed.), *Mediating discourse online* (pp. 305–327). Amsterdam: John Benjamins.

PART I

New literacies

English in cyberspace

Negotiating digital literacies in a climate of educational accountability

Heather Lotherington, Deanna Neville-Verardi, and Natalia Sinitskaya Ronda

This chapter explores the educational gap between contemporary cyberspace communications that bring youth of diverse linguistic and cultural backgrounds together in an era of local-global synergies, and resources and approaches used in English language and literacy teaching and testing, and questions the political agenda to gate-keep restrictive literacy attainment which creates unhelpful divisions between L1 and L2 users. The authors raise relevant communicative issues for second language users in this discussion of contemporary digital genres and platforms that are growing in global popularity, such as contending with the shifting orthographic conventions used in digital conversations which at the same time facilitate conversational practice free from the stigma of an identifying "foreign" accent.

1.   Introduction

Over the past two decades, the rapid development of networked digital communications media has radically altered everyday literacies, introducing new social trends, cultural practices and linguistic norms that call into question the standards used to teach and test language and literacy in formal education. Educational practice has been slow to recognize that textual norms provide inadequate preparation for contemporary communication. Following Graddol's (1999) problematizing the hegemonic position of the native speaker in establishing language norms in a rapidly globalizing world, this study queries assumptions about authentic literacies in the 21st century, given the intercultural co-creation of online genres, and examines the legitimacy of monolingual print conventions underwriting definitions of literacy for the millennium learner.

In the Canadian province of Ontario, high school students, no matter what their linguistic profile, must successfully navigate the Ontario Secondary School Literacy Test (OSSLT), established by the Educational Quality and Accountability Office (EQAO), to be eligible for graduation. This chapter examines how this high stakes mandatory test is out of sync with contemporary literacy practices, and underlines its particular unfairness to English as a second language users. The chapter descriptively documents the English-medium digital literacies of two groups of teenagers living in the greater Toronto area (GTA) who wrote the OSSLT in different years, and analyzes their critical comments on the 2007 test, and on a mock literacy test that utilizes knowledge of digital literacies.

In the process, we explore and overview contemporary conceptions of literacy, discussing digital social networking interfaces that selectively engage novel orthographic, syntactic, and discursive values contributing to the emergence of a shifting, alternative standard of digital communication (see Baron, 2004; Crystal, 2006; Herring, 2004; Lotherington, 2005; Lotherington & Xu, 2004; Warschauer, 2006), and necessitate increased sensitivity to genre and platform-based language and literacy needs on the part of the user. We raise relevant communicative issues for second language users in this discussion of contemporary digital genres and platforms that are growing in global popularity, such as contending with the shifting orthographic conventions used in digital conversations which at the same time facilitate conversational practice free from the stigma of an identifying "foreign" accent.

The chapter addresses the educational gap between contemporary cyberspace communications that bring youth of diverse linguistic and cultural backgrounds together in an era of local-global synergies, and resources and approaches used in English language and literacy teaching and testing, and questions the political agenda to gate-keep restrictive literacy attainment which creates unhelpful divisions between L1 and L2 users. The study provides an important focus on and overview of new literacies and authentic communication in a post-industrial era.

2.   Background

Neoconservative political trends towards "accountability" in language and literacy education across North America, exemplified in such government institutions as No Child Left Behind (U.S. Dept. of Education, 2004) in the United States, and the Educational Quality and Accountability Office (EQAO/OQRE, 2006) in the Canadian province of Ontario, have instituted and promoted standardized test mechanisms to assess "literacy" attainment. As Kelly, Luke, and Green (2008) explain:

> [in] current debates between media and politicians, policymakers and researchers, disciplinary experts and educationists, questions about knowledge, or rather, knowledges, have been taken as given: that there is a corpus of "basic skills," core knowledges or competencies that have self-evident educational value; or the assumption that there is a corpus of canonical disciplinary and cultural knowledge, received wisdom, that is beyond criticism and is "essential" for cultural literacy, citizenship, national identity, and so forth. These assumptions have, in turn, been translated into key criteria, standards, and benchmarks for legal-juridical, technical-scientific, and ethical-moral assessments of school efficiency in the production of educational 'outcomes'. (p. viii)

In the case of the EQAO, literacies are quantitatively assessed on paper in one of the two official languages of the country: English or French, depending on the majority language of the school. In 2002, the EQAO introduced a mandatory literacy test that provincial secondary school students must satisfactorily write in order to graduate (EQAO/OQRE, n.d.c). Cheng, Fox and Zheng (2007) describe the Ontario Secondary School Literacy Test as a cross-curricular test of secondary school literacy achievement constructed for native English speakers, and determine that ESL students systematically score well below the average, with mean scores consistently in the failure range. The OSSLT is written on paper in English, capturing a narrow monocultural band of linguistic performance. The test does not discriminate between native English speakers and those children who enter the public school system at some stage of acquiring English as a second language (ESL) which creates an unfair bias against learners of English, who currently make up nearly half of the school population in Toronto.

The greater Toronto area (GTA) is a metropolis that has been described, perhaps metaphorically, as "the most multicultural city in the world" (Government of Ontario, 2005). According to the 2006 census, 49% of Toronto's residents claimed one or more of 147 languages other than English or French as mother tongue (Statistics Canada, 2008). In the Toronto District School Board (TDSB), the largest in Canada, and one of the largest in North America, children come from 175 different countries, and native English speakers form a bare majority (53%) of the school population (TDSB, n.d.). This means that the majority of children in school in the TDSB are at some stage of acquiring ESL.

Classrooms in Toronto typically bring together students of diverse language and cultural backgrounds, including children who are native speakers, cyberneration 1.5 learners, and recent arrivals, including those who have been in Canada past the narrow margins qualifying them for ESL specialist instruction. Harklau, Losey and Siegal (1999) characterize as Generation 1.5 those learners whose "traits and experiences … lie somewhere in between those associated with the first or second generation" (p. vii), and discuss how Generation 1.5 learners, as nonnative

English speakers socialized into the host culture have particular problems and issues in literate expression that can fall between the educational cracks.

Research clearly indicates that children engaged in second language learning benefit from building on their extant language and literacy foundation, rather than suppressing and replacing it in subtractive learning (Cummins, 1981; 1991; 2000; 2004). Given that increasingly fewer "native" speakers of English are entering school in Toronto, it is the majority of the student body who is affected by perennially shrinking educational budgets that diminish the resources available for ESL assistance, and erode opportunities for linguistically supportive "international" language classes, currently funded as continuing education, while putting tens of millions of dollars (EQAO/OQRE, n.d.a.) into literacy testing that has been statistically shown to be systematically biased against ESL learners. This flies in the face of Canada's political stance of welcoming and supporting multiculturalism.

School children everywhere are, at this point in the 21st century, what Prensky (2001, p. 1) terms "digital natives": those born in the digital age. These children are culturally and linguistically conversant in digital genres, which form a social bridge across their diverse physical and linguistic cultures. Though digital literacies do find their way into formal literacy education in enterprising Canadian schools (Cummins, 2004; Early, 2005; Kist, 2005; Lotherington, 2008), digital inclusion is not universally welcomed into, or even acknowledged as a fundamental part of curricular literacy education. Cyberspace literacies and digital culture are conspicuously absent from the gate-keeping tests that determine literacy attainment, and ultimately, educational success, for all public school children (Asselin, Early, & Filipenko, 2006; Coiro, Lankshear, Knobel, & Leu, 2008; Lotherington, 2003). This is unacceptable.

The disconnect between test takers and test makers is multifaceted: for the majority, children's home language and culture will be at odds with the Anglo-Canadiana assessed in literacy test questions (Darragh, 2007); their digital literacies, which engage navigation and programming, downplaying English grammatical proficiencies and emphasizing collaborative communication, will not be tapped by test questions or objectives that are oriented towards independent, individual responses on paper; and their knowledge of prescriptive English grammar will be tested regardless of their multimodal literacies. Cheng, Fox, and Zheng's (2007) investigation of the typically skewed performance of ESL learners on the OSSLT, found that students complained about vocabulary difficulty, and relied heavily on test-taking strategies and logic to manage comprehension questions. Though they suggested that cultural schemata were not a particular problem, the students' insistence on vocabulary difficulty in fact relates closely to background knowledge.

"Literacy" as tested in the OSSLT is disconnected from contemporary multimodal literacy practices, unaccommodating of multicultural perspectives, focused on industrial era expectations, and limited to written English. Our response to the OSSLT's mandatory testing of restricted school literacies was to offer a counterbalancing test of contemporary English medium digital communication proficiencies to teenage students who had written the OSSLT. Utilizing November's (2001; 2005) information literacy resources, the mock literacy test, which is modeled on the OSSLT format, was constructed to assess the language conventions, digital genres, and platforms familiar to contemporary digital natives. We canvassed teenagers' critiques of both the OSSLT and the mock literacy test.

3. Literacy and the Millennium Learner

> In the Anglo/European imagination, literacy education is part of a larger onto/ phylogenetic logic at the centre of models of cultural, societal, technological and individual psychosocial development that literacy as a technology enables both the development of the individual psyche and the simultaneous extension of the project of nation, Western science and modernity.   (Luke, 2008, p. 246)

According to the Oxford English Dictionary, "literacy" is a 19th century coinage, formed in antithesis to its predecessor, "illiteracy," which has described since 1660 a condition of ignorance of letters and want of learning. Barton (1994), in examining social metaphors for literacy in the late 20th century, retrieved a host of comparisons made to an antithetical state of sickness, handicap, ignorance, incapacity, oppression, deprivation and even deviance (p. 13) which could be alleviated, adjusted, corrected or otherwise improved by attaining literacy. During the 20th century prominent theorists made well-researched cases for understanding literacy as far more than a cognitive tool-kit for decoding and encoding print and ideas contained therein. Despite views on literacy as social practice (Gee, 1990; Heath, 1983; Street, 1995), and politically emancipatory only as critical engagement (Freire 1998/1970), it seems that little has changed in the public discourse on literacy.

Literacy has been associated with market forces and economic progress since the Industrial Revolution, when reading and writing – heretofore skills of the educated socially elite – were repackaged as workforce preparation through the modern project of mass education (Agnello, 2001). The current climate of standardized assessment in literacy harks back to a commodified perception of literacy, promoting a "back-to-basics" mentality. The "basics" are narrowly conceptualized as the "three Rs" of 19th century instruction: reading, writing, and (a)rithmetic. The standardized testing apparatus is built around this ideology, masking a gatekeeping agenda with discourses of accountability and the importance of "going back to the basics."

In the emerging knowledge economy and the changing realities of what knowledge, collaboration, and education look like, there is a call for conceptualizing the "new basics" (Kalantzis, Cope, & Harvey, 2003). Kalantzis, Hope, and Harvey (2003) argue that the new communication technologies are redefining the skills that will be required of effective learners and workers in the future: flexibility, collaboration, problem-solving skills, the ability to work with diversity, and independent thinking abilities (p. 23). The new basics thus focus not only on learning new metalinguistic repertoires of multimodal and multimedia consumption and production, but most importantly on new kinds of learning that will promote the development of individuals who "will be able to navigate change and diversity, learn-as-they-go, solve problems, collaborate and be flexible and creative" (p. 23).

According to de Castell and Jenson, "[t]he primary instrument of our times is digital code" (2003, p. 48). Literacies in the 21st century include forms and social uses of digital communications unrecognizable as essential literacy only a decade ago. Ong (1995) explained in the mid-nineties that interpretation in electronic cultures – which follow oral, chirographic and typographic interpretive eras – "operates in and on and out of the open, electronic text" (p. 12). Bolter (2007) emphasizes the importance of hybridity in "an age of hypermediacy: with forms ranging from handwriting and print to film and 3D games" (p. 27). Prensky (2006) stresses that education must include programming as an essential element of emergent literacy in this day and age. Students, regardless of first language, need to be as familiar with technological grammar as they are with print-based writing conventions, which are, in turn, developing appropriate domains.

Sefton-Green (2001) observes that though educational institutions are faced with significant challenges in how they bring together school activities and digital culture, to ignore the needs for schools to engage digital literacies, or to expect such knowledge to "spontaneously erupt from young people" (p. 728) is blinkered. "New literacies" require urgent research and pedagogical attention that extends to the political domain of assessment, particularly in the multicultural and multilingual contexts that this chapter addresses.

4.   Is there a native speaker online?

The "four skills" analysis of communication as reading, writing, listening and speaking typically employed in language education is rooted in a modernistic conceptualization of communicative competence, and is inadequate to the reach of online communication. As Crystal (2006) notes, "[t]he Web is graphically more eclectic than any domain of written language in the real world" (p. 205). Crystal has tagged online chat as "Netspeak" (p. 19), which he characterizes as a new variety of language. In online chat and cell phone texting, there is neither a speaker nor a writer but an interlocutor communicating with a flexible but sufficiently stable range of graphic conventions that eventuate in speech-timed conversations (Lotherington, 2004; 2005). How can there be a native "speaker" where there is no speech? It is argued that "nativeness" in texting rests on a confluence of factors, including knowledge of

1. the language – what is novel is the orthography not the language being communicated;
2. the graphic interface; and
3. the digital interface, which Prensky (2001) alludes to in his notion of "digital natives."

Coiro et al. (2008) pose a challenge to educational stake-holders about the meaning of "new" in literacy education, and the place of these new literacies in the curriculum. New literacies, they argue, "are identified with an epochal change in technologies and associated changes in social and cultural ways of doing things, ways of being, ways of viewing the world" (p. 7). This description aptly captures not only the "newness" of digital media, but also the profound effects they are having on our social practices. Reading on screens, accessing news via Web interfaces, communicating electronically via email and instant messenger, relying on cell phones for both verbal and "texted" communications have all become normal everyday practices.

Contemporary understandings of digital media were shaken yet again with the emergence of sociable media – digital media that stress user-driven content production and connection among individuals, such as blogging, or online journal-writing, which serves as a public forum for self-expression and identity exploration (Herring et al., 2007; Huffaker & Calvert, 2005; Lankshear & Knobel, 2006); collaborative writing, i.e., wikis, that foster collective knowledge-building where authority and writing conventions are renegotiated (Emigh & Herring, 2005; Pfeil, Zaphiris, & Ang, 2006); multiplayer online gaming which offers a "third space" for social interactions and connectivity (Steinkuehler & Williams, 2006; Taylor, 2006); video logging, or vlogging (i.e., creating video journals and posting them on public websites such as YouTube); and, finally, social networking sites, such as MySpace, and Facebook, which is currently the fastest growing social networking site in the world (Hartley, 2007), with a diverse multinational contingent (Ostrow, 2007). These environments are redefining familiar categories of participation, authorship, and text, and have had a particularly significant effect on our understanding of the role of technologies in social and educational practice. Participation in these media opens new avenues for identity engagement and development (boyd, 2008), writing and authorship (Black, 2008), citizenship and democratic participation (Boler, 2008), social capital and connectivity (Ellison, Steinfield, & Lampe, 2007), as well as intercultural and multilingual communication (Thorne, 2008). These technological platforms provide rich communicative opportunities in multiple languages for native speakers and second language users alike by creating a base for participatory digital culture that brings together individuals of diverse physical cultures. This participatory digital culture is acquiring an increasingly multicultural and multilingual flavor, reflecting glocalization trends (Robertson, 1995) that combine the social and economic drive towards global expansion with growing local diversity. In this rapidly developing global environment of co-constructed, multiply edited texts; of collective, anonymous contributions, remixing and authorship, we reassert Graddol's (1999) question: what is the place of the "native speaker"?

The expanding digital universe opens up a new dimension in human communication that begs us to rethink the why, what, where, when and how of teaching and learning language and literacy. Reflecting on the challenge to "old" literacies posed by digital gaming, Squire (2008) argues the following:

> [t]he literacies that schools are based around include "mastery" over predetermined, increasingly federally mandated content, reading and writing traditional school-based genres of text (i.e. the five-paragraph essay, the term paper), ritualized performance on decomposed tasks, participation in activity cleaved from other social processes and institutions. Game-based literacies include a constellation of literacy practices that are quite different: texts are spaces to inhabit, learning as a productive, performative act, knowledge is legitimized through its ability to function in the world, participation requires producing as well as consuming media, expertise means leveraging digital spaces to further one's goals, and social systems have permeable boundaries with overlapping trajectories of participation. (pp. 662–663)

Jean-Luc, one of our teenaged participants, expressed his dissatisfaction with the highly structured and decontextualized expectations of the OSSLT, captured in the following question from the 2007 test (Figure 1):

Writing a Series of Paragraphs

1	**Task:**	Write a **minimum** of **three paragraphs** expressing an **opinion** on the topic below. Develop your main idea with supporting details (proof, facts, examples, etc.).
	Purpose and Audience:	an adult who is interested in your opinion
	Length:	The lined space provided for your written work indicates the approximate length of the writing expected.
	Topic:	**Should every student be required to take a Physical Education class every year of high school?**

Write your series of paragraphs on the lines provided on the following two pages.

Rough Notes

Use the space below for rough notes. Nothing you write in this space will be scored.

Figure 1. A question from the 2007 OSSLT

Excerpt 1 is a comment from Jean-Luc.

Excerpt 1.

… they limit this to a minimum of three paragraphs. I feel when you're writing you shouldn't be limited to how much you write or what you're saying… What I don't understand [is] you're supposed to get your opinion across; who are you to say how long it should take? That's what I don't like.

5. Literacy assessment and educational accountability in Ontario: The OSSLT

What is assessed in the Ontario Secondary School Literacy Test? The OSSLT is a standardized literacy test that Ontario high school students write in Grade 10. The OSSLT framework (EQAO/OQRE, 2007) states that the purpose of this test is "to determine whether a student has the literacy (reading and writing) skills required to meet the standard for understanding reading selections and communicating in a variety of writing forms expected by The Ontario Curriculum across all subjects up to the end of Grade 9" (p. 6). The definition of literacy put forward by the Ontario Curriculum for English in Grades 9 and 10, however, encompasses different ways to view and represent information, both in print and in media forms, and shares the responsibility for literacy development as "a communal project", across the curriculum (Ontario Ministry of Education, 2007a, p. 3).

There are several course options in the English curriculum, including academic, applied and open courses. Locally developed credit courses are also eligible. All courses subscribe to a broad, multimodal approach to literacy.

> In the core English curriculum (the compulsory courses offered in every grade), the overall expectations outline standard sets of knowledge and skills required for effective listening and speaking, reading, writing, and viewing and representing. They encompass the types of understanding, skills, approaches, and processes that are applied by effective communicators of all ages and levels of development, and are therefore described in constant terms from grade to grade.
>
> (Ontario Ministry of Education, 2007a, p. 12)

ESL learners follow a separate curriculum for grades 9 to 12 that "has been developed to ensure that English language learners have the maximum opportunity to become proficient in English and achieve the high levels of literacy that are expected of all Ontario students" (Ontario Ministry of Education, 2007b, p. 3). The curriculum mandate pursues English language proficiency in a transitional model that does not offer opportunities for simultaneous maintenance of the home language, though antidiscriminatory principles are upheld, recommending active acknowledgment and utilization of multicultural communication practices in inclusive class teaching and learning (p. 51).

In both English and English as a Second Language curriculum documents, digital multimodalism is recommended for literate expression incorporating both individual and collegial learning.

> [S]tudents should be encouraged to use ICT to support and communicate their learning. For example, students working individually or in groups can use computer technology and/or Internet websites to gain access to museums and archives in Canada and around the world. Students can also use digital cameras and projectors to design and present the results of their research to their classmates.   (Ontario Ministry of Education, 2007a, p. 35; 2007b, p. 53)

The OSSLT, on the other hand, limits literacy to print-based reading and writing in English. This narrow focus firmly grounds literacy assessment in Ontario in the "old basics" paradigm, and effectively excludes any media, digital, or linguistic forms that do not conform to the dominant modern-era literacy model of reading and writing in standard English. Literacy is conflated with English language proficiency, as exemplified in questions such as the following grammar check (Figure 2) taken from the 2007 OSSLT test.

■ Choose the correct option to fill in the blank.

________________ got wet when it rained.

A He and I

B Him and I

C He and me

D Me and him

Figure 2. A grammar check question from the 2007 OSSLT

In Excerpt 2, Heidi picks up this issue in critiquing the validity of test questions.

Excerpt 2.

If I had a question showing a picture of a stop sign asking do you know what this means, or how to use an ATM machine, the usual reaction is yes, why are you asking. But if it was "he and I", that's not my everyday goings-on. "He and I", or "he and she", you have to stop and do that. If they asked me this on the test, I'd be like, what is this?

Whereas digitally-mediated conversations invite collaboration, even as a means to text construction, such as a wiki, and particular grammatical competencies are not expressly registered as originating in first or second language users, the OSSLT structure validates only individual textual decoding and encoding as a timed performance on paper and pencil in English. The English conventions expected are normed on print standards, and emphasize "correctness", focusing on such mechanical details as placement of punctuation, as can be seen in the following test question (Figure 3).

■ Select the sentence that is written correctly.

A "Yes, it is." she replied.

B "My friend writes songs" I said, "as well as music."

C "Where did he learn to write songs and music" asked Ranjit?

D "Isn't that the song that your friend wrote for you?" asked Jan.

Figure 3. A question from the 2007 OSSLT

Testing knowledge of English grammatical and mechanical conventions as literacy indicates another significant gap: the communicative language teaching practices of the past several decades value socially appropriate and functionally effective communication as well as grammatical exactitude. As Giuseppe comments, "[t]hey don't really want my opinion, they want to see if I know where to put a comma."

The EQAO website (EQAO/OQRE, n.d.b) leaves no doubt as to how results on individual test performance are rated: There are only two student outcomes on the OSSLT – successful or unsuccessful. Either a student has met the minimum standard for literacy or has not. Heidi, for example, in Excerpt 3, indicates how transparent this attitude is to test-takers.

Excerpt 3.

It's a question; you come up with some kind of answer. It's a test, so there's wrong and right, and you want to be right, so you say, alright, I'm going to pretend that I have some kind of an opinion and I'm going to try and write it in a lovely flowing way with proper grammar and spelling that I know I will be marked on.

6.   A digital take on the OSSLT: The mock test

Lotherington (2003) outlines the disparity between the digital literacies being acquired by multicultural children and the modern print literacy "skills" being examined formally in school, stating that "[l]earning for the future is not the focus of the EQAO tests" (2003, p. 316). This observation was the impetus for the development of a mock literacy test (see Appendix 1) that focused on multimodal activities familiar to school children.[1] Content was drawn from Alan November's Information Literacy Quiz (2005), and the strategy guide for the video game: *The Legend of Zelda, Majora's Mask* (Hollinger & Ratkos, 2000). The "comprehension" questions mimicked the format of the OSSLT based on sample questions from the EQAO website. The technology practice section required the test-takers to use Game Boys, rather than paper and pencil, and focused on tasks that students would be familiar with. The final writing assignment followed the digital activities of the students described in Lotherington (2003).

The mock test was created to demonstrate how out of sync the OSSLT is with the literacies students are rapidly developing, not as a replacement for the OSSLT. The test was administered, in the first instance, to a group of classroom teachers, whose responses indicated scattered familiarity with digital practices and with the literacies required to operate common digital devices. This experience gave these teachers the opportunity to experience how students feel when the frame of refer-

---

1.   This test was constructed by Deanna Neville-Verardi for a graduate course in Multilingual Education taught by Heather Lotherington at York University.

ence for test questions relates to a world divorced from their usual literacy practices, and raised awareness of the digital metaliteracies students are developing.

The following commentary, in Excerpt 4, by high school students Tallie and Giuseppe gives a clue as to why the teachers involved in this exercise may have demonstrated poor digital literacies.

Excerpt 4.

HL: Do your teachers give you any direction as to where you should get your information [re: using Google]?

Giuseppe: I definitely do not get any directions as to where to get my information.

Tallie: My teachers don't really care. Some teachers wouldn't even notice if a student bought an essay on the Internet and handed it in. They'd probably give you 100%.

HL: Would you be able to get hold of your teacher through the Internet?

Tallie: I have one teacher that had his own website and he would post assignments, test reviews, notes, and he had an email so we could contact him.

DN-V: The Union has advised teachers to not communicate with parents or students through the Internet…because…writing things could be misconstrued and it could come back to haunt you.

7.   A case study of teenagers' literacy experiences

Two groups of teenagers who had written the OSSLT in different years participated in our study as described in Table 1. Focus group 1 comprised 2 high school students who attended the same Catholic high school in an outer suburb to the north of metropolitan Toronto: Tallie[2] who took the 2007 OSSLT, and Giuseppe who had failed the 2006 test and retaken it in 2007. Group two comprised 4 university students who had successfully completed the OSSLT in 2005. Focus group 2 students had attended three different high schools in different areas of Toronto. Wolfgang and Jean-Luc had finished their high school in a bilingual (English-French) program at the same high school; Cornelius had taken an international baccalaureate program in another school; and Heidi had graduated from an arts-focused high school. All students had studied French. Additionally, Tallie had studied Italian in heritage language classes and had participated in an exchange program in Switzerland. Wolfgang and Heidi had studied German as an international language in high school; Wolfgang had also studied Japanese in external classes. All students would be described as fluent and dominant speakers of English.

---

2.   All names are pseudonyms.

Table 1. Case study participants

Pseudonym	Sex	Family language profile	Institution	Location	Current studies
Tallie	F	English, Italian	St. X HS	Northern suburban GTA	High school grade 12
Giuseppe van Nistelrooy	M	English	St. X HS	Northern suburban GTA	High school grade 12
Wolfgang Maus	M	English, German, French	Université A (bilingual English/French)	Midtown Toronto	BA linguistics
Heidi Banks	F	English, Polish	University A	Northwest Toronto	BFA theatre
Jean-Luc Guimauve	M	English, Jamaican Patwa	University B	Downtown Toronto	BSc science
Cornelius Archibald	M	English	University C	Downtown Kingston	BA political science

The students were interviewed in focus groups jointly by the three researchers, following a semi-structured interview protocol. Meetings were informal, centred around a shared meal. Participants were questioned about their everyday digital practices, their opinions on the 2007 OSSLT (the version that Tallie and Giuseppe had both written), and their opinions of the mock literacy test.

The interviewers recorded the interviews, took individual field notes, and captured demonstrations of digital literacies in still and moving images. Field observations were shared, and taped interview conversations were transcribed, individually coded using the software package ATLAS.ti version 5.2 (Muhr, 2006), then compared and merged into a unified coded data set. Data were qualitatively analyzed, focusing on students' daily digital literacies, their comments on the OSSLT and their reactions to the mock test.

8.   Discussion

8.1   Daily digital literacy practices

The teens in our sample were highly proficient in a variety of digital media, though these proficiencies did not necessarily overlap. They were conversant in different digital genres, including social networking, video sharing, using portable electronic devices such as mobile phones, gaming devices and media players, and using the Web for academic and recreational purposes. They were very active digital communicators (Excerpt 5).

Excerpt 5.

Cornelius: I am a big text messenger, I use it at least 20 times a day on my cell phone, I use Facebook a lot, MSN a great deal.

Wolfgang: Same, most people I know and definitely me go on Facebook at least once or twice a day. MSN a lot, checking my email, text-messaging is big.

Their discussions of the different digital media revealed the complexity and sophistication behind choices of particular recreational media and technologies (Excerpt 6).

Excerpt 6.

Jean-Luc: For me personally, I like Facebook because I actually understand how to use it better than MySpace. MySpace completely confuses me. Even though I took a computer programming class, I still don't understand how to configure the MySpace page to make it look cool. And most of my friends have Facebook, so there's a connection right there. I believe at least in Canada MySpace isn't as popular as Facebook, that's another aspect to it too. And also I love sharing pictures on Facebook as well. That's why I prefer Facebook over other websites.

Cornelius: I just want to add about Facebook vs. MySpace. If you are on Facebook you have to be in a network, be it a school network or a region network, whereas on MySpace it's just an account. You're just in a giant sea of MySpace accounts, whereas Facebook is more like talking to your friends. It's an easier way to communicate for example if they are not online on MSN, you can just send them a message – it's easier than email sometimes.

They exploited the technology they had access to (Excerpt 7).

Excerpt 7.

HL: You're into cell phones. So what would you do with a cell phone?

Tallie: You call. You take pictures. Listen to music. Take videos.

HL: I didn't know you could listen to music on a cell phone.

Tallie: Well that is what the card is for that phone.

Giuseppe: A vibe.

Tallie: It has an mp3 player.

Giuseppe: There is like live video chat now … You hold your cell phone and you can see the people you are talking to.

Tallie: And like video messaging.

They were resourceful self-reliant learners (Excerpts 8a & 8b).

Excerpt 8a.

Jean-Luc: Oh, another thing I forgot to mention that you will probably find interesting is that at the cottage I discovered how to use Facebook and MSN on my cell phone, which actually saved my life right now because [my] computer is down at the moment … I had two bars which is enough to get [a] signal.

Excerpt 8b.

Tallie: Well, you have to go to LimeWire and download an mp4.

Giuseppe: I have a converter … It's just a program that converts video files like mpeg to mp4 … I researched it. I googled 'how do you put a video on an iPod' and it showed me the program.

Teenagers socially gauged appropriate and necessary digital literacy skills. Peer learning was highly effective (Excerpt 9).

Excerpt 9.

Cornelius: I had a couple of friends tell me about T9. My phone isn't automatically programmed to T9, and I actually never heard of it until maybe Grade 11 when two of my friends have mentioned it, because they noticed how slow I was… So clearly I had to speed up. So they taught me about that.

They were creative with digital media as well as being intelligent consumers of it (Excerpts 10a & 10b).

Excerpt 10a.

Heidi: Me and Wolfgang use it [T9] as a joke… We have interesting linguistic theories, and we love messing around with words. So I would type something in T9 mode without looking, and I know that's how you type it in the non-T9 mode, and it comes out, because it makes up words, and it's just so funny.

Excerpt 10b.

Giuseppe: PSP is the best by far. I do a lot of hacking for it. I put Gameboy games on the PSP. I learned it through Google. The instructions are still complicated. I didn't pay for any of it. I downloaded it and then used [X] to do that. I got homebrew games.

A number of prominent scholars and media gurus support videogame play-ing as a powerful means for even young students to learn social, strategic, and problem-solving skills (cf: Gee, 2003; 2004; Johnson, 2005; Prensky, 2006). The research, problem-solving, creative, skills sourcing and sharing proficien-cies these teenagers discuss here, though, fly completely under the radar of the OSSLT and like tests. Prensky (2006) describes programming as fundamental to 21st century literacy (p. 49) and refers to millennium learners as the "new scribe tribe" (p. 50). Sadly, the most proficient programmer in our network, Giuseppe, failed the OSSLT the first time he took it.[3]

8.2   Students' critique of the OSSLT

Teenagers commented on the validity, relevance, and authority of the OSSLT. They were largely critical of the test, though they conceded that education in-cluded such measures (Excerpts 11a & 11b).

Excerpt 11a.

Cornelius: I kind of feel in some ways the EQAO is kind of realistic in fact that you go through school and you do tests, and you always have this pressure.

Excerpt 11b.

Jean-Luc: I think the testing material was highly irrelevant to me, but the testing method was [relevant]. With science, 90% of my tests and exams are multiple choice.

Both groups critically reflected upon the validity of the test questions, framing their discussion through academic and personal interests, including their expec-tations of what a test should look like. They felt testing literacy as reading and writing in English was particularly unfair to ESL learners (Excerpts 12a & 12b).

Excerpt 12a.

Heidi: What about ESL students? Everybody from different languages and cultural backgrounds at the same point in Grade 10 has to take the test; everybody has to do it… When you're faced with articles on Avril Lavigne and airbags, and then it says write three pages about what you think how they use "I" and "my", you'd be confused. I think the standard is just not fair from that standpoint.

---

3.   He subsequently passed the test on the second try.

Excerpt 12b.

Jean-Luc: Just because you failed the literacy test doesn't mean that you're illiterate. What if English isn't your first language, yet you're taking a test in English?

Their comments on the subject matter of comprehension questions were mixed (Excerpts 13a & 13b).

Excerpt 13a.

HL: The last one was about how air bags work. Was this interesting or relevant?
Tallie: I learned this in drivers' ed.
Giuseppe: I slept in drivers' ed.

Excerpt 13b.

HL: And what about this question: Do Canadians benefit from people becoming honorary citizens? Explain your answer using information in the selection and your own ideas.
Cornelius: That one I can accept I think that's thought-provoking … That actually interests me. But something like that rather than 'How do you feel in winter?' feels a little more thought-provoking.
Wolfgang: For me personally, if I were writing this when I see a question like this I panic. I'm someone who isn't very interested in politics, and just because I've been taking different courses doesn't mean I can… I feel like I would have to randomly pick an opinion right there.

Participants felt strongly, though, that the OSSLT generally lacked relevance for their age group. This, of course, affects content validity (Excerpts 14a, 14b, & 14c).

Excerpt 14a.

Jean-Luc: I find the content to be so irrelevant and so unnecessary. It's supposed to be relevant to the age group that is writing it but it's really not.
HL: Who do you think it's relevant to?
Jean-Luc: To no one.

Excerpt 14b.

Tallie: I helped grade 3 and 6 get ready for EQAO. And it's the same stuff.

Excerpt 14c.

Cornelius: Well, the first multiple [choice] question after the Nelson Mandela article, "What question isn't answered in paragraph 1 of this news report? A. Who? B. Why? C. What? D. Where?" I feel like this was welded in my head when I was 8.

They gave the opinion that the test was inauthentic, and unhelpful – a hurdle to be overcome rather than a means of learning or of assessing educational progress (Excerpts 15a & 15b).

Excerpt 15a.

Giuseppe: It was my first time writing it. I regret writing it – I wish I took the class.[4] In class I could have learned something. With the test I didn't really learn anything, 'cause I haven't seen the mistakes that I made and can't learn from it.

Excerpt 15b.

Jean-Luc: I take my education seriously, and I know I'm smarter than this test is giving me credit for. And who are you to say that I'm illiterate because I can't pass this test, that's nonsense. This test isn't actually doing anything, at least in my eyes.

Their critical comments indicated that students provided equally inauthentic test-worthy answers in order to pass, rendering the test-taking exercise one of tedium, extraneous to real communicative concerns (Excerpts 16a, 16b, & 16c).

Excerpt 16a.

Giuseppe: Both tests I told them what they want to hear. I don't think they want to hear what you think. They just worry about spelling, punctuation, and sentence structure.

Excerpt 16b.

Cornelius: Yeah, like the political question you could also be scared that your opinion is stupid and not right, or not the one that your marker agrees with.

Excerpt 16c.

Jean-Luc: I don't know about other people, but I usually make up some flowered BS. I don't actually believe it but that's what they want me to say. I think it actually defeats the purpose of the test.

On the whole, the teenagers felt that the purpose of the literacy test was obscure (Excerpts 17a & 17b).

---

4. Students who have failed the OSSLT at least once, and are still eligible to rewrite the test, may opt to take the Ontario Secondary School Literacy Course (OSSLC) in lieu.

Excerpt 17a.

Heidi: All of it seems just... dumb.

Excerpt 17b.

Jean-Luc: Even though we are the first group of students to go through all of the
             EQAO testing, I still don't understand the point of the EQAO.

8.3   Students' critique of the mock literacy test

The mock literacy test, which was developed to highlight inherent limitations in
the OSSLT format and content, targeted the relevance of content, and in so doing
appealed to greater authenticity, given that the format remained the same and the
media of communication were similarly limited. Excerpt 18 shows that reactions
were mixed, possibly indicating differences in age group interests.

Excerpt 18.

HL: Next question about Zelda.
Giuseppe: I love that game. Classic.
DN-V: We got Zelda for Wii.
Tallie: We have a cheat book for Zelda.
HL: If you were asked that [as a reading comprehension passage], would it be
             interesting?
Tallie: You rarely come upon a teen who hasn't played a videogame. So we will
             have an opinion about it. We have experience.
Giuseppe: It brings back memories.
HL: Would those be easy questions for you to write?
Giuseppe: Yes.
HL: Would it be a waste of time?
Giuseppe: Less so.
Tallie: Not that I would be excited about it, but it would be less of a waste of my
             time.

Interestingly, basing reading comprehension and writing questions on a gaming
text was felt to be inauthentic to the educational project by the older teenagers
who were now in university. School "stuff" was assumed to be somewhat irrelevant to life, but using pop culture to judge reading comprehension and writing
"skills" was felt to be culturally invasive and of suspect educational value (Excerpts 19a & 19b).

Excerpt 19a.

Heidi: Yeah, who are you to be telling me that because I don't know how an airbag works, I'm not literate. But if you were to do the test on some other kind of material, like PlayStation or Xbox, how would you feel?

Excerpt 19b.

Wolfgang: If I failed that, I'd be like, so because I don't know about Xbox I cannot graduate high school?

The game and platform-based questions in the mock literacy test were shown to be easily outdated, given the gaming industry's relentless push for new and improved products, though using technology to complete the test was felt to be an improvement (Excerpt 20).

Excerpt 20.

HL: If you were to take this test on the computer would it make a difference?
Tallie: Using the technology – there would be familiarity. It won't put you to sleep.
Giuseppe: It will be more relevant, more familiar.

Asked how they would update the content, students were ambivalent (Excerpt 21).

Excerpt 21.

Tallie: You can add in more things such as like different types of games. Some people don't play on PlayStation – they might have a PSP or a Gameboy, or play games on their computer.
Giuseppe: You can't be too specific. That would be too narrow for some people. Like some people would not be able to relate to that.

Interestingly, their debates offered the kind of argumentation literacy tests try, and in this case both tests failed, to achieve (Excerpt 22).

Excerpt 22.

Tallie: It is like problem solving, because you have to go on Google and everything and try to figure it out. That makes more sense than 'talk about Flavia's book' or put the comma in the right place – who cares if you can't put the comma in the right place, there are editors and spell checkers that will fix that. That is what Microsoft Word is for.
Giuseppe: No, spell checker is bad … If I don't know how to spell a word, I'm not going to be able to pick the right one out properly.

Both groups of teenagers were asked for their suggestions on how to improve assessments of literacy (Excerpts 23a, 23b, 23c, & 23d).

Excerpt 23a.

Tallie: I would do an ISU [Independent Study Unit] because it has more creativity. With tests they are looking for specific answers. ISUs you can present and conduct it in many different ways

Giuseppe: I would work on an ISU too. Just because there is more time and you get to choose what you are doing instead of having it chosen for you I guess.

Excerpt 23b.

Jean-Luc: I would use more real life examples, like can you read a receipt? Could you read a return policy sign at a store, something like that. Do you know what the stop sign means, stuff like that. Not everybody is going to pull out an essay, and say I have to understand this, because not everybody reads essays in the first place. But there is stuff that should be common knowledge for the better of mankind, if you will, if you know how to read it or pull information from it.

Excerpt 23c.

Wolfgang: I would feel better about writing an essay.

Excerpt 23d.

Jean-Luc: I think it's kind of impossible to do, but if the EQAO actually had personalized tests, that would be better.

The focus group's commentary on the mock test shed interesting light on whether utilizing teenagers' digital competencies as the base material for the set of reading and writing skills tested in the OSSLT could ameliorate test relevance, validity or authenticity. The answer, in short, was no, but the case for the need for an alternative means of assessment was clearly stated (Excerpts 24a & 24b).

Excerpt 24a.

Heidi: It's not like 'who am I, what am I doing?" They make it quite plain and simple, it is the literacy test. Am I literate according to certain level, a standard.

Excerpt 24b.

Jean-Luc: And things like the EQAO test don't take into account what's going on in the school, what's going on in the classroom. And when they do get this test, they are making every student taking the test the same person, which they're not. You're a number when you're doing this test, you are not a person which is I think really wrong.

9.   Conclusions

> [T]here is a growing recognition that we are educating current students for jobs, pathways, and life worlds that are still in formation – and some that have yet to come into existence. This challenges long-standing curriculum directions that have their roots in modernist traditions where the boundaries of knowledge were assumed to be known and the skills needed for future learning and work taken as identifiable and quantifiable. (Kelly et al., 2008, p. viii)

Shohamy (2007) points out that language tests have undergone a shift over the past decade, from "tools used to measure language knowledge" (p. 117) to "instruments connected and embedded in political, social and educational contexts" (p. 117). This chapter has investigated one such instrument: the OSSLT from the perspective of two groups of teenagers who wrote it, with both successful and unsuccessful outcomes. The teenagers agreeing to discuss both the OSSLT and a mock literacy test, modeled directly on the OSSLT but grounded in an alternative curriculum of digitally accessible pop culture, represented urban and suburban, monolingual and multilingual populations, though all would position themselves as dominant English speakers. They spoke candidly about their social literacies and their experiences writing the OSSLT, and where and whether these two domains – school and "everyday stuff" – should meet in terms of literacy education.

The teenagers in this study were all proficient and critical consumers of a variety of digital platforms and programs, regular social networkers using combined text and online chat modes, familiar with various games, able to program and access their favourite sites using the technology they had at hand, and even ready to tailor commercial media to their preferred purposes, which requires imagination, creativity, and sophisticated programming abilities. None of these skills were tested in the OSSLT, which focused on "correctness" in prescriptive grammar, multiple choice answers, and rigidly timed, spatially limited essay writing keyed to ad hoc topics of the test-makers' choosing, many of which were found to be irrelevant or boring by the teenagers we consulted. The modern notion of correctness and focus on prescriptive print-based conventions biases against all contemporary learners, but particularly penalizes those for whom English is nonnative. Given that nearly half of the student population of the Toronto District School Board comprises nonnative speakers, this limited notion of "literacy" is outdated and punitively unfair.

Standardized testing, relying on individual answers in timed, written conditions is a poor fit to new literacies, which are networked, collaboratively constructed, and multimodal, more dependent on the grammar of programming than the conjugation of verbs. Bolter and Grusin (1999) note that new literacies have evolved. "New digital media are not external agents that come to disrupt an unsuspecting culture. They emerge from within cultural contexts, and they refashion other media, which are embedded in the same or similar contexts" (p. 19).

Literacy was never limited to language: school children learn to read music, mathematics, diagrams, charts, maps, photographs, and artistic styles across language borders. Conflating literacy with dominant languages is elitist, even racist; children learn other languages in school, predominantly through textual media, they come to school speaking, and sometimes reading community languages, and lay claim to multilingual and multicultural heritages that offer a rich panorama of orthographies and texts. Narratives are borrowed and adapted from culture to culture. Multimodality in illustrated storybooks is centuries old. Networked media go back to genre adaptations.

The information era has created the conditions for postmodern communication to flourish. Digital natives communicate in complex interactive, interculturally co-constructed digital genres that defeat individualistic interpretations of literacy "skills" and modally limited English language "attainment." What is "native" now rests on a more complex synergy of digital and graphic interfaces alongside traditional language proficiencies.

Language policy makers need to critically rethink how literacy is evaluated for millennium learners who read and write across media, modes and genres, programming, linking, problem-solving, critically assessing, collaborating, and creating. Educators and test-makers need to confront political agenda that gatekeep modern notions of restrictive print-based standard English language and literacy attainment and create unhelpful and invalid divisions between L1 and L2 users. Contemporary cyberspace communications that bring multicultural kids together in an era of glocalization confound modern expectations of communicative competence, language conventions, and, all too often, the resources used in English language and literacy teaching.

Appendix
The Mock Literacy Test

**THE NEW REVISED LITERACY TEST
PILOT PROJECT FOR TECHNOLOGY LITERACY
BOOKLET 1**

**Part A: General Technology Knowledge.
Written responses.**

1. List 4 major search engines.

2. What is a blog?

3. Why might you use quotation marks when conducting a search?

4. What does the following emoticon mean?   **;-P**

5. What does the following say and where would you normally see it?

Part B: Reading

Reading 1

> ## The Legend of Zelda
> ### How to Survive the Impending Doom
>
> After defeating the mighty Ganondorf and saving the land of Hyrule, our hero decides to take a more personal journey. However, he finds himself in a precarious position when a devious little imp steals the Ocarina of Time and his steed, Epona. And with this event, our hero finds himself caught up in yet another adventure of grand proportions.
>
> *TIP:* Targeting an enemy with $\boxed{Z}$ not only allows you to track that creature's movements, but also prevents any other enemies in the vicinity from attacking you while you're engaging the targeted creature. This can be extremely helpful when you enter a room filled with creatures and your Health Meter is low.

Reading 1:

Multiple Choice: (Circle the letter next to the best or most correct answer for each question.)

1. What is the best meaning for "devious" as used in paragraph 1.
a) tricky   b) Machiavellian   c) stupid   d) ugly

2. Who is the hero they are talking about in this reading?
a) Pikachu   b) Zelda   c) Link   d) Epona

Written Answers

3. Why would the hero be caught in "yet another adventure of grand proportions?"

4. What is the usefulness of the "Tip" that is offered in this reading?

5. Based on your reading of this selection, do you think the hero will be successful yet again? Explain.

Pact C:

Technology Practice:

1. Circle the image of the technology that you have in your package. Locate the "ON" switch for the device. Draw an arrow to indicate the location of the "ON" switch in the image below.

2. What is the following button used for?  OR  OR 

3. What is the title of the game you have and describe how you play it?

4. What is the following Game Boy accessory used for?

a) a speaker   b) a light   c) a microphone   d) a snake charm

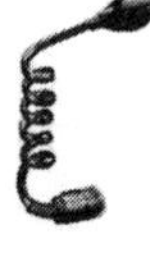

5. What is the following Game Boy accessory used for?

a) a light   b) a microphone   c) a camera   d) a rumble pack

Part D: Writing Task

Opinion

> **Task:** Write a series of paragraphs (a minimum of three) expressing an opinion on the topic below. Develop your main idea with supporting ideas (proof, facts, examples).
>
> **Purpose and audience:** a friend who is interested in your opinion.
>
> **Topic:** Which of the following game systems is better and why? Xbox, GameCube, Playstation, Playstation2.
>
> **Length:** The lined space provided for your written work indicates the approximate length of the writing expected.

References

Agnello, M. F. (2001). *A postmodern literacy policy analysis.* New York, NY: Peter Lang.

Asselin, M., Early, M., & Filipenko, M. (2006). Accountability, assessment, and the literacies of information and communication technologies. *Canadian Journal of Education, 29,* 670–689.

Baron, D. (2004). *Technologies of the word: Reading and writing in the digital age.* Paper presented at the Illinois Library Association Annual Conference Chicago, IL. Retrieved February 15, 2007, from http://www.english.uiuc.edu/-people-/faculty/debaron/essays/wordtech.htm

Barton, D. (1994). *Literacy: An introduction to the ecology of written language.* Oxford: Blackwell.

Black, R. W. (2008). Just don't call them cartoons: The new literacy spaces of anime, manga, and fanfiction. In J. Coiro, C. Lankshear, M. Knobel, & D. Leu (Eds.), *Handbook of research on new literacies* (pp. 583–610). New York, NY: Lawrence Erlbaum.

Boler, M. (2008). Introduction. In M. Boler (Ed.), *Digital media and democracy* (pp. 1–50). Cambridge, MA: The MIT Press.

Bolter, J. D. (2007). Remediation and the language of new media. *Northern Lights, 5,* 25–37. doi: 10.1386/nl.5.1.25_1

Bolter, J. D., & Grusin, R. (1999). *Remediation: Understanding new media.* Cambridge, MA: The MIT Press.

boyd, d. (2008). Why youth ♥ social network sites: The role of networked publics in teenage social life. D. Buckingham (Ed.), *Youth, identity, and digital media* (pp. 119–142). The John D. and Catherine T. MacArthur Foundation Series on Digital Media and Learning. Cambridge, MA: The MIT Press.

Cheng, L., Fox, J., & Zheng, Y. (2007). Student accounts of the Ontario Secondary School Literacy Test: A case for validation. *The Canadian Modern Language Review, 64,* 69–98.

Coiro, J., Lankshear, C., Knobel, M., & Leu, D. (2008). Central issues in new literacies and new literacies research. In J. Coiro, C. Lankshear, M. Knobel, & D. Leu (Eds.), *Handbook of research on new literacies* (pp. 1–22). New York, NY: Lawrence Erlbaum.

Crystal, D. (2006). *Language and the Internet* (2nd ed.). Cambridge, England: Cambridge University Press.

Cummins, J. (1981). *Bilingualism and minority language children.* Toronto: Ontario Institute for Studies in Education of the University of Toronto.

Cummins, J. (1991). Interdependence of first- and second language proficiency. In E. Bialystok (Ed.), *Language processing in bilingual children* (pp. 70–89). Cambridge: Cambridge University Press.

Cummins, J. (2000). *Language, power and pedagogy: Bilingual children in the crossfire.* Clevedon: Multilingual Matters.

Cummins, J. (2004). Multiliteracies pedagogy and the role of identity texts. In K. Leithwood, P. McAdie, N. Bascia & A. Rodigue (Eds.), *Teaching for deep understanding: Towards the Ontario curriculum that we need* (pp. 68–74). Toronto: Ontario Institute for Studies in Education of the University of Toronto and the Elementary Federation of Teachers of Ontario.

Darragh, J. (2007). Universal design for early childhood education: Ensuring access and equity for all. *Early Childhood Education Journal, 35,* 167–171.

de Castell, S., & Jenson, J. (2003). Serious play: Curriculum for a post-talk era. *Journal of the Canadian Association for Curriculum Studies, 1,* 47–52.

Early, M. (2005). *From literacy to multiliteracies: Implications for lifelong learning and work.* Paper presented at The Future of Lifelong Learning and Work International Conference, Ontario Institute for Studies in Education of the University of Toronto, Ontario. Available from http://lifelong.oise.utoronto.ca/papers/rEarlyPaper.pdf

United States Department of Education. (2004). *No child left behind: Overview.* Available from http://www.ed.gov/nclb/ overview/intro/4pillars.html

Ellison, N., Steinfield, C., & Lampe, C. (2007). The benefits of Facebook "friends": Exploring the relationship between college students' use of online social networks and social capital. *Journal of Computer-Mediated Communication, 12*(4). doi: 10.1111/j.1083–6101.2007.00367.x

Emigh, W., & Herring, S. C. (2005). Collaborative authoring on the Web: A genre analysis of online encyclopedias. *Proceedings of the Thirty-Eighth Hawai'i International Conference on System Sciences (HICSS-38).* Los Alamitos: IEEE Press. Retrieved June 12, 2008, from http://ella.slis.indiana.edu/~herring/wiki.pdf

EQAO/OQRE. (2006). *About the EQAO.* Available from http://www.eqao.com/AboutEQAO/AboutEQAO.aspx?Lang=E

EQAO/OQRE (2007). *Framework: Ontario Secondary School Literacy Test.* Available from http://www.eqao.com/pdf_e/08/Xe_Framework_07.pdf

EQAO/OQRE. (n.d.a). *Annual Report 2004–2005.* Available from http://www.eqao.com/pdf_e/06/06P013e.pdf

EQAO/OQRE. (n.d.b). *Ontario province-wide tests: Ontario Secondary School Literacy Test.* Available from http://www.eqao.com/Test/OSSLT/index.aspx?Lang=E

EQAO/OQRE. (n.d.c). *Ontario Secondary School Literacy Test: Frequently asked questions.* Available from http://www.eqao.com/Educators/Secondary/10/10FAQ.aspx? Lang=E&gr=10

Freire, P. (1998/1970). *Pedagogy of the oppressed* (M. B. Ramos, Trans.). London: Continuum.

Gee, J. P. (1990). *Social linguistics and literacies: Ideology in discourses.* London: Falmer Press.

Gee, J. P. (2003). *What video games have to teach us about learning and literacy.* New York, NY: Palgrave Macmillan.

Gee, J. P. (2004). Learning by design: Games as learning machines. *Interactive Educational Multimedia, 8,* 15–23. Retrieved September 3, 2008, from http://greav.ub.edu/iem/index.php?journal=iem&page=article&op=view&path[]=51&path[]=70

Government of Ontario (2005). *About Ontario: People and culture – Language, heritage and religion.* Retrieved February 8, 2007, from http://www.ontario.ca/en/about_ontario/004564?openNav=people_and_culture

Graddol, D. (1999). The decline of the native speaker. In D. Graddol & U. H. Meinhof (Eds.), *English in a changing world* (pp. 57–68). *AILA Review 13.*

Harklau, L., Losey, K. M., & Siegal, M. (1999). Preface. In L. Harklau, K. M. Losey, & M. Siegal (Eds.), *Generation 1.5 meets college composition: Issues in the teaching of writing to US-educated learners of ESL* (pp. vii-ix). Mahwah, NJ: Lawrence Erlbaum.

Hartley, M. (2007, November 3). Why Microsoft really wanted Facebook. *The Globe and Mail,* p. B3.

Heath, S. B. (1983). *Ways with words: Language, life and work in communities and classrooms.* Cambridge: Cambridge University Press.

Herring, S. C. (2004). Computer-mediated discourse analysis: An approach to researching online behavior. In S. A. Barab, R. Kling, & J. H. Gray (Eds.), *Designing for virtual communities in the service of learning* (pp. 338–376). Cambridge: Cambridge University Press.

Herring, S. C., Paolillo, J. C., Ramos Vielba, I., Kouper, I., Wright, E., Stoerger, S., Scheidt, L. A., & Clark, B. (2007). Language networks on LiveJournal. *Proceedings of the Fortieth Hawaii International Conference on System Sciences*. Los Alamitos, CA: IEEE Press. Retrieved June 11, 2008, from http://ella.slis.indiana.edu/~herring/hicss07.pdf

Hollinger, E., & Ratkos, J. (2000). *The Legend of Zelda, Majora's Mask, Prima's official strategy guide*. Roseville, CA: Prima Games.

Huffaker, D. A., & Calvert, S. L. (2005). Gender, identity, and language use in teenage blogs. *Journal of Computer-Mediated Communication, 10*. doi: 10.1111/j.1083–6101.2005.tb00238.x

Johnson, S. (2005). *Everything bad is good for you: How today's popular culture is actually making us smarter*. New York, NY: Riverhead.

Kalantzis, M., Cope, B., & Harvey, A. (2003). Assessing multiliteracies and the new basics. *Assessment in Education, 10*, 15–26.

Kelly, G. J., Luke, A., & Green, J. (2008). Introduction: What counts as knowledge in educational settings: Disciplinary knowledge, assessment, and curriculum. *Review of Research in Education, 32*, vii-x.

Kist, W. (2005). *New literacies in action: Teaching and learning in multiple media*. New York, NY: Teachers College Press.

Lankshear, C., & Knobel, M. (2006). *New literacies: Everyday practices and classroom learning* (2nd ed.). Berkshire, England: Open University Press.

Lotherington, H. (2003). Emergent metaliteracies: What the Xbox has to offer the EQAO. *Linguistics and Education, 14*, 305–319.

Lotherington, H. (2004). What four skills? Redefining language and literacy skills in the digital era. *TESL Canada Journal, 22*, 64–78.

Lotherington, H. (2005). Authentic language in digital environments. In J. L. Egbert & G. M. Petrie (Eds.), *CALL research perspectives* (pp. 109–127). Mahwah, NJ: Lawrence Erlbaum.

Lotherington, H. (2008). Digital epistemologies and classroom multiliteracies. In T. Hansson (Ed.), *Handbook of digital information technologies: Innovations and ethical issues* (pp. 263–282). Hershey, PA: IGI Global.

Lotherington, H., & Xu, Y. (2004) How to chat in English and Chinese: Emerging digital language conventions. *ReCALL, 16*, 308–329.

Luke, A. (2008). On the situated and ambiguous effects of literacy. *International Journal of Bilingual Education and Bilingualism, 11*, 246–249.

Muhr, T. (2006). ATLAS.ti (Version 5.2) [Computer software]. Berlin: ATLAS.ti Scientific Software Development GmbH.

November, A. (2001). *Empowering students with technology*. Glenview, IL: LessonLab SkyLight.

November, A. (2005). *Resources: Information literacy quiz*. Retrieved March 19, 2005, from http://novemberlearning.com/resources/information-literacy-resources/i-information-literacy-quiz/

Ong, W. J. (1995). Hermeneutic forever: Voice, text, digitization, and the "I". *Oral Tradition, 10*, 3–26.

Ontario Ministry of Education (2007a). *The Ontario Curriculum, Grades 9 and 10: English*. Retrieved July 11, 2008, from http://www.edu.gov.on.ca/eng/curriculum/secondary/

Ontario Ministry of Education (2007b). *The Ontario Curriculum, Grades 9 and 10: English as a Second Language and English Literacy Development*. Retrieved July 11, 2008, from: http://www.edu.gov.on.ca/eng/curriculum/secondary/

Ostrow, A. (2007, October 2). Facebook boasts about international growth. *Mashable: Social networking news.* Retrieved November 2, 2007, from http://mashable.com/2007/10/02/facebook-international-2/

Pfeil, U., Zaphiris, P., & Ang, C. S. (2006). Cultural differences in collaborative authoring of Wikipedia. *Journal of Computer-Mediated Communication, 12*(1). doi: 10.1111/j.1083-6101.2006.00316.x

Prensky, M. (2001). Digital natives, digital immigrants. *On the Horizon, 9*(5), 1–6. Retrieved September 3, 2008, from http://www.marcprensky.com/writing/

Prensky, M. (2006). *Don't bother me mom, I'm learning.* St. Paul, MN: Paragon House.

Robertson, R. (1995). Glocalization: Time-space and homogeneity-heterogeneity. In M. Featherstone, S. Lash & R. Robertson (Eds.), *Global modernities* (pp. 25–44). London: Sage.

Sefton-Green, J. (2001). Computers, creativity, and the curriculum: The challenges for schools, literacy and learning. *Journal of Adolescent and Adult Literacy, 44,* 726–728.

Shohamy, E. (2007). Language tests as language policy tools. *Assessment in Education, 14,* 117–130.

Squire, K. D. (2008). Video-game literacy: A literacy of expertise. In J. Coiro, C. Lankshear, M. Knobel, & D. Leu (Eds.), *Handbook of research on new literacies* (pp.635–670). Mahwah, NJ: Lawrence Erlbaum.

Statistics Canada (2008). Language. Retrieved July 10, 2008, from http://www12.statcan.ca/english/census06/data/profiles/community/Details/Page.cfm?Lang=E&Geo1=CSD&Code1=3520005&Geo2=PR&Code2=35&Data=Count&SearchText=toronto&SearchType=Begins&SearchPR=35&B1=Language&Custom

Steinkuehler, C., & Williams, D. (2006). Where everybody knows your (screen) name: Online games as "third places." *Journal of Computer-Mediated Communication, 11*(4). doi: 10.1111/j.1083-6101.2006.00300.x

Street, B. (1995). *Social literacies: Critical approaches to literacy in development, ethnography and education.* London: Longman.

Taylor, T. L. (2006). *Play between worlds: Exploring online game culture.* Cambridge, MA: The MIT Press.

Thorne, S. L. (2008). Transcultural communication in open Internet environments and massively multiplayer online games. In S. Magnan (Ed.), *Mediating discourse online* (pp. 305–327). Amsterdam: John Benjamins.

Toronto District School Board (n.d.) About us: TDSB Fact sheet. Retrieved August 29, 2010, from http://www.tdsb.on.ca/_site/ViewItem.asp?siteid=308&menuid=4721&pageid=4131

Warschauer, M. (2006). Literacy and technology: Bridging the divide. In D. Gibbs & K. L. Krause (Eds.), *Cyberlines 2: Languages and cultures of the Internet* (pp. 163–174). Albert Park, Australia: James Nicholas.

Navigating and interpreting hypertext in French

New literacies and new challenges

Lawrence Williams

As a point of departure for exploring the challenges of reading and interpreting digital texts, this chapter provides an analysis of the use of the French second-person pronouns *tu* and *vous* in French-language hypertext. The results of this study suggest that fundamental differences (e.g., traditional linearity versus multilinearity; frequency and ease of editing) between traditional, printed text and hypertext create an environment susceptible to producing conflicting uses of these pronouns. Pedagogical applications for examining second-person pronoun use and critical framing of various features of French-language hypertext are provided as means for promoting electronic literacy and language awareness.

1. Introduction

This chapter explores various genres of French-language hypertext within the broader scope of promoting electronic literacy in the teaching and learning of French. Prior to the widespread accessibility and expansion of the Internet, hypertext (organized originally in a somewhat traditional, linear fashion) was the only type of discourse readily available in reader-friendly format; however, since the late 1990s, web browsers have become capable of displaying not only text, but also still and moving images and embedded applications for many different types of communication and discourse. The website has become the host or vehicle for practically all other types of discourse since it allows cybernauts to access and use search engines, e-mail, podcasts, blogs, chat rooms, wikis, discussion forums, etc. This means that any successful user of the Internet must be able to find and navigate through sites and within pages on the World Wide Web in order to access information and discourse.

How important is electronic literacy for understanding new technologies that can be used as tools for communication and learning? According to the list of standards elaborated by the (U.S.) National Standards in Foreign Language Education Project and the framework produced by the Council of Europe, learners must be given access to and opportunities to use new technologies in order to understand their current or potential uses for learning, online communication, and information dissemination and retrieval. In the *Common European Framework of Reference for Languages (Framework)* (2001), the Council of Europe adopts a general, flexible approach that allows curriculum designers and instructors to make specific decisions regarding the extent to which new technologies will be integrated into language learning. The *Framework* mentions "technology" or "new technologies" specifically fewer than ten times, and there are fewer than five references to "electronic" discourse or communication; however, it is clear that new technologies could be used for most types of pedagogical and communicative tasks. The advantage of this general, flexible approach is that the focus remains on communication and learning in a variety of contexts, as stated in one of the aims of the *Framework* (p. xi):

> To encourage practitioners of all kinds in the language field, including language learners themselves, to reflect on such questions as:
> - What do we actually do when we speak (or write) to each other?
> - What enables us to act in this way?
> - How much of this do we need to learn when we try to use a new language?
> - How do we set our objectives and mark our progress along the path from total ignorance to effective mastery?
> - How does language learning take place?
> - What can we do to help ourselves and other people to learn a language better?

Although the *Framework* generally avoids mentioning specific technologies, the notion of electronic or digital literacy (see Lankshear & Knobel, 2008) is indeed presented as a valuable heuristic skill (*Framework*, p. 108), especially as students move toward becoming autonomous learners.

> 5.1.4.4 Heuristic skills
> These include:
> - the ability of the learner to come to terms with new experience (new language, new people, new ways of behaving, etc.) and to bring other competences to bear (e.g. by observing, grasping the significance of what is observed, analysing, inferencing, memorising, etc.) in the specific learning situation;
> - the ability of the learner (particularly in using target language reference sources) to find, understand and if necessary convey new information;
> - the ability to use new technologies (e.g. by searching for information in databases, hypertexts, etc.).

Although the emphasis here is placed on using new technologies for information retrieval and the navigation of hypertexts, it should be obvious to teachers and students that networked computers and other types of networked devices now also play a central in the act of communication itself. Computers and computer networks are no longer limited to providing quick access to data.

Like the *Framework*, the *Standards for Foreign Language Learning in the 21st Century (Standards)* (1999) only recommend at a general level the incorporation of new technologies into the foreign language learning experience. Technology – as a concept and a collection of tools for communication and language learning – is interwoven with other curricular elements (i.e., language system, cultural knowledge, communication strategies, critical thinking skills, learning strategies, other subject areas) to create the fabric of language learning. The weave serves as a metaphor in which each element remains identifiable, yet at the same time becomes part of the whole. The elements in the curricular weave expand the focus beyond "the memorization of words and grammar rules," and "[t]he exact form and content of each of these elements is not prescribed. … Instead, the standards provide a background, a framework for the reflective teacher to use in weaving these rich curricular experiences into the fabric of language learning" (p. 32). Technology, specifically, is meant to include both "old" and "new" devices and textual formats.

> Access to a variety of technologies ranging from computer-assisted instruction to interactive video, CD-ROM, the Internet, electronic mail, and the World Wide Web, will help students strengthen linguistic skills, establish interactions with peers, and learn about contemporary culture and everyday life in the target country. In addition, students can expand their knowledge of the target culture via edited and unedited programs available on short-wave radio, satellite broadcasts, and cassette or video recordings.
> (*Standards*, p. 35)

The emphasis in the *Standards* remains on providing "[a]ccess to authentic sources of language, through technology or other means, [since such access] helps establish the necessary knowledge base for language learners" (p. 36).

In this chapter, the analysis focuses on the use of second-person French pronouns *tu* (T) and *vous* (V) in hypertext in order to highlight the communicative nature of the interpretive mode of communication. The guide to the *Standards* (1999) defines the interpretive mode of communication in the following way: "Receptive communication or oral or written messages; Mediated communication via print and non-print materials; Listener, viewer, reader works with visual or recorded materials whose creator is absent" (p. 37). Although this mode of communication is defined with a term such as "receptive" and as having an absent author, reading – as a part of the interpretive mode of communication – is indeed just as communicative as the other modes of communication (i.e., interpersonal and presentational). This point is important to make because some definitions or perceptions of the interpretive mode of communication place too much emphasis on the "receptive" nature of the task, which often only focuses on the end-user (i.e., the reader/viewer/listener), thereby completely or partially disregarding the creator (or designer) and the context of the text.

> Texts – written, oral, visual, audio-visual – offer more than something to talk about (i.e. content for the sake of practicing language). They offer learners the chance to 'stand between two viewpoints and between two cultures'. They can be the locus of the thoughtful and creative act of making connections between grammar, discourse, and meaning, between language and content, between language and culture, and between another culture and one's own. In short, the reading, writing, and discussion of texts can lead students to become aware of the complex webs, rather than isolated strands, of meaning in human communication.   (Kern, 2000, p. 46)

Although readers do not directly interact with the author of a text, readers must at least be aware of the "Available Designs (grammar, vocabulary, formal conventions, schemata)" (Kern, 2000, p. 60; see also New London Group, 1996, pp. 74–75) that have been or could have been used by the author as he or she was engaged in the act of writing as part of the presentational mode of communication (i.e., organizing, editing, and writing or uttering one's ideas). In the case of hypertext (including both text, still images, and moving images of different kinds), website designers could, for example, avoid second-person pronouns altogether, using only the first and/or third-person form(s).

There are certainly other features of discourse that could have been used as a lens for exploring some of the new challenges involved in reading, interpreting, and navigating hypertext; however, the use of second-person pronouns allows for a rather clear way of demonstrating to learners at all levels both obvious and subtle differences between traditional printed text and hypertext.

2.   Differences between text and hypertext

Many of the differences between text and hypertext are self-evident. For instance, the fact that one is printed and one is digital – appearing on a computer screen – is certainly the most obvious difference, and although students and teachers certainly recognize this, understanding the consequences of these differences can be rather difficult when the analysis of these two different types of texts remains superficial and general, especially if hypertext is used only as a tool for vocabulary building and treated as a typical text to be exploited for the primary purpose of reading comprehension. As such, this section of the chapter focuses on co-occurrences of T and V forms in order to demonstrate how they appear to be used in conflicting ways since both are used to address the reader (i.e., the person visiting the site), often on the same webpage, yet sometimes in different zones. It is possible that many uses of V forms could be analyzed as plural by interpreting V forms as a reference to all people looking at a particular page within a site in a way that traditional printed advertisements could use V forms to address several people collectively looking at an advertisement posted in public or on television; however, for most people, computer use is an individual activity. Therefore, advertisements as well as announcements – and the discourse on webpages in general – could be considered interactions with one reader/viewer at a time. In many cases it is clear that the individual reader is being addressed with a V form when a singular adjective is used, as in Excerpt 1, which has been reproduced in text format below with V forms underlined. Since this is an excerpt taken from a Flash advertisement, each screen appears for a few seconds, then the next screen appears, and the sequence is repeated as long as the person viewing the page remains on the page or does not click the "refresh"/"reload" button of the browser, in which case the same advertisement could begin playing again, or a different one could appear and begin playing. (The excerpts of discourse represented here and in the rest of this chapter have been reproduced as they were transcribed directly from screen captures saved as image files. Therefore, capitalization, punctuation, and spelling might not always seem correct from a prescriptivist perspective.)

Excerpt 1. Online Flash advertisement for Yootribe site (now Azaim), Sept. 2006

Screen 1:	Pour être toujours connecté[1] …
Screen 2:	à <u>vos</u> amis !
Screen 3 (top):	<u>cliquez</u> ici
Screen 3 (middle):	[yootribe logo, which includes the text *yootribe.com*]

Even when the singular/plural distinction is not made explicit by one or more grammatical features of the discourse, the very nature of computer use favors an individual, singular interpretation of V forms. However, this distinction (i.e., V-sing. and V-pl.) is only important to make when V is the sole focus of the analysis. In this chapter, T forms – which are necessarily singular in French – are compared to V forms that are clearly intended for the individual visitor of a site.

---

1.   The adjective *connecté* is singular, so this is clearly not a case of V forms being used for the plural.

2.1   Format and organization of content

One of the most noticeable differences between (printed) text and hypertext is the organization of content, which is often made known to the reader of hypertext through the use of typographical features such as font type and size, spacing, and different colors. Whereas the typical printed text (e.g., newspaper, novel, magazine, owner's manual, and so forth) would be prepared in such a way the reader would read and/or scan from the left to right and top to bottom (in English, French, and many other languages), hypertext is often organized by zones that can be read in any order. Kress (2003) prefers the term "block" (p. 136) instead of zone; however, the concept is the same: each zone or block contains words, phrases, sentences, and/or images that "have a uniform function (and structural meaning) across occasions and sites, irrespective of [the] content" (p. 136). One way to analyze the use of formatting and typographical features that create zones is to find an advertisement on a webpage, since an online advertisement is often a self-contained smaller version of a full page. For example, Figure 1 below shows the layout of an advertisement template that was used by Yahoo!® Canada en français (which has since been renamed Yahoo!® Québec) in order to promote their redesigned site in March 2007.

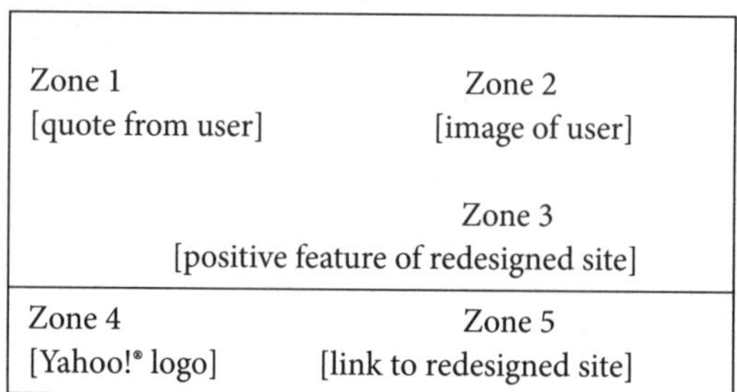

Figure 1.   Advertisement template for the redesigned site Yahoo!® Canada en français

Zones 1 and 2 are on the same horizontal level, indicating that the text in Zone 1 is closely linked (here, as a quote) to Zone 2. Slightly lower is Zone 3, which indicates a feature of the redesigned site that would appeal to the particular type of user whose image is displayed and who has been quoted. The font used in Zone 3 is the same color as the text in Zones 1 and 4; however, the size of the font in Zone 3 is noticeably smaller, and the background is somewhat lighter than the similar purple hue in Zones 1 and 4. The word *Yahoo!*®, as part of the logo in Zone 4, has the largest font in the entire advertisement, which seems reasonable if the company wants viewers to identify its brand immediately as the sponsor of the advertisement. Although the link button in Zone 5 is at the same horizontal level as Zone 4, it is clear that this button (black text on a yellow background) is a separate zone since this is the only text in the advertisement that is not white on a purple background. Although this template – with five clear zones – is relatively simple to analyze, consistency is deceivingly difficult to maintain since only Zones 4 and 5 are permanent in all three versions of the advertisement that were apparently created from the same template. In one version of the advertisement, a T form was used in the text of Zone 3 (*LE NOUVEAU YAHOO! À <u>TON</u> GOÛT*) even though the link – which appears in all three versions of the advertisement – to the redesigned welcome page of the site, Zone 5, uses a V form (<u>*Découvrez*</u> *la page d'accueil*).

Seemingly conflicting uses of T and V forms can also be found on the welcome (i.e., main) page of the Carambar site, which has a greater number of zones than the Yahoo! Québec advertisements, and since Carambar has an entire site, there are necessarily more layers than any advertisement on a single page (or even those presented in Flash with multiple screens that are set to loop and always play the screens in the same order). A sketch of the zones on the Carambar welcome page is provided in Figure 2. It is important to note that for this outline, although the title bar (i.e., the very top of the browser window, often a border with a blue background) and the URL bar (i.e., the box with the address of the webpage) are not listed as zones in Figure 2, they could certainly be added to any analysis of the organization of hypertext content, especially when analyzing an entire page.

<table>
<tr><td colspan="2">Zone 1 [Carambar logo]</td><td colspan="2">Zone 2 [navigational toolbar for product-related information]</td></tr>
<tr><td colspan="2" rowspan="3">Zone 3
[Text "Découvre la blague du jour avec Elie Semoun" and image of E.S. holding a wrapped Carambar between his teeth.]</td><td colspan="2">Zone 4
[Images of Carambar candies with text indicating that each piece of candy is a link to product-related information, the same as the links in Zone 2.]</td></tr>
<tr><td>Zone 5 [public service message about food]</td></tr>
<tr><td>Zone 6 [Carambar logo and slogan "Qu'est-ce qu'on se marre !".]</td></tr>
<tr><td colspan="2"></td><td colspan="2">Zone 7 [links to HTML version, website credits, legal notice, information about the Cadbury group and how to contact them]</td></tr>
</table>

Figure 2. Layout of the Carambar welcome page, Feb. 2008

In this example of hypertext (Figure 2), the zones are clearly distinguishable from each other through the use of different text and/or background colors, font sizes, dividing lines, and empty space. In Zone 3, a T form is used (*découvre*, an imperative meaning *discover* in English), yet in Zone 5, two V forms are used (*votre*, a possessive determiner and *mangez*, an imperative meaning *eat*) in the public service announcement encouraging the viewer/reader of the hypertext to eat at least five fruits and vegetables per day. Although it is quite clear that Zones 3 and 5 are different spaces on this webpage, there is nonetheless a conflicting use of second-person pronouns since T and V are being used to address the same person. However, it could be argued that this is not too problematic since most people who live in France and visit websites frequently would understand that this public service announcement is the same (i.e., text with V forms) no matter where it is used (e.g., television, magazines, websites, and so forth). This argument might have held in the past with printed text, but the very nature of the Web allows people from around the world to access the site, so it cannot be considered as having only residents of France as its target audience. This same type of conflicting T/V use can be found on many food and beverage sites that use (primarily) T forms, yet the public service advertisement always uses V forms.

The map in Figure 2 showing the zones of the Carambar site also highlights an issue related to what Kress (2003) calls the "notion of 'entry'" (p. 136). Kress notes the following:

> 'Screens' have points of entry; traditional pages do not. Or maybe the better way to put this is to say that in screens the point of entry is a problematic issue, whereas for the traditional page it was not. The 'point of entry' for the page is so much a part of conventions that it has ceased to be visible. Here, however, in relation to the [typical webpage], there is no principle by which we could treat and read this as a (conventional/traditional) page. (p. 136)

Multiple points of entry exist on a webpage not only because there is text of different sizes, but also because text is mixed with images, some of which can be hyperlinks. The Coca-Cola France site is another good example of hypertext with multiple points of entry. A sketch of the zones of the welcome page from late 2008 is provided below in Figure 3.

<table>
<tr><td colspan="2">Zone 1 [Title bar]</td></tr>
<tr><td colspan="2">Zone 2 [Address bar]</td></tr>
<tr><td>Zone 3 [Product links]</td><td>Zone 4[Navigation bar for logging in]</td></tr>
<tr><td rowspan="3">Zone 5 [Eight items in a vertical navigation bar to help users find content related to products, TV advertisements, "goodies," etc.]</td><td>Zone 6 [Five items in a horizontal navigation bar that are also found in Zone 4. This is the largest zone of the page.]</td></tr>
<tr><td>Zone 7 [Image of Coca-Cola® bottle and slogan "Prends la vie côté Coca-Cola®" (Live on the Coke side of life.)]</td></tr>
<tr><td colspan="2">Zone 8 [Navigation bar for corporate information, legal information, and contact information]</td></tr>
</table>

Figure 3. Layout of the "welcome" page of Coca-Cola® France site, December 2008

The issue related to multiple points of entry is highlighted here since all the items in Zone 6 can also be found in Zone 5. The selection of certain items from Zone 5 to be placed in a larger, more prominent place (Zone 6) appears to have been a marketing decision. The five items displayed in Zone 5 are anchored on either end by links to permanent areas of the site: the secret formula and corporate information (which is also available in Zone 8). However, the three items in the middle seem to be seasonal in nature (e.g., Christmas, soccer, and festivals sponsored by this company). The rather complex nature of the organization of content on this large website leads to a discussion of the next main difference between traditional, printed text and hypertext: linearity, which is discussed below.

2.2   Linearity

Linearity is not problematic for most genres of written discourse in the form of printed text. The reader of English, French, Spanish, and many other languages often learns at a young age – usually in school – that all "stories" (and, by extension, all or most printed texts) have a beginning and an end. Children also learn that something interesting will probably happen at some point in the story, or a secret will be revealed only to the reader, so that there is some interest in continuing to read the story in order to know how the problem is resolved or if – and how – the secret is revealed. Boardman (2005) compares the linear structures of text and hypertext in the following way:

> Traditional narratives are basically linear: there may be more than one line of development (as in the various storylines of a soap opera) but the plots follow a line and are heading (eventually) for some kind of conclusion. In contrast, a better way of imagining hypertext discourse would be to think of it resembling one of those spider diagrams that we have all been taught to use for planning essays. A [web] page can be connected [with no particular hierarchy or apparent linearity] to ten other pages, using hyperlinks, and then each of those ten pages can be connected to ten others, either on the same site or another site maybe thousands of miles away (distance is not important on the Web). (p. 15)

The lack of a traditional, linear narrative in hypertext is a direct result of having multiple points of entry, which then necessarily leads to having multiple points of resolution or completion. In other words, Boardman notes that "we have a problem with hypertext because in a real sense the narrative is never finished, and there are more ways of navigating the available paths than a reader can pursue in a lifetime" (p. 14).

Returning to the Coca-Cola® France website's welcome page outlined above in Figure 3, from December 2008, it is easy to see conflicting uses of T and V forms in many of the non-linear paths that a visitor to the site might choose. The first example involves a page-internal conflict between the T forms in Zones 4 (the area for visitors to log in) and 7 (advertising slogan) and the V forms in Zone 6, as shown in Table 1. The translation of each phrase is not important here. Instead, the focus is on the use of T or V, which has been indicated in the second column, and the forms of T and V used have been underlined in each excerpt provided.

Table 1. Coca-Cola® France welcome page, Dec. 2008

Zone	T or V	Excerpt
4	T	<u>Inscris-toi</u> vite sur coca-cola.fr
4	T	<u>Ton</u> E-mail
4	T	<u>Ton</u> mot de passe
6	V	<u>Découvrez</u> l'univers de Coca-Cola France.
6	V	<u>Donnez</u> vie aux rêves des enfants malades
6	V	<u>Partagez</u> la magie de Noël avec [Coca-Cola® logo]
6	V	<u>Découvrez</u> le meilleur de Noël
7	T	<u>Prends</u> la vie côté [Coca-Cola® logo]

Although it is impossible to predict where the viewer's eyes will look first when the page appears, it does seem reasonable to suggest that most people would look at the largest and most colorful zones (6 and 7, in this case) first, or at least relatively early in their initial perusal of the hypertext. In such a case, there would be an immediate viewing of two zones with clearly conflicting uses of T and V.

Frequent visitors to the site might also decide relatively quickly to log in to their account in Zone 4, which also has conflicting uses of T and V when compared to one of the largest and most colorful zones, Zone 6.

Another non-linear path with differences between the use of T and V forms would involve the selection of links from the Coca-Cola France welcome page (where there are already page-internal conflicts), such as *La formule secrète* (the secret formula), *Football* (soccer), and *Coca-Cola light*™ (diet Coke) or Coca-Cola BlāK™ (a mix of Coca-Cola and coffee extract). The conflicting T and V forms are shown in Table 2, in which the T and V forms underlined.

Table 2. T and V forms in the Coca-Cola® France site, Dec. 2008

Page	T or V	Excerpt
La formule	T	<u>Prends</u> la vie côté [Coca-Cola® logo]
La formule	V	<u>TELECHARGEZ</u>
La formule	V	<u>PARTAGEZ</u> / AJOUTER A <u>VOTRE</u> BLOG
Football	T	<u>Entre</u> dans le stade avec l'équipe de France !
Football	T	<u>Entre</u> sur le terrain !
Football	T	<u>Tente ta</u> chance !
Football	T	<u>Entre</u> dans le stade !
Football	T	<u>Entre</u> dans les gradins !
Football	T	<u>DECOUVRE</u> LES GAGNANTS DU JEU !
Football	T	<u>Découvre</u> leur aventure.
BlāK™	V	<u>Entrez</u> dans l'univers mystérieux et inattendu …
BlāK™	V	Une inspiration nouvelle <u>vous</u> envahit déjà …
BlāK™	V	<u>Entrez</u>
light™	V	<u>Découvrez</u> Coca-Cola light Plus (vitamines / avec antioxydant)
light™	V	<u>Découvrez</u> toute la gamme Coca-Cola light !

Although the separate pages for Football, Coca-Cola BlāK™, and Coca-Cola light™ are consistent with the use of T, V, and V forms, respectively, the visitor to this site will undoubtedly notice the conflicting use of these pronouns of address in most of the non-linear paths that could be followed throughout the site. This now leads to the next main difference between text and hypertext, namely the issue of authorship.

2.3   Authorship

Although many pieces of evidence point to the Coca-Cola corporation as the owner of the Coca-Cola France website, no single person or team appears to be credited with the creation of the various pages within the site. This immediately draws attention to authorship, which is normally indicated clearly somewhere (usually at the beginning) in a traditional printed text and even in some types of hypertext that model themselves after a genre that has, in the past, typically appeared in printed (e.g., magazine, newspaper, political poster) or handwritten (e.g., diary, travel log) form. Instead of having a single author, hypertext seems likely to have many different authors. Nonetheless, some consistency has been found on specific pages of the Coca-Cola France website, which may be the result of a single author or a team having created those pages, yet the authors and teams might not have considered to what extent their page(s) would be integrated into the website as a whole.

Another type of ambiguity related to authorship can be seen in one of the games created for the Carambar (candy) site, a memory game called *Le Mémorable*. The goal of this game is to observe the different types of Carambar candy in order to memorize the types and flavors in anticipation of a question about them. Once again, the translation is not important, but the T and V forms have been underlined in each excerpt.

Table 3. T and V use in the Carambar game *Le Mémorable*

T or V	Excerpt
	Instructions (*Comment jouer ?*)
T	<u>Tu</u> as 5 secondes pour mémoriser l'image.
T	<u>As-tu</u> bonne mémoire ? Pour le savoir <u>réponds</u> à la question …
	Initial playing screen
	[player is supposed to memorize the items in the game window]
V	<u>Mémorisez</u>
	Second playing screen
	[appears once the time for memorizing has expired]
V	<u>Répondez</u> à la question !
	Third playing screen
	[provides feedback based on answer; several different possibilities]
T	Joli ! <u>Réessaie</u> pour voir si ce n'était pas un coup de chance
T	Super ! <u>Tu</u> es vraiment incollable, j'en suis scotché !
T	Super ! Si c'est facile pour <u>toi</u>, <u>essaie</u> les yeux fermés
T	Perdu ! <u>Tu</u> vois à quoi ça ressemble un Carambar ?
T	Perdu ! <u>T'as</u> un Carambar dans l'œil ou quoi ?
T	Perdu ! <u>T'as</u> la mémoire qui Flex ?

The conflicting patterns of T and V use in this table suggest three possible scenarios. First, a single author may have designed the instructions and each of the different screens or sections of the game at different times. Another possibility is that different programmers might have worked on different parts of the game, which could also account for the intra-screen or intra-section consistency while still producing an inconsistent pattern overall. The third scenario involves the issue to be treated in the next section: editing, which highlights yet another main difference between (traditional, printed) text and hypertext.

2.4   Editing

The Carambar game *Le Mémorable* demonstrates how individual zones or parts of a webpage can be consistent (here, in the case of the use of T and V forms), yet when viewed as a whole, a pattern of conflicting use emerges. This can result from having one or more editors who work on the same hypertext at many different times. When a change has been made on a website, there is no indication to the viewer/reader which part(s) of the page was modified, neither is there anything to indicate if or when changes were made. It is also important to understand that the games, including *Le Mémorable*, are part of the Carambar website created with Adobe Flash (formerly Macromedia Flash), a type of technology that allows content (text and images) to be animated. The Adobe Flash webpage[2] states the following: "Adobe Flash Player is the standard for delivering high-impact, rich Web content. Designs, animation, and application user interfaces are deployed immediately across all browsers and platforms, attracting and engaging users with a rich Web experience." According to the Internet for Beginners[3] area of the website About.com, there are, however, disadvantages associated with the use of Flash, one of which is the inability to edit quickly.

> **Downside #3: Flash .swf movies can be very time consuming to edit.** It is very laborious work to change a Flash webpage quickly. For this reason, you will almost never see a dynamic content page like a news site utilizing Flash for its rapidly-changing content. Instead, Flash is used more for decorative purposes, and for advertising and online gaming purposes.

Such difficulty involved in editing a Flash section of a website means that even if there were only a single author of the game *Le Mémorable*, it might have been decided by the author or the corporate owner that "fixing" the T/V consistency issue would not be worth the extra cost. However, it is impossible to know with certainty if the author(s) or the corporate owner are even aware of the conflicting uses of these address pronouns.

---

2.   http://www.macromedia.com/software/flash/about/

3.   http://netforbeginners.about.com/od/f/f/flash.htm

A similar pattern of inconsistency can, in some cases, be found on the same webpage (i.e., the same URL) when content is edited over a period of months or years. This type of editing often goes unnoticed because websites do not also publish the previous version(s) of each page. In most cases, corporate sites update their content on a regular basis in order to display or provide current information only about new products, contests, or special offers. Table 4 provides an overview of the use of T and V forms (which are underlined in the excerpts) at three different times: late 2006, late 2008, and early 2009.

Table 4. T and V forms on the Coca-Cola France website (2006–2009)

Period	T or V	Zone
		Advertising slogan
2006	T	<u>Prends</u> la vie côté Coca-Cola®
		Main zone
2006	T	Coke + iTunes – TALENT BRUT en scène – <u>Découvre</u> de jeunes talents …
2006	T	<u>Découvre</u> l'univers de la nouvelle pub Coca-Cola …
		Les goodies, le jeu pour <u>ton</u> mobile …
		Horizontal content navigation zone (below main zone)
2006	V	Coke + iTunes – TALENT BRUT en scène – <u>Découvrez</u> les Podcasts
2006	T	<u>Découvre</u> la charte *On parle tous Football*
2006	T	Site internet mobile – <u>découvre</u> le site wap.coca-cola.fr
		Advertising slogan
2008	T	<u>Prends</u> la vie côté Coca-Cola®
		Main zone
2008	V	<u>Découvrez</u> l'univers de Coca-Cola France.
2008	V	<u>Donnez</u> vie aux rêves des enfants malades
2008	V	<u>Partagez</u> la magie de Noël avec [Coca-Cola® logo]
2008	V	<u>Découvrez</u> le meilleur de Noël
		Advertising slogan
2009	T	<u>Prends</u> la vie côté Coca-Cola®
		Main zone
2009	T	<u>Découvre</u> l'univers de Coca-Cola France.
2009	T	<u>Entre</u> dans le stade
2009	T	<u>Entre</u> dans le stade avec l'équipe de France !

It is clear in Table 4 that although the advertising slogan remained consistent with the use of a T form, the main zone of the site switched from having primarily T forms to exclusively V forms, then to exclusively T forms. (Sometime between 2006 and 2008, the horizontal content bar near the bottom of the page was displaced to the left side of the page as a vertical bar on which there were no T or V forms in 2008 and 2009.) The zone for logging in – not shown in Table 4 – also remained consistent with T use during this period from 2006 to 2009. In fact, no words or phrases in the zone for logging in have been changed over the past several years, yet the graphics, colors, and fonts have been updated to match the site's new design elements.

Conflicting uses of second-person pronouns over time could be considered one of the most subtle differences between text and hypertext since hypertext can be edited selectively, and visitors to the site might not happen to notice changes immediately if they do not look at all parts of the site on every visit. Nonetheless, such changes over time are common, especially on the site of a product or service sold by an international corporation such as the Coca-Cola Company if there is, for example, a mix of local and corporate control over content.

2.5   Spatial affordances and constraints

Over the past few years the pop-up window has added an extra dimension of complexity to the discourse of hypertext. In many cases, the pop-up window is always activated by a specific action such as clicking on a hyperlink or visiting (sometimes returning to) the main page of a site. For the Coca-Cola France site, a customer/visitor survey sometimes appears as a pop-up window, but the timing of its appearance does not seem to be activated by a specific action on the part of the visitor. Instead, this pop-up can appear at any time. When this customer survey window appears, the visitor can either accept the invitation to take the survey (*Répondre au questionnaire*) or reject it (*Non merci*). The text from this pop-up window is reproduced below in Excerpt 2. For this excerpt, it is not important to understand the entire text of the message about the survey. Instead, the focus is on demonstrating the presence of both T and V forms, which have been underlined.

Excerpt 2. Coca-Cola® site survey pop-up window[4]

<u>prends</u> la vie côté Coca-Cola®
[advertising slogan in red with the words *Coca-Cola®* superimposed on the likeness of a Coca-Cola® bottle, as is the case wherever the slogan appears on the site]

Bonjour !

Pour améliorer en permanence le service que nous <u>vous</u> apportons sur coca-cola.fr, nous souhaitons mieux <u>vous</u> écouter.

En passant quelques minutes pour remplir ce questionnaire, <u>vous</u> nous aiderez à mieux <u>vous</u> connaître pour répondre toujours mieux à <u>vos</u> attentes.

Merci d'avance pour <u>votre</u> participation !
L'équipe coca-cola

---

4.   http://www.crmmetrix.fr/projects/2007/sc/closcfrq37/sitecrm/exit.htm

Although this text appears in a single pop-up window, there is a mix of T and V forms; however, this may not seem to surprising because the T form *prends* (an imperative meaning *take*) is clearly set off by the color red as being in a different zone since the message about the survey appears as black text. Nonetheless, the use of V forms as the primary way of addressing the visitor to the site creates a stark contrast between the overwhelming use of T forms on the welcome page of the site, which are normally still visible in the background since the pop-up window – as is usually the case – only covers a small part of the computer screen.

Although this section has demonstrated many of the differences between text and hypertext, there are indeed also many similarities between these two types of text, especially when a conscious effort is made to render hypertext less "hyper." A document (*Research-Based Web Design & Usability Guidelines*, 2006) prepared by the U.S. government[5] on webpage design, page and site navigation, graphics and images, effective Web-based content writing, and searching is just one example of guidelines that remind authors of the differences between text and hypertext in order to reduce the e-literacy learning curve that the typical citizen might encounter. The perceived need itself for such a document demonstrates the extent to which both reading/interpreting and writing/designing hypertext present new challenges.

3.   Pedagogical applications

The tasks presented in the following sections are designed to create different types of learning opportunities for students based on a pedagogical framework of multiliteracies first proposed by the New London Group (NLG) (1996). Each task involves engaging students in learning opportunities designed as situated practice, overt instruction, critical framing, or transformed practice. There is no specific order recommended in the NLG framework, and in some cases a particular task might not fit exactly into one of these four categories. However, it is important to keep in mind that the goal is to provide students with different types of learning opportunities as a way of "addressing the full range of learners' literacy needs" (Kern, 2000, p. 133). Kern (2000) summarizes these four curricular components in the following way:

> *Situated practice* is immersion in language use. The focus is on communicating in the 'here and now', on learners' own lives and experiences, and on the spontaneous expression of their thoughts, opinions, and feelings. (p. 133)

---

5.   http://usability.gov/pdfs/updatedguidelines.html

Overt instruction involves developing 'an explicit metalanguage of Design' (New London Group 1996: 83) so that various elements contributing to meaning can be identified, talked about, and learnt explicitly. In terms of the design model, overt instruction focuses learners' attention explicitly on Available Designs and their use. (p. 133)

Critical framing has to do with the reflective dimension of literacy instruction. Whereas situated practice focuses on the immediate 'here and now', critical framing involves stepping back and looking at the 'then and there' of communication. (p. 133)

Transformed practice involves acts 'in which students transfer and recreate Designs of meaning from one context to another' (New London Group 1996: 83). In concrete terms, this means creating new texts on the basis of existing ones, or reshaping texts to make them appropriate for contexts of communication other than those for which they were originally intended. (pp. 133–134)

Although the NLG framework does not prescribe an order for these different types of learning opportunities, nor does it recommend specific ratios for including them in lesson planning and assignments, teachers of learners at all developmental levels should seriously consider the importance of all four components. Kern (2000) notes – using a "nutritional needs" (p. 134) metaphor – that, "[u]nfortunately, the complementary nutritional elements of critical framing and transformed practice are all too often either reserved for the elite in advanced level literature courses or not provided at all" (p. 134).

3.1   Situated practice

The starting point for this task is to have each student do a pencil sketch of the zones of the welcome page of any website. Since webpages offer a combination of textual, visual, and audio-visual features, a first level of reading, analysis, and interpretation should include an overview of the zone with the largest amount of space, the text with the largest font (or the largest image), and the text/images with colors that make a zone stand out, even if it is not one of the largest zones of the hypertext. Once these three items have been identified, there are at least two possibilities for further analysis: (1) a comparison of a site's welcome page to pages that are further "within" the site (i.e., a page that requires several clicks in order to find it); or (2) a comparison of the site's welcome page and the welcome pages of sites with the same type of product or theme (e.g., beverages, automobiles, universities, governments, search engines).

Students should be able to answer the following questions after having spent 15–20 minutes visiting a website:

1. On the welcome page that you have sketched, how many zones are there?
2. How were you able to distinguish one zone from another?
3. Were there cases where the border between two or more zones was not clear?
4. Are the same features used to create zones on both the welcome page and the other pages "inside" the website?
5. Do the webpages on this site use second-person pronouns to address visitors? If so, take some notes on the consistency of their use and the general pattern, if any, so that you can compare T and V use on websites that other students in the class visit.
6. Now go to a different website with a similar theme. (If possible, find at least one other student in the class who wants to visit the site.) Keep a Website Visit Log indicating the zones you read and the links you used to go to other parts of the site or to external sites.

These questions will immerse students not only in language use, but also in the approach to teaching reading as design. Students will be forced to confront the notion that the pages of hypertext they have viewed, read, and interpreted were indeed created by someone for a specific purpose (e.g., provide information, promote a product, and so forth). The list of questions provides only the beginning of a module using situated practice.

3.2   Overt instruction

If the lesson includes finding T and V forms in order to analyze their consistency, the best way to incorporate overt instruction might be a combination of two different participation structures: one-on-one as students are working on Question 5 above and teacher-fronted (although not teacher-centered) once the students have all identified some examples of T and V forms on their own. By combining one-on-one overt instruction as the students are working on the list of questions that are part of situated practice, the teacher can interact with students who have questions or comments, and students should benefit from an overlapping (as opposed to linear) relationship between reading, writing, and talking (see Kern, 2000, pp. 130–132). During the teacher-fronted overt instruction, students will be able to hear or see other students' examples of T and V forms, and the teacher can help students work through hypotheses about their own examples or those of other students. In addition to discussing T and V forms in the examples of hypertext that the students have found, the teacher could also provide students with some of the examples presented above in Section 2 in order to see if the same inconsistencies are still present.

Overt instruction could also focus on the use of colors, fonts, geographical shapes, and other design-related features that help visitors to a website distinguish one zone from another. Teachers should also draw students' attention to the use of symbols in hypertext that represent navigational or content-related information, such as the image of a house to indicate a link to the home or welcome page; the image of an envelope representing a link to contact someone; or an image in the form of a question mark to indicate a link to the FAQ (Frequently Asked Questions). Although many children now begin using the Internet for information retrieval at a very young age, there are certainly still many learners who could also benefit from overt instruction on using search engines and web portals for information gathering.

3.3   Critical framing

For these critical framing tasks, if students have seen some of the websites mentioned in the analysis in section 2 of this chapter, these same sites can be used as points of reference. The Coca-Cola France corporate[6] website is a good place to begin for critical framing since there is a great deal of consistency in the use of V forms. An immediate comparison with the Coca-Cola France beverage website also displays a great deal of consistency (since early 2009), but here the use of T forms is prevalent. After seeing (or reviewing, as the case may be) this comparison, students can use the corporate site's link "Nos boissons" in order to see the list of products (i.e., beverages). When each beverage is selected (except Nestea and Chaudfontaine bottled water), there is a link to that beverage's separate website. After visiting each product's website in order to analyze T and V use (in addition to vocabulary, syntax, images, sounds, etc.), students could answer the following questions individually, in small groups, or with the entire class:

1. Which product sites used T predominantly, and which ones used V?
2. What kinds of inferences could be made regarding T and V use on the websites of these products?
3. Would you have designed each of these pages in the same way, specifically regarding the use of T and V forms?
4. How – if at all – would different patterns of T and V use change the "feel," the image, or the perception of each of these websites?

---

6. http://www.coca-cola-france.fr/ (Note that the same URL without "-france" is the welcome page of the Coca-Cola beverage site.)

5.   Which features other than T and V use create the overall linguistic or communicative essence, theme, or tone of each product's website?

These are only a few of the questions that could be asked in order to promote critical framing so that learners have an opportunity to think "about relations and interactions among … design, communicative context, and sociocultural context …" (Kern, 2000, p. 133).

Critical framing is ideal for asking students to hypothesize and formulate questions about features of language and genres of text that are beyond the current task, yet still related. This would be an appropriate time for the teacher to introduce the use of T and V forms in other types of authentic discourse, such as audio or video interviews, advertisements, film clips, and so forth, and then the teacher could extend the examples to non-T/V forms (i.e., the infinitive) that are used to address people in texts such as instruction manuals and recipes. Although the majority of critical framing could focus on the use of second-person pronouns in hypertext and other types of texts or communicative environments, students could certainly also be asked to reflect on the effect of the use of specific fonts, colors, geometric shapes on websites with a variety of themes and types of information.

3.4   Transformed practice

There are two different lessons that could involve transformed practice based on the analysis provided earlier in this chapter: one focusing on electronic literacy and the other on the French second-person pronoun paradigm. The lesson that would promote electronic literacy is rather simple to explain, yet perhaps slightly complicated to complete. For such a lesson, all students in the class would be asked to visit the same website (preferably one with many levels, products, and/or types of information), and each student would keep a Website Visit Log indicating which links were used to navigate to different pages within the site as well as external sites and pages. The log would also include an approximate amount of time spent reading various zones on the pages and sites visited. Ostensibly, each student's log would represent one possible path for visiting the site, and then students will switch logs with another student in order to follow the other student's path through the site (and possibly beyond). This type of task will reinforce the notion that hypertext is necessarily multilinear, and this creates the potential for each student to experience one or more websites in an entirely different way.

In addition to the task focusing on multilinearity, students could compare the use of T and V on the websites of the Coca-Cola products to the use of these second-person pronouns on a corporate site that also has microsites for each of its own products. An obvious corporate site to compare with be that of Pepsi-Cola France; however, students might want to explore the French version of the Cadbury Group's corporate and product sites or those of the Nestlé Group. Most international conglomerates have websites providing corporate information and then independent or microsites for different divisions or products. Students should be reminded of the hypothesizing they engaged in as part of critical framing since this type of transformed practice would give them opportunities to test their assumptions and guesses about other beverage and food sites.

3.5   Summary of pedagogical applications

The tasks presented in this section of the chapter are by no means the only possibilities for organizing lessons involving the interpretive mode of communication and the promotion of electronic literacy. Instead, these tasks should be viewed as a part of a flexible model that tries to create a balance among situated practice, overt instruction, critical framing, and transformed practice, regardless of specific tasks that may be used.

4.   Conclusion

This chapter has provided an overview of only some of the issues and challenges learners (and teachers) face as they try to read, interpret, and navigate hypertext within the World Wide Web. Of course this is only one small part of the many types of literacies (electronic and other) today's learners might need. Given the exponential increase in the amount of information available on line, the ability to locate, organize, filter, and synthesize this information as efficiently as possible has become a necessity. Kern (2000) notes that "critical reading on the Web requires asking *who* designed the webpage and *for whom*" (p. 230). From a wider perspective viewing literacy as a socio-political construct, it is perhaps best to remember that literacy is never a stable concept or a finite set of skills. Instead, different types of literacies are necessary in different fields, for a variety of purposes, and they will undoubtedly change over time since "digital literacy is itself an element in the ongoing construction, in a social context, of individual identity" (Martin, 2008, p. 173).

References

Boardman, M. (2005). *The language of websites*. London: Routledge.

Council of Europe. (2001). *Common European framework of reference for languages: Learning, teaching, assessment*. Cambridge: Cambridge University Press.

Lankshear, C., & Knobel, M. (2008). Introduction: Digital literacies – concepts, policies and practicies. In C. Lankshear & M. Knobel (Eds.), *Digital literacies: Concepts, policies and practices* (pp. 1–16). New York, NY: Peter Lang.

Kern, R. (2000). *Literacy and language teaching*. Oxford: Oxford University Press.

Kress, G. (2003). *Literacy in the new media age*. London: Routledge.

Martin, A. (2008). Digital literacy and the "Digital Society." In C. Lankshear & M. Knobel (Eds.), *Digital literacies: Concepts, policies and practices* (pp. 151–176). New York, NY: Peter Lang.

National Standards in Foreign Language Education Project. (1999). *Standards for foreign language learning in the 21st century*. Lawrence, KS: Allen Press.

New London Group. (1996). A pedagogy of multiliteracies: Designing social futures. *Harvard Educational Review, 66*, 60–92.

Web-based translation for promoting language awareness

Evidence from Spanish

Lee B. Abraham

This chapter reports on a study that explored how students in a Spanish conversation course worked collaboratively to evaluate sentences translated from English to Spanish by a Web translation site. An analysis of language-related episodes (Swain & Lapkin, 1998) indicated that learners' offline collaborative dialogue provided opportunities to become aware of and to correctly solve many of the grammatical and lexical problems in the translations. Recommendations for adapting this study's task in order to show affordances and limitations of translation tools for reading and writing are provided. This chapter also analyzes translations from English to Spanish using selected parts of speech in different morphosyntactic environments to compare the overall quality of three Web translation sites. Future research could examine two or more grammatical features such as tense, mood, or aspect, the effectiveness of translations of idiomatic expressions and false cognates, or the quality of online translations of narratives, expository texts, and other genres.

1. Introduction

This chapter presents the results of an empirical study using machine-translated sentences as the basis for a task developed to raise language awareness and familiarity with online translation sites among third-year U.S. university-level learners of Spanish. Although Web-based machine translation sites, online dictionaries, and language-related websites are sources that may be frequently consulted and used by foreign language learners, formal training in understanding and using these types of sources does not appear to be commonplace in U.S. higher education. As such, this chapter demonstrates how sentences translated via the popular online site AltaVista Babel Fish (prior to its merger with Yahoo!) can be incorporated into the foreign language curriculum.

1.1   Objectives

The main focus of this chapter is the development of language awareness in learners of Spanish; however, tasks and empirical research using translation sites could certainly be designed for learners of the other languages commonly available in translation software (e.g., Chinese, French, German, Greek, Italian, Portuguese, Russian, and so forth). The rationale for choosing language awareness as the main objective of this study stems from the Comparisons standards of the U.S. *Standards for foreign language learning in the 21st century* (*Standards*) (National Standards in Foreign Language Education Project, 1999). "Students benefit from language learning by discovering different patterns among language systems and cultures" (Standards, p. 57). The use of the preposition "among" is important here because the Comparisons standard involves understanding patterns, anomalies, and forms found in both the L1 and the L2.

> For example, students often come to the study of another language with the assumptions that all languages are like their own. Shortly, they discover categories that exist in other languages (e.g., neuter gender) that do not exist in their own. They discover that elements to which they gave scant attention (e.g., ends of words) may be quite important in another language. (p. 57)

The Comparisons standards are the following:

> Standard 4.1: Students demonstrate understanding of the nature of language through comparisons of the language studied and their own. (p. 58)

> Standard 4.2: Students demonstrate understanding of the concept of culture through comparisons of the cultures studied and their own. (p. 60)

Any task using sentences produced by a translation site could be designed to align more closely with Standard 4.1 or 4.2, but ideally, such a task would at least touch on both standards.

Although the *Common European Framework of Reference for Languages* (*CEFRL*) (Council of Europe, 2001) is organized somewhat differently than the *Standards*, the *CEFRL* also states clearly that the comparison of a learner's two (or more) linguistic systems (L1 and L2) should play an important part in developing communicative competence.

> 5.1.4.1 Language and communication awareness
> Sensitivity to language and language use, involving knowledge and understanding of the principles according to which languages are organized and used, enables new experience to be assimilated into an ordered framework and welcomed as an enrichment. The associated new language may then be more readily learnt

and used, rather than resisted as a threat to the learner's already established linguistic system, which is often believed to be normal and 'natural'. (p. 107)

In addition to raising students' awareness of the similarities and differences between L1 and L2, this study has as a secondary objective to demonstrate the advantages and limitations of the use of online language and reference tools, specifically translation sites.

1.2   Background

Learners' use of Web-based technologies brings new challenges and opportunities for research in second language learning and teaching. One area of increasing attention has been the use of Web-based machine translation sites in both language learning and the training of professional translators (Somers, 2003). Alley (2005) provides a number of examples illustrating the disadvantages of translation Web sites and recommends tasks involving vocabulary and syntax with beginning language learners so that they are aware of such limitations. Williams (2006) examines a number of specific linguistic constraints of translation in French and provides concrete pedagogical recommendations for its use as a tool to enable learners to understand certain complexities of language (e.g., potentially false cognates, polysemy). He also points to the importance of teaching students to be able to recognize the benefits and limitations of technology-mediated tools such as translation as well as other tools such as monolingual and bilingual print and electronic dictionaries and software.

Despite recent attention given to the misuse of translation for language learning, there has been relatively little research on its use as a tool that can be used to raise students' language awareness. Niño (2008) compared the accuracy of an experimental group who edited a text produced by a translation site with a control group who translated the same text from English to Spanish. Students in the experimental group (those revising the text originally produced by the translation software) had fewer grammatical and lexical errors than the control (translation) group. As such, Niño suggests that when appropriately introduced into the curriculum, editing of texts produced by machine translation software "can provide an excellent form-focused activity that can help the students develop their grammatical and lexical accuracy" (p. 42).

Collaborative dialogue has been found to support language learning and occurs when "learners work together to solve linguistic problems and/or co-construct language or knowledge about language" (Swain, Brooks, Tocalli-Beller, 2002, p. 172). Studies of collaborative dialogue have shown that it enhances writing ability (Qi & Lapkin, 2001), revision skills (Swain & Lapkin, 2002), and grammatical development (Lapkin, Swain, & Smith, 2002). Much less is known about the ways in which collaborative dialogue or interaction around computer-mediated tasks promotes language learning (Chapelle, 2007, p. 108).

Kitade (2008) examined students' offline peer dialogue while they wrote messages that were later posted on an electronic discussion board. The study analyzed the type and quantity of talk about lexical and grammatical questions (defined as language-related episodes, see Section 3.1) generated by peers' offline dialogue and demonstrated that learners of English as a Second Language helped each other to solve linguistic problems in messages that were subsequently posted online. As Kitade (2008) points out, "Previous studies on CMC have paid less attention to the role of offline interaction in language learning; however, the potential of offline interactions to create a collaborative context, not only among online interlocutors but also among offline peers, should be investigated in future studies" (p. 80). The study reported later in this chapter seeks to extend Kitade's (2008) framework by examining the role of peer dialogue in offline interactions to raise students' language awareness while evaluating and revising English to Spanish Web-based translations.[1]

1.3   Organization of the chapter

This chapter analyzes translations from English to Spanish using selected parts of speech in different morphosyntactic environments and structures to compare the overall quality of three Web-based translation sites. The second part of this chapter presents the results of a study in which third-year learners of Spanish worked in pairs to correct sentences that had been translated from English to Spanish on the Babel Fish website. The objective of the study is to understand the potential of translation tasks for promoting students' awareness of grammatical and lexical features in L2 learning. Students who use translation sites, electronic dictionaries, and other types of software (e.g., grammar and spelling checkers) often do not understand the complexities involved in cross-linguistic transfer of meanings, which may or may not happen to coincide with a transfer of forms. As Kern (2000) points out,

> … many beginning language learners assume a one-to-one correspondence between words in their native language and words in their target language, what Bland, Noblitt, and Kay refer to as the "naive lexical hypothesis". This assumption

---

1.   In the present study, language awareness is defined as "an understanding of the human faculty of language and its role in thinking, learning, and social life" (van Lier, 2001, p. 160). For an overview of recent research in language awareness, see Svalberg (2007).

> is reinforced by textbook glossaries, which generally provide one-word transla-
> tions. Sometimes of course, there is no lexical equivalent as when a student looks
> up the Spanish word for 'would', only to find a note about the use of imperfect or
> conditional forms of verbs .... (p. 74)

The importance of learners' awareness of differences in vocabulary and grammar
for developing learners' communicative competence, discussed by Kern (2000),
has also been underscored by the *Standards* and the *CEFRL*. As such, the final section of the chapter provides concrete suggestions for adapting this study's task as a
model for language educators in order to show the limitations of translation tools
for writing and reading not only in Spanish, but also in other languages. Specific
recommendations for further research of translation tasks in language learning
are also provided.

2.   Method

2.1   Research questions

The research questions guiding the present study are as follows:

1. Do learners become aware of problems with grammatical, lexical or ortho-
    graphic features when evaluating Web-based English to Spanish translations?
2. Which linguistic elements form the basis of learners' offline collaborative dia-
    logue?
3. Do learners successfully correct grammatical, lexical, and orthographic prob-
    lems in Web-based translations?

2.2   The participants

Data in the present study are drawn from 16 learners enrolled in a third-year
Spanish composition and conversation class at a relatively small private university
in the northeastern United States. Learners were placed into this course based on
their score on the University placement test that measures grammar and vocabulary knowledge. The instructor of the course, trained with the proficiency guidelines of the American Council of the Teaching of Foreign Languages (Breiner-
Sanders, Lowe, Miles, & Swender, 2000; Breiner-Sanders, Swender, Terry, 2002;
Liskin-Gasparro, 2003), indicated that all participants had at least an intermedi-
ate-high level of oral proficiency. Participants had studied Spanish in high school
for an average of 4 years. All learners were native speakers of English who had

neither studied nor lived abroad in a Spanish-speaking country. A questionnaire asking students to report their use of different types of computer-mediated technologies (synchronous chat, discussion forums, and search engines in Spanish), indicated that none of participants had used a Web-based machine translation site prior to participating in the study reported here.[2]

2.3   The task

Learners were randomly paired and were provided with the results of 12 sentences translated from English into Spanish by AltaVista's Babel Fish translation Web site (Appendix). Each pair was asked to discuss in their L1 (English) whether or not the sentence was translated correctly from English to Spanish, and if they believed the translation to be incorrect, they were instructed to talk about a correct solution. Students were not specifically directed to focus on vocabulary, grammar, or spelling. All pairs were given 25 minutes to complete the task that was audiorecorded. Learners did not have access to the Internet, nor were they permitted to use dictionaries during the task, in order to encourage collaborative dialogue.

2.4   The source

At the time of this study, Babel Fish was widely known as the translation tool of the AltaVista site, but it has now become part of Yahoo!©.[3] Before turning to a discussion of the student-produced data, this section reports the quality of the translations of selected terms and phrases produced by Babel Fish as well as two other popular Web-based translation sites.[4] In Tables 1, 2, and 3, an asterisk has been inserted in cases where there is a grammatical and/or semantic problem with the translated word/phrase. The examples in these tables are merely illustrative, not exhaustive.

---

2.   It is, of course, possible that some students had used or at least were familiar with online translation sites prior to doing this task even if they chose not to self-report this, for whatever reason.

3.   Software used for translation sites seems to be updated on a regular basis. Therefore, problems related to the translation of specific grammatical, lexical, or sociopragmatic features of a language will necessarily change over time.

4.   Yahoo!© Babelfish: http://babelfish.yahoo.com/, Free Translation©: http://www.freetranslation.com/, Google© Translate: http://translate.google.com/

Table 1 presents the variation in the translation of nouns in three translation Web sites.[5] The word *fall* in Example 1 demonstrates the problems that translation sites have with words that have more than one meaning. Babel Fish translates *fall* as the falling of a person or object from one point to another, but Free Translation uses the equivalent that refers to the season (i.e., the period of the year following summer). Google's site uses the infinitive meaning *to fall* with regard to the movement of objects and individuals. All three Web sites translate *time* (Example 2) which has a multitude of meanings in Spanish rather than selecting what perhaps could be considered a semantically more restricted equivalent *hora* commonly used to measure time [(*¿Qué hora es?* What time is it?)] or the noun *vez* [(a realization of something one time or on more than one occasion, two times (twice), etc.]. Example 3 shows the difficulty that translation sites have in distinguishing mass nouns from count nouns.[6] A compound noun in English in Example 4 is translated word for word by Free Translation (*vidrio* typically refers to glass as a material from which something is made) and Example 5 presents an example of the difficulty of expressing possession in a noun phrase.

Table 1. Nouns

	Babel Fish	Free Translation	Google
1. fall	caída	otoño	caer
2. time	tiempo	tiempo	tiempo
3. a piece of furniture	*un pedazo de muebles	un mueble	*una pieza de mobiliario
4. a drinking glass	*un vidrio de consumición	*un vidrio potable	un vaso
5. the lawyer's case	*el lawyer' caso de s	el caso del abogado	*el abogado del caso

The two copular verbs, *ser* and *estar*, express multiple meanings and variation exists in their use across a range of contexts (Butt & Benjamin, 2004; Vañó-Cerdá, 1982). Students who use translation Web sites may quickly discover that they are not necessarily appropriate for translating *to be*. As indicated in Table 2, Babel Fish selects the appropriate verb for use with health (*estar*) but cannot distinguish punctuation from the abbreviation for the state of Illinois. Free Translation correctly translates *to be* with *estar* but incorrectly uses the masculine ending on the adjective when referring to the female names (i.e., Marisol and Cristina). Singular subjects of Google's translations are correct, but plural subjects are translated with

---

5. For a corpus-based study comparing noun phrases in English and Spanish, see Ramón García (2006).

6. See Whitley (2002) for an extensive discussion of differences in noun phrases in English and Spanish.

the incorrect copula (*ser enfermo* generally means *to be mentally ill*) and adjective (*malos*, meaning *badly behaved* when used with *ser*).

Table 2. The verbs *ser* and *estar*

		Babel Fish	Free Translation	Google
1.	José is ill.	*José es Illinois.	José está enfermo.	José está enfermo.
2.	Marisol is ill.	*Marisol es Illinois.	*Marisol está enfermo.	Marisol está enferma.
3.	Marisol and José are ill.	*Marisol y José son Illinois.	Marisol y José están enfermos.	*Marisol y José son los malos.
4.	Marisol and Cristina are ill.	*Marisol y Cristina son Illinois.	*Marisol y Cristina están enfermos.	*Marisol y Cristina son los malos.
5.	Marisol and Pablo are ill.	*Marisol y Pablo son Illinois.	Marisol y Pablo están enfermos.	*Marisol y Pablo son malos.

Other difficulties with translation sites are prevalent with regard to aspect (preterite/perfective versus imperfective), mood (subjunctive vs. indicative), and false cognates and are presented in Table 3. In Example 1, we find the problem of the translation of false cognates in two of the three translation sites (*realizar* = to fulfill, carry out vs. *darse cuenta de (que)* = to realize something).[7] In Example 2 the Free Translation uses *agarrar el autobús* which is less formal than *tomar el autobús* but generally acceptable in colloquial Spanish. Google's translation means *We are trapped in the bus at 9:00 a.m.* The Babel Fish site uses the verb *coger* (which has a vulgar connotation in some Spanish-speaking countries) but does not use the correct prepositional phrase (i.e., *a las 9:00 a.m, at nine o'clock*). All three translations in Example 4 in Table 3 may be considered correct and show an important limitation of translation sites for translating polysemous verbs. *Querer* in the preterite form (*quisieron*) generally means *wanted to and failed*, i.e., *quisieron pedirle, they wanted to and failed to ask you* but in the imperfect indicative (*querían*), i.e., *querían pedirle, they wanted to ask you (and they may or may not have done so)* does not imply that this happened.[8] Example 3 shows the difficulty of translating verbs that require the preposition *a* (often referred to as the *personal a*) before a direct object that refers to a specific person. Google included the *personal a* but the word order is incorrect. Both Babel Fish and Free Translation omit the required *personal a*. The

---

7.   Although the verb *realizar* is considered a false cognate, it may be found in everyday, conversational Spanish (Real Academia Española, 2005).

8.   All three Web sites provide the equivalent of the formal *you* (*usted*), never the informal 2nd person singular (*tú*), the informal 2nd person plural (*vosotros/vosotras*), or the formal 3rd person plural (*ustedes*).

subjunctive mood is correctly translated by Babel Fish in Example 5 (*partido* generally refers to a party in terms of political affiliation or a sporting event), but both Free Translation and Google incorrectly use the future tense form of the verbs (*vendrá* = will come; *llegará* = will arrive).

Table 3. Other linguistic features

	Babel Fish	**Free Translation**	**Google**
1. Jorge realized that he had left his keys on the kitchen table.	*Jorge realizó que él había dejado sus llaves en la tabla de cocina.	*Jorge se dio cuenta de que él había dejado sus llaves en la mesa de cocina.	Jorge se dio cuenta de que había dejado las llaves en la mesa de la cocina.
2. We caught the bus at 9:00 a.m.	*Cogimos el autobús en el 9:00 mañana.	Agarramos el autobús a las 9:00 de la mañana.	*Estamos atrapados en el autobús a las 9:00 a.m.
3. Ana invited Felipe and Claudia to dinner.	*Felipe y Claudia invitados anecdotario a la cena.	*Ana invitó Felipe y Claudia a la cena.	*Ana Claudia invitó a Felipe y para la cena.
4. They wanted to ask you if you could buy a few things at the store.	Quisieron preguntarle si usted podría comprar algunas cosas en el almacén.	Ellos quisieron preguntarle si usted podría comprar unas pocas cosas en la tienda	Querían preguntarle si podría comprar un par de cosas en la tienda.
5. My wife and I hope that Julia will come to the party.	*Mi esposa y yo esperamos que Julia venga al partido.	*Mi mujer y yo esperan que Julia vendrá al partido.	*Mi esposa y yo esperamos que Julia llegará a la fiesta.

3.   Results

3.1   The data

The audio recordings from the eight pairs were transcribed by the author and a second, Spanish instructor who did not teach the course in this study. Transcripts were then analyzed for the occurrence of language-related episodes. Following Swain and Lapkin (1998), a language-related episode (LRE) is defined as "any part of a dialogue where the students talk about the language they are producing, question their language use, or correct themselves or others" (p. 326).

As illustrated in Example 1 below, Web-translations often resulted in discussions of the correct verb tense and form, which had a direct link to subjects that were or were not possible.

Example 1. Grammatical LRE

Jessica: It's like we were robbed. [9]
Robert: Nosotros. No, wait.
[Robert: We. No, wait.]
Jessica: Hemos? How about "have been"?
[Jessica: We have? How about "have been"?]
Robert: Nosotros, uhm …
[Robert: We, uhm …]
Jessica: Robamos? Alguien?
[Jessica: We stole? Someone?]
Robert: Alguien nos robó?
[Robert: Someone stole from us?]

Example 2 illustrates a pair's discussion of the correct equivalent for letter as a type of correspondence (*carta*) versus a letter of the alphabet (*letra*).

Example 2. Lexical LRE

Kristen: Letra? Is *letra* a letter?
Ana: No, isn't that letter of the alphabet? I think letter of the alphabet is *letra*.
Kristen: Isn't it carta?
Ana: Yeah, carta is like the letter or the document that you actually write to someone.

Learners also reflected on orthographic problems with the translations as shown in Example 3 in which learners discussed the changes required for the irregular verb *poder* (*to be able to*).

Example 3. Orthographic LRE

Charles: So you take the first person, pueda and then puedamos
Emma: And that one is not irregular, is it?
Charles: Puedamos. So "espero que mis amigos y yo puedamos". Wait. I don't know if you can use coger right after it.
Emma: So wait. How are we spelling it?
Charles: Puedamos

---

9. All names are pseudonyms. This study was approved by the University's Institutional Review Board (HS01518) and implemented in full compliance with this protocol.

Following Lesser (2004) and Storch (2007), a LRE was coded as *correctly solved* or *incorrectly solved*.[10] *Correctly solved* LREs were those in which the dyads correctly solved any grammatical, lexical, or spelling problems. The category *incorrectly solved* was defined as a LRE in which a grammatical, lexical or orthographic problem was identified, but the solution was not correct. The researcher and a Spanish instructor (who was not the same instructor of the course in this study) independently read the transcripts and identified lexical, grammatical and orthographic LREs. The interrater reliability for LREs was as follows: lexical = .96, grammatical = .93, and .98 for orthographic. Disagreements with coding were resolved through discussion.

3.2   Analysis

The first research question sought to determine whether off-line talk while discussing English-to-Spanish translations from a popular Web-based translation site would allow learners to become aware of problematic linguistic features. As shown in Table 4, the translation task in this study allowed learners to become aware of grammatical, lexical, and orthographic problems. 118 language-related episodes were found in the present study, with more than half focusing on grammatical aspects in the Web-based translations followed by lexical and orthographic elements.

Table 4. Summary of LREs

	Sum	% Total LREs
Grammatical	66	55.93
Lexical	49	41.53
Orthographic	3	2.54
Total	118	100

The second research question focuses on the types of grammatical and lexical features that formed the basis of the language-related episodes in the translation task. Table 5 shows that morphology (tense, aspect, mood, word order, and subject-verb agreement) accounted for 74% of learners' language-related episodes.[11]

---

10. Previous studies have included a third category *not resolved* but this was not found in this data.

11. Comparisons of the distribution of grammatical, lexical, and orthographic LREs with those of previous studies using dictogloss, text reconstruction, or jigsaw tasks are difficult to make, particularly since the task type may result in different quantities and types of LREs (Alegría de la Colina & García Mayo, 2007).

Table 5. Type of Grammatical LREs

	Sum	%	% Total LREs
Word Order	13	20	11.0
Verb Tense	12	18	10.2
Verb Phrase	12	18	10.2
Verb Aspect	8	12	6.8
Agreement (Subject-Verb)	6	9	5.1
Preposition	6	9	5.1
Verb Mood	4	6	3.4
Agreement (Noun-Adjective)	2	3	1.7
Pronoun	2	3	1.7
Definite Article	1	2	0.8
Total	**66**	**100**	**55.9**

Table 6 indicates that learners primarily discussed problems with the types of words produced by the Web-based translator, including false cognates (*letra*, a letter of the alphabet vs. *carta*, a letter mailed at a post office) and subtle yet important differences in the meaning of words (*golpear la puerta*, 'to bang on the door' vs. *tocar la puerta* 'to knock on the door'). Discussions of the word meanings were not restricted to a particular part of speech and included verbs (e.g., *conseguimos, acabo de*) as well as nouns (e.g., *dining room*).

Table 6. Type of Lexical LREs

	Sum	%	% Total LREs
Word choice	36	73	30.51
Word meaning	13	27	11.02
Total	**49**	**100**	**41.53**

Table 7. Type of Orthographic LREs

	Sum	%	% Total LREs
Spelling	2	67	2
Accent marks	1	33	1
Total	**3**	**100**	**3**

Research question 3 addresses whether or not learners were able to solve the grammatical and lexical problems originating in the language-related episodes. As Table 8 illustrates, learners were able to correctly solve almost two-thirds of all of the LREs. Further comparisons in Tables 9 and 10, reveal that the learners correctly solved more than half of the grammatical problems and 71% of lexical errors in the translations. Table 11 shows that, while fewer in number than grammatical and lexical LREs, learners also solved most of the orthographic problems identified in their off-line collaborative dialogue.

Table 8. Resolution of All LREs

	Sum	%	*M*	*SD*
Correctly solved	74	63		
Incorrectly solved	44	37		
Total	118	100	.61	.49

Table 9. Resolution of Grammatical LREs

	Sum	%	% of total LREs	*M*	*SD*
Correctly solved	37	56.06	31.36		
Incorrectly solved	29	43.94	24.57		
Total	66	100	55.93	.56	.50

Table 10. Resolution of Lexical LREs

	Sum	%	% of total LREs	*M*	*SD*
Correctly solved	35	71.43	29.66		
Incorrectly solved	14	28.57	11.87		
Total	49	100	41.53	.67	.47

Table 11. Resolution of Orthographic LREs

	Sum	%	% of total LREs	*M*	*SD*
Correctly solved	2	67	1.69		
Incorrectly solved	1	33	.85		
Total	3	100	2.54	.67	.58

When comparing lexical and grammatical LREs, the lower number of solutions to grammatical problems with the translations may be attributable to the difficulty of 2 of the 12 sentences: *I hope that my friends and I are able to catch that flight.* and *We got robbed last week.* (Appendix). All of the eight dyads identified these sentences as grammatically incorrect, but none was able to provide a correct solution.

3.3   Summary of results

Overall, the results of this study suggest that learners' offline collaborative discourse provided opportunities for them to become aware of and correctly solve many of the problems in the output generated by a commonly-used translation site. The finding of the potential benefits of learners' offline talk for promoting language awareness of grammatical and lexical problems matches that of Kitade (2008) and is consistent with the benefits of peer collaboration for revising machine translations that were observed by Niño (2008). The results of the present study indicate that offline peer dialogue allows learners to become aware of differences in English and Spanish, a stated goal in both the *Standards* and the *CEFRL*.

4.   Pedagogical applications

There are two general approaches that teachers could adopt regarding the use of online translation sites either for similar or different tasks. The first option is to use a single site, and the second would be to use several sites. There are advantages and disadvantages to both approaches, so the choice might depend on a variety of factors that will be different for each educational context. One possible compromise would be to use the same translation website each time there is an in-class activity, but whenever the students have to work on a project either in the language lab or outside of class they could be instructed to use any other site. This option would allow all students to become quite familiar with a single site, which would provide a common point of reference for the class.

4.1   Recommendations for replication or using a similar task

In Tables 1, 2, and 3 above, nouns, *ser/estar*, and other linguistic features were tested in three different online translation sites. An extension of the words and phrases analyzed in these three tables could be done by examining the results with students and asking them which other words or phrases could cause similar problems for one or more of the translation sites. This will challenge them to think in terms of grammatical categories (i.e., parts of speech and the organization of linguistic systems in both languages), and at the same time they will have to begin developing hypotheses about the affordances and constraints of translation software. Even though the tasks mentioned in the sections below use examples from Spanish, these are readily adaptable to grammatical, lexical, and sociopragmatic features of other languages.

Awareness through the analysis of differences and similarities in languages is a stated component of the *Standards* and the *CEFRL* discussed previously (see Section 1.1). As such, for the category of nouns (Table 1), teachers could design exercises with words that have similar spelling in both languages yet are different in meaning (such as *cuestión* = matter; *éxito* = success; *pariente* = relative), as well as for other parts of speech: adjectives (*actual* = present/right now; *embarazada* = pregnant, *sensible* = sensitive) and verbs (*asistir* = to attend; *atender* = to take care of/attend to). Learners could also use translation sites to find and then identify any limitations involved in the translation of true cognates.

In addition to the verb *invitar* (*to invite*) presented in Table 3, it would certainly be helpful for students to work on other verbs with the "personal *a*" (e.g., *llamar a Gabriela, ver a Eduardo,* etc.). Learners should also work with translations of other verbs that require prepositions before an infinitive (e.g., *comenzar/ empezar a* = to begin to; *dejar de* = to stop; *tratar de* = to try to/to deal with; *consentir en* = to consent to; *soñar con* = to dream of) as well as verbs that require a preposition in Spanish that is not the same in English (e.g., *depender de* = to depend on; *consistir en* = to consist of; *casarse con* = to get married to). An extension of this task could involve asking students to use the results of their findings on differences in the use of prepositions in order to hypothesize about which other verbs and structures require prepositions in Spanish, but not in English, and vice versa.

Students could also test the lexicon of the online software in an attempt to determine how much technical vocabulary is included. Any domain or area of expertise could be chosen, and if students themselves choose the subject area (business, medical, or legal Spanish) and are responsible for supplying the vocabulary, they will begin to understand the difference between electronic (and even print) resources that provide only one answer and those that provide multiple answers and actual examples of words and phrases used in more than one context. Once again, students could be asked to hypothesize about the lexicon. Are all sports, musical instruments, and countries included? Why some and not others? Are the same (or different) sports, musical instruments, and countries included in all the online translation software? Does the software produce different results depending on whether an isolated lexical item vs. a contextualized lexical item (e.g., a noun as part of a noun phrase, clause, or sentence) is entered? These are only a few of the questions students could be asked to reflect on regarding the lexicon.

5.   Conclusion

Findings from the research reported in this chapter suggest a number of possibilities for additional empirical studies in Spanish and other languages. A study could compare a group of students who are given lists of sentences that highlight problematic features of the sentences (or the number of errors in each sentence) produced by a translation site with a group of students who are only given a list of sentences without such guidance. Studies could focus on one or two grammatical features (e.g., tense, mood, aspect) or lexical equivalents (idiomatic expressions, false cognates, terminology in courses emphasizing medical, legal, or business language) and compare the outcomes of students' collaborative dialogue using different translation sites for these features. Future research could also study and compare students' evaluation or revision of translations of larger stretches of different types of texts/genres (Niño, 2008). Studies investigating (and evaluating) the effectiveness of translation sites for politeness and other aspects of sociopragmatic variation (requests, invitations, refusals, apologies, compliments) provide another possible line of research.

References

Alegría de la Colina, A., & García Mayo, M. P. (2007). Attention to form across collaborative tasks by low proficiency learners in an EFL setting. In M. P. García Mayo (Ed.) *Investigating tasks in formal language learning* (pp. 91–116). Clevedon: Multilingual Matters.

Alley, D. C. (2005). Using computer translation websites to further the objectives of the foreign language standards. In C. M. Cherry & L. Bradley (Eds.), *Languages and language learners: Dimension 2005* (pp. 63–74). Valdosta, GA: Southern Conference on Language Teaching.

Breiner-Sanders, K. E., Lowe, P., Jr., Miles, J., & Swender, E. (2000). ACTFL proficiency guidelines – Speaking: Revised 1999. *Foreign Language Annals, 33,* 13–18.

Breiner-Sanders, K. E., Swender, E., & Terry, R. M. (2002). Preliminary proficiency guidelines – Writing: Revised 2001. *Foreign Language Annals, 35,* 9–15.

Butt, J., & Benjamin, C. (2004). *A new reference grammar of modern Spanish* (4th ed.). New York, NY: McGraw-Hill.

Chapelle, C. (2007). Technology and second language acquisition. *Annual Review of Applied Linguistics, 27,* 98–114.

Council of Europe. (2001). *Common European framework of reference for languages: Learning, teaching, assessment.* Cambridge: Cambridge University Press.

Kern, R. (2000). *Literacy and language teaching.* Oxford: Oxford University Press.

Kitade, K. (2008). The role of offline metalanguage talk in asynchronous computer-mediated communication. *Language Learning and Technology, 12,* 64–84. Available from http://llt.msu.edu/vol12num1/kitade/default.html

Lapkin, S., Swain, M., & Smith, M. (2002). Reformulation and the learning of French pronominal verbs in a Canadian French immersion context. *Modern Language Journal, 86,* 485–507.

Liskin-Gasparro, J. E. (2003). The ACTFL proficiency guidelines and the Oral Proficiency Interview: A brief history and analysis of their survival. *Foreign Language Annals, 36,* 483–490.

Leeser, M. J. (2004). Learner proficiency and focus on form during collaborative dialogue. *Language Teaching Research, 8,* 55–81.

National Standards in Foreign Language Education Project. (1999). *Standards for foreign language learning in the 21st century.* Lawrence, KS: Allen Press.

Niño, A. (2008). Evaluating the use of machine translation post-editing in the foreign language class. *Computer Assisted Language Learning, 21,* 29–49.

Qi, D. S., & Lapkin, S. (2001). Exploring the role of noticing in a three-stage second language writing task. *Journal of Second Language Writing, 10,* 277–303.

Ramón Garcia, N. (2006). Mapping meaning onto form: A corpus-based contrastive study of nominal modification in English and Spanish. *Languages in Contrast, 6,* 307–334.

Real Academia Española & Asociación de Academias de la Lengua Española (2005). *Diccionario panhispánico de dudas.* Bogotá, Colombia: Santillana.

Somers, H. (2003). Machine translation in the classroom. In H. Somers (Ed.), *Computers and translation: A translator's guide* (pp. 319–340). Amsterdam: John Benjamins.

Storch, N. (2007). Investigating the merits of pair work on a text editing task in ESL classes. *Language Teaching Research, 11,* 143–159.

Svalberg, A. (2007). Language awareness and language learning. *Language Teaching 40,* 287–308.

Swain, M., Brooks, L., & Tocalli-Beller, A. (2002). Peer-peer dialogue as a means of second language learning. *Annual Review of Applied Linguistics, 22,* 171–185.

Swain, M., & Lapkin, S. (2002). Talking it through: Two French immersion learners' response to reformulation. *International Journal of Educational Research, 37,* 285–304.

Swain, M., & Lapkin, S. (1998). Interaction and second language learning: Two adolescent French immersion students working together. *Modern Language Journal, 82,* 320–337.

van Lier, L. (2001). Language awareness. In R. Carter & D. Nunan (Eds.), *The Cambridge guide to teaching English to speakers of other languages* (pp. 160–165). Cambridge: Cambridge University Press.

Vañó-Cerdá, A. (1982). *Ser y estar + adjetivos: Un estudio sincrónico y diacrónico.* Tübingen: Gunter Narr.

Whitley, M. S. (2002). *Spanish/English contrasts: A course in Spanish linguistics* (2nd ed.). Washington, DC: Georgetown University Press.

Williams, L. (2006). Web-based machine translation as a tool for promoting electronic literacy and language awareness. *Foreign Language Annals, 39,* 565–578.

Appendix
Web-Based Translation Task

Decide if you and your partner accept the sentence as translated from English to Spanish by AltaVista's on-line translation software *Babel Fish*.

If you accept it, write "okay" in the space provided and continue to the next number on the list below. If you do <u>not</u> accept it, discuss what needs to be changed and explain why to each other. Write the correct version in the space provided. Please translate one sentence at a time and please do not use your dictionary for this activity.

1. *There are two chairs in the dining room.*
Result from Babel Fish: Hay dos sillas en el cuarto que cena.
Your final version of the acceptable/correct Spanish sentence:

---

2. *I've just written a letter to Paul.*
Result from Babel Fish: Acabo de escribir una letra a Paul.
Your final version of the acceptable/correct Spanish sentence:

---

3. *Me and my brother play at the park on Tuesdays.*
Result from Babel Fish: Yo y mi juego del hermano en el parque el martes.
Your final version of the acceptable/correct Spanish sentence:

---

4. *When I go to Canada, I play golf. When I visit my friends in Spain, I play tennis.*
Result from Babel Fish: Cuando voy a Canadá, juego golf. Cuando visito a mis amigos en España, juego a tenis.
Your final version of the acceptable/correct Spanish sentence:

---

5. *I have been working here since September.*
Result from Babel Fish: He estado trabajando aquí desde septiembre.
Your final version of the acceptable/correct Spanish sentence:

---

6. *I hope that my friends and I are able to catch that flight.*
Result from Babel Fish: Espero que mis amigos y yo poder coger ese vuelo.
Your final version of the acceptable/correct Spanish sentence:

---

7. *My brother does not know the neighbors, but I do.*
Result from Babel Fish: Mi hermano no conoce a los vecinos, pero .
Your final version of the acceptable/correct Spanish sentence:

---

8. *Yesterday I woke up at 5 in the morning.*
Result from Babel Fish: Desperté ayer en 5 de la mañana.
Your final version of the acceptable/correct Spanish sentence:

---

9. *Have you seen The Man Who Knew Too Much?*
Result from Babel Fish: ¿Usted ha visto a hombre que sabía demasiado?
Your final version of the acceptable/correct Spanish sentence:

---

10. *My wife and I want to buy a house soon.*
Result from Babel Fish: Mi esposa y yo deseamos comprar una casa pronto.
Your final version of the acceptable/correct Spanish sentence:

---

11. *He was cooking when I knocked on the door.*
Result from Babel Fish: Él cocinaba cuando golpeé en la puerta.
Your final version of the acceptable/correct Spanish sentence:

---

12. *We got robbed last week.*
Result from Babel Fish: Conseguimos la semana pasada robada.
Your final version of the acceptable/correct Spanish sentence:

PART II

Chat

Learner noticing, negative feedback, and uptake in synchronous computer-mediated environments

Susana M. Sotillo

This study analyzes a subset of data from chat logs and transcribed voice chats from a previous investigation by Sotillo (2005) of exchanges between tutors and English as a Second Language (ESL) learners as they collaborated on four learning tasks in an instant messaging environment, Yahoo! Instant Messenger (YIM). Given the characteristics of learner-interlocutor exchanges and negotiation work documented by previous Second Language Acquisition (SLA)/ Computer-Mediated Communication (CMC) researchers (e.g., Blake, 2000; Jepson, 2005; Smith, 2003), this study focuses on the characteristics of repair work in language-related episodes, type and quality of negative feedback, and learner uptake. The purpose of this study is to identify how learners notice linguistic forms (both erroneous output and target-like linguistic forms) during naturally occurring negotiation work in an online environment using voice and text-based chat.

1. Introduction

1.1 Second language acquisition and the cognitivist-interaction framework

Research focusing on negotiation of meaning and modifications of learner output by Pica, Holliday, Lewis, and Morgenthaler (1989) and Pica, Lincoln-Porter, Paninos, and Linnell (1996) provides evidence that various types of negotiation or repair moves bring about different kinds of interlanguage modifications. In addition, researchers have used tasks designed to encourage interaction and negotiation in dyad work. Interaction in dyads consisting of native speakers (NSs) and English as a Second Language/second language (L2) learners has been compared to that of dyads of English L2 learners. Pica (1994) and Gass, Mackey, and Pica (1998) argue that task-based negotiation plays a powerful role in language learning because it draws learners' attention to linguistic gaps in their knowledge. The results of subsequent studies, including meta-analyses that combine quantitative findings across many similar studies into statistical aggregations, have established that interaction during task completion between learners and interlocutors facilitates second language learning (Mackey & Goo, 2007).

Recent SLA investigations focusing on negotiated interaction and output have stressed psycholinguistic factors and learner-initiated repair moves. For instance, Izumi (2003) used Levelt's (1989) psycholinguistic framework to analyze learner output, and Shehadeh (2001) drew attention to the importance of self-initiated repair or output modification, a feature often ignored in SLA.

Though communicative classrooms encourage learner output, second language learners continue to experience linguistic problems. As a result, a group of SLA researchers refined and extended the focus on form (FonF) approach originally proposed by Long (1996), who argued that instruction in a communicative classroom that includes focus on linguistic form can increase the salience of positive evidence. FonF is also a means of providing essential negative evidence as negative or corrective feedback to learners.

1.2 Language-related episodes and attention to form

Various studies have reported that focusing on form in meaning-centered language classrooms is an instructional option that leads to instances of successful learner uptake or learner acknowledgment of an interlocutor's or a teacher's negative feedback (Ellis, Basturkmen, & Loewen, 2001; Loewen, 2004). More recent FonF studies have shown that incidental focus-on-form, as opposed to direct or explicit focus-on-form, may be beneficial to learners if they incorporate problematic linguistic forms targeted during negotiated interaction into their own output, and are later able to recall these targeted linguistic items following the administration of immediate and delayed post-tests (Loewen, 2005; Williams, 2001). One recent study showed that in student-initiated preemptive focus-on-form, there was a significant relationship between the presence of metalanguage and the incidence of successful learner uptake (Basturkmen, Loewen, & Ellis, 2002).

Research on the provision of error correction or negative information, orally or in writing, is now referred to as negative feedback since intentionality cannot be assumed. Various SLA researchers have pointed out that implicit negative feedback in the form of recasts is beneficial to learners' short-term development of the grammatical forms targeted (Braidi, 2002; Doughty & Varela, 1998; Iwashita, 2003). Others, however, have suggested that negotiation moves, such as clarification requests, are more beneficial to learners than recasts because they are more effective in drawing learners' attention to linguistic forms (Lyster & Ranta, 1997).

Recent negotiation of form studies that examine the provision of indirect or explicit negative feedback by teachers or interlocutors have been carried out in a variety of computer-mediated environments that allow for both asynchronous and synchronous communication.

Swain and Lapkin (1995) investigated how learners negotiated form during collaborative writing tasks and labeled these negotiation-of-form activities language-related episodes (LREs). Since LREs allow learners to focus on various aspects of language while collaborating on meaning-focused tasks, Swain (1995, 1997, 2000) claimed that LREs provided researchers with a means of observing the cognitive process of noticing, viewed as a major component of language acquisition by Schmidt (1990, 1995, 2001).

The original LREs were redefined by Williams (1999) as learner-initiated episodes that focused on negotiation of either meaning or form. The results of her FonF SLA investigations showed that the degree and type of learner-initiated attention to form was related to proficiency level and the nature of the learning activity. Ellis, Basturkmen, and Loewen (2001) used the term Learner-Initiated Focus on Form in their investigations of learner language and attention to form in second language classrooms. The results of FonF investigations into second/foreign language classrooms show that negotiation of form facilitates metareflection and learner self-regulation processes. Also, negative feedback provided to learners, whether explicit or implicit, encourages these processes which seem to facilitate language learning as evidenced by immediate and delayed post-test gains reported in the FonF SLA literature.

2.   Computer-mediated communication (CMC) and SLA

Computer-mediated communication or CMC, whether synchronous or asynchronous, oral or written, has been shown to offer learners a potentially rich environment for language learning. In recent years, CMC studies carried out in classrooms and laboratory settings have adapted theoretical frameworks and methodologies from SLA face-to-face (F2F) investigations.

Investigations of networked language learning in the 1990s reported that more equitable learner participation and more opportunities to use more complex language were among the major benefits found in this type of environment (Beauvuois, 1992; Chun, 1994; Kelm, 1992; Kern, 1995; Warschauer, 1996). CMC studies also investigated the development of linguistic complexity in students' asynchronous and synchronous discussions, and adjustments to the communicative setting (Davis & Thiede, 2000; Schultz, 2000; Sotillo, 2000).

Studies have also examined language learning outcomes and differences between F2F and CMC interaction (Abrams, 2003; Fernández-García & Martínez-Arbelaiz, 2002; Warschauer, 1996). From a sociocultural perspective, CMC has been investigated as a site where participants co-construct a dynamic and student-centered discourse community (Darhower, 2002).

Methodologies from F2F SLA research, such as the Varonis and Gass (1985) schema, which includes a trigger, indicator, response, and reaction, have been used for coding negotiation work in mixed dyads. For example, in his investigation of negotiated interaction, Blake (2000) found that CMC provided many of the benefits for language learning predicted by the Interaction Hypothesis, as well as opportunities to maximize language learning claimed by Warschauer (1997) and Warschauer and Kern (2000). His research also showed that the focus on most negotiation work involved lexical items and not morphosyntax.

Others have investigated the quantity and quality of language produced by learners in negotiation work while engaged in jigsaw, decision-making, and free-discussion tasks (Oskoz, 2004; Smith, 2003). CMC negotiation work among children learning a foreign language has also been examined. For example, Morris (2005) found that children participating in a CMC Spanish immersion program provided over 50% of implicit negative feedback in the form of recasts and negotiation moves, and that most corrections involved lexical items.

Though the methodology of previous SLA interactionist studies has been used in these technology-mediated investigations, as Smith (2005, 2008) points out, many challenges remain concerning the design of these studies and operationalization of key concepts.

Two recent studies by Lai and Zhao (2006) and Shekary and Tahririan (2006) have investigated noticing in online negotiated interaction. These studies were partly motivated by Warschauer's (1997) observations that the text-based aspect of synchronous-computer-mediated communication (SCMC) amplified students' attention to linguistic form or noticing.

3.   Video and audio modalities in SCMC

Only a handful of studies have explored the advantages of video and audio in current SCMC that would allow learners to focus on both meaning and form. Additionally, a limited number of studies have explored these modalities during interaction work outside classroom settings and across national borders (see Belz

& Thorne, 2006; Lee, 2006; Levy & Kennedy, 2004; Sotillo, 2005). Jepson (2005) was among the first to investigate nonnative speaker (NNS)-nonnative speaker (NNS) conversational repair moves in both text and voice synchronous chat rooms. He found that self-correction, which is considered evidence of noticing, was not found in SCMC. He claimed that the NNS-NNS SCMC context was not conducive to self-correction; however, Smith (2008) has challenged these findings and argues that SCMC interaction needs to be captured using video, audio, and screen capture tools in order to highlight its many nuances. According to Smith and Gorsuch (2004), relying on printed chat scripts is insufficient to document the important cognitive process of noticing for language learning.

4.   Methodology

This study utilizes a subset of data from chat logs and transcribed voice chats from a previous investigation by Sotillo (2005) of exchanges between tutors and ESL learners as they collaborated on four learning tasks in an instant messaging environment *Yahoo! Instant Messenger* (YIM).

Voice and text-based chat data obtained from four dyads – two NS-L2 learners and two advanced NNS (ANNS)-L2 learners – were analyzed. The study was motivated by recent investigations on noticing and repair work in SCMC voice and text-based chats (Jepson, 2005; Smith 2003; Shekary & Tahririan, 2006), as well as by student-initiated preemptive FonF research (Basturkmen, Loewen, and Ellis, 2002). Three research questions are addressed and the categories used in the methodology section are adapted from previous work by Williams (1999), Loewen (2004), and Shekary and Tahririan (2006). The unit of analysis utilized is the LRE, which is defined as an instance where a learner notices an error in his/her L2 output, self-corrects, or requests direct or indirect information about a linguistic form or lexical item in negative feedback provided by a tutor during the process of completing a learning task. Indirect negative feedback is provided to learners through negotiation moves and recasts during task collaboration, whereas direct feedback is provided as explicit error correction, metalinguistic explanations, explicit provision of linguistic form or lexical item by tutor. Given the characteristics of learner-interlocutor exchanges and negotiation work documented by previous SLA-CMC researchers (Blake, 2000; Jepson, 2005; Smith, 2003), this study focuses on the characteristics of repair work in LREs, type and quality of negative feedback, and learner uptake.

4.1   Research questions

Voice and text SCMC chats have been shown to have the potential to benefit language learners outside traditional classroom contexts and to possibly facilitate L2 learning processes. The examination of noticing in what Swain (1997, 2000) refers to as mini-dialogs is an important first step in determining how learners indicate lack of knowledge of specific linguistic items. In this study, no tailor-made immediate or delayed post-tests were administered to participants following the completion of collaborative learning tasks. Thus, it was not possible to evaluate the effectiveness of noticing and uptake on subsequent language learning.

The purpose of this study is to identify how learners notice linguistic forms (both erroneous output and target-like linguistic forms) during naturally occurring negotiation work in an online environment using voice and text-based chat. The following research questions are addressed:

1. Do English L2 learners notice linguistic forms while negotiating meaning with their tutors in an SCM environment?
2. Which modality, voice or text-based chat, affords learners more opportunities for noticing linguistic forms?
3. What type and quality of negative feedback is provided by tutors engaged in repair work, and is there evidence of immediate or successful uptake?

4.2   Participants and tasks

Negotiation work in these SCMC voice and text-based chats occurred naturally since participants were not monitored by the researcher or any ESL instructor. Furthermore, this was not a quasi-experiment taking place in a language laboratory. The participants were collaborating on various tasks from the comfort of their own homes while using *Yahoo!* Instant Messenger and a Webcam that had been provided to 12 individuals who had initially volunteered for this study. Two dyad members dropped out because of scheduling conflicts and technical problems. The aim of the original pilot study was two-fold: (a) to encourage negotiation work and language use via a specific type of SCMC, instant messaging, and (b) to provide learners with opportunities to request corrective or negative feedback from their partners during negotiation work while completing several 45-minute tasks.

The data used in this study were obtained from two NS tutors and two advanced-NNS (ANNS) tutors who were enrolled in an undergraduate course required for TESL certification. The ANNS tutors spoke Spanish and Brazilian Portuguese, respectively, and the NNSs who participated in this pilot project, three females and one male, were volunteers not enrolled in ESL classes at the time.

They ranged in age from 18 to 36. One of the participants was a male student who lived in Sao Paolo, Brazil, and spoke Brazilian Portuguese as a first language. Other first languages spoken included: Korean, Spanish, and Vietnamese.

The NS and ANNS tutors, one male and three females, ranged in age from 24 to 32. They were not instructed by the researcher or staff to favor either the provision of direct or indirect negative feedback to learners. They were simply asked to encourage learners to use the L2 during interaction via *YIM* or in both voice and text-based chats.

In exchange for their participation in this pilot study, all volunteers were loaned *LogiTech* Webcams and the accompanying software for up to five months. All participants, tutors and English L2 learners, first filled out a questionnaire developed by the Office of Information Technology (OIT) staff in order to determine whether or not they had the required hardware and Internet connections for SCMC collaborative work. Next, they were shown how to use the equipment on a one-on-one basis. An OIT staff member and the researcher spent two consecutive weeks with members of each of the dyads, showing them how to initiate chat sessions, record their voice chats, and save chat logs for subsequent analysis.

Participants completed the following 45-minute collaborative tasks: (a) jointly filling out a career goals questionnaire, (b) synthesizing information inferred from reading a newspaper or magazine article, (c) negotiating individual perceptions about the content of a movie or documentary each student had seen separately, and (d) discussing and evaluating the usefulness of instant messaging as a language learning tool. All dyad members interacted outside a laboratory or traditional classroom setting using similar equipment, resources, and tasks.

4.3   Coding procedures: LREs, negative feedback, and learner uptake

A subset of text and voice chat data from the original pilot project was analyzed separately by the researcher and a trained assistant. In addition, 30 additional minutes of two short oral exchanges were transcribed, coded, and analyzed. The transcribed voice chats were separated from the text-based chat logs in order to identify instances of noticing in negotiation work between tutors and learners. This allowed for more reliable identification and coding of the type and quality of negative feedback provided to learners, and instances of learner uptake and successful uptake. The interrater reliability coefficient obtained was .95.

Language-related episodes (LREs), characteristics of negative feedback, and learner response traditionally employed in F2F SLA interaction research were identified, coded, and subsequently tagged for analysis in a 16,525-word corpus, which consisted of voice and text-based chats. A concordancer, MonoConc

(Barlow, 2002), was used to obtain tagged LREs, types of negative feedback, and instances and types of learner uptake.

Table 1. LREs (adapted from Loewen, 2004; Shekary & Tahririan, 2006), negative feedback, and learner uptake

Features or Characteristics	Definition	Categories
Language-Related Episodes	A LRE is instantiated when attention is momentarily shifted from focusing on content or meaning to linguistic form while collaborating on a task (e.g., finding out about each other's career goals). It normally consists of a trigger, a response, and a learner acknowledgement or uptake. These are often classified as either reactive or preemptive in the SLA literature.	Learner-Initiated LREs: Attention shift to linguistic form is initiated by the ESL learner during negotiation work. Other-Initiated LREs: LREs initiated by the NS or ANNS tutor during negotiation work in reaction to lexical, morphosyntactic or phonological difficulty.
Type of Negative Feedback (NF) – Quality of Feedback	Negative or corrective feedback provided to learner.	Direct, Indirect Direct feedback includes metalinguistic explanations, definitions of terms, or the provision of explicit information. Indirect feedback involves implicit responses to a linguistic item through the use of recasts, clarification requests (e.g., *What do you mean?*), repetitions (*horror, horror*), confirmation checks (e.g., *Heaven is where happiness is?*), or comprehension checks (e.g., *Does that make sense?*) Accurate: Feedback conforms to Standard (or academic) American English (SAE) lexical, morphosyntactic, and phonological conventions. Inaccurate: Feedback does not conform to SAE conventions.
Learner Response	NNS's response to feedback	Uptake, No Uptake
Characteristics of Learner Response	Whether the learner incorporated or failed to incorporate NF as evidenced in subsequent turns	Successful Uptake, Unsuccessful Uptake

Noticing as used in this study is defined as either the learner's act of detecting a problematic grammatical/lexical feature in his/her output or requesting information or clarification from the tutor concerning a specific linguistic form or lexical feature during negotiation work. An LRE may be initiated by the learner as either a self-correction, a clarification request, a request for information concerning a linguistic form, or it may also constitute the learner's reaction to a tutor's clarification request, comprehension check, confirmation check or exact repetition. In such instances, attention is shifted momentarily from the content or meaning being negotiated to a linguistic form.

Language-related episodes (LREs) are examined within the context of negotiation work between English L2 learners and their tutors (see Swain & Lapkin, 1995; Williams, 1999). For example, in a text-based chat, a learner may express nonunderstanding (trigger) while completing a learning task or activity with his/her tutor or engage in self-repair by rephrasing or restructuring an utterance in voice chats. Following Shekary and Tahririan's (2006) reformulation, each LRE is defined as consisting of three basic moves: trigger (self-correction or indicator of nonunderstanding), response or feedback, and uptake or learner response (optional move).

Excerpt 1 from a text-based chat illustrates an LRE which occurred in response to an error as the learner and her tutor were collaborating on a task that involved synthesizing information. Instances of self-correction, negative feedback, and learner response (uptake) are indicated in this excerpt. Learner errors appear in italics and negative feedback and instances of self-correction in bold.

Excerpt 1. LRE, text-based chat

003L <ANNS>   Okay, do you think that this new system will help the government get rid of terrorism?

004L <ANNS>   What about getting information on everything we do so they could detect terrorist[s]?

005A <NNS>   not *completly*, but like I say *febore,* something has to be done to at least, stop these people from doing something *worst thatn* what they have *allready* done

006L <ANNS>   **worse** (recast)

007A <NNS>   I *misspell - before-* (**self-correction**)

008L <ANNS>   **than** (recast)

009L <ANNS>   that's okay.

010L <ANNS>   Ana what did you think about the historical trend though?

011A <NNS>   worse (uptake), when I say worse (uptake) I am *reffering* to the attack *to* the Towers

In Excerpt 2 from a voice chat, I and L are discussing a controversial article about the rights of atheists. L, the English L2 learner, requests clarification of the term "Amish" and receives explicit information about this vocabulary entry from her NS partner but fails to use the new word during the exchange (no uptake).

Excerpt 2. LRE, voice chat

7I <NS>	Well, um, the idea was that not America – I don't know about America – specifically, but I know that places like Pennsylvania were founded to keep… well, no it's true
8I <NS>	The Puritans came to America and colonized because they were being persecuted in England. People didn't like their religion. And then Pennsylvania was founded by a man who wanted Amish people and Quakers.
8L <NNS>	What's Amish? (clarification request)
9I <NS>	An Amish person…It's a Christian based religion. They give up Electricity and modern things and they don't leave their own people. And then the Quakers are similar but they have electricity and cars and things like… The Amish are all farmers

I and L continue to discuss and synthesize information from a magazine article as shown in Excerpt 3, but L is unable to find the correct expression when trying to explain why she feels compelled to convert unbelievers. I, the NS, provides the appropriate word, which L immediately acknowledges and uses.

Excerpt 3. LRE, voice chat

48L <NNS>	Um, to me, if I see Atheist, I go for *Evangelist* because personally, it's my personal opinion, but as a Christian if I leave Atheist leaving like that, *it's sin*
49L <NNS>	I have to convert that person to become a Christian to go to heaven
50L <NNS>	I can not leave a person *if I am given to be a Christian* and become converted to a child of God, I have a duty to do
51L <NNS>	God gave me ability…not ability…God gave me some kind of work…
52I <NS>	**responsibility?** (explicit provision of appropriate word)
53L <NNS>	Yeah, responsibility (uptake) to take care of people around Me… So, that's my opinion

4.4   Type and quality of negative feedback

As was mentioned in Section 1.2, negative feedback is the term currently in use for the provision of error correction or negative information, orally or in writing. The provision of negative feedback can be done either indirectly through the use of recasts (i.e., a repetition of a learner's utterance that corrects the error), clarification requests, confirmation checks, repetitions of learners' exact utterances, and comprehension checks, or directly via metalinguistic explanations, definition of terms for clarifying lexical confusion, or by supplying explicit information concerning vocabulary or morphosyntax.

In Excerpt 4, T (an intermediate-advanced ESL learner) and D, her NS partner, are discussing cultural differences and personal information. D politely provides indirect negative feedback in the form of recasts (shown in bold), which T sometimes implicitly acknowledges (uptake). However, the transcribed oral exchanges show that D does not address T's pronunciation errors.[1]

Excerpt 4. LRE, voice chat (transcribed oral exchange)

027T <NNS>	Especially because *you [dʒu]* need to listen to me a little bit more.
028T <NNS>	My parents are worried about me because they might be thinking that I'm living in a horrible place because news in my country *are* always about this country and always related *to big cities big problems.*
029T <NNS>	Maybe, problems in the border in a way… I don't know… Americans are *presented [prisɛntɛd]* differently, and American life too.
030D <NS>	Well, American life is very different.
031T <NNS>	Yeah, it's very very different. I know that. But, they're also *too worried* and they don't understand that I'm also *too worried.*
032T <NNS>	And, maybe I'm not even enjoying being here. To be honest, that's the truth. I'm *too worried* about everything. I don't know. Maybe because *I'm thinking in them.*
033D<NS>	**You're thinking…**
034T<NNS>	*In my parents*
035D<NS>	**About your parents**
036T<NNS>	The people *suppose to be waiting for me*… etc. etc.
037D<NS>	(laughing) **Supposed to be waiting for you?**
038T<NNS>	No, no well, I'm talking about relationships. I did have a very good relationship but *that* doesn't exist anymore. So, I don't know. It's just that *people starts getting you [dʒu] feel worried too?*

---

1. Morphosyntactic and lexical errors appear in italics.

039D<NS>   **making**
040T<NNS>   making you feel worried too? (uptake)
041D<NS>   I suppose. Well, yeah

In contrast, K addresses her partner's pronunciation and grammar in their voice and text-based chats, but on many occasions she provides explicit nontarget-like or inaccurate feedback to R or fails to address morphosyntactic problems. In Excerpt 5, she provides inaccurate negative feedback, which includes common expressions and vocabulary used in both spoken and written American English:

Excerpt 5. LRE, text-based chat: Quality of negative feedback

060K <ANNS>   *"in the other hand"* is an expression that means *"but in the other side"*, understand? (inaccurate feedback)
061R <NNS>   ok do you want that I *answered* again? (learner error not addressed)
062K <ANNS>   yes please
063K <ANNS>   Yes, I would you like if you answered again.
064R <NNS>   I think the article is very interesting, but it has a good and a bad side.
065R <NNS>   It is good because *it might terrorism* but *in the other hand the government* (**learner uptake of inaccurate feedback**) takes away our privacy
066K <ANNS>   You forgot the word "fight" before terrorism. Can you see that? DO you understand this whole sentence?
067R <NNS>   *I think that initial is vey expensive and a dont belive that it can to happen now?*
069K <ANNS>   ok … I'll be correcting this sentence too.
070R <NNS>   ok
071K <ANNS>   YOU should say … I think that initially this project would be Very expensive and I don't believe it could happen now.

In LREs initiated by this ANNS interlocutor, inaccurate negative feedback was often provided to the English L2 learner. In Excerpt 6, R acknowledges K's negative feedback, but is unable to detect inaccuracies in the feedback. In this LRE, K misspells "all right" and leaves out the definite article [the] in line 114 (in bold), and the indefinite article [a] in 117 (in bold):

Excerpt 6. LRE, voice chat (K is also typing): Quality of negative feedback

114K <ANNS>   *alright,* can you see this sentence. Can you say that to me? Say after me…'**I have never been in [ ] United States**' (inaccurate feedback)

115R <NNS>   I have never been in [the] United States (uptake)
116K <ANNS>   yes, it sounds good, you just should practice more – you are by
                 yourself in a loud voice. I did this when I didn't know either.
117K <ANNS>   It's easier to learn. When you read English, **read in [ ] loud voice.**
                 (inaccurate feedback)
118K <ANNS>   o.k. I sent an e-mail to show you how to take your picture.

5.   Results and discussion

The answer to the first research question – whether or not English L2 learners notice linguistic forms while negotiating meaning with their tutors in an SCM environment – is in the affirmative, and the results are displayed in Figures 1 and 2. A total of 98 LREs were identified in this 16,525-word learner corpus consisting of voice and text-based chats.

As shown in Figure 1, learners initiated 65% (24) of all LREs in voice chats, whereas tutors initiated only 35% (13) of all the LREs, and 71% of learner-initiated LREs were in response to tutors' direct and indirect forms of negative feedback.

Though learner-initiated LREs in voice chats were fewer than those found in text-based chats, which are shown in Figure 2, (24 vs. 33, respectively), it is important to keep in mind that only one pair of the two ANNS-ESL learner dyads tape recorded voice exchanges via YIM. Voice chat data from the other ANNS-ESL learner dyad were not available. In fact, the ANNS and English L2 learner collaborating on tasks in voice chats spent more time negotiating both form and meaning than members of the two NS-ESL learner dyads (140 minutes vs. 70 minutes, respectively).

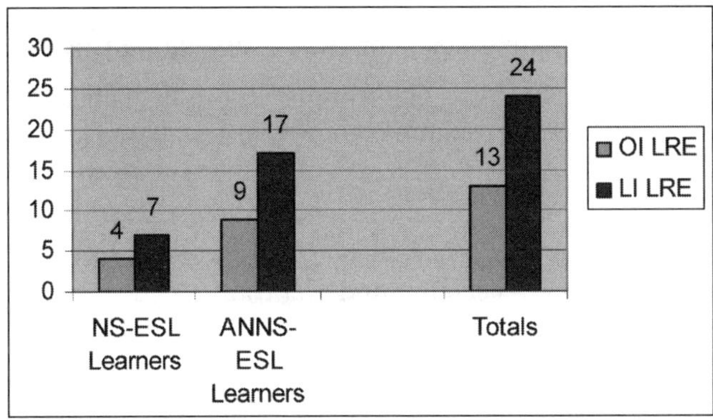

Figure 1. LREs in voice chats

Figure 2 displays raw frequencies for LREs in text-based chats. Again, members of NS-ESL learner dyads spent considerably less time interacting in an SCMC environment than members of ANNS-ESL learner dyads (60 minutes vs. 355 minutes, respectively). Learners initiated 54% of all LREs identified in text-based chats, whereas tutors initiated 46% of all LREs. Most of the other-initiated LREs occurred in ANNS-ESL dyads. The word count for the ANNS-ESL learner dyads was twice that obtained for the NS-ESL learner dyads (6327 vs. 3098, respectively). A close examination of NS-ESL dyad voice and text-based chat data reveals that NS tutors often spent between 15–20 minutes on negotiation work. They completed tasks in a rush and often ended their sessions abruptly. In contrast, the ANNS tutors spent between 45–60 minutes collaborating on each task with their ESL partners. There were 33 instances of self-correction, code-switching, and clarification requests in text-based, learner-initiated LREs as shown in Figure 2.

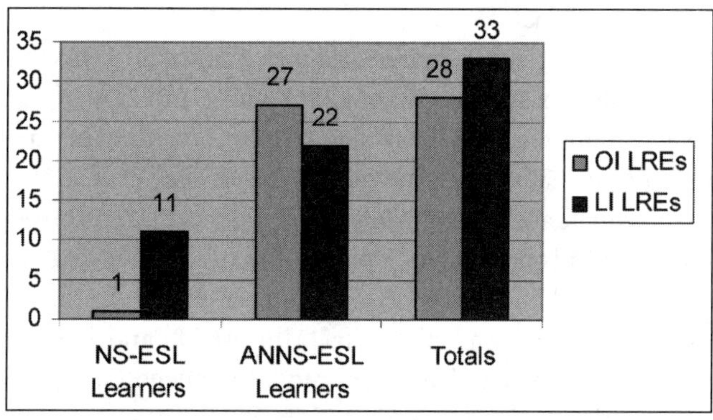

Figure 2. LREs in text-based chats

With respect to the second research question – Which modality, voice or text-based chat, affords learners more opportunities for noticing linguistic forms? – raw frequencies displayed in Figure 3 show that text-based chats afford considerably more opportunities for learners to shift attention to linguistic forms in both their own L2 output and in their tutors' reaction to lexical and morphosyntactic difficulties than voice chats (61 LREs vs. 37 LREs, respectively). However, it is important to keep in mind that transcribed voice chat data were available for only one of the two ANNS-ESL learner dyads. These results contradict findings reported by Jepson (2005) who observed 10 groups of NNSs and obtained significant differences between the higher number of total repair moves made in voice chats and the smaller number in text-based chats. They do support the findings of Shekary and Tahririan (2006) that significant numbers of LREs were present in text-based SCMC. Their study included 16 Persian L2 learners who were asked to complete a variety of language tasks that had been used in previous studies of F2F and computer-mediated interaction: dictogloss, jigsaw, and free discussion tasks.

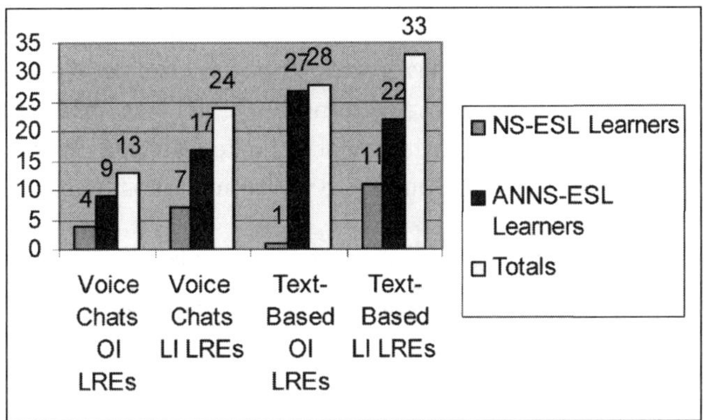

Figure 3. LREs of voice chat vs. text-based chat

Concerning the third research question – What type and quality of negative feedback is provided by tutors engaged in repair work, and is there evidence of immediate or successful uptake? – Table 2 shows that in the subset of chat and voice data analyzed, direct feedback, which includes metalinguistic explanations, definitions, clarification of lexical confusion, and explicit information, accounts for 61% of all negative feedback to learners in voice chats. In contrast, 39% of all negative feedback is of an indirect type, primarily in the form of recasts, requests for clarification, confirmation checks, or exact repetitions. Raw frequencies and percentages displayed in Table 2 also show that 89% of the feedback in voice chats is provided immediately following the trigger.

Table 2. Type and timing of negative feedback to learners in voice chat LREs

Dyads	Type of negative feedback		Timing of negative feedback	
	Indirect	Direct	Immediate	Deferred
NS-ESL Learner (2 dyads)	7	3	9	1
ANNS-ESL Learner (1 dyad)	7	19	23	3
Total	14 (39%)	22 (61%)	32 (89%)	4 (11%)

In text-based chats, direct and indirect feedback frequencies and percentages are displayed in Table 3. These figures show that direct feedback accounts for 77% of all negative feedback, compared with 23% for indirect feedback, and that 85% of all feedback occurs in the turn immediately following the trigger in these LREs. There are few instances of deferred feedback or negative feedback involving more than two turns after the trigger. This is in keeping with observations made by SLA researchers who have often emphasized the importance of providing immediate negative feedback to learners in order to minimize the possibility of their internalizing nontarget like features, which would make restructuring of their interlanguage system quite difficult (Doughty, 2001; Doughty & Long, 2003).

Table 3. Type and timing of negative feedback to learner in text-based chat LREs

Dyads	Type of negative feedback		Timing of turns	
	Indirect	Direct	Immediate	Deferred
NS-ESL Learner (2 dyads)	1	11	9	3
ANNS-ESL Learner (2 dyads)	13	36	43	6
Total	14 (23%)	47 (77%)	52 (85%)	9 (15%)

Table 4 displays overall frequency counts for both accurate and inaccurate or inappropriate negative feedback provided to learners by NS and ANNS tutors. ANNS tutors provided inaccurate negative feedback to ESL learners 37 times in the synchronous voice and text-based chats analyzed. There are possible implications concerning the provision of this type of feedback in that learners run the risk of internalizing nontarget-like morphosyntactic, lexical, or phonological features if their instructors, language resource staff, or trained tutors fail to provide prompt adjustments when responding to ungrammatical learner output. In many cases, inaccurate learner output that deviates from L2 language norms may be the result of nontarget-like negative feedback by peers.

Table 4. Quality of negative feedback provided by tutors in LREs

Dyads	Quality of feedback in both voice and text-based chats	
	Accurate	Inaccurate
NS-ESL Learner (2 dyads)	19	3
ANNS-ESL Learner (2 dyads)	38	37
Total	57	40

In terms of addressing the second part of the third research question – whether or not there is evidence of learner uptake and subsequent successful uptake in voice and text-based online chats – raw frequencies displayed in Table 5 show that there were 31 instances of learner uptake in voice chats that often involved negative feedback targeting lexical, grammatical, and phonological features. Successful learner uptake was 45% or 14 out of 31 instances of all learner uptake identified. English L2 learners appeared to incorporate linguistic forms, phonological features, and L2 vocabulary into their evolving interlanguage as evidenced by their use of specific forms or vocabulary in subsequent exchanges with tutors. Since no immediate or delayed post-tests were administered, we are unable to determine whether this integration or incorporation is long-lasting or short-lived. Though negative feedback on pronunciation errors was provided by only one ANNS tutor, the results show that when learners are encouraged to collaborate on tasks that include opportunities to focus on the pronunciation of specific words or phrases during negotiation work, successful uptake of target-like pronunciation is indeed possible in voice chat LREs.

Table 5. Learner response and type of uptake in voice chats

Dyads	Learner response		Type of uptake	
	Uptake	No uptake	Successful	Unsuccessful
NS-ESL Learners	10	1	2	8
ANNS-ESL Learners	21	5	12	9
Total	31	6	14 (45%)	17 (55%)

Concerning learner response or uptake in text-based chats, the raw frequencies displayed in Table 6 show 36 occurrences of learner uptake or acknowledgement following the provision of negative feedback, and 24 instances of no uptake. Successful learner uptake represents 75% of all uptake found in text-based chats. This type of uptake is corroborated by instances of learners' incorporation of target-like linguistic forms, which are found in subsequent collaborative task work with their tutors. The results of learner uptake and successful uptake displayed in Table 6 support Shekary and Tahririan's (2006) findings concerning the nature of reactive LREs in text-based chats, which focus primarily on grammar. In a previous SCM study, Sotillo (2005) found that the corrective or negative feedback to English L2 learners focused primarily on grammar (42%), vocabulary (38%), spelling (18%), and pronunciation (2%). Language learners were reported by Shekary and Tahririan (2006) to be more likely to repeat the same successful uptake of grammatical structures in subsequent turns, and thus reinforce previous noticing and incorporation of the correct linguistic form provided by an interlocutor reacting to a learner's error (Shekary & Tahririan, 2006, p. 569).

Table 6. Learner response and type of uptake in text-based chats

Dyads	Learner Response		Type of Uptake	
	Uptake	No Uptake	Successful	Unsuccessful
NS-NNS	9	2	6	3
ANNS-NNS	27	22	21	6
Total	36	24	27 (75%)	9 (25%)

6.   Conclusion and implications

This analysis of LREs identified in voice and text-based chat data shows that these SCMC modalities do indeed amplify learners' attention to linguistic form as noted by Warschauer (1997) and challenge current notions of meaning negotiation as applied to negotiated interaction in SCMC environments (Kern, Ware, & Warschauer, 2004, p. 246). As computer-mediated investigations of negotiation work and noticing from a sociocultural perspective have shown, learners and their partners use scaffolding as a tutoring strategy that makes it possible for the language learner to build on prior knowledge (Darhower, 2002). It is often claimed that this tutoring strategy will eventually allow learners to internalize new information. This type of scaffolding was observed in negotiation work between ANNS-ESL learners in these SCMC modalities. As demonstrated during interaction and negotiation work in the two-different types of dyads, successful uptake or incorporation of target-like word order, grammatical features (e.g., articles, prepositions), and vocabulary provided as negative feedback to learners was feasible.

Motivation for the present study included recent FonF studies as well as investigations on noticing and repair work in SCMC oral and text-based chats. In addressing the questions posed, the results of this small-scale exploratory study suggest that different modalities of SCMC, voice and text-based chats, enhanced the learners' cognitive process of noticing, which was operationalized as LREs where the focus momentarily shifts from meaning negotiations to linguistic form(s) during the completion of various tasks in SCMC dyad work.

Caution must be exercised concerning these findings since neither immediate nor delayed post-tests – designed to test learners' interlanguage restructuring or incorporation of new linguistic forms – were administered to the English L2 learners participating in this pilot study. Thus, claims cannot be made that noticing leads to subsequent L2 learning.

Despite these limitations, the results show that negotiation work in synchronous voice and text-based chats, supplemented by the occasional use of visual input via webcams, provides further opportunities for learners to notice linguistic forms or unknown vocabulary. Such was the case when an ANNS tutor asked the learner to pay attention to the screen as she was explaining the present perfect to him. Thus, an SCMC environment appears to maximize opportunities for task collaboration and negotiation of both form and meaning outside the traditional classroom or language laboratory. Learners in this technology-mediated environment were able to self-correct and often requested negative feedback from their tutors concerning a linguistic item, acknowledged the feedback provided, and often modified their output in subsequent task completion activities with their tutors. These results support similar findings by Shekary and Tahririan (2006) in their study of text-based online chats. Their study showed that SCMC interaction enhanced the process of noticing and this was associated with subsequent L2 learning. Furthermore, successful uptake in LREs was the strongest predictor of correct responses in immediate and delayed post-tests (Shekary and Tahririan, 2006, p. 570).

Since the popularity of voice chats has increased as a result of recent innovations and software improvements made by providers of commercial products (e.g., Elluminate and Wimba Classroom), as well as by those offering free online chats (e.g., AIM, MSN, NetMeeting, Skype, Windows Live, and Yahoo!), this and other studies of SCMC have important pedagogical implications. The results show that interaction and language practice are possible between members of two different types of dyads (NS-English L2 learners and ANNS-English L2 learners) in these online environments, but that language instructors and tutors need to develop and use appropriate communicative or learning tasks. As Pica, Kang, and Sauro (2006, p. 301) maintain, two-way information gap tasks have been shown to encourage attention to form, function, and meaning, which often results in modified interaction among learners and their interlocutors. LREs in SCMC environments also afford learners opportunities to notice nontarget-like features in their own output. However, the results of this exploratory study have also shown that learners' momentarily shifting attention to form while negotiating meaning with their partners does not necessarily result in the incorporation of a targeted linguistic form. Even if it is shown in the chat logs or transcribed voice chats that a modified linguistic form or new word is subsequently used in the completion of other tasks, this does not constitute evidence that it has been successfully acquired/learned.

Another important pedagogical implication involves the quality of negative feedback provided by tutors to L2 learners. In this study, 40 occurrences of incorrect or inappropriate feedback to learners by both NS and ANNS tutors were identified. Thus, it is important that second- and foreign-language instructors or teachers-in-training monitor the quality of tutor input to learners, as well as learner output in SCMC. This is something that has not been adequately addressed to date in SLA studies of negotiated interaction in classroom settings or quasi-experiments in language labs. Chat logs and transcribed voice chats allow learners and tutors to focus on a specific linguistic form or reflect on feedback provided in response to clarification requests or explanations regarding lexical or morphosyntactic confusion. Printouts of text-based chats or chat logs are helpful to both learners and tutors. In this study, chat logs were particularly helpful to Participant A, who had lived in the U.S. mainland for more than seven years and had had limited exposure to formal instruction. In general, text-based and transcribed voice chat data are also helpful to instructors and teachers-in-training because they can provide evidence of a learner's developmental stage and evolving interlanguage grammar. Tutors need to be aware of learners' developmental errors and feedback needs. These data can be used in preparing lesson plans or developing new simple and complex online tasks.

With respect to the use of ANNS tutors in SCMC, research on English L2 learners' interaction with other learners and with NSs by Pica, Lincoln-Porter, Paninos, and Linnel (1996) showed that NNS partners could not meet the modified input or negative feedback needs of English L2 learners as well as NS partners could. This seemed to be the case with respect to ANNS input and feedback to English L2 learners in this pilot study. However, NS tutors were unwilling to provide explicit negative feedback to learners, even though they were familiar with SLA research in classroom settings that highlights the value of occasional focus on form. It is possible that NS tutors did not want to discourage learners from using their L2 by providing explicit negative feedback and interrupting the flow of the exchange while solving a technical problem or negotiating meaning in a free discussion task. In addition, since NS tutors were teachers-in-training, it appears that they were already familiar with English L2 learner speech and were thus able to understand the intended meaning of the learners' utterances or written output. This allowed them to immediately fill in linguistic gaps in learner output, a process which was first described by Gass and Varonis (1984) in a study of NS-NNS interaction.

The various modalities of SCMC should be used for collaborative language learning while taking into consideration task demands and learner factors. On-line chatting in its various modalities provides learners enormous opportunities for language practice, metareflection, and noticing outside the traditional classroom environment or language lab setting. In order to encourage L2 usage and the acquisition of linguistic knowledge, task designers must take into consideration the need for user friendly and simple instructions when designing either simple or complex tasks in technology-mediated learning environments. If the learning curve associated with a software program or CMC tools is high and the task instructions are exceedingly lengthy or complicated, learner frustration and anxiety will increase resulting in diminished opportunities for productive L2 language practice and learning.

References

Abrams, Z. I. (2003). The effect of synchronous and asynchronous CMC on oral performance in German. *Modern Language Journal, 87,* 157–167.

Barlow, M. (2002). MonoConc Pro (Version 2.2) [Computer software]. Houston: Athelstan.

Basturkmen, H., Loewen, S., & Ellis, R. (2002). Metalanguage in focus on form in the communicative classroom. *Language Awareness, 11,* 1–13.

Beauvois, M. H. (1992). Computer-assisted classroom discussion in the foreign language classroom: Conversation in slow motion. *Foreign Language Annals, 25,* 455–464.

Belz, J. A., & Thorne, S. L. (2006). Introduction: Internet-mediated intercultural foreign language education and the intercultural speaker. In J. A. Belz., & S. L. Thorne. (Eds.), *Internet-mediated intercultural foreign language education* (pp. viii–xxv). Boston, MA: Heinle & Heinle.

Blake, R. (2000). Computer mediated communication: A window on L2 Spanish interlanguage. *Language Learning & Technology, 4,* 120–136. Available from http://llt.msu.edu/vol4num1/blake/

Braidi, S. M. (2002). Reexamining the role of recasts in native-speaker/non-native-speaker interactions. *Language Learning, 52,* 1–42.

Chun, D. M. (1994). Using computer networking to facilitate the acquisition of interactive competence. *System, 22,* 17–31.

Darhower, M. (2002). Instructional features of synchronous computer-mediated communication in the L2 class: A sociocultural case study. *CALICO Journal, 19,* 249–277.

Davis, B., & Thiede, R. (2000). Writing into change: Style-shifting in asynchronous electronic discourse. In M. Warschauer & R. Kern (Eds.), *Network-based language teaching: Concepts and practice* (pp. 87–120). Cambridge: Cambridge University Press.

Doughty, C. (2001). Cognitive underpinnings of focus on form. In P. Robinson (Ed.), *Cognition and second language instruction* (pp. 206–257). Cambridge: Cambridge University Press.

Doughty, C. J., & Long, M. H. (2003). Optimal psycholinguistic environments for distance foreign language learning. *Language Learning & Technology, 7,* 50–80. Available from http://llt.msu.edu/vol7num3/doughty/

Doughty, C., & Varela, E. (1998). Communicative focus on form. In C. Doughty & J. Williams (Eds.), *Focus on form in classroom second language acquisition* (pp. 114–138). Cambridge: Cambridge University Press.

Doughty, C., & Williams, J. (Eds.). (1998). *Focus on Form in classroom second language acquisition.* Cambridge: Cambridge University Press.

Ellis, R., Basturkmen, H., & Loewen, S. (2001). Learner uptake in communicative ESL lessons. *Language Learning, 51,* 281–318.

Ellis, R., Basturkmen, H., & Loewen, S. (2002). Doing focus on form. *System, 30,* 419–432.

Fernández-García, M., & Martínez-Arbelais, A. (2002). Negotiation of meaning in nonnative speaker-nonnative speaker synchronous discussions. *CALICO Journal, 19,* 279–294.

Gass, S. M., & Varonis, E. (1984). The effect of familiarity on the comprehension of nonnative speakers. *Language Learning, 34,* 65–89.

Gass, S. M., Mackey, A., & Pica, T. (1998). The role of input and interaction in second language acquisition: Introduction to the special issue. *Modern Language Journal, 82,* 299–307.

Iwashita, N. (2003). Negative feedback and positive evidence in task-based interaction. *Studies in Second Language Acquisition, 25,* 1–36.

Izumi, S. (2003). Comprehension and production processes in second language learning: In search of the psycholinguistic rationale of the Output Hypothesis. *Applied Linguistics, 24,* 168–196.

Jepson, K. (2005). Conversations – and negotiated interaction – in text and voice chat rooms. *Language Learning & Technology, 9,* 79–98. Available from http://llt.msu.edu/vol9num3/jepson/default.html

Kelm, O. R. (1992). The use of synchronous computer networks in second language instruction: A preliminary report. *Foreign Language Annals, 25,* 441–454.

Kern, R. (1995). Restructuring classroom interaction with networked computers: Effects on quantity and quality of language production. *Modern Language Journal, 79,* 457–476.

Kern, R., Ware, P., & Warschauer, M. (2004). Crossing frontiers: New directions in online pedagogy and research. *Annual Review of Applied Linguistics, 24,* 243–260.

Lai, C., & Zhao, Y. (2006). Noticing and text-based chat. *Language Learning & Technology, 10,* 102–120. Available from http://llt.msu.edu/vol10num3/laizhao/default.html

Lee, L. (2006). A study of native and nonnative speakers' feedback and responses in Spanish-American networked collaborative interaction. In J. Belz & S. Thorne (Eds.), *Internet-mediated intercultural foreign language education* (pp. 147–176). Boston, MA: Heinle & Heinle.

Levelt, W. (1989). *Speaking: From intention to articulation.* Cambridge, MA: The MIT Press.

Levy, M., & Kennedy, C. (2004). A task-cycling pedagogy using stimulated reflection and audio-conferencing in foreign language learning. *Language Learning & Technology, 8,* 50–68. Available from http://llt.msu.edu/vol8num2/levy/default.html

Loewen, S. (2004). Uptake in incidental focus on form in meaning-focused ESL lessons. *Language Learning, 54,* 153–188.

Loewen, S. (2005). Incidental focus on form and second language learning. *Studies in Second Language Acquisition, 27,* 361–386.

Long, M. H. (1996). The role of the linguistic environment in second language acquisition. In W. Ritchie & T. Bhatia (Eds.), *Handbook of research on second language acquisition* (pp. 413–469). New York, NY: Academic Press.

Long, M. H., & Robinson, P. (1998). Focus on form: Theory, research, and practice. In C. Doughty & J. Williams (Eds.), *Focus on form in classroom second language acquisition* (pp. 15–41). Cambridge: Cambridge University Press.

Lyster, R. (1998). Negotiation of form, recasts, and explicit correction in relation to error types and learner repair in immersion classrooms. *Language Learning, 48,* 183–218.

Lyster, R., & Ranta, L. (1997). Corrective feedback and learner uptake: Negotiation of form in communicative classrooms. *Studies in Second Language Acquisition, 19,* 37–66.

Mackey, A. (1999). Input, interaction and second language development: An empirical study of question formation in ESL. *Studies in Second Language Acquisition, 21,* 557–587.

Mackey, A., & Goo, J. (2007). Interaction research in SLA: A meta-analysis and research synthesis. In A. Mackey (Ed.), *Conversational interaction in second language acquisition: A collection of empirical studies* (pp. 407–452). Oxford: Oxford University Press.

Morris, F. (2005). Child-to-child interaction and corrective feedback in a computer mediated L2 class. *Language Learning & Technology, 9,* 29–45. Available from http://llt.msu.edu/vol-9num1/morris/default.html

Oskoz, A. (2004, June). Negotiation of meaning in jigsaw and free discussion in synchronous computer-mediated communication (S-CMC). Paper presented at *CALICO 2004,* Carnegie-Mellon University, Pennsylvania, USA.

Pica, T., (1994). Research on negotiation: What does it reveal about second-language learning conditions, processes, and outcomes? *Language Learning, 44,* 493–527.

Pica, T., Holliday, L., Lewis, N., & Morgenthaler, L. (1989). Comprehensible output as an outcome of linguistic demands on the learner. *Studies in Second Language Acquisition, 11,* 63–90.

Pica, T., Lincoln-Porter, F., Paninos, D., & Linnell, J. (1996). Language learner interaction: How does it address the input, output, and feedback needs of second language learners? *TESOL Quarterly, 30,* 59–84.

Pica, T., Kang, H. S., & Sauro, S. (2006). Information gap tasks: Their multiple roles and contributions to interaction research methodology. *Studies in Second Language Acquisition, 28,* 301–338.

Robinson, P. (1995). Attention, memory, and the "noticing" hypothesis. *Language Learning, 45,* 283–331.

Schmidt, R. (1990). The role of consciousness in second language learning. *Applied Linguistics, 11,* 129–158.

Schmidt, R. (Ed.) (1995). *Attention and awareness in foreign language learning.* Technical Report No. 9. Honolulu, HI: University of Hawai'i Second Language Teaching & Curriculum Center.

Schmidt, R. (2001). Attention. In P. Robinson (Ed.), *Cognition and second language instruction* (pp. 3–32). Cambridge: Cambridge University Press.

Schultz, J. M. (2000). Computers and collaborative writing in the foreign language curriculum. In M. Warschauer & R. Kern (Eds.), *Network-based language teaching: Concepts and practice* (pp. 121–150). Cambridge: Cambridge University Press.

Shehadeh, A. (2001). Self- and other-initiated modified output during task-based interaction. *TESOL Quarterly, 35,* 433–457.

Shekary, M., & Tahririan, M. H. (2006). Negotiation of meaning and noticing in text-based online chat. *Modern Language Journal, 90,* 557–573.

Smith, D. B. (2003). Computer-mediated negotiated interaction: An expanded model. *Modern Language Journal, 87,* 38–57.

Smith, D. B. (2004). Computer-mediated negotiated interaction and lexical acquisition. *Studies in Second Language Acquisition, 26,* 365–398.

Smith, D. B. (2005). The relationship between negotiated interaction, learner uptake, and lexical acquisition in task-based computer-mediated communication. *TESOL Quarterly, 39,* 33–58.

Smith, D. B. (2008). Methodological hurdles in capturing CMC data: The case of the missing self-repair. *Language Learning & Technology, 12,* 85–103. Available from http://llt.msu.edu/ vol12num1/smith/default.html

Smith, D. B., & Gorsuch, G. J. (2004). Synchronous computer mediated communication captured by usability lab technologies: New interpretations. *System, 32,* 553–575.

Sotillo, S. (2000). Discourse functions and syntactic complexity in synchronous and asynchronous communication. *Language Learning & Technology, 4,* 82–119. Available from http:// llt.msu.edu/vol4num1/sotillo/

Sotillo, S. (2005). Corrective feedback via Instant Messenger learning activities in NS-NNS and NNS-NNS dyads. *CALICO Journal, 22,* 467–496.

Swain, M. (1995). Three functions of output in second language learning. In G. Cook & B. Seidlhofer (Eds.), *Principle and practice in applied linguistics: Studies in honour of H. G. Widdowson* (pp. 125–144). Oxford: Oxford University Press.

Swain, M. (1997). Collaborative dialogue: Its contribution to second language learning. *Revista Canaria de Estudios Ingleses, 34,* 115–132.

Swain, M. (2000). The output hypothesis and beyond: Mediating acquisition through collaborative dialogue. In J.P. Lantolf (Ed.), *Sociocultural theory and second language learning* (pp. 97–114). Oxford: Oxford University Press.

Swain, M., & Lapkin, S. (1995). Problems in output and the cognitive processes they generate: A step towards second language learning. *Applied Linguistics, 16,* 371–391.

Varonis, E., & Gass, S. M. (1985). Non-native/non-native conversations: A model for negotiation of meaning. *Applied Linguistics, 6,* 71–90.

Warschauer, M. (1996). Comparing face-to-face and electronic discussion in the second language classroom. *CALICO Journal, 13,* 7–26.

Warschauer, M. (1997). Computer-mediated collaborative learning: Theory and practice. *Modern Language Journal, 81,* 470–481.

Warschauer, M., & Kern, R. (Eds.). (2000). *Network-based language teaching: Concepts and practice.* Cambridge: Cambridge University Press.

Williams, J. (1999). Learner-generated attention to form. *Language Learning, 49,* 583–625.

Williams, J. (2001). The effectiveness of spontaneous attention to form. *System, 29,* 325–340.

Teaching language variation in French through authentic chat discourse

Rémi A. van Compernolle and Isabelle Pierozak

In this chapter, we provide a glimpse into the nature of moderated and non-moderated French-language chat in public, non-educational contexts, and we enumerate and explain a number of pedagogical applications aimed at helping learners of French participate in and have greater access to this type of authentic discourse beyond the classroom. We first present a corpus-based analysis of language variation in moderated and nonmoderated chat discussions, focusing in particular on orthography, the second-person pronouns *tu* and *vous*, the first-person plural pronouns *nous* and *on*, and verbal negation, in order to demonstrate the amount and types of variation that exist in these two different types of synchronous computer-mediated communication. We then provide a number of pedagogical recommendations for teaching sociolinguistic variation in French using computer-mediated communication data. The sample tasks and task components are conceptualized to include one or more spheres of learning opportunities proposed by the New London Group (1996).

1. Introduction

In recent years, the use of technology in the foreign language classroom has become an integral part of language instruction in many parts of the world. While the benefits of using various forms of new technologies (e.g., discussion fora, real-time chat, weblogs, and so forth) in the classroom have been extensively promoted, the primary focus has been on discourse produced by language learners in electronic environments within a structured, formal learning context. Recent writings on foreign language learning and literacy (e.g., Kern, 2006 and references therein) have, however, stressed the need for access to and use of authentic (electronic) discourse in foreign language education. In this chapter, we provide a glimpse into the nature of moderated and non-moderated French-language chat in public, non-educational contexts, and we enumerate and explain a number of pedagogical applications aimed at helping learners of French participate in and have greater access to this type of authentic discourse beyond the classroom. We focus specifically on the teaching and learning of sociolinguistic and pragmatic variation in French, and we provide a number of example tasks and task components aimed at raising learners' awareness of this type of language variation.

Our analysis focuses on two types of synchronous (i.e., real-time) chat: "non-moderated" Internet Relay Chat (IRC) and "moderated" chat, during which a moderator fields questions from participants for an invited guest (see discussion below). The IRC data were collected over the course of four days, selected at random, during both weekday and weekend times. The corpus constitutes approximately 16 hours of chat and a variety of discussion topics from each of the two channels divided by age (*#18-25ans* and *#25-35ans*).[1] The corpus of moderated chat data consists of 20 randomly selected archives of moderated chat sessions held by online news sites in France (ten sessions each from *Le Monde* and *Libération*). In analyzing the data, we considered selected linguistic norms and language variation in this type of communication environment. This analysis of linguistic variation in chat environments illustrates the radical difference between informal varieties of French and the prescriptive (and often very formal) variety that is presented and portrayed in most U.S. pedagogical materials. Since explanations and examples of language variation are seldom included in beginning and intermediate textbooks and ancillaries for teachers and students of French (Etienne & Sax, 2006), the analysis presented in this chapter will enable teachers and learners of French to understand and analyze critically language variation as it occurs in non-educational chat environments.

2.   The nature of moderation in chat

In the interest of convenience, we have made a distinction between "moderated chat" and "non-moderated chat," even if there is moderation in both of these types of online chat on some level. Generally speaking, moderation implies the presence of one or several moderators (called *opérateurs* or *ops* in some public French-language chat spaces) whose role is to ensure that the chat runs smoothly. The requirements for becoming a moderator are technical but also – and perhaps more importantly – sociolinguistic, because it is also necessary to know the relative status of the various chat participants within a given community.

---

1.   There is, however, no way of verifying the actual age of any of the chat participants given the degree of anonymity provided by the IRC environment. Further, given the public, free-access nature of IRC channels, any person of any age can log in to the channel of his or her choosing.

The two types of chat considered in this chapter differ on several levels, which has provided us with a point of departure for defining each as a particular context of communication analyzed in terms of variable levels of discourse (or register, formality, etc.). The principle medium and social features (see Herring, 2007) used to define and compare moderated and non-moderated chat are summarized in Table 1.

Table 1. Medium and social features of moderated and non-moderated chat

	Moderated chat	Non-moderated chat
Sociotechnical factors	1. Non-autonomous (linked to a web site) → no particular technical competence required 2. Reputed web sites (e.g., newspapers)	1. Autonomous → certain technical competence required 2. Non-reputed channels
Duration of the chat	Predefined, punctual (i.e., the length of the interview)	Indefinite, lasting, persistent (i.e., no clear beginning or end)
Development of community	Limited	Important: community development ensures the progeny of the chat
Participants	A guest, moderator, and connected Internet users	Chatters, some of whom are *opérateurs* (or *ops*) depending on their level of access
Status of participants	Heterogeneous (i.e., fixed and distinct participant roles and "hierarchies")	Homogenous (i.e., chatters are equal) then heterogeneous since some chatters can become *ops*
Type of exchanges	Question-response, interview style, public poses questions to guest	"Equal" participation, in that all participants have equal opportunity to send and respond to different types of messages (conversation style)
Goal of moderation	Accept or reject messages in advance of posting → filtering	Sanction (positively or negatively) messages after they appear in the chat → regulation of the chat
Type of moderation	Explicit	Implicit
Status of moderation	Essential: without moderation, the chat does not exist	Non-essential: moderation is only a plus

In the sense that the question of moderation is central to the analysis presented in this chapter, we will use this notion as a means of easily distinguishing between the two types of chat considered here. As such, we will refer to the chat conversations from the archives of *Le Monde* and *Libération* as "moderated chat" while our corpus of IRC will be labeled as "non-moderated chat." This distinction is principally motivated by the fact that a moderator for *Le Monde*, for example, has the power to accept or reject messages, and thus controls which messages appear in the exchange, whereas *ops* on IRC can only react to messages that have appeared in the public discussion window. The end result of these differences in moderator and participant roles is sociolinguistic in nature, in that there exists a sharp contrast in the level of discourse produced in one and the other of these types of chat. As we show in the analyses presented below, moderated chat tends to align with more formal (written or spoken) language, whereas non-moderated chat tends to align with more informal registers of language.

3.   Analysis of the corpus

3.1   Orthographic variation

Orthographic systems (and other graphic phenomena) are among the most researched aspects of French-language computer-mediated communication (Pierozak, 2003; van Compernolle & Williams, 2007). In most cases, researchers have commented on new orthographic norms (or "neography") in non-moderated chat and text messages sent via mobile telephony. In fact, this is often the first feature of online chat discourse that many chat users (as well as the general public) notice about this type of communication, according to surveys conducted in France (Pierozak, 2003). These "remarkable phenomena" ("phénomènes remarquables," Pierozak, 2003) include two principle, superficial categories of variation: unintentional variation (e.g., typos, spelling mistakes, punctuation errors, etc.) and intentional variation (e.g., accent deletion, acronyms, truncation, etc.).

Table 2. Classification of intentional orthographic variation

Example	Traditional form	Type of variation
deja	déjà ('already')	Accent suppression
tjrs	toujours ('always')	Vowel deletion
c	c'est ('it is')	Syllabogram
tlm	tout le monde ('everyone')	Acronym
bon app	bon appétit	Truncation
y'a	il y a ('there is/are')	Oralization

Instances of intentional orthographic variation can be categorized as one of six main types provided in Table 2 along with an example of each type. Accent suppression simply refers to the absence of an accent where one would be expected in traditional writing and vowel deletion occurs when only the consonant "skeleton" of a word is written. A syllabogram is a single-character representing a multi-letter sound, word, or subject-verb sequence. Acronyms are used for certain lexicalized phrases, whereby only the first letter of each word is present. Truncation refers to the shortening of a word, which means either the first or last part of the word is omitted. Finally, oralizations are orthographic representations of spoken forms, which are generally used to imitate non-standard pronunciation.

Despite the widespread belief that chat – and Internet communication more generally – is characterized by non-standard or non-traditional orthography (Crystal, 2001), the use of non-standard orthographic forms is relatively infrequent. Baron (2004) and Tagliamonte and Denis (2008), who have investigated the use of CMC "acronyms" in English-language instant messaging, report that these non-standard forms account for less than 5% of their respective corpora, the remaining words being spelled/written in a more traditional way. The same is true in our corpus of IRC (there was no variation in moderated chat). Table 3 displays the observed and relative frequencies of some common non-standard orthographic forms (see Pierozak, 2003; van Compernolle & Williams, 2007). What emerges from our limited analysis is that despite their status as "remarkable phenomena" (Pierozak, 2003) these non-standard forms are not always as frequent as one might expect. In fact, for *dans*, *mais*, and *tout*, the standard written form is overwhelmingly preferred to the chat form/remarkable phenomenon. For other examples, non-standard forms can account for up to 50% or more, but they are never overwhelmingly preferred to the standard form.

Table 3. Frequencies of selected orthographic variants

Form	n	%
pk	27	47.4%
pourquoi	26	45.6%
pourkoi	4	7.0%
ds	15	6.8%
dans	207	93.2%
ms	2	0.4%
mais	459	99.6%
tt	47	14.2%
tout	283	85.8%
bcp	9	50%
beaucoup	9	50%
koi	83	40.1%
quoi	124	59.9%

It is also important to note that some of the most frequently occurring non-standard forms are those that can be observed in non-electronic contexts, such as note-taking and shorthand writing (Pierozak, 2003) and the informal spoken language (van Compernolle & Williams, 2007). Thus, *tt, bcp, ds, qqch,* for example, originate from other forms of writing, most notably note-taking and dictionary entries, while the use of the letter *k* for phonetic /k/ and the use of syllabograms are more closely associated with electronic discourse. Writing *t'es* for the subject-verb sequence *tu es,* while orthographically variable, comes directly from a spoken form, and the use of the syllabogram *t* in lieu of *t'es* is arguably a hybrid of spoken and electronic variation (i.e., the contraction of *tu* and *es* > *t'es* in speech represented by the letter *t* [pronounced /te/] in chat).

Problematic for learners, however, are the numerous polysemous non-standard forms. Decontextualized *c,* for example, can function as the subject-verb sequence *c'est,* the verb forms *sais/sait,* reflexive *s'est* or nearly any other occurrence of phonetic /se/. As such, the contextualization of orthography is necessary for the interpretation of many variants. For example, in the phrase *je c pas qui c,* the first *c* can only be read as the verb form *sais* while at the same time the second occurrence of *c* must be interpreted as *c'est.* Thus, for teachers and learners interested in exploring electronic discourse, memorization of lists of acontextual orthographic forms is insufficient; instead, participants new to this type of communication should be able to first know what types of variation exist (e.g., which phenomenon is at play and what are the possible interpretations) and interpret orthography appropriately based on the context of occurrence. In other words, learners (and teachers who are unfamiliar with chat or other forms of electronic discourse) should recognize that there is not always a one-to-one equivalency between the form written and its meaning.[2] This active critical framing of orthography is particularly important when learners are confronted with "variations of variants" used (almost) exclusively by one or a small group of chatters, which enables them to identify themselves and be identified by others. Pierozak (2003) thus proposes analyzing orthographic variation in terms of "sociodiscursive capital" available to vested chat room participants over time, which allows them to adopt a certain linguistic identity in a communication space with limited paralinguistic and non-verbal features of communication.

---

2.   It should be noted that polysemy also occurs in standard writing. For example, the word *vous* decontextualized can be a subject pronoun, an object pronoun, or a disjunctive pronoun, but its meaning is clear when it is contextualized in its syntactic environment.

3.2   Sociolinguistic and pragmatic variation

We have selected three well known sociolinguistic features of discourse that have been extensively analyzed in the sociolinguistics literature: the second-person pronouns *tu* and *vous*, the use of *on* at the expense of *nous* for first-person plural reference, and the variable deletion (i.e., omission) of the negative particle *ne*. Table 3 illustrates the relative sociolinguistic or stylistic status of each form, or variant, to be explored in our data. Although the stylistic continuum includes perhaps more degrees of formality (i.e., colloquial, informal, neutral, formal, hyperformal; see Nadasdi, Mougeon, & Rhener, 2005), we present the variants as either "less formal" or "more formal" for simplicity.

Table 3. Sociolinguistic status of features of discourse

	Sociolinguistic status	
Features of discourse	**Less formal variant**	**More formal variant**
Second-person pronoun	*tu*	*vous*-singular
First-person plural pronoun	*on*	*nous*
Negation	*ne* absent (e.g., Paul *vient pas* ce soir 'Paul isn't coming tonight')	*ne* present (e.g., Paul *ne vient pas* ce soir 'Paul is not coming tonight')

It is important to note that second-person pronoun use is constrained by a very different set of factors than the other two variables presented here. While the *on* versus *nous* variable and *ne* deletion or retention are predominately conditioned by the context of communication (e.g., formality, audience, style), and every speaker in every context can, theoretically, use one form or the other freely, *tu* (T) and *vous*-singular (V-sg) use is determined by the relationship between two or more speakers, or what Morford (1997) labels as "social indexicality." Thus, the choice of one address pronoun or the other in our data will inform us about the (perceived) relationship and degree of familiarity permitted between interlocutors in these contexts. The distribution of *nous* vs. *on* and *ne* retention vs. deletion, on the other hand, will provide an indication of formality / register in these contexts of communication. The distribution of each variant in moderated and non-moderated chat discussions is provided in Table 4. The data indicate a stark difference between moderated and non-moderated chat discourse. In moderated chat, the more formal variants (i.e., V-sg, *nous*, *ne* presence) are overwhelmingly preferred, while more informal variants (i.e., T, *on*, *ne* absence) are much more frequent in non-moderated chat discussions.

Table 4. Distribution of formal and informal features of discourse

Features of discourse	Moderated chat		Non-moderated chat	
	n	%	*n*	%
Second-person pronoun				
V-sg	210	99.5	1	0.2
T	1	0.5	617	99.8
First-person plural pronoun				
nous	102	90.3	6	4.8
on	11	9.7	119	95.2
Negation				
ne present	382	100	156	15.9
ne absent	0	0	825	84.1

The rates of T and V-sg use in non-moderated chat match those reported by Williams and van Compernolle (2007) (i.e., rates as high as 99% for T). Only one example of V-sg was used as a subject pronoun in the non-moderated chat data. Another example of V-sg (not represented in Table 4) was used in a tag question, which provoked the interesting response shown in Excerpt 1.

Excerpt 1.

[16:07] <Tom_Pouce> tu peux me tutoyer si je suis la seule personne a qui tu t'es adressé ['you can use *tu* with me if I'm the only person you're talking to']

This explicit request for *tutoiement* (i.e., the use of T as opposed to V-sg) illustrates that online non-moderated chat is an environment in which inappropriate address pronoun use can lead to ambiguity, or even a questioning of the pronoun chosen. In the moderated chat data, however, V-sg was overwhelmingly preferred to T (V-sg = 99.5%). The only example of T was in a question posed by an emotional fan of a television personality. Previous studies of the use of T and V in press interviews, which are similar to moderated chat discussions, have shown similar patterns of T / V use, where T may be used when a shared interest or a common goal exists between the interviewer and his or her interlocutor (Claudel, 2004). Thus, it seems clear that non-moderated chat provides an environment in which T use contributes to a shared sense of familiarity, while V-sg dominance in moderated chat discussions indicates a certain level of deference and / or social distance between participants and the interviewee.

In the case of the grammatical variables *nous* vs. *on* and *ne* presence vs. absence, the data clearly show the stylistic divide between moderated and non-moderated chat. The rates of *on* use in non-moderated chat align closely those reported for everyday conversational French (Blondeau, 2003; Coveney, 2000;

Fonseca-Greber & Waugh, 2003; see also van Compernolle, 2008b for an in-depth analysis of IRC). Likewise, *ne* is absent in the vast majority of verbal negations (84.1%), and these rates are similar to those reported by Ashby (2001), Coveney (1996), and Hansen and Malderez (2004) who have analyzed informal speech, as well as van Compernolle (2008a) for IRC. On the other hand, the exact opposite trends can be observed in the moderated chat discussions, where *nous* is over-whelmingly preferred to *on* and *ne* is categorically retained. These norms move in the direction of the formal spoken or written language, or *bon usage*, which may be more familiar to many learners of French.

4.   Pedagogical recommendations

The analysis presented above has highlighted the stark stylistic difference between moderated and non-moderated chat contexts. The discourse of moderated chat may present few – if any – difficulties for learners of French, given that it aligns very closely with formal or written norms as presented in learner textbooks; how-ever, the preponderance of non-traditional orthography and other more informal sociolinguistic features of discourse in non-moderated chat might prove more difficult for learners since these forms may be unfamiliar to them. Despite the widespread, and often-stated, opinion that learners may become confused if pre-sented with other "options" in a foreign language (i.e., other linguistic variants), we believe that awareness of variation is necessary for authentic and appropriate interaction in online (as well as off-line) environments. More generally, learning to "manage" ('gérer') (Valdman, 2000) variation in a variety of registers and genres constitutes a powerful catalyst for the development of communicative (and socio-linguistic) competence in the target language (see also Train, 2003). As Williams (2004) notes, "As participants in virtual communities, language learners need to understand not only what is acceptable, but also what is expected of members who share a common communication space" (p. 163). Such is also naturally true for offline communication, such as everyday conversation.

The pedagogical recommendations provided below aim to raise learners' awareness of the sociosituational factors (i.e., the context of communication) that determine the use of linguistic variants. We have situated our recommenda-tions within the framework of the New London Group (1996), which includes four "spheres of learning opportunities": Overt Instruction, Situated Practice, Critical Framing, and Transformed Practice. We discuss each of these spheres in turn, and we provide a number of sample task components that fit within each of them. However, we wish to note that there is no prescribed order or sequence of tasks; language teachers could easily adapt any of our recommendations to their individual teaching objectives, or try any of our sample task components from any of the spheres of learning opportunities independently.

The New London Group (1996) defines Overt Instruction as "all those active interventions on the part of the teacher and other experts that scaffold learning activities that focus the learner on the important features of their experiences and activities within the community of learners" (p. 86). For teachers interested in raising students' awareness of linguistic variation in and through the use of moderated and non-moderated chat discourse, an ideal way to engage in Overt Instruction is through a whole-group, teacher-fronted task in which learners and the teacher identify instances of linguistic variation.

The teacher, using a transparency with numbered lines, for example, identifies specific examples of intentional and non-intentional orthographic variation, T / V use, *on* and *nous* when used as first-person plural subject pronouns, and the absence versus the presence of *ne*. The students, with assistance from the teacher and still in a whole-group setting, then identify additional examples of these variables, quantify them, and then compare the frequencies of each variant found in these two types of discourse (i.e., moderated and non-moderated chat). Alternatively, the teacher could divide the class into small groups, each assigned to a specific variable (e.g., orthography, *on* versus *nous*, negation, etc.). The small groups could work independently of each other as the teacher circulated from one group to the next to offer assistance. At the end of the task, each group would report its findings to the others. Then, in a whole-group, teacher-fronted participation structure, the teacher could lead a discussion of the social significance of the different variants identified in the transcripts of moderated and non-moderated chat. The objective of this type of Overt Instruction is, in addition to making students aware that variation exists, to demonstrate the degree to which linguistic variation is determined by the communicative context in which language is used. This is often achieved relatively quickly by comparing rates of orthographic variation, *tu* use, *on* use, and *ne* deletion in the moderated and non-moderated chat excerpts.

A second sphere of learning opportunities identified by the New London Group (1996) is that of Situated Practice. Situated Practice is "the part of pedagogy that is constituted by immersion in meaningful practices within a community of learners who are capable of playing multiple and different roles based on their background and experiences" (New London Group, 1996, p. 85). For students exploring and comparing sociolinguistic norms and variation in moderated and non-moderated chat, an ideal context for engaging in Situated Practice is inter-learner online chat activities in small groups (3–4 students) within a structured educational setting. Activities within the sphere of Situated Practice should also reflect a real-world situation in which students might (eventually) need to apply what they have learned.

In small group, inter-learner chat discussions, students have the opportunity to use new or rather unfamiliar forms (e.g., orthographic variants) in "an area in which all learners are secure in taking risks and trusting the guidance of others – peers and teachers" (New London Group, 1996, p. 85). These small group chat discussions should be framed as an informal context for communication in order to encourage the use of non-standard or informal variants, which students may not otherwise use in a formal, structured pedagogical setting.[3] Alternatively, students could engage in role-play activities similar to the moderated chat discussions they had previously analyzed. In such cases, one student would act as the guest and the others would send the guest their questions. Students engaged in a role-play such as this would be expected to produce a level of discourse similar to what they had observed and analyzed in the moderated chat transcripts. As a combination of Situated Practice and Overt Instruction, the teacher could review the chat transcripts and, in a teacher-fronted setting during a subsequent class meeting, lead a discussion about the use of sociolinguistic features of discourse in the students' chat tasks. In this way, the teacher could identify examples of sociolinguistic inappropriateness (e.g., using *ne* in casual, conversational chat or using *tu* to address a "guest" during a role-play of moderated chat), as well as appropriate uses of sociolinguistic features of discourse. This type of follow-up lesson may have the potential to raise students' awareness of their own use of these features of discourse. If no chat server is available for students to use at school, another option would be to have students chat on the *French Chat* website,[4] which encourages native and non-native speaker exchanges in a relatively authentic context as a means of practicing to "speak" French.

The third component of our pedagogical sequence involves Critical Framing (New London Group, 1996). In line with our recommendation that teachers review student-produced chat discourse and lead discussions about sociolinguistic appropriateness, we believe that students could engage in tasks aimed at fostering their critical reflexive skills when presented with authentic discourse.

> The goal of Critical Framing is to help learners frame their growing mastery in practice (from Situated Practice) and conscious control and understanding

---

3.   It is important to note that the non-use of a particular form or structure does not necessarily mean that the student does not know how to use or that is can be used; rather, in many instances, the student may not chose to use it because he or she is not comfortable with the form or believes it is inappropriate in a formal, structured learning environment.

4.   http://www.french-chat.com/

> (from Overt Instruction) in relation to the historical, social, cultural, political, ideological, and value-centered relations of particular systems of knowledge and social practice. Here, crucially, the teacher must help learners to denaturalize and make strange again what they have learned and mastered.
>
> (New London Group, 1996, p. 86)

In the case of orthography, pronouns, and negation in French-language chat, students could be asked if similar types of variation exist in English-language chat (or any other language they know or are familiar with). This is especially important because the recognition of one's own competency in a first language may be necessary for the construction of new competencies in a second or foreign language. If, for example, students recognize that similar forms of orthographic variation exist in English chat (e.g., *u = you, r = are,* or *c u l8r = see you later*), they would be able to begin to compare the different types of orthographic variation found in English-language and French-language chat. In addition, students could compare address forms in English-language moderated and non-moderated chat. Although English does not have two second-person pronoun forms, students could explore the use of titles and honorifics (e.g., *Mr., sir,* etc.). If they noticed that titles and honorifics were used more often in moderated chat discussions with politicians or other guests than in non-moderated chat conversations, they might also recognize that the *tu / vous* system in French operates in much the same way. Whatever the comparison, it is during Critical Framing that students should begin to realize that variation exists not only in French, but in their first language as well. They should also become aware that the types of variation and the purposes of these variations are not always the same in all languages. These types of tasks could be done in teacher-fronted brainstorming units, small groups, or as individual assignments during class or for homework. Students could also be asked during Critical Framing to expand the types of variation explored by identifying other features of discourse that are used differently in moderated and non-moderated chat (e.g., interrogative structures, discourse markers, or anything else that may seem "strange" or different from what they have learned from their textbooks).

A fourth component of our pedagogical sequence involves Transformed Practice, where students can "apply and revise what they have learned [during Overt Instruction, Situated Practice, and Critical Framing]" (New London Group, 1996, p. 87). Transformed Practice includes "[t]ransfer in meaning-making practice, which puts transformed meaning to work in other contexts or cultural sites" (p. 88). One way that students concentrating on sociolinguistic and pragmatic variation in French chat could engage in Transformed Practice would be to participate in some form of non-educational moderated or non-moderated chat discussion (see our list of online resources at the end of this chapter). Initially, the teacher could, for example, ask students to spend 10 minutes (or more if desired) in a public chat room and to make observations about orthography, pronoun use, and grammatical variation, or any other area of online communication, as they actively participate in a discussion. In an ideal situation, the students would then have an opportunity to report back to the class (perhaps the next day) and to discuss, compare, and contrast their experiences with those of their classmates. This could be done through short, two to three minute mini-reports or as part of a whole-class, teacher-fronted discussion during which similarities and differences are highlighted and explained by students and the teacher. In addition, teachers could find an upcoming moderated chat on a newspaper website, such as *Le Monde* or *Libération*, and, as a class, write one or several questions to send to the moderator. Of course, Transformed Practice should (hopefully) continue once students have left the formal educational setting, either after class or once they are no longer enrolled in French-as-a-foreign-language courses, if they choose to explore non-educational chat (or other types of authentic electronic discourse) further. Ideally, this participation may become legitimized over a certain period of time, such that learners are accepted as members of the online communities they chose to explore.

5.   Other recommendations

As advocates of the teaching and learning of sociolinguistic and pragmatic variation in foreign language education, we believe that using authentic moderated and non-moderated chat in the classroom can help students to become aware of and possibly use appropriately sociolinguistic features of discourse. However, we do not wish to imply that non-standard features of discourse should become the focal point of foreign language education, nor do we wish to suggest that detailed analyses of electronic French (or any other foreign language being learned) discourse should become central areas of language learning at all levels in all programs. Rather, we argue that using authentic moderated and non-moderated chat in the French-as-a-foreign-language classroom could help learners to contextualize language use – both formal and informal forms and structures – in order to raise their awareness of how language (and other types of) variation functions in authentic interactions. Incidentally, non-educational chat rooms are often viewed by learners as a means of familiarizing oneself with informal, everyday, conversational speech (Pierozak, 2007), a variety of language largely absent from most formal, structured educational settings.

While we believe that learning to understand and use non-standard or informal linguistic forms and structures is central to language learners' communicative competence, perhaps more important is their ability to distinguish between and use appropriately the sociolinguistic features of discourse (i.e., sociolinguistic competence; see Savignon, 1997). Thus, whenever language variation is included in foreign language education, we argue that these units should include at a minimum a comparison of language use in two or more contexts. Our analysis comparing moderated and non-moderated chat discourse is one way in which such a comparison could be made. Other options include classroom-based lessons on variation in one type of electronic discourse (e.g., non-moderated chat) with a follow-up homework assignment where students would visit a discussion forum or read a transcript of a moderated chat session and compare selected areas of variation. Alternatively, students could compare electronic discourse to speech in different contexts, for example, through the use of film, radio broadcasts, or other sources,[5] as a means of introducing sociolinguistic (and other types) of variation in French.

6.   Online resources for teachers

There are many resources available on the Internet for teachers (and students) interested in exploring moderated and non-moderated French-language chat in more detail. The website addresses below provide some useful information about chat (and other forms of electronic discourse) as well as accessing authentic chat discourse.[6]

–   The homepage for the IRC network *EpikNet*. Includes information about IRC in general, statistics for the network, and an overview of expected behaviors and practices when engaged in chat discussions. URL: http://www.epiknet.org/
–   *Voila T'Chat*. Includes Web-based (non-moderated) chat rooms and information about Web-based or Java chat. URL: http://tchat.voila.fr/
–   *French Chat*. This chat site is for native and non-native French speakers where students can chat and practice chatting in French. URL: http://www.french-chat.com/

---

5.   See Etienne and Sax (2006) for recommendations for using film to sensitize students of French to stylistic variation.

6.   In addition to these online resources, readers are encouraged to read Gerbault (2007); Lamy, Mangenot, & Nissen (2007); and volume 27 of the *Annual Review of Applied Linguistics*: *Language and Technology*.

- *Libération.fr* moderated chat page. Announcements for upcoming chats and archived transcripts of previous chats. URL: http://www.liberation.fr/interactif/chats_home/
- *ALSIC*, a French online journal with research and practitioner articles as well as *fiches pédagogiques* focusing on using technology in foreign language learning. URL: http://alsic.u-strasbg.fr/

References

Ashby, W. (2001). Un nouveau regard sur la chute du *ne* en français parlé tourangeau: S'agit-il d'un changement en cours? *Journal of French Language Studies, 11,* 1–22.

Blondeau, H. (2003). The old *nous* and the new *nous*. A comparison of 19th and 20th century spoken Quebec French. *University of Pennsylvania Working Papers in Linguistics, 9,* 1–15.

Baron, N. (2004). See you online: Gender issues in college student use of instant messaging. *Journal of Language and Social Psychology, 23,* 397–423.

Claudel, C. (2004). De l'utilisation du système d'adresse dans l'interview de presse écrite française. *Langage & Société, 108,* 11–26.

Coveney, A. (1996). *Variability in spoken French: A sociolinguistic study of interrogation and negation.* Exeter, UK: Elm Bank.

Coveney, A. (2000). Vestiges of *nous* and the 1st person plural verb in informal spoken French. *Language Sciences, 22,* 447–481.

Crystal, D. (2001). *Language and the Internet.* Cambridge: Cambridge University Press.

Etienne, C. & Sax, K. (2006). Teaching stylistic variation through film. *The French Review, 79,* 934–950.

Fonseca-Greber, B., & Waugh, L. (2003). On the radical difference between the subject personal pronouns in written and spoken European French. In P. Leistyna & C. F. Meyer (Eds.), *Corpus analysis: Language structure and language use* (pp. 225–240). Amsterdam: Rodopi.

Gerbault, J. (Ed.). (2007). *La langue du cyberspace: de la diversité aux normes.* Paris: L'Harmattan.

Hansen, A., & Malderez, I. (2004). Le *ne* de négation en région parisienne: Une étude en temps réel. *Langage & Société, 107,* 5–30.

Herring, S. C. (2007). A faceted classification scheme for computer-mediated discourse. *Language@Internet, 4,* Article 1 [np]. Available from http://www.languageatinternet.de/articles/2007.

Kern, R. (2006). Perspectives on technology in learning and teaching languages. *TESOL Quarterly, 40,* 183–210.

Lamy, M.-N., Mangenot, F., & Nissen, E. (Eds.). (2007) *Actes du colloque «Echanger pour apprendre en ligne»* (EPAL). Grenoble: Université Stendhal. Available from http://w3.u-grenoble3.fr/epal/actes.html

Morford, J. (1997). Social indexicality in French pronominal address. *Journal of Linguistic Anthropology, 7,* 3–37.

Nadasdi, T., Mougeon, R., & Rehner, K. (2005). Learning to speak everyday (Canadian) French. *Canadian Modern Language Review, 61,* 543–563.

New London Group. (1996). A pedagogy of multiliteracies: Designing social futures. *Harvard Educational Review, 66,* 60–92.

Pierozak, I. (2003). *Le français tchaté: Une étude en trois dimensions – sociolinguistique, syntaxique et graphique – d'usages IRC.* Unpublished doctoral dissertation, Université d'Aix-Marseille I, France. Available from http://www.u-picardie.fr/LESCLaP/ spip.php?rubrique43

Pierozak, I. (2007). Communication électronique et construction de compétences en langue autre, hors contexte pédagogique, *Lidil, 36,* 189–209.

Savignon, S. (1997). *Communicative competetnce: Theory and classroom practice. Texts and contexts in second language learning* (2nd ed.). New York, NY: McGraw-Hill.

Tagliamonte, S., & Denis, D. (2008). Linguistic ruin? LOL! Instant Messaging and teen language. *American Speech, 83,* 3–24.

Train, R. (2003). The (non)native standard language in foreign language education: A critical perspective. In C. Blyth (Ed.), *The sociolinguistics of foreign-language classrooms: Contributions of the native, the near-native, and the non-native speaker* (pp. 3–40). Boston, MA: Heinle.

Valdman, A. (2000). Comment gérer la variation dans l'enseignement du français langue étrangère aux Etats-Unis. *The French Review, 73,* 648–666.

van Compernolle, R. A. (2008a). Morphosyntactic and phonological constraints of negative particle variation in French-language chat discourse. *Language Variation and Change, 20*(2), 317–339.

van Compernolle, R. A. (2008b). *Nous* versus *on*: Pronouns with first-person plural reference in synchronous French chat. *Canadian Journal of Applied Linguistics, 11*(2), 85–110.

van Compernolle, R. A., & Williams, L. (2007). De l'oral à l'électronique: La variation orthographique comme ressource sociostylistique et pragmatique dans le français électronique. *Glottopol, 10,* 56–69.

Williams, L. (2004). Preparing students for real-time chat in language-learning environments. In J. Cooke-Plagwitz & L. Lomicka (Eds.), *Teaching with technology* (pp. 162–170). Boston, MA: Heinle & Heinle.

Williams, L., & van Compernolle, R. A. (2007). Second-person pronoun use in French-language chat environments. *The French Review, 80,* 804–820.

Exploring native and nonnative interactive discourse in text-based chat beyond classroom settings

Lina Lee

This paper reports on a study that explored how nonnative speakers (NNSs) interacted with native speakers (NSs) in a chat room. Fifteen university students worked collaboratively with expert speakers to complete six task-based activities. The findings indicated that online communication fostered high levels of interaction using various types of negotiation strategies. Students benefited from being exposed to a wide range of functional discourse produced by the NSs. Further, expert scaffolding increased students' awareness of linguistic forms that led to modified output including self-repairs. Students, however, experienced difficulties comprehending linguistic variations including regionalisms. Students also failed to perform certain tasks, such as direct and indirect speech acts. The results suggest that learners not only need to work toward maintaining a balance between fluency and accuracy, but also develop their intercultural communication skills in order to successfully engage in online exchanges with NSs. Expert speakers, on the other hand, need to be aware of not over intervening in the interaction. The study concludes that text-based chat involving NSs is a powerful mediating tool for the enrichment of language learning that goes beyond a traditional classroom setting.

1. Introduction

Communicative language teaching aims to develop learners' ability to use the language correctly and appropriately to achieve communication goals. Interaction through negotiation of meaning in real-life situations, therefore, is imperative. Given the limited access to NSs that many students have in the regular classroom, synchronous computer mediated communication (CMC) affords unique learning conditions, supporting both meaning-oriented communication and form-focus reflection (e.g., Lee, 2005, 2006; O'Rourke, 2005; Sotillo, 2005).

Research on CMC has shown beneficial effects on learners' interactions and outcomes (e.g., Jepson, 2005; Lai & Zhao, 2006; Lee, 2001, 2004a; Smith, 2008). However, relatively few studies have included NSs for chat exchanges (Darhower, 2008; Lee, 2004b, 2006; Toyoda & Harrison, 2002; Tudini, 2003). The utterances of NSs are original and authentic, embedded in a variety of social functions, speech acts and discourse types that occur outside of class. It is only through real contexts and natural discourse that classroom-learned language becomes meaningful for real-world communication, something not available through a single textbook or instructor within formal classroom settings (Furstenberg et al., 2001). Importantly, learners increase cross-cultural awareness and further develop skills and strategies for intercultural exchanges with NSs (Belz, 2002; O'Dowd, 2003).

To gain insight into the ways in which learners interact with NSs in synchronous CMC environment, this study builds on Lee's (2006) original examination of NNS and NS networked interaction, focusing on exploring various discourse dimensions (e.g., linguistics, pragmatics, discourse markers and negotiation strategies). The current study involved 15 expert-to-novice pairs (n = 30) who carried out six two-way information exchange tasks via a chat room. The expert speakers were 15 NSs from different Spanish-speaking countries, whereas the novices were 15 students from a fourth-semester Intermediate Spanish class.[1] Negotiation types and strategies generated by both NSs and NNSs during online exchanges were examined. In addition, linguistic, social and cultural dimensions of NS-NNS collaborative interaction that affected the process of online negotiation were explored.

2.   Communicative features of written discourse in CMC

One popular form of CMC that permits participants to interact with each other in real time is text chat. Text chatting creates a kind of semi-speech that is between talking and writing. Hence, it is comparable to face-to-face (FTF) exchange in terms of interactivity. CMC is human-to-human exchange involving negotiation of meaning using various types of strategies to achieve mutual understanding (see next section for further discussion). Text chat presents written discourse in conversational style with a variety of speech acts including greeting, request, compliment, apology and gratitude, as well as discourse markers (Sykes, 2005; Tudini,

---

1.   It should be noted that although the students were in the fourth-semester intermediate Spanish course, it does not mean that they had attained language skills at the Intermediate level on the ACTFL proficiency scale prior to the study.

2003). Both direct and indirect speech acts form an important part of pragmatic competence that demonstrates learners' appropriate use of the target language in social context (see also Kasper & Rose, 2001). In contrast to e-mail, online chat is a fast paced exchange similar to FTF conversation that places pressure on learners to produce the L2 in a timely fashion (less waiting time and quick response). As a result of the spontaneity, learners tend to write briefly and informally with abbreviations, unconventional punctuation and misspelling (Lee, 2002b; Toyoda & Harrison, 2002).

CMC is different from spoken discourse in its textual representation, which relies heavily on writing and reading skills; thus, learners may need more time to process input and output (Abrams, 2003). Electronic communication also requires skills and strategies that are different from the ones employed for FTF exchange (Chun, 1994, Lee, 2006). Unlike FTF interaction, CMC cannot take advantage of certain social aspects of oral interaction, such as nonverbal cues (facial expressions) and prosodic features (intonation). Thus, learners use other means to express meaning and emotions. Invented linguistic devices including onomatopoeia (e.g., lol = laugh out loud, btw = by the way) and keyboard symbols using smiley faces (e.g., ☺!) are commonly found in CMC to make up for the absence of paralinguistic features of real time exchange (Lee, 2001, 2006; Smith, 2003). Moreover, context and reference of written discourse may not be clear and the problem of misunderstanding may be hard to overcome.

L2 studies have reported the potential benefits of using CMC to extend learners' use of the target language. In their CMC studies, Chun (1994) and Kern (1995) found that learners produced a wide range of discourse structures and enhanced their sociolinguistic and interactive competence. Other studies revealed that learners increased language output (Abrams, 2003; González-Bueno & Pérez, 2000) and produced both lexically and syntactically complex language (Warschauer, 1997). Furthermore, students improved their grammatical competence (Dussias, 2006; Lee, 2002a; Pellettieri, 2000), as well as written and oral skills (e.g., Abrams, 2003; Blake, 2000; Kitade, 2000; Lee, 2002a; Payne & Whitney, 2002).

3.   Negotiation of meaning, feedback and responses in CMC

CMC promotes interaction that plays an essential role in the development of learners' interlanguage. Learners negotiate meaning by responding to corrective feedback and further modifying output in a way similar to that which they would experience through FTF interaction (Lee, 2001, Sotillo, 2005). According to Lee (2006), students are exposed to real language discourse, rich lexical items and correct grammatical structures through interacting with NSs. The burden of negotiation through written discourse without non-verbal cues pushes L2 learners to use a wide range of negotiation strategies to solve communication breakdowns (Lee, 2001, 2002b; Pellettieri, 2000). L2 researchers have found that learners employ negotiation strategies similar to the ones used in FTF conversation, such as confirmation checking, L1 use, and self-repair to provide and attend to feedback (e.g., Blake, 2000; Darhower, 2002; Fernández-García & Martínez-Arbelaiz, 2003; Lee, 2002a, 2006; Smith, 2003, 2008). González-Lloret (2003), for example, found that clarification requests were the preferred way to provide feedback among NNSs during the online exchange. In their CMC study of heritage speakers and NNSs of Spanish in online interaction, Blake and Zyzik (2003) revealed that lexical negotiations through the use of recasts and clarification requests had a positive effect on vocabulary use. More recently, Lee (2008) found that intermediate learners tended to use the L1 to negotiate for meaning. She suggests that it is fairly difficult to explain an advanced grammatical concept in the target language. Until students gain more knowledge of the target language, the L1 seems to be a good option to resolve linguistic problems and to keep the flow of conversation going.

Another affordance of synchronous CMC is a focus-on-form procedure through corrective feedback that brings learners' awareness of linguistic problems – a process hypothesized to be necessary for second language acquisition (Long & Robinson, 1998; Schmidt, 1995). One of the most common ways of drawing learners' attention to focus on form is the use of recasts, especially within NS-NNS exchanges. Recasts involve a partial or full reformulation of an utterance (see Long 1996; Oliver 1995, for a comprehensive discussion of recasts). L2 studies using CMC have shown that the visual salience of written discourse and the self-paced setting increase learners' opportunities to take notice of errors and make output modifications (e.g., Blake & Zyzik, 2003; Lai & Zhao, 2006; Lee, 2006; Smith, 2008; Sotillo, 2000). However, learners tend to resolve lexical problems that are the main triggers for negotiation of meaning rather than syntactic errors (e.g., Blake & Zyzik, 2003; Lee, 2002b; 2006; Morris, 2002). Linguistic problems that do not impede mutual understanding tend to go by the wayside (Lee, 2001, Meskill & Anthony, 2005; Ware & O'Dowd, 2008). Loewen and Erlam (2006) argue that learners may not be at a developmental stage that allows them to notice linguistic features. Available studies seem to suggest that synchronous CMC encourages fluency rather than accuracy.

4.   Social interaction and collaborative scaffolding in CMC

Apart from the understanding of negotiation of meaning through input, feedback, focus on form and modified output from psycholinguistic perspectives, it is important to take into account how social interaction through a joint activity supports online learning including a focus-on-form procedure (see also Lee, 2008). From a sociocultural point of view, individuals use the language as a cognitive tool to construct meaning by collaborating with online partners (Lee, 2004a). Social interaction is more than the action of one person delivering information to another; rather, it shapes and constructs learning through collaborative efforts (Lantolf & Thorne, 2006). The individual is apprenticed by scaffolding from an expert in reconstructing linguistic forms through noticing the gap between L1 and L2 (e.g., Foster & Ohta, 2005; Lee, 2004b, Swain, 2000). Lee (2008), for example, found that expert assistance fostered the development of learners' interlanguage by activating their zone of proximal development (ZPD) (see also Lee, 2004b; Nassaji & Swain, 2000 for further discussion of ZPD). Both the expert and the learner, however, need to maintain an intersubjectivity by means of which they establish common goals within a shared communicative context (Darhower, 2002; De Guerrero & Villamil, 2000; Lee, 2008). Researchers have also found other factors that affect the quality and results of online exchanges. Lee (2007), for instance, reports that the role of the expert affects the ways learners respond to corrective feedback. The expert has the tendency to dominate the interaction. Other researchers argue that while CMC is less anxiety provoking than FTF interaction (Blake, 2000; Lee, 2002a), it does not guarantee the interactivity due to the lack of social presence and cohesiveness (Darhower, 2002; Lee, 2008). Individuals' linguistic, academic and cultural backgrounds also play an essential role in the process of online interaction.

Based on the above discussion on negotiation of meaning from a cognitive approach of the interactionist tradition and collaborative scaffolding from a sociocultural perspective, the study addresses three major questions:

1.   What negotiation types and strategies do NSs and NNSs generate during online chatting?;
2.   What variables influence negotiated interaction between NSs and NNSs?;
3.   What are the pedagogical implications for utilizing the NS-NNS online chatting based on findings in (1) and (2)?

5.   Methodology

5.1   Participants

The study was conducted over ten weeks involving 15 NSs and 15 NNSs in the northeastern United States. The NNS group consisted of 15 students, ranging in age from 19 to 21, who had attained the intermediate level of language proficiency based on the results of the Spanish Oral Proficiency Test – SOPT (Lee, 2000). Most students had a minimum of three years of Spanish in high school and one semester of Intermediate Spanish in college prior to the study. They did not have opportunities to use the target language outside of class, as they lived in small New England towns and cities where English is the only language used for daily communication. None of the students had studied in a Spanish-speaking country nor had they had the experience of dealing with NSs prior to the study.

Fifteen NSs, ranging in aging from 23 to 42, who lived or studied in the United Stated voluntarily took part in this study. The majority of them (n = 12) were recruited from the ESL program at the university and a few (n = 3) were from the local community. The NSs were from different Spanish-speaking countries (Columbia = 3; Mexico = 3; Argentina = 3; Spain = 2; Puerto Rico = 2; Costa Rica = 1; Peru = 1). In terms of the technological knowledge and skills, the majority of the participants were comfortable with e-mail and text-chat (e.g., *Yahoo Messenger, Skype*). Therefore, no training of how to use a chat room was needed prior to the study.

5.2   Tasks

For this project, two-way interactive tasks were designed that involved the exchange of information between two interlocutors and provided opportunities for both parties to contribute input and generate and receive feedback through modified output (Long, 1996; Pica, Kanagy, & Falodun, 1993). Tasks were also chosen not only to ensure a primary focus on meaning but also to allow for incidental attention to linguistic form (see also Ellis, 2003; Swain & Lapkin, 1998). Three types of two-way exchange tasks that elicit negotiation of meaning through collaborative efforts were included in this study (see Table 1).

According to Skehan (2003), two-way exchanges with one closed outcome promote negotiation of meaning and form because learners need to exchange information in order to complete the task. For instance, one of the goal-oriented activities requires learners to work together to identify 15 differences between two drawings of a Christmas party, whereas the jigsaw task features a set of

Table 1. Topic, task type, and description of task

Topic	Task type	*Description of task
Chat #1: Community service Chat #4: Adventures in Machu Picchu	Jigsaw	Information gap; convergent; one closed outcome
Chat #2: Christmas party Chat #5: At the airport	Spot-the-differences	Goal-oriented; convergent; one closed outcome
Chat #3: Home schooling Chat #6: Euthanasia	Open-ended question	Opinion exchange; divergent; multiple outcomes

*The description of each task is based on Pica, Kanagy and Falodun (1993).

drawings depicting Maria's adventures in Machu Picchu. It is likely that specific lexical items or grammar points are required to achieve mutual comprehension. In contrast, open-ended questions with multiple outcomes allow free responses that may not necessarily require precise information to complete the task. To this end, task type influences the amount of corrective feedback received from the expert during synchronous CMC.

5.3   Procedure

As part of their coursework, students carried out six chats[2] with their NS partners using the *Group Pages* of *Blackboard*. The type of task was alternated each week (see Table 1). All activities took place in the language lab outside of class time and consisted of several steps described below:

Step 1: The researcher randomly paired each student with a NS partner, made an initial contact to all participants via e-mail and provided them with instructions of how to log in to *Blackboard*. Pair groups were asked to set up a common time to introduce each other using the chat room in *Group Pages* prior to the study. If after several attempts the participant had trouble connecting with his/her partner, the researcher would find a replacement.

Step 2: Participants spent the first week chatting on the topics about their school, personal life and plans for the future in order to become acquainted with each other. Students were strongly encouraged to use the target language to chat with their NS partners. When necessary, the researcher sent e-mails to remind the participants to make contact with each other prior to the project.

---

2. The type of task was alternated each week. Table 1 shows the number of each chat indicating the week that the task was executed.

Step 3: The researcher informed the participants about the chat project as well as the types of tasks they would be doing in the language lab via e-mail. The researcher made up the schedule based on the availability of pair groups. A lab assistant contacted all participants via e-mail to remind them of the scheduled times for each assignment.

Step 4: Upon arriving at the lab, each pair[3] received a manila envelope containing instructions for carrying out the task. The lab assistant also briefly explained the chatting procedure to the participants. Participants were allowed 5–7 minutes to read the instructions and view the drawings or questions. The researcher reminded them that they were not allowed to use dictionaries or notes. Participants were encouraged to focus on the topic and allow each other to contribute as much as possible. Each session lasted approximately 40 minutes. The lab assistant was present to solve any technical problems. Chats were automatically saved in *Blackboard*'s archives and were retrieved later for data analysis.

Step 5: After the last chat, the lab assistant asked participants to write a brief reflection log in their native language[4] to report their observations of online exchanges. The participants were given the following instructions to guide their reports:

1. Describe your overall experience of chatting online with your partner.
2. Tell me how you worked with your partner to complete the task. Were there moments that you felt were particularly helpful or challenging?
3. Explain how your partner provided feedback to you and whether you found expert feedback useful or confusing during the exchange. If so, how?
4. Comment on three types of tasks (jigsaw, spot-the-differences, open-ended question) that you used for this project. What role and impact did each task have on the way you interacted with your partner?
5. Write additional observations on beneficial and challenging aspects of online chats.

6.   Data collection and analysis

Selective chat data[5] and reflective essays were used to provide evidence to support findings and make additional observations. Combining qualitative and quantitative

---

3. Both NS and NNS were in a different room that physically separated them from each other.

4. It should be noted that the use of L1 allows participants to fully express themselves through their own observation about CMC.

5. Chat logs from the fourth, fifth and sixth sessions were selected to reduce the amount of data in order to maintain consistent and systematic analysis.

data lends confirmability and credibility to the findings. Three types of task-based activities; one jigsaw, one spot-the differences and one open-ended question were included for data analysis. Representative examples were chosen because they illustrated a fair amount of negotiation of meaning using various types of strategies to solve communication problems. Using Varonis and Gass' (1985) coding scheme[6] involving trigger, indicator, response and reaction, chat transcripts were analyzed to examine interactive negotiation routines in synchronous CMC. The researcher and a trained graduate student coded the data to ensure consistency. Each coder first worked individually and then both coders compared and discussed the discrepancies until they reached final agreement.

Example 1, taken from the current study,[7] illustrates the scheme during lexical negotiation:

Example 1.
1.   **NS:** El hombre lleva un bastón. (The man carries a cane.) [**trigger**]
2.   **NNS:** que es baston? No se. (what is baston? I don't know.) [**indicator**]
3.   **NS:** Creo que se dice "cane" en inglés. (I think it is called "cane" in English.) [**response**]
4.   **NNS:** o.k. tiene sombrero? (o.k. does he have hat?) [**reaction**]

In this example, the unfamiliar word *bastón* (cane) serves as the trigger for negotiation. Upon encountering communication difficulty, the NNS expressed the need for clarification of the unknown word by using the Spanish for "what is" (line 2). The NS then responded to the incomprehensible message using L1 to explain the meaning of the lexical item (line 3). Finally, the NNS brought closure to the negotiation by acknowledging the response using "o.k." (line 4). In this case, the NNS used the clarification request, one typical negotiation strategy to elicit feedback.

Three types of negotiation triggers were considered for this study; lexical, syntactic and sociolinguistic issues. Following Tudini (2007), lexical problems included unknown words and idiomatic expressions (see Examples 1, 6). Grammar errors including morphological and structural features were coded as syntactic

---

6.   The author is aware of other Interactionist coding schemes in application to CMC including Smith's (2003) and Tudini's (2007) identified negotiation routines. However, the current study is building on the author's previous studies (Lee, 2001, 2002b, 2006) drawing on a similar set. Thus, the same coding scheme created by Varonis and Gass (1985) is used for this study.

7.   All examples presented in this paper were taken from the current study and without any correction. While accents, tildes and umlauts are supported in *Blackboard*, participants often do not use them.

triggers (see Example 3). Socially inappropriate use of the target language including pragmatic issues (e.g., politeness) was coded as sociolinguistic triggers. Example 2 illustrates the negotiation triggered by an inappropriate opening on the part of NNS:

Example 2.

1. **NNS:** Que quieres hacer primero? (What do you want to do first?)
2. **NS:** Hola! Como esta? Quiero saludarle primero ☺!! (Hi! How are you? I want to greet you first ☺!!)
3. **NNS:** Si, lo siento. hola! (Yes, I'm sorry, hi!)

Despite the fact that the NNS produced a correct sentence (line 1), certain type of greetings as opening remarks for a conversation are often expected to establish the interaction. The NS, therefore, politely and openly made her point to address the issue using the sentence "I want to greet you first" with a smiling face in line 2. The NNS then realized the problem and responded to the NS using *lo siento* (*I'm sorry*) in line 3.

Building on Lee's (2006) CMC study of NNS-NS interaction, six types of negotiation strategies were coded: (1) confirmation check which includes parts of the statement to ensure understanding (e.g., On the top, right?), (2) clarification request which indicates confusion and asks for help (e.g., What is *cicatriz*?), (3) recast which reformulates all or part of non-target form (e.g., *fueron* instead of *fuieron*), (4) L1 use, (5) request for help which requires additional information (e.g., I don't really understand. Can you explain more?), and (6) use of keyboard symbol or onomatopoeia to express ideas and emotions (e.g., guau guau = dog barking, WOW!, ☺!).

Learners' responses to NSs' corrective feedback were coded: (1) acknowledgment without repeating the recast and continue the task (e.g., o.k. What else do you have?), (2) repetition of the recast which confirms the reformulated target form, and (3) repair which indicates the immediate correction upon receiving corrective feedback, as shown in Example 3:

Example 3.

1. **NNS:** La chica dormió en el autobus. (The girl slept on the bus.)
2. **NS:** *dormió?* (Slept? = wrong conjugation) [**Confirmation check**]
3. **NNS:** Ah, *durmió*. Lo siento. (Ah, slept = correct form. I'm sorry.) [**Repair**]

In this case, the confirmation check used by the NS (line 2) drew the learner's attention to focus on the non-target-like verb *dormió*. The learner then immediately made the correction (*durmió*) in line 3.

7.   Findings and discussion

7.1   Negotiation types and strategies used by NSs and NNSs

The results showed that like face-to-face interaction, online chatting called for a variety of speech acts (greeting, leave-taking) and discourse markers ("really," "me too!"). Keyboard symbols (e.g., ☹!) or uppercase letters (e.g., COOL!) were used to make up for the missing paralinguistic elements of text chats.[8] Despite the fact that linguistic incorrectness and pragmatic inappropriateness occurred throughout the exchange, the NNSs generated various types of strategies to negotiate meaning with the NSs. Table 2 shows that overall more than 50% of negotiations were triggered by lexical problems (56%), whereas less than 30% of negotiations occurred due to the syntactic (25%) or sociolinguistic issues (19%). The analysis yielded a total of 34 negotiation occurrences (40%) made by the NSs and 51 negotiations (60%) initiated by the NNSs (see Table 3). The results indicated that the NNSs initiated more negotiations than the NSs, as Tudini (2007) reported in her recent CMC studies.

Table 2. Negotiation occurrences per negotiation type

Negotiation type	Number and percentage
Lexical	48 (56%)
Syntactic	21 (25%)
Sociolinguistic	16 (19%)
Total	85 (100%)

Table 3. Negotiation occurrences per speaker type

Speaker type	Negotiation occurrences
NSs	34 (40%)
NNSs	51 (60%)
Total	85 (100%)

In some cases, lexical problems were colloquial expressions used by the NSs, such as *¿Qué onda?* (What's up?), *Eso es el colmo* (That's the limit), *Tener mala leche* (To be very bad tempered) or *Es un rollo* (It's a bore). Table 4 illustrates that the lack of lexical knowledge on the part of NNSs provoked a high rate of negotiations (71%).

---

8. Both NNSs' and NSs' discourse markers and speech acts were manifested throughout the examples used for this study.

Table 4. Negotiation type: NSs and NNSs

Negotiation type	NSs (n = 15)	NNSs (n = 15)
Lexical	11 (32%)	36 (71%)
Syntactic	17 (50%)	4 (8%)
Sociolinguistic	6 (18%)	11 (21%)
Total	**34 (100%)**	**51 (100%)**

On contrast, the NSs generated a high frequency of corrective feedback on the NNSs' syntactic problems (50%), especially morphological errors. It is likely that interlocutors solve lexical problems before syntactic errors because the latter contain less communicative value. It is also logical that NSs would initiate negotiations on syntactic problems rather than the NNSs, as the latter would not have sufficient knowledge to detect grammar errors. These findings corroborated those found in the recent studies of NS-NNS chat interaction conducted by Lee (2006) and Tudini (2007).

In terms of sociolinguistic issues, both groups respectively had equal opportunities to make intercultural negotiations (NS = 18% vs. NNS = 21%). The findings showed that the NNSs experienced difficulty understanding colloquial expressions that contained pragmatic features of the Spanish language, as shown in Example 4:

Example 4.

1. **NS:** ¿Cómo andan las cosas? Listo? Quizás, podrías empezar. (How are things going? Ready? Maybe you would start.)
2. **NNS:** Hmm…*andar* es caminar, si? (Hmm…*andar* means to walk, right?) **[Confirmation check]**
3. **NS:** Si, pero en este caso es una forma de saludar. Significa "how are things going?" (Yes, but in this case it is a form of salutation. It means "how are things going?") **[L1 use]**
4. **NNS:** Oh, no se esto. Es interesante. (Oh, I don't know this. It is interesting.)
5. **NS:** En México se usa "¿cómo andas?" para decir "¿cómo estás?" (In Mexico one uses "how's it going?" to say "how are you?")

The evidence showed that the NNS misinterpreted a causal opening remark in a Spanish conversation that demonstrated her lack of pragmatic competence.

Another common pragmatic issue found in this study is the incorrect register between formal and informal you, as shown in Example 5. The underlined and bold words illustrate the inappropriate use of the informal you (*tú*) and incorrect possessive pronoun (*tu* and *tus*) in Spanish.

Example 5.

1. **NNS:** No comprendo. <u>Tú</u> puedes explicar mas <u>tu</u> *pintura*? [I don't understand. Can you explain more your picture?]
2. **NS:** Claro. En mi *dibujo* el policía está platicando con la chamaca que lleva anteojos. [Sure. In my picture the policeman is talking to the girl who wears glasses.] **[Recast]**
3. **NNS:** No comprendo <u>tus</u> palabras platicando y chamaca. [I don't understand your words platicando and chamaca]
4. **NS:** Bueno, platicar es hablar y chamaca quiere decir niña o chica. [Well, platicar is to speak and chamaca means kid or girl in México.]
5. **NNS:** Gracias. En mi *dibujo* un hombre está corriendo muy rápido. [Thanks. In my picture a man is running very fast.] **[Repetition]**
6. **NS:** ¿Para recuperar la bolsa? [To rescue the bag?]

Clearly, the NNS was not aware of inappropriate social conventions by using informal you (*tú*) instead of formal you (*usted*) to address someone who she had contacted only once via e-mail in line 1 and consequently, the incorrect possessive pronoun you (*tus*) appears in line 3. Similar to the comments made by the NSs in Lee's (2007) study, the NS noted on her reflective log that she was reluctant to intervene in the conversation and point out the student's pragmatic infelicities in regard to address forms because she did not want to make the student feel uncomfortable.

Table 5 shows that both NSs and NNSs used various types of strategies for negotiation of meaning. Recasts resulted in the highest rate of corrective feedback (44%) initiated by the NSs, whereas the clarification request (45%) was the most frequent negotiation strategy used by the NNSs. Both groups used other types of negotiation strategies as well (see Table 4).

Table 5. Negotiation strategies

Type of strategy	NSs (n = 15)	NNSs (n = 15)
Confirmation check	7 (20%)	11 (21%)
Clarification request	4 (12%)	23 (45%)
Recast	15 (44%)	0 (0%)
L1 use	4 (12%)	8 (16%)
Request for help	2 (6%)	5 (10%)
Use of keyboard symbol	2 (6%)	4 (8%)
Total	34 (100%)	51 (100%)

Interestingly, there was a similarity found in the distribution of confirmation checks (NS = 20% vs. NNS = 21%). It seems logical that the NNSs employed more L1 to negotiate meaning than the NSs (NNS = 8 occurrences vs. NS = 4 occurrences), as they were at the developmental stages of interlanguage and may have encountered difficulty in expressing meaning. L1 was mainly used to negotiate advanced grammatical points, such as the differences between the preterit and imperfect. Lee (2006) in her CMC study suggested that the use of L1 might be related to learners' language skills as well as their personal learning style. In contrast, the NSs tended to give the English equivalent of Spanish lexical items (see Examples 1, 4).

When a lexical item was incomprehensible to the NNSs, they asked for clarification, such as "What is x?" "What do you mean x?" or "I don't understand what you said." For instance, they did not know words such as *mala pata* (bad luck in Spain), *¡qué padre!* (cool! in Mexico), *chorro* (thief in Argentina), *chibolo* (kid in Peru) *aventón* (ride in Mexico) and *jugo de china* (orange juice in Puerto Rico). Example 6 is typical of many clarification requests used by the NNSs to negotiate unfamiliar idiomatic expressions:

Example 6.

1. NS: La niña está sonriendo porque la comida está para chuparse los dedos. (The girl is smiling because the food is finger licking good.)
2. NNS: que es chuparse los dedos? (what is chuparse los dedos?) [**Clarification request**]
3. NS: Ah, "chuparse los dedos" es una expresión para decir que la comida está muy muy buena; absolutamente deliciosa!! (Ah, "chuparse los dedos" is an expression to say that the food is very very good; absolutely delicious!!)
4. NNS: Ella tiene hambre y quiere comer la comida deliciosa. (She is hungry and wants to eat the delicious food.)

The unknown expression *chuparse los dedos* (to lick the fingers) in line 1 was not understood by the NNS. The use of clarification request in line 2 sent the signal to the NS that pushed her to successfully explain the meaning in Spanish in line 3. In the reflection log, some students noted how important it was for them to increase lexical knowledge; especially expressions commonly used by the NSs, as it was the main trigger for negotiation of meaning. Although these findings corroborate those found in Lee's (2006) and Smith's (2003) studies of CMC, further research is needed in order to confirm the long-term effect of clarification requests on the acquisition of L2 vocabulary.

During the negotiation routines, the NSs showed a strong tendency to use recasts (44%) to provide corrective feedback on non-target-like forms. Similar to the findings reported in Morris's (2002) and Lee's (2006) studies, syntactic errors favored recasts. Example 7 illustrates how a NS utilized the recast to correct a syntactic error made by a NNS:

Example 7.

1. **NNS:** Venio a ayudar ella. Corrio detras de thief. No se la palabra. (He came to help her. He ran after the thief. I don't know the word.)
2. **NS:** ¿Quien vino a ayudar a la chica? (Who came to help the girl?) [**Recast**]
3. **NS:** Se dice ladrón en español. Tenía la bolsa de la chica? (It is called ladrón in Spanish. Did he have the girl's bag?)
4. **NNS:** Su novio vino a ayudar pero no podia tomar el ladron. (Her boyfriend came to help but he couldn't take the thief.) [**Repetition**]
5. **NS:** ¿Que pasó despues? (What happened after?)
6. **NNS:** La chica fue muy furioso y llamaba la policia. (The girl was very furious and called the police.)

The evidence showed that the recast drew the learner's attention to the non-target-like form *venio* in line 1. After reading the verb reformulated by the NS partner in line 2, the NNS noticed the mismatch between input and output and immediately repeated the same verb (*vino* = he came) in line 4. By resorting to the use of recasts, the NS avoided embarrassing the learner. The recast is more salient in CMC than in face-to-face interaction, as the learner reads the correct written text on the screen. Moreover, written discourse can easily be retrieved by the use of the vertical scroll bar (Lee, 2006). While this study makes no claim on the positive effect of recasts for L2 development, the data seems to suggest that the recast did reorient the learner's attention toward the accuracy, as the learner repeated the correct form (also see Example 5).

The results revealed that the NNSs responded to 56% (19 occurrences) of their NS partners' feedback. This aligns with the findings reported by Lee (2006), that expert feedback led to learners' responses. However, the results showed that a high percentage of NS feedback (44%; 14 occurrences) was not responded to by the NNSs. Despite the fact that NS partners provided feedback on syntactic errors, the NNSs tended to ignore them in order to maintain the conversational flow (Blake & Zyzik, 2003; Lee, 2006). In some cases, students initiated another topic to avoid error correction. The results seemed to imply that students were more interested in lexical items than making corrections on grammar errors. Example 8 is a typical lexical repair made by the NNS upon receiving the confirmation check from the NS partner in line 3:

Example 8.

1. **NS:** Hay que distinguir entre suicidarse y terminarse la vida a causa de cuestiones físicas que le impide a alguien participar de una vida satisfactoria.
    (It is necessary to distinguish between committing suicide and ending life because of physical matters that prevents somebody from participating from a satisfactory life.)

2. **NNS:** Creo que la gente tiene *la derecha* de decidir su vida. Alguno gente prefiere morir que sufrir. (I believe that people has right-hand side to decide their life. Some people prefer to die than to suffer.)

3. **NS:** La derecha??? El punto de quitarse la vida porque está sufriendo es interesante. Tambien es una carga para la familia, no? (The right-hand side??? The point of taking one's own life because he/she is suffering is interesting. It is also a burden for the family, right? [**Confirmation check**]

4. **NNS:** Lo siento. El derecho es importante. ¿Que es una carga? (I'm sorry. The right is important. What is una carga?) [**Repair**]

5. **NS:** Es que la familia necesita cuidar al paciente como el caso de Terri. Que opina del caso de Terri? (It is that the family needs to take care of the patient like the case of Terri. What do you think of the case of Terri?)

6. **NNS:** Es muy triste pero creo que el esposo no queria que ella sufria mas. (It is very sad but I believe that the husband did not want her to suffer more.)

7. **NS:** De acuerdo. Creo que el caso de Terri abrio una ventana al futuro en relacion a la eutanasia. (Agree! I believe that the case of Terri opened a window to the future regarding euthanasia.)

This study also found evidence that English was the preferred response move used by the NNS when Spanish as the first attempt to try to solve communication problem was not successful. In the reflective essay, some students admitted that it was not possible for them to express meaning without using L1 due to their insufficient knowledge of Spanish. As pointed out previously, the L1 shaped the route taken by NSs and NNSs alike to negotiate L2 forms for both syntactic and lexical problems. L1 seemed to be a quick way to solve communication difficulties without interrupting the flow of conversation. The question remains whether the amount of L1 decreases as learners advance their language proficiency. The long-term effect of L1 on feedback negotiation in relation to learners' performance is an issue worthy of further research.

Based on the above discussion, students benefited from negotiating meaning with NSs in real-time exchanges. However, the observations made by both NSs and NNSs based on their reflective logs revealed critical factors that affected the way they interacted with each other. Due to the limited space permitted in this discussion to provide a detailed analysis of each participant's observations, two accounts that played a significant role in collaborative interaction are highlighted: (1) the role of tasks and (2) expert scaffolding.

7.2   The role of tasks

Regarding task type, both NSs and NNSs praised the effectiveness of task-based instruction for the study. Participants pointed out that two-way information exchange tasks fostered more balanced turn-taking and equalized contributions. In this study, three types of tasks (jigsaw, spot-the-differences, open-ended question) were employed to promote negotiation. For instance, the jigsaw featured a set of drawings on cards depicting an adventure. Each party was given a different portion of the complete set of drawings. Each pair had to collaboratively work together in order to produce a story based on the pictures. Participants commented that both jigsaw and spot-the-differences tasks were like puzzles that kept them curious and involved, as they were required to contribute parts of exchange in order to attain one possible outcome. They found jigsaw and spot-the-differences fun and stimulating for problem-solving tasks that led to high level of negotiated interaction, as suggested in Blake's CMC study (2000).

Open-ended questions regarding controversial issues challenged students to formulate their ideas. Some students admitted that they did not have sufficient content knowledge and language skills to fully express themselves. For example, one student maintained: "Although topics like home schooling and euthanasia were interesting, I experienced great difficulty in conveying ideas because I really did not know much about these topics. Thus, I was not able to provide substantial commentary." Similarly, NSs expressed the concern about not having the depth of discussions on debating issues, as this expert speaker wrote: "I did not find discussions on controversial topics engaging and fulfilling. Rather, they were somewhat brief and superficial. I think you have to have a high level of language skills to engage in this kind of discussion." Clearly, the degree of familiarity with the topic and language proficiency influenced the interactivity between NSs and NNSs. Controversial topics may be more suitable for advanced language learners. It would be worthwhile to explore how debating topics affect the meaning is negotiated involving students at an advanced level of proficiency in synchronous CMC.

7.3   Expert scaffolding

One important aspect of social engagements is expert scaffolding through which learners receive help from more capable individuals (e.g., teacher, native speaker). The findings indicated that NSs played a facilitator role in providing effective assistance to mediate collaborative interaction, a result that has repeatedly been supported in previous studies (e.g., Iwasaki & Oliver, 2003; Lee, 2008). During the interaction, learners use the target language as a cognitive tool for collaboration to complete a shared task (Lee, 2004a). Students' observations of the expert role were mixed in this study. While some students admitted that the expert scaffolding enhanced their understanding of Spanish language and increased their awareness of pragmatic issues, others did not find expert scaffolding effective. Anecdotal evidence based on comments made on reflective logs suggests that linguistically strong students appreciated and benefited from expert scaffolding, as they were able to reconstruct L2 forms after receiving feedback from their NS partners. More importantly, expert scaffolding pushed learners to reflect on linguistic forms using cognitive skills. One student remarked: "I felt quite comfortable chatting with my NS partner. I found her feedback helpful. I learned cool things, such as *güera* (a blond girl) and *¿qué onda?* (what's up?) that I did not know nor did I learn from my previous Spanish classes." Another student made a remark on how well his expert partner explained to him the usage of *por* and *para*[9] with examples. These comments highlight the necessity of understanding authentic language for meaningful real-world contexts.

Just as previous studies have shown that expert speakers have a tendency to dominate the discussion (Lee, 2004a), some students in this study expressed the same concern. They did not find an equal power relationship, as they felt that their NS partners did not allow them to fully express their opinions by leading the exchange. One explanation could be that the majority of the NSs in this study had lived in the United States for a short period of time. They may not have become accustomed to dealing with American students who were learning a foreign language. One student reported on her reflective log: "I did not think my NS partner knew how to help me out when I got stuck. She kept asking me the same questions." The same student further suggested that the instructor should provide NSs with training on how to provide constructive feedback. Another student addressed that too much negative feedback was given to her that discouraged her from contributing and made her feel incompetent. CMC is human-to-human interaction that needs both affective and cognitive supports for social interchanges. Despite the fact that pragmatically the NS was polite using phrases, such as *No estoy convencido. Me gustaría ver algunos ejemplos* (I'm not convinced. I'd like to see some examples.), the student viewed the act as face-threatening in the social setting. It is likely that the student may not have the self-confidence or self-determination to maintain the face. It should be noted that most of the students in this study had never had the experience of dealing with the NSs. Thus, they might not know how to converse with people from other cultures. To this end, it is important to build interpersonal relationships that demonstrate trust and casualness to support socio-emotional CMC.

---

9. The Spanish prepositions *por* and *para* have a variety of meanings. They often cause confusion for English speakers learning Spanish, since both of them can be translated as "for."

8.   Pedagogical implications

Although the short duration of one-to-one chat interaction with NSs did not directly transfer to the improvement of students' language skills and intercultural awareness, the evidence of chat data and observations made by the participants offer the following pedagogical implications.

1. As mentioned previously, the interaction with expert speakers exposes students to a wide range of functional language discourse within social contexts. Instructors are strongly encouraged to incorporate NSs into the use of CMC to increase authentic interaction. Expert speakers can be recruited among the international students and scholars on campus and from the local community (see also Darhower, 2008 for bilingual chat community). In order to use CMC effectively and efficiently, both students and NSs need to learn how to interact within the electronic environment. For instance, due to the reduced non-verbal cues in CMC, NSs should learn when and how to provide corrective feedback to help learners cope with communication breakdowns. On their part, students need to be aware of pragmatic appropriateness, rather than just linguistic accuracy.

2. Grammar accuracy and lexical growth are equally important for developing learners' L2 language competence. While negotiations are mainly triggered by lexical problems in communicative situations, it is essential for instructors to create appropriate awareness-raising activities through which focus-on-form is guaranteed while meaning-oriented interaction is shared during the CMC. Students should be advised to focus on form (syntactic errors) with the assistance of the expert speaker when the opportunity arises to maintain a balance between fluency and accuracy.

3. A task-based approach focuses on conveying ideas contextually using the target language rather than practicing L2 through mechanical drills. Jigsaw and spot-the-differences tasks have proven highly effective for negotiated interaction (also see, Lee, 2006). Thus, designing tasks that are meaning-driven and at the same time support form-focus reflection should be one of the primary objectives of network-based instruction. While other types of tasks including decision-making and opinion exchange are also useful for two-way exchange, certain topics may not be suitable for students with less language proficiency. Instructors, therefore, need to carefully choose topics to avoid learners' frustration that may discourage them from being active in the discussion.

4. Using one-to-one text chat affords students additional opportunities to use the target language for real time exchanges outside of class. In addition to text chats, teachers are encouraged to explore other possibilities. For instance, the *Horizon Wimba* software is a multi-channel-mediated communication tool that allows users to add audio and visual interaction to current online courses

(e.g., *Blackboard, WebCT, Moodle*). Other options are to use cost-effective voice and video tools including *NetMeeting* and *Skype*. Internet technology continues to play an ever-increasing role in foreign language teaching and learning. Freely available social networking programs, such as *Blogger, Facebook, Myspace* and *Wikispaces* should be explored, as they have the potential to create a stimulating online learning environment that is conducive to collaborative exchanges (see also Lee, 2009, for discussion on Web 2.0 tools).

5. Establishing interpersonal relationships and building up mutual trust are essential for the success of online interaction. Teachers need to provide opportunities for participants to get acquainted with each other to raise the comfort level and self-confidence of learners in order to surmount linguistic and sociolinguistic barriers via synchronous CMC. As task-based activities rely on the use of meta-cognitive skills, learners may encounter difficulty in expressing meaning. Affective supports from expert speakers that show empathy – the ability of putting oneself into someone else's shoes – are needed to motivate learners to fully engage in the negotiation process.

9.   Conclusion

Interacting with NSs affords learners a variety of authentic language discourse that would not be available during learner-to-learner exchange. The current study explored native and nonnative interactive discourse in text chat. This study clearly showed that online chats presented both promises and challenges for NS-NNS interaction. The evidence showed that the text chat not only enabled students to negotiate meaning using various types of strategies, but also reinforced their understanding of idiomatic expressions as well as pragmatic issues including speech acts. Importantly, NS feedback using recasts played a facilitative role in making learners aware of linguistic forms using repetitions in their follow-up responses (Examples 5, 7). The findings revealed that the task type affected how participants negotiated meaning during CMC. While participants generated a high level of interactive negotiation using jigsaw and spot-the-differences tasks, students at the intermediate level experienced difficulty expressing ideas using open-ended questions regarding controversial topics.

The ability to function interculturally is an important asset to language learning that goes beyond solely linguistic fluency to include intercultural communicative competence (see also Byram, 1997). The findings suggest that negotiation of linguistic problems is only part of interaction that promotes L2 acquisition. It is important to bring students' awareness of pragmatic issues and teach them politeness strategies for effective intercultural communication (Kinginger &

Belz, 2005). Further studies might include cross-cultural exchanges to bring intercultural sensitivity involving NSs who reside in Spanish-speaking countries rather than in the United States. In closing, this study offers an insightful perspective of the practicalities of implementing synchronous CMC for the extension of the target language communication beyond classroom limits.

References

Abrams, Z. (2003). The effect of synchronous and asynchronous CMC on oral performance in German. *Modern Language Journal, 87,* 157–167.

Belz, J. A. (2002). Social dimensions of telecollaborative foreign language study. *Language Learning & Technology, 6,* 60–81. Available from http://llt.msu.edu/vol6num1/belz/

Blake, R. (2000). Computer mediated communication: A window on L2 Spanish interlanguage. *Language Learning and Technology, 4,* 120–136. Available from http://llt.msu.edu/vol4num1/blake/

Blake, R., & Zyzik, E. (2003). Who's helping whom?: Learner/heritage speakers' networked discussions in Spanish. *Applied Linguistics, 24,* 519–544.

Byram, M. (1997). *Teaching and assessing intercultural communicative competence.* Clevedon: Multilingual Matters.

Chun, D. (1994). Using computer networking to facilitate the acquisition of interactive competence. *System, 22,* 17–31.

Darhower, M. (2002). Interactional features of synchronous computer-mediated communication in the intermediate L2 class: A sociocultural case study. *CALICO Journal, 19,* 249–277.

Darhower, M. (2008). The role of linguistic affordances in telecollaborative chat. *CALICO Journal, 26,* 48–69.

De Guerrero, M., & Villamil, O. S. (2000). Activating the ZPD: Mutual scaffolding in L2 peer revision. *Modern Language Journal, 84,* 51–68.

Dussias, P. E. (2006). Morphological development in Spanish-American telecollaboration. In J. Belz & S. Thorne (Eds.), *Internet-mediated intercultural foreign language education* (pp. 121–146). Boston, MA: Thomson & Heinle.

Ellis, R. (2003). *Task-based language learning and teaching.* Oxford: Oxford University Press.

Fernández-García, M., & Martinez-Arbelaiz, A. (2003). Learners' interactions: A comparison of oral and computer-assisted written conversations. *ReCALL, 15,* 113–136.

Foster, P., & Ohta, A. (2005). Negotiation for meaning and peer assistance in second language classrooms. *Applied Linguistics, 26,* 402–430.

Furstenberg, G., Levet, S., English, K., & Maillet, K. (2001). Giving a voice to the silent language of culture: The *cultura* project. *Language Learning & Technology, 5,* 55–102. Available from http://llt.msu.edu/vol5num1/furstenberg/default.html

González-Bueno, M., & Pérez, L. (2000). Electronic mail in foreign language writing: A study of grammatical and lexical accuracy, and quantity of language. *Foreign Language Annals, 33,* 189–198.

González-Lloret, M. (2003). Designing task-based CALL to promote interaction en busca de esmeraldas. *Language Learning & Technology, 7,* 86–104. Available from http://llt.msu.edu/vol7num1/gonzalez/

Iwasaki, J., & Oliver, R. (2003). Chatline interaction and negative feedback. *Australian Review of Applied Linguistics, 17*, 60–73.

Jepson, K. (2005). Conversations and negotiated interaction in text and voice chatrooms. *Language Learning & Technology, 9*, 79–98. Available from http://llt.msu.edu/ vol9num3/jepson/

Kasper, G., & Rose, K. (2001). Pragmatics in language teaching. In K. Rose & G. Kasper (Eds.), *Pragmatics in language teaching* (pp. 1–9). Cambridge: Cambridge University Press.

Kern, R. (1995). Restructuring classroom interaction with networked computers: Effects on quantity and characteristics of language production. *Modern Language Journal, 79*, 457–476.

Kinginger, C., & Belz, J. (2005). Socio-cultural perspectives on pragmatic development in foreign language learning: Microgenetic and ontogenetic case studies from telecollaboration and study abroad. *Intercultural Pragmatics, 2*, 369–422.

Kitade, K. (2000). L2 Learners' discourse and SLA theories in CMC: Collaborative interaction in Internet chat. *Computer Assisted Language Learning, 13*, 143–166.

Lai, C., & Zhao, Y. (2006). Noticing and text-based chat. *Language Learning & Technology, 10*, 102–120. Available from http://llt.msu.edu/vol10num3/laizhao/default.html

Lantolf, J. P., & Thorne, S. L. (2006). *Sociocultural theory and the genesis of second language development.* Oxford: Oxford University Press.

Lee, L. (2000). Evaluating intermediate Spanish students' speaking skills through a taped test: A pilot study. *Hispania, 83*, 127–138.

Lee, L. (2001). Online interaction: Negotiation of meaning and strategies used among learners of Spanish. *ReCALL, 13*, 232–244.

Lee, L. (2002a). Enhancing learners' communication skills through synchronous electronic interaction and task-based instruction. *Foreign Language Annuals, 35*, 16–23.

Lee, L. (2002b). Synchronous online exchanges: A study of modification devices on nonnative discourse interaction. *System, 30*, 275–288.

Lee, L. (2004a). Perspectives of nonnative speakers of Spanish on two types of on-line collaborative exchanges: Promises and challenges. In L. Lomicka & J. Cooke-Plagwitz (Eds.), *Teaching with technology* (pp. 248–261). Boston: Heinle & Heinle.

Lee, L. (2004b). Learners' perspectives on networked collaborative interaction with native speakers of Spanish in the U.S. *Language Learning & Technology, 8*, 83–100. Available from http://llt.msu.edu/vol8num1/lee/

Lee, L. (2005). Using web-based instruction to promote active learning: Learners' perspectives. *CALICO Journal, 23*, 139–156.

Lee, L. (2006). A study of native and nonnative speakers' feedback and responses in Spanish-American networked collaborative interaction. In J. Belz & S. Thorne (Eds.), *Internet-mediated intercultural foreign language education* (pp. 147–176). Boston, MA: Thomson & Heinle.

Lee, L. (2007). Fostering L2 oral communication through constructivist interaction in desktop videoconferencing. *Foreign Language Annals, 40*, 635–649.

Lee, L. (2008). Focus-on-form through collaborative scaffolding in expert-to-novice online interaction. *Language Learning & Technology, 12*, pp. 94–113. Available from http://llt.msu.edu/vol12num3/lee.pdf

Lee, L. (2009). Using wikis, blogs and podcasts in the foreign language classroom: A task-based approach. In L. Stone & C. Wilson-Duffy (Eds.), *Task-based III: Expanding the range of tasks with online resources* (pp. 49–70). International Association for Language Learning Technology.

Loewen, S., & Erlam, R. (2006). Corrective feedback in the chatroom: An experimental study. *Computer Assisted Language Learning, 19,* 1–14.

Long, M. H. (1996). The role of linguistic environment in second language acquisition. In W. Richie & T. Bhatia (Eds.), *Handbook of research on language acquisition: Vol. 2. Second language acquisition* (pp. 413-468). New York: Academic Press.

Long, M. H., & Robinson, P. (1998). Focus on form: Theory, research and practice. In C. Doughty & J. Williams (Eds.), *Focus on form in second language acquisition* (pp. 15–41). Cambridge: Cambridge University Press.

Meskill, C., & Anthony, N. (2005). Foreign language learning with CMC: Forms of online instructional discourse in a hybrid Russian class. *System, 33,* 89–105.

Morris, F. (2002). Negotiation moves and recasts in relation to error types and learner repair in the foreign language classroom. *Foreign Language Annals, 35,* 395–404.

Nassaji, H., & Swain, M. (2000). A Vygotskian perspective on corrective feedback in L2: The effect of random versus negotiated help on the learning of English articles. *Language Awareness, 1,* 34–52.

O'Dowd, R. (2003). Understanding the "other side": Intercultural learning in a Spanish English exchange. *Language Learning and Technology, 7,* 118–144. Available from http://llt.msu.edu/vol7num2/odowd/

Oliver, R. (1995). Negative feedback in child NS/NNS conversation. *Studies in Second Language Acquisition, 17,* 459–483.

O'Rourke, B. (2005). Form-focused interaction in online tandem learning. *CALICO Journal, 22,* 433–466.

Payne, S., & Whitney, R. (2002). Developing L2 oral proficiency through synchronous CMC: Output, working memory and interlanguage development. *CALICO Journal, 20,* 7–32.

Pellettieri, J. (2000). Negotiation in cyberspace: The role of chatting in the development of grammatical competence. In M. Warschauer & R. Kern (Eds.), *Network-based language teaching: concepts and practice* (pp. 59–86). Cambridge: Cambridge University Press.

Pica, T., Kanagy, R., & Falodun, J. (1993). Choosing and using communication tasks for second language instruction. In G. Crookes & S. Gass (Eds.), *Tasks and language learning: Integrating theory and practice* (pp. 9–34). Clevedon: Multilingual Matters.

Schmidt, R. (1995). Consciousness and foreign language learning: A tutorial on the role attention and awareness in learning. In R. Schmidt (Ed.), *Attention and Awareness in Foreign Language Learning* (pp. 1–63). Technical Report No. 9. Honolulu, HI: University of Hawaii, Second Language Teaching and Curriculum Center.

Skehan, P. (2003). Focus on form, tasks and technology. *Computer Assisted Language Learning, 16,* 391–411.

Smith, D. B. (2003). Computer-mediated negotiated interaction: An expanded model. *Modern Language Journal, 87,* 38–57.

Smith, D. B (2008). Methodological hurdles in captures CMC data: The case of the missing self-repair. *Language Learning & Technology, 12,* 85–103. Available from http://llt.msu.edu/vol12num1/smith/default.html

Sotillo, M. S. (2000). Discourse functions and syntactic complexity in synchronous and asynchronous communication. *Language Learning & Technology, 4,* 82–119. Available from http://llt.msu.edu/vol4num1/sotillo/

Sotillo, M. S. (2005). Corrective feedback via instant messenger learning activities in NS-NNS and NNS-NNS dyads. *CALICO Journal, 22,* 467–496.

Swain, M. (2000). The output hypothesis and beyond: Mediating acquisition through collaborative dialogue. In J. P. Lantolf (Ed.), *Sociocultural theory and second language learning* (pp. 97–114). Oxford: Oxford University Press.

Swain, M., & Lapkin, S. (1998). Interaction and second language learning: Two adolescent French immersion students working together. *Modern Language Journal, 82,* 320–337.

Sykes, J. M. (2005). Synchronous CMC and pragmatic development: Effects of oral and written chat. *CALICO Journal, 22,* 399–432.

Toyoda, E., & Harrison, R. (2002). Categorization of text chat communication between learners and native speakers of Japanese. *Language Learning & Technology, 6,* 82–99. Available from http://llt.msu.edu/vol6num1/toyoda/

Tudini, V. (2003). Using native speakers in chat. *Language Learning & Technology, 7,* 141–159. Available from http://llt.msu.edu/vol7num3/tudini/

Tudini, V. (2007). Negotiation and intercultural learning in Italian native speakers chat rooms. *Modern Language Journal, 91,* 577–601.

Varonis, E., & Gass, S. (1985). Non-native/non-native conversations: A model for negotiation. *Applied Linguistics, 6,* 71–90.

Ware, P., & O'Dowd, R. (2008). Peer feedback on language form in telecollaboration. *Language Learning & Technology, 12,* 43–63. Available from http://llt.msu.edu/vol12num1/wareodowd/default.html

Warschauer, M. (1997). A sociocultural approach to literacy and its significance for CALL. In K. Murphy-Judy & R. Sanders, (Eds.), *Nexus: The convergence of research and teaching through new information technologies* (pp. 88–97). Durham, NC: University of North Carolina.

PART III

Podcasts

Podcasts and second language learning

Promoting listening comprehension
and intercultural competence

Kara McBride

This chapter discusses how podcasts that were not originally made specifically for second language (L2) learners can be used in L2 classes to promote listening comprehension and intercultural competence. The chapter first defines and describes podcasts and offers strategies for locating useful ones. Next, listening comprehension is examined in order to identify practices that may improve bottom-up and top-down skills and the automaticity by which these are executed. The topic of authenticity is reviewed in terms of how authentic podcasts are a rich source of cultural and pragmatic information, and when students learn how to find podcasts of interest to them, they are likely to become more motivated and autonomous learners. The issue of how to avoid potentially offensive materials is also touched upon. Finally, this chapter outlines activities that can be done in class and out, keeping in mind potential curricular- and time-related restrictions and giving suggestions for how the above-mentioned skills can be targeted, as well as vocabulary building, collaboration, and pronunciation practice.

1.   Introduction

Podcasts were first produced in 2004 (Hegelheimer & O'Bryan, 2008), and by 2005, nearly a third of all owners of mp3 players had downloaded one (Rainie & Madden, 2005). Podcasts represent yet another way in which the Internet has made available to its users vast quantities of information in the form of a new medium. Presented with this new linguistic resource, second language (L2) pedagogy should investigate whether and how podcasts can be used to promote second language acquisition (SLA). There have been published articles that give broad overviews of types and possible pedagogical uses of podcasts (McCarty, 2005; Rossell-Aguilar, 2007; Sze, 2006; Young, 2007) and how best to incorporate podcasts into L2 classes (Abdous, Camarena, & Facer, 2009; Craig, Paraiso, &

Patten, 2007; Schmidt, 2008), while others discuss more specific uses, such as podcasts created by language learners for the purpose of improving their pronunciation skills (Lord, 2008) and podcasts created by instructors for teaching academic listening skills (O'Bryan & Hegelheimer, 2007).

This chapter focuses on the use, in L2 classes, of podcasts that were made by third parties without the original intention of them being used by language learners. The two main objectives of such a practice are to improve listening comprehension (LC) and to teach intercultural competence. I begin with a definition of podcasts, choosing to define that term in a wider sense that has come into popular usage. I then discuss L2 LC and its development in order to examine how listening to podcasts can most advantageously be approached by teachers and learners. This leads into a discussion of the use of authentic materials and the teaching of intercultural competence. Finally, specific class-related activities are proposed.

2.   A definition

Podcasts are audio files, usually in mp3 format, that can be downloaded from the Internet.[1] Several authors have insisted that only files that are syndicated count as podcasts (e.g., Abdous, et al., 2009; Godwin-Jones, 2005; Rossell-Aguilar, 2007; Stanley, 2006; but see Lu, 2008). This means that where the podcast is published, there is an option for subscribing to it. Subscription is often accomplished as easily as clicking on a button, so that every time a new audio file is added to the collection of a particular podcast series, subscribers can be automatically notified, or, more commonly, automatically receive a downloaded copy of the new episode on their computer and/or mp3 player. The most widely used program for such automatic delivery is iTunes, but a site such as Podcatchermatrix[2] directs one to many, alternative aggregators or podcatchers, as they are called. Like iTunes and other programs for downloading, playing, organizing, and transferring podcasts, almost all podcasts are free.

The term *podcast* has been extended in some popular usage to include most downloadable sound files on the Internet, without them needing to be either syndicated, nor one in a series of episodes, although both features are common. By adopting the broader meaning of "podcast," we include more potential resources for teachers.

---

1.   There are also video podcasts, although these are less common. Their usage does not afford users the same mobility, and V. Askildson (2008) found that language learners were much less interested in using video rather than audio podcasts.

2.   http://www.podcatchermatrix.org

Many corporations (e.g., McDonald's[3]) and professional groups (e.g., TESOL[4]) post podcasts on their webpages with some regularity, to provide an alternative form of update about their organization. This is also a common practice among libraries and universities, with many universities doing so through iTunes U. Other entities that regularly post podcasts are radio stations (e.g., National Public Radio,[5] which provides full transcripts for most stories), professional journals, especially in the sciences (e.g., *Molecular Medicine*[6]), and news organizations. Some periodicals, for example, *The Economist*, provide versions of their publications in mp3 format, but the download is only available to paying subscribers, while others, like *The New Yorker*,[7] provide free audio versions of selected articles. All of these examples are referred to as podcasts.[8]

So far, professionally-made podcasts have been highlighted, but probably far more of all podcasts are made by private individuals who publish not for commercial purposes but instead for personal, social, and entertainment reasons. Frequently they follow a talk radio format, dominated by commentary, mixed in with occasional songs. Like radio shows, they often include interviews with guests and responses to listeners who have called or left voice or text messages over the Internet.

Podcast directories are described by some (e.g., Rossell-Aguilar, 2007; Schmidt, 2008; Stanley, 2006) as the primary way of locating podcasts. However, performing a Google search for the keyword "podcast" plus other search terms of interest should be just as, if not more, effective.[9] Also, podcatchers facilitate but are not essential for downloading the sound files.[10] Files in mp3

---

3.   http://www.mcdonalds.com/corp/podcasts.html

4.   http://www.tesol.org/

5.   http://www.npr.org/

6.   http://www.molmed.org/

7.   http://www.newyorker.com/

8.   Another source of online sound files which has great potential educationally are the spoken versions of Wikipedia articles, <http://en.wikipedia.org/wiki/Wikipedia:Spoken_articles>, although these fall outside of even most loose usages of the term "podcast."

9.   This can be especially effective in looking for podcasts in languages other than English. By using search terms in the language one is interested in, one is directed to podcasts produced in that language. Although the examples listed earlier in this article are all English examples, podcasts are widely available in many languages. Also important to note is that most podcast directories, including the iTunes Store, do not allow one to do a search based on language.

10.   With PCs, right-clicking on the link to the sound file will bring up a menu that includes "Save link as…", which then allows one to save the file locally. With Macs, holding down the option key and clicking on the link to the mp3 file allows downloading.

format can easily be copied onto mp3 players and many other mobile devices, such as most cell phones. Some of these devices can play other audio formats as well, and when they cannot, conversion is possible via a number of free or low-priced programs.[11]

This is the other major advantage that podcasts present potential users with: besides expanding people's access to recorded materials to a practically limitless amount of up-to-date materials from all over the world, podcast technology allows the listener to be mobile. Of course personal stereos existed before, but few people had access to materials that lent themselves easily as L2 lessons. Such materials used to be mostly the property of language laboratories, requiring students to go to the technology. Now technology, especially in its more recent, small, and convenient form, can travel with the learner. Being available when and where the L2 learner wants, makes listening to materials less burdensome and more attractive to the student (Windham, 2007; Young, 2007). Mobile learning solutions also alleviate institutions of some of the needed hours of available language lab space, thus presenting a possible financial benefit.

Students belonging to the Net Generation – born between 1977 and 1997 – typically are (or feel) extremely busy but are fond of and fairly good at multitasking (Tapscott, 2009). They are likely to own, carry with them, and be familiar with the workings of a device that plays sound files (Rainie & Madden, 2005; Schmidt, 2008). For all of these reasons, podcasts appear to be an excellent format for delivering L2 materials to students of the Net Generation, as well as other students who study through distance learning programs, who typically also are pressed for time, unable to regularly attend a (physical) language lab or perhaps even classroom, and need alternative formats for the delivery of educational materials. Finally, using podcasts in language lessons has indeed been found to be in itself motivating for many learners (Craig, et al., 2007; Windham, 2007).

Still, podcasts should not be used for teaching L2 except in pedagogically sound ways that fit with SLA theory. Decoo (2001) warns that "... quite often 'the media makes the method'" (p. 9) – meaning that educators sometimes allow a new technology to dominate choices about approaches to language teaching, when instead one should begin from a clear understanding of what kinds of activities promote SLA, and then find and use whatever tools best support those activities. The rest of this chapter aims to demonstrate that for the purpose of teaching LC, transcultural competence, and strategic and autonomous L2 study skills, podcasts are a valuable resource.

---

11. One way of doing this is to use the "Convert selection to mp3" option in iTunes, found in menus connected to importing preferences.

3.   Listening comprehension

LC is achieved through the employment of a combination of top-down and bottom-up skills (Rost, 2002; Vandergrift, 2004). Bottom-up skills involve listening to sounds, perceiving words and sentences among them, and parsing these. Top-down skills are those that use general world knowledge and background information to activate appropriate schemata through which to interpret spoken messages. Both types of skills are required for all LC.

The way in which top-down and bottom-up skills interact is variable, depending on the task, context, and listener (Flowerdew & Miller, 2005; Wu, 1998). Successful L2 LC is accomplished through an orchestration of strategies, using those that best match a given task (McBride, 2008; Vandergrift, 2003b). Learners benefit from training in metacognitive awareness about LC and in top-down processes such as using background information to form hypotheses about the spoken message (Vandergrift, 2003a, 2004). Top-down listening skills can largely compensate for incomplete bottom-up processing when there is a good match between the listener's expectations and what is said, but when this is not the case, skilled bottom-up processing is what distinguishes more skilled listeners from less successful ones (Tsui & Fullilove, 1998). Therefore, bottom-up skill development is also essential.

L2 students often fail to recognize in a spoken text words they do in fact know (Field, 2000), and even successful retrieval of words may be excessively slow. Bottom-up skill building takes the form of moving the learner towards automatized word recognition and parsing. When these processes are not yet automatized, they can present such a strain to working memory that they short-circuit LC (Carpenter, Miyake, & Just, 1994; Hulstijn, 2003), blocking the listener's ability to remember properly or make connections between parts of the message.

L2 learners, especially in a classroom environment, learn many words in the written form first and then must learn to associate their knowledge about the words with the way the words sound when spoken. They also must learn a great deal about how words sound when strung together and are pronounced in natural, faster, and less careful speech. The teaching of these bottom-up skills ought to be approached from two sides: (1) through focused listening activities which direct the learner's attention on specific features of the aural input, and (2) through extensive exposure to authentic speech.

4.   Authentic materials

As Little (1997) says, " … we cannot expect learners to cope with target language communication in the world outside the classroom if we do not prepare them by bringing examples of that communication into the classroom" (p. 226). L2 classes provide students with the opportunity to encounter authentic language while receiving support from the scaffolding that is provided by a well-planned lesson. Learners at first will only be able to perform the task when given a large amount of assistance, but as practice continues, the teacher's support is needed less and less, until the student is able to do the task on his or her own (Lantolf & Thorne, 2007).

If students gain the skills to work with authentic aural texts through their L2 classes, they are more likely to also listen to such texts on their own. Thus, teaching students both how to find interesting podcasts, and how to approach listening to authentic texts through strategic listening and generally improved LC skills, allows students to be autonomous learners. Getting learners in the habit of accessing interesting target language podcasts gives the learners a dual purpose in continuing to access these materials on their own: not only does it help them in their SLA, but the materials themselves will be a draw.

L2 learners find working with authentic listening materials motivating and useful (Dupuy, 1999). Vandergrift (2004) also describes two studies that support this: "Both elementary school students (Vandergrift, 2002) and university students of French (Vandergrift, 2003a) found it motivating to learn to understand rapid, authentic texts and responded overwhelmingly in favor of this approach" (p. 9). Successfully working with an authentic speech sample is exciting. Being able to listen to discussions of topics of personal interest to one is also very important. Finally, podcasts give learners many more opportunities to hear speech from the particular social group that they wish to learn about and perhaps identify with. This reference group may be defined by age, lifestyle, ethnic group, accent, or otherwise. The diversity of podcast producers makes it likely that materials from within this group can be found, and such material will be of especially high interest to the learner, promoting SLA (Beebe, 1985). Listening to a social group's podcasts can allow students to feel more a part of that culture (Craig, et al., 2007). Further, it can provide valuable lessons in pragmatics. Often L2 learners acquire excessively formal speech habits that are inappropriate for the social situations that they will later find themselves in. Interviews, phone calls, and other kinds of social exchanges are common features of podcasts and can serve as models for the L2 listener.

Authentic texts also give students vital ways of connecting with the culture of study. The Modern Language Association's (MLA) 2007 report urges language educators to teach intercultural competence, which entails being able to "comprehend and analyze the cultural narratives that appear in every kind of expressive form" (p. 238). Instead of adhering to the monolithic narrative of an education based exclusively on canonical texts, one needs exposure to a variety of voices within a culture in order to approach an understanding of it.

5.   Lesson plans

5.1   Avoid overwhelming participants

Having looked at the construct of LC and discussed reasons for incorporating authentic, recently made materials in the form of podcasts into an L2 class, this last part of the chapter discusses specific activities that can be introduced by a teacher into L2 classes. One of the guiding concerns in designing this kind of a lesson will be the need to avoid overwhelming either the student or the teacher. The student runs the risk of being overwhelmed because the materials used are authentic and not made with L2 learners in mind. To address this potential problem, the teacher must create listening tasks at an appropriate level of difficulty. Frequently this is determined by the nature of the materials with which the students work. When working with authentic materials, this can be controlled somewhat (for example by choosing more familiar topics, or a certain type of genre or accent), but not entirely. It is instead the nature of the task that will determine the level of difficulty.

L2 learners should not be expected to achieve full comprehension of authentic listening passages. Instead, they should be given tasks divided into small enough steps and reasonable goals so that they can be successful at each stage. As is common in the teaching of L2 reading comprehension, students can be given texts that are in one sense well above their level, and then be asked to perform tasks that do not require full textual comprehension, such as summarizing main ideas or identifying key words (Grabe & Stoller, 2001). It is important to communicate to the students the worth of such exercises and reasonableness of the expectations. Pointing out the frequently incomplete nature of first language (L1) LC – given, for example, that it is possible for two people to come away with different interpretations of the same conversation – can help to illustrate this point.

Another way that LC with authentic materials can be made more attainable is through the manipulations of recordings that technology affords (Hulstijn, 2003; Robin, 2007). Learner control over speech rate and pausing enhances immediate LC (Zhao, 1997), and repetition (Jensen & Vinther, 2003) and adjustments in rate of speech (Jensen & Vinther, 2003; McBride, 2007) can aid in the development of L2 LC over time. In several ways the digitized nature of podcasts can be exploited to allow L2 learners of all levels to use authentic listening materials to extract meaning and improve their LC.

The instructor is also in danger of being overwhelmed by working with podcasts. Incorporating podcasts into class activities will require some teachers to first become familiar with new technology. This, fortunately, is mostly a one-time commitment and can be done fairly quickly with the help of a personal tutorial or online guides. The other problem is that of finding appropriate materials, creating lessons to go along with them, and responding to students in ways that will support their language acquisition. Ideas for accomplishing all of this without resulting in a much greater workload are incorporated into the suggestions given below. One overarching principle that needs to be kept in mind is to avoid treating technology-based activities as mere additions to a course and instead seek ways to fully integrate them into the course. When technology-based activities are an integral part of a course, they prove to be of greater benefit to the students (Abdous, et al., 2009; Craig, et al., 2007; Richards, 2005; Schmidt, 2008).

5.2   Using podcasts of the teacher's choosing

Creating podcast-based lessons presents the teacher with the burden of finding the podcast ahead of time. One way of addressing this problem is for the teacher to find a podcast that he or she enjoys listening to and then incorporating this into his or her regular routine. Listening to podcasts in the language that one teaches, one frequently encounters instances of the grammatical structures, functional concepts, and vocabulary that one is about to cover in class. Because mp3 players are in fact so convenient, one can listen to podcasts when walking down the street or driving to work. Listening regularly to a podcast, therefore, does not necessarily represent much extra time for the teacher. Alternatively, teachers might look for podcasts on specific topics. This can be done by entering well-chosen keywords along with the keyword "podcast," as described previously. Students in beginning classes will not be in a position to follow conversations about many topics. However the sorts of themes that are normally covered in beginning classes, such as salutations, descriptions of people, and telling time, can be found quite easily in podcasts. Salutations, for example, are common in interviews and when speakers send greetings out to family and friends. Podcasts discussing celebrities or reviewing movies will frequently yield descriptions of people.

By also including the word "transcript" in an Internet search, one can find podcasts that are accompanied by these.[12] The advantages of transcripts are many: one can review the contents more quickly; one can be certain of exactly what

---

12.   Some likely sources for these are US embassies, NPR, NASA, science journals, and others. Unfortunately, transcripts appear to be much less common in languages other than English.

was said; and transcripts can be used in lessons for read-along activities,[13] cloze exercises, pronunciation exercises, and so on. Other podcasts do not come with a transcript but are published next to articles that present basically the same information.

5.3   Leading classroom-based podcast activities

A teacher may choose to run a podcast-based activity during which everyone in the class listens and works together. One advantage of this method is that the teacher can model each step and respond to students' questions and concerns as they arise. This might be particularly useful for the first time a class works with authentic recordings. A teacher might instead choose to have students work largely independently in a lab together. The teacher could still be available to answer questions, but students would have the freedom to proceed at their own pace, controlling playback, rewind, and perhaps speed. Since L2 learners can have quite different ways of arriving at LC, this would allow students to experience a lesson more precisely suited to their needs (Vandergrift, 2004). This would also address the common problem of having students with different levels of listening proficiency. In this case, a teacher might devise a lesson around a core activity to be done with a shorter segment of a podcast, but provide additional activities for more advanced students to work with other segments of the podcast.

The lesson ought to start with a pre-task activity to activate background knowledge and appropriate schemata. Since many podcasts are available on their own web pages, one could show the web page to the students and discuss visual cues and what information it is possible to ascertain about the makers of the podcast. In rare cases, such as NASA[14], both video and audio-only versions of podcasts are available. Teachers could view part of the video with the students with the sound turned off and discuss what the images are and predict the content of the podcast.

5.4   Tasks

Generally one will want to work with a short (1–4 min.) segment of a podcast instead of its full length, which typically can range between eight minutes and an hour. A teacher may choose to edit the sound file down to only the part of the recording that is to be worked with. This can be done easily with a number of sound

---

13. The practice of reading while listening to a recording of the same text has been shown to improve reading (L. Askildson, 2008).

14. http://www.nasa.gov/multimedia/podcasting/twan_index.html

editing software programs, for example the freeware Audacity,[15] which works with the same copy-paste paradigm that most people are familiar with through Word, or Garage Band, which is a standard program on Macs. Another even simpler solution would simply be to tell the students where in the file to listen, for example between 1:13 and 2:46.

During the first few times that beginning and intermediate students listen to authentic recordings, they will probably understand little of what is being said, but there are still many ways students can work with the listening passage. The following is a list of questions learners could answer (perhaps, depending on their proficiency and the course goals, in their L1) at this stage.

1.   What do you think is the general topic of this podcast?
2.   What kind of people do you imagine the speakers are? What might they look like? How old are they? Are they highly educated? Etc.
3.   Where were the speakers, probably, when they recorded this podcast?
4.   How did the speakers probably feel when they were recording?

These questions target top-down listening skills. To target bottom-up listening skills, students could be asked to write a list of some of the words that they understood. Students might be encouraged to do this without rewinding or pausing, but instead seeing what can be understood just in the first try. Although the list may be short, the exercise can show that some comprehension is achieved even early on. Later, students can be provided with a list of some key terms and asked to indicate where in the sound file they heard those key terms. They can indicate this by writing down the time (for example 1:37) at which they heard a particular word.

To develop bottom-up skills, students need to learn how native and advanced speakers of the target language speak. To do this, quite a bit of time should be spent on listening carefully and repeatedly to a limited amount of speech. At the earliest stages of listening, students could simply be asked to describe their impression of how the speech sounds. This is an activity that can be fun, gets beginning learners engaged with authentic speech, and yet makes it clear that the LC activities need not cause high anxiety or a sense of failure.

Individual words or phrases can be isolated and listened to several times, optionally at a slowed-down speed,[16] allowing the students to understand how the word is spoken in naturally occurring speech. In a related activity, students could attempt to imitate the podcast speakers' pronunciation. This will allow them to

---

15. http://audacity.sourceforge.net

16. A program such as 2xAV™ Plug-in for RealPlayer & RealOne can be purchased to slow speech rate without affecting pitch much. Recent copies of Window Media Player also allow one to adjust speeds, but this results in often radical changes in pitch.

understand better how the pronunciation is performed by the model speakers, and it may also help their pronunciation. They might also be encouraged to express in words the differences that they perceive between the podcasts speakers and other models they have heard before. As students gain a better understanding of how words in the target language are spoken in natural speech, their ability to follow authentic speech will improve dramatically.

As students comprehend more of the contents of a podcast, they can answer questions based more on the content of the message. They might be asked to give an outline of what they believe is said in the recording, or answer some comprehension questions about it. Asking about very specific details of a conversation, however, should generally be avoided. These kinds of trivial questions, as they are called, are not accurate indicators of LC and function more like tests of memory (Shohamy & Inbar, 1991).

To promote and exploit the idea that extensive listening improves LC and that students are not always expected to experience full comprehension of authentic passages, students could be given copies of the sound file and asked to listen to it several times on their own, on their mp3 players or on a computer. Students might write their reflections on the experience, noting if after a few repetitions they began to understand more. Students might also journal about questions that have come up from listening to the passage. These might be questions about pronunciation, vocabulary, or something about the target culture. Reading these kinds of questions can give teachers excellent insight into the confusions and interests that students have.

After students have been able to extract some meaning from the podcast, they could share their impressions with the class. Students could exchange strategies and cues that they used to understand the podcast, thus enhancing each other's repertoires of strategies. If several students contribute different insights into the podcast, then the next time they listen to the podcast, they will understand more. The teacher's contributions of some additional information (perhaps keywords, background information, or cultural insights) would also be valuable. One or two iterations of adding to the collective understanding of the podcast in this way could lead the group to a relatively high level of comprehension of the recording in the end, and this successful ending could be quite satisfying and motivating to the students. Following multiple episodes of the same podcast might lead to even deeper understandings, as well as ensure that students begin their listening exercises with background knowledge of the storyline.

Sharing among classmates impressions and reactions to the podcast could also be a springboard for discussions and offer many opportunities for follow-up speaking and writing assignments. As Little (1997) says, "Once learners have derived some meaning, however slight, from their encounter with the authentic text, it can be used as an object of linguistic exploration and a quarry from which learners can borrow words and phrases in order to construct meanings of their own" (p. 229).

5.5   Student-found podcasts

Since one important advantage of podcasts is that students have the chance to find materials of particular interest to them, teachers ought to consider incorporating activities that make use of podcasts that the students have chosen. This might most beneficially be done after students have experienced a group-supported lesson involving some of the activities described in the previous section.

This type of activity will require more technical work on the part of the student. In all cases when students are expected to use technology, it is essential to spend the needed amount of time to train students on the technology (Schmidt, 2008; Young, 2007). Students may need to be trained on not only how to download podcasts and transfer them on to whatever device they are going to listen to them on, but they will also need to be taught how to find podcasts and choose keywords wisely. Unfortunately, even well-chosen search terms may results in hits on inappropriate material (Schmidt, 2008), and this may be reason enough for some teachers in some contexts to decide not to use this kind of activity. However students need to develop the skills to find materials that are appropriate for them, and if the instructor intends to teach the students skills that will enable them to become autonomous learners, then helping them to learn how to find appropriate listening materials can be of great benefit.

The activities that the students would then work through could be many of the same activities that were suggested above, but individual work makes listening to longer segments of a podcast more appropriate. In this, students will inevitably encounter many new words and expressions. Students should be encouraged to listen for words that they hear often and then try to look those words up. Looking up an unknown term in Google would be more likely to succeed than looking up a new term in a dictionary, because when one enters a word that is slightly misspelled into Google, many times one is then asked if one instead meant a related but correctly spelled word. Students who are successful in discovering interesting new terms might do an online image search on that word and then find out what that word represents visually in the target culture when the word is expressed in the target language. Similarly, they might look up newly learned phrases via the Internet by putting quotation marks around a phrase. They could then skim a few of the pages where the phrase is used and learn more about what kinds of contexts the phrase is used in.

After finding and working with podcasts, students could write about their podcasts or talk about their podcasts orally in class. They could give a critique of the podcasts and discuss what related information they learned, linguistically or culturally. By sharing this information, other students' interest may be sparked, potentially leading them to engage more with the target language. It might also be an occasion for students to share learning strategies. An exchange between classmates about common interests could promote a sense of community (Lord, 2008) and provide an important opportunity for meaningful interaction, which is essential to SLA. Discussions about student-found podcasts might include sharing small segments of the podcast with the whole class. This would provide other students with further listening practice and could be an occasion for the teacher to supply additional information or clarifications.

6.   Conclusion

The last suggestion, of encouraging students to engage in a type of show-and-tell with their podcasts, would not be appropriate with some less mature students, nor a comfortable activity for teachers who are not confident about their own LC skills. However, in some situations this would be an appropriate and effective way of promoting meaningful interaction, while saving the teacher from having to listen to every podcast students worked with. It is not necessary that the teachers monitor all of the listening activities of their students. Nor is it necessary that students achieve accurate comprehension in every LC exercise. Listening, like reading, is improved through extensive practice. By teaching students how to locate materials of potential interest to them, along with developing skills for approaching authentic materials, the instructor raises interest and motivation, increases the opportunities for intercultural understanding, improves LC, and enables students to be autonomous, lifelong learners of both language and culture.

References

Abdous, M., Camarena, M. M., & Facer, B. R. (2009). MALL Technology: Use of academic podcasting in the foreign language classroom. *ReCALL, 21*, 76–95.

Askildson, L. R. (2008). Phonological bootstrapping in word recognition and whole language reading: A composite pedagogy for L2 reading development via concurrent reading-listening protocols and the extensive reading approach. *Dissertation Abstract International, 69*(3), 303A. (UMI No. AAT 3297984) Retrieved March 21, 2009, from Dissertations and Theses database.

Askildson, V. (2008). What do teachers and students want from a foreign language textbook? *Dissertation Abstract International, 69*(3), 274A. (UMI No. AAT 3297985) Retrieved March 21, 2009, from Dissertations and Theses database.

Beebe, L. M. (1985). Input: Choosing the right stuff. In S. M. Gass & C. G. Madden (Eds.), *Input in second language acquisition*. New York, NY: Newbury.

Carpenter, P. A., Miyake, A., & Just, M. A. (1994). Working memory constraints in comprehension: Evidence from individual differences, aphasia, and aging. In M. A. Gernsbacher (Ed.), *Handbook of psycholinguistics* (pp. 1075–1122). San Diego, CA: Academic Press.

Craig, D., Paraiso, J., & Patten, K. B. (2007). *eLiteracy and literacy: Using ipods in the ESL classroom*. Paper presented at the Society for Information Technology and Teacher Education International Conference, Chesapeake, VA.

Decoo, W. (2001, Nov.). *On the mortality of language learning methods*. Paper presented as the James L. Barker Lecture at Brigham Young University, Provo, UT. Retrieved February 27, 2009, from http://webh01.ua.ac.be/didascalia/mortality.htm

Dupuy, B. (1999). Narrow Listening: An alternative way to develop and enhance listening comprehension in students of French as a foreign language. *System, 27*, 351–361.

Field, J. (2000). Finding one's way in the fog: Listening strategies and second language learners. *Modern English Teacher, 9*, 29-34.

Flowerdew, J., & Miller, L. (2005). *Second language listening: Theory and practice*. Cambridge: Cambridge University Press.

Godwin-Jones, R. (2005). Skype and podcasting: Disruptive technologies for language learning. *Language Learning & Technology, 9*, 9–12. Available from http://llt.msu.edu/vol9num3/emerging/default.html

Grabe, W., & Stoller, F. L. (2001). Reading for academic purposes: Guidelines for the ESL/EFL teacher. In M. Celce-Murcia (Ed.), *Teaching English as a second or foreign language* (pp. 171–186). Boston, MA: Heinle & Heinle.

Hegelheimer, V., & O'Bryan, A. (2008). Mobile technologies, podcasting and language education. In M. Thomas (Ed.), *Handbook of research on Web 2.0 and second language learning* (pp. 331–349). Hershey, PA: Information Science Reference.

Hulstijn, J. H. (2003). Connectionist models of language processing and the training of listening skills with the aid of multimedia software. *Computer Assisted Language Learning, 16*, 413–425.

Jensen, E. D., & Vinther, T. (2003). Exact repetition as input enhancement in second language acquisition. *Language Learning, 53*, 373–428.

Lantolf, J. P., & Thorne, S. L. (2007). Sociocultural theory and second language learning. In B. VanPatten & J. Williams (Eds.), *Theories in second language acquisition* (pp. 201–224). Mahwah, NJ: Lawrence Erlbaum.

Little, D. (1997). Responding authentically to authentic texts: A problem for self-access language learning? In P. Benson & P. Voller (Eds.), *Autonomy and independence in language learning* (pp. 225–236). New York, NY: Longman.

Lord, G. (2008). Podcasting communities and second language production. *Foreign Language Annals, 41*, 364–379.

Lu, J. A. (2008). Podcasting as a next generation teaching resource. In M. Thomas (Ed.), *Handbook of research on Web 2.0 and second language learning* (pp. 350–366). Hershey, PA: Information Science Reference.

McBride, K. (2007). The effect of rate of speech and CALL design features on EFL listening comprehension and strategy use. *Dissertation Abstract International, 68*(2), 401A. (UMI No. AAT 3254885) Retrieved March 21, 2009, from Dissertations and Theses database.

McBride, K. (2008). Adaptive and maladaptive strategy use in computer-assisted language learning activities for listening comprehension. *Indian Journal of Applied Linguistics, 34*, 65–86.

McCarty, S. (2005). Spoken Internet to go: Popularization through podcasting. *The JALT CALL Journal, 1*, 67–74.

MLA Ad Hoc Committee. (2007). Foreign languages and higher education: New structures for a changed world. *Profession, 12*, 234–245.

O'Bryan, A., & Hegelheimer, V. (2007). Integrating CALL into the classroom: The role of podcasting in an ESL listening strategies course. *ReCALL, 19*, 162–180.

Rainie, L., & Madden, M. (2005). Podcasting catches on. *Pew Internet & American Life Project*. Retrieved February 26, 2009, from http://www.pewinternet.org/PPF/r/194/ report_display.asp

Richards, C. (2005). The design of effective ICT-supported learning activities: Exemplary models, changing requirements, and new possibilities *Language Learning & Technology, 9*, 60–79. Available from http://llt.msu.edu/vol9num1/richards/default.html

Robin, R. (2007). Learner-based listening and technological authenticity. *Language Learning & Technology, 11*, 109–115.

Rost, M. (2002). *Teaching and researching listening*. London: Pearson.

Rosell-Aguilar, F. (2007). Top of the pods – In search of a podcasting "Podagogy" for language learning. *Computer Assisted Language Learning, 20*, 471–492.

Schmidt, J. (2008). Podcasting as a learning tool: German language and culture every day. *Die Unterrichtspraxis/Teaching German, 41*, 186–194.

Shohamy, E., & Inbar, O. (1991) Validation of listening comprehension tests: The effect of text and question types, *Language Testing, 8*, 23–40.

Stanley, G. (2006). Podcasting: Audio on the Internet comes of age. *TESL-EJ, 9*, np. Retrieved February 27, 2009, from http://www-writing.berkeley.edu/TESL-EJ/ej36/int.html

Sze, P. M.-M. (2006). Developing students' listening and speaking skills through ELT podcasts. *Education Journal 34*, 115–134.

Tapscott, D. (2009). *Grown up digital: How the net generation is changing your world*. New York, NY: McGraw-Hill.

Tsui, A., & Fullilove, J. (1998). Bottom-up or top-down processing as a discriminator of L2 listening performance. *Applied Linguistics, 19*, 432–451.

Vandergrift, L. (2002). "It was nice to see that our predictions were right:" Developing metacognition in L2 listening comprehension. *Canadian Modern Language Review, 58*, 555–575.

Vandergrift, L. (2003a). From prediction through reflection: Guiding students through the process of L2 listening. *Canadian Modern Language Review, 59*, 425–440.

Vandergrift, L. (2003b). Orchestrating strategy use: Toward a model of the skilled second language listener. *Language Learning, 53*, 463–496.

Vandergrift, L. (2004). Listening to learn or learning to listen? *Annual Review of Applied Linguistics, 24*, 3–25.

Windham, C. (2007). Confessions of a podcast junkie. *EDUCAUSE Review, 42*, 50–65.

Wu, Y. (1998). What do tests of listening comprehension test? A retrospection study of EFL test-takers performing a multiple-choice task. *Language Testing, 15*, 21–44.

Young, D. J. (2007). iPods, MP3 players and podcasts for FL learning: Current practices and future considerations. *The NECTFL Review 60*, 39–49.

Zhao, Y. (1997). The effects of listener's control of speech rate on second language comprehension. *Applied Linguistics, 18*, 49–68.

Discourse analysis of podcasts in French

Implications for foreign language listening development

Janel Pettes Guikema

This chapter examines the discourse of French-language podcasts to discover their potential for use in facilitating the development of listening proficiency in the foreign language classroom. Through detailed analysis of authentic podcast transcripts, the chapter highlights linguistic, lexical, and cultural features of this type of discourse in order to demonstrate how such a tool can be used both in and outside the classroom. Of the various types of podcasts in French, the news archive receives the most attention largely because it is always current but also because of its cultural and linguistic authenticity and wide availability. A variety of practical suggestions for implementing news archive podcasts at various levels of French instruction are provided, including how to find and select appropriate podcasts and how to guide students in listening to authentic spoken French.

1. Introduction

With new technologies come new possibilities for foreign language learning and for connecting with students in ways that are relevant to them. The ubiquitous podcast may no longer be cutting-edge technology; however, the potential for its implementation in language learning remains largely unexplored by language educators and students. In this chapter, the podcast will be defined and analyzed in order to highlight its versatility and accessibility to the language learning community. Specifically, the chapter focuses on the podcast as *authentic discourse,* a central component of foreign language learning (Kinginger, 2000; Kramsch, A'Ness & Lam, 2000; Van Lier, 1996), and argues that this technology has tremendous potential as a tool (Richardson, 2006; Thorne & Payne, 2005) in the development of foreign language listening skills (see Buck, 2001; Flowerdew & Miller, 2005).

The chapter begins with a typology of the podcast, presenting an explication of various terms used around the French-speaking world. This is followed by a brief presentation of the general characteristics and format of three main types of podcasts available in French: pedagogical, personal, and the news and information archive (Williams, 2007). The last of these three, essentially a recording of a previous radio broadcast, is the focus of this study due to its current wide availability on the Internet and particularly for its culturally-rich content and potential for interest to French language teachers and students.

Analysis of several news archive podcasts will illustrate their overall structure and particular features of spoken discourse in order to show what teachers and students can expect to find in French podcasts and how these cultural artifacts can be put to practical use inside and outside the classroom. The chapter concludes by featuring sample listening activities and suggestions for increased access to podcasts in French.

2.   Typology of the podcast

The word *podcast* has rapidly risen to the forefront in the realm of everyday conversation about technology. The term emerged in 2004 as a combination of *iPod* and *broadcast*, essentially referring to a pre-recorded audio file available for download from the Internet (King & Gura, 2007, p. 8; see also Terdiman, 2004). So when a radio or television news show announces that the broadcast is "available on podcast," this means that with a few clicks of the mouse, the program can be downloaded immediately, enabling listeners to tune in at their convenience with a computer or handheld device, wherever and whenever they desire. This is the essence of the acronym *pod*, which stands for "portable on demand." Some may view this technology as superfluous; however, this paper argues that the podcast is an invaluable tool for language and culture learning simply because it is "portable, personal and powerful" (King & Gura, 2007, p. 10; see also Jardin, 2005).

> *Ode to a Podcast*
> A podcast is portable, personal and powerful.
> The MP3 format makes it portable.
> The XML makes it personal because you select it and it is delivered to your desktop.
> The combination makes it *anytime, anywhere* and therefore a powerful combination for teaching and learning. (p. 10)

A podcast's portability is indeed an attractive feature, providing teachers with greater opportunities to engage learners in listening activities. However, even more appealing is the access to an extremely vast and ever-changing inventory of *authentic* language audio texts. This means that the text type itself is authentic, and the speech is not slowed or otherwise altered for language learners, providing students with exposure to and practice with how native speakers speak and listen. Vandergrift (2007) underscores the importance of authentic materials in the following:

> The ultimate goal of listening instruction is to help L2 listeners understand the target language in everyday situations. Authentic listening materials are best suited to achieve this goal because they reflect real-life listening, they are relevant to the learners' lives, and they allow for exposure to different varieties of language. (pp. 199–200)

Celce-Murcia and Olshtain (2000) also highlight the importance of using authentic discourse in the classroom to help learners become more aware of the discourse context and of the various features of spontaneous speech (p. 108, 114).

3.   Terminology

In France, the most common term currently in use is *le podcast,* which designates, as it does in English, the actual audio (or video) file downloadable from the Internet. This term showcases an obvious connection with Apple technology, in spite of the fact that no particular Apple technology is necessary to listen to or to create a podcast. The term *le podcasting* is also currently in use, referring to the diffusion of the audio file via a digital media player application. The French radio network Europe 1 uses these terms on its website[1] offering at least fifty different podcast series with downloadable programs ranging from news summaries to shows on art and literature. Recently Radio France Internationale has widely expanded its programs available on podcast. In the fall of 2007, they announced that their podcasting was on a trial run and asked for suggestions from listeners:

> Face à la demande d'internautes de plus en plus nombreux, nous vous proposons trois des émissions de RFI disponibles en podcast à titre expérimental. Merci de nous faire connaître vos commentaires, critiques et suggestions pour nous permettre d'améliorer ce service durant cette phase de test. (Retrieved August 16, 2007)

Having evidently received positive feedback from listeners and recognizing the trend, Radio France Internationale now has over thirty programs available on podcast.

In Québec, where there is an intense effort to defend the French language from English borrowings, the Office québécois de la langue française (OQLF)

---

1.   Website URLs are provided in Appendix A.

has proposed French terms, often neologisms (see Williams, 2008), for podcast vocabulary: *la baladodiffusion* (podcasting) and *la baladoémission* or *le balado* (podcast). These are the most common terms currently in use in Québec. According to the OQLF's Bibliothèque virtuelle (Virtual Library), the terms to avoid (due to misspelling in French or borrowing from English) are *le podcast, la balladodiffusion, la balladiffusion, le podcastage,* and *le podcasting*. In Switzerland, *podiffusion* is currently the most widely accepted term, but websites also use *le podcast* and *la baladodiffusion* to refer to their audio programs available for download. These are just a few examples of podcast terminology currently in use in the French-speaking world, but it should be noted that there is variation among users who, for whatever reason, prefer the English borrowing or one of the many available French terms.

4.   Types of podcasts in French

4.1   Pedagogical podcasts

The pedagogical podcast is usually organized in lesson format for beginner or intermediate-level learners. These programs, created by both individuals and organizations, are designed to teach self-motivated learners how to speak French. The podcasts are often divided into lessons so that listeners can download each lesson individually (or subscribe to the series) as they progress in the language. The episodes may not necessarily follow a specific order but may simply be a collection of various themes and/or functions of the language. One feature unique to this type of podcast is that it is most often commented (introduction, instructions, breaks, conclusion) in English.

Examples of French lessons currently available on podcast include *FrenchPodClass*, where each weekly lesson includes a culture topic, grammar lesson, and a film and/or music review. *Podcast en français facile* is another website providing podcasts of varying lengths and interests as well as activities designed for learners of French as a foreign language. One podcast might focus on how to read a recipe while the next podcast presents a poem or a grammatical item. It reflects the variety inherent in classroom learning, where activities and materials change any number of times during one lesson. Transcripts for all recordings, as well as dictations and grammar exercises, can all be found on the website.

4.2   Personal podcasts

The personal podcast is essentially a recording made by an individual on any topic using audio software such as Audacity[2] (for PC) or Garageband (for Macintosh). There is no particular structure, although they usually start with a brief introduction to identify the topic and the person(s) responsible for producing the recording. These podcasts are often incorporated into personal blogs, and the level of language is informal, oriented toward an online community sharing a similar interest. This is different from corporate podcasts which are incorporated within websites that promote a company's products or provide customer service information.

4.3   News podcasts

The news archive podcast is of particular interest in this chapter for its potential appeal to language teachers and learners. Unlike pedagogical, personal, and corporate podcasts, the French news archive is most often a recording of an earlier broadcast designed to be re-disseminated for audiences to listen at their convenience. The general format of the news archive is probably familiar and predictable to listeners, since it follows the same presentational structure as a news program in any other language. Most importantly, this type of podcast is authentic, and the content itself is always current, as some news archive podcasts are updated and made available up to three times daily. Furthermore, given the limitless variety of topics covered by this type of podcast, the possibilities for implementation in foreign language learning are vast and very exciting. The type of program also varies (news broadcast, weather report, sports or cultural update, etc.), giving the instructor even more options to choose a podcast appropriate for the students' levels and interests.

5.   Analysis of podcast discourse

For teachers and students who are interested in using podcasts as a tool to enhance language learning, it is important first to consider what the actual podcast discourse looks like. This section of the chapter will look at structure and typical formulas and patterns of the discourse of a news archive podcast in order to preview this type of tool and to provide suggestions for implementation in the classroom, with particular attention paid to listening comprehension. The analytical approach to authentic discourse is based on Fairclough's (1995) concept of

---

2. http://audacity.sourceforge.net

critical discourse analysis, which considers both the linguistic properties of the audio text as well as the social effects. This approach focuses on discourse as the context in which the complex interplay of power relations in society becomes visible. It analyzes the linguistic and intertextual aspects of text, spoken or written, as a form of social analysis to arrive at a better understanding of issues of ideology, power, and identity.

5.1   Europe 1: *L'essentiel de l'info*

This series, a news summary, is a weekly broadcast from the French radio network Europe 1. The program always begins with the weather, as is the case in Excerpt 1 (25 January, 2006).[3]

Excerpt 1.

1   L'essentiel de l'info d'Europe 1 + partout tout le temps
2   Alors dites-nous Laurent Cabrol on va continuer à geler?
3   Euh on va avoir froid effectivement à Paris en particulier parce que Paris-Ile-de-
4   France en grande banlieue parisienne et là le froid s'est accentué. C'est un peu +
5   euh mm c'est c'est un peu soulagé j'allais dire dans les régions de l'est où il
6   faisait un petit peu moins froid qu'hier mais en Ile-de-France en Saulogne + sur
7   la partie plus centrale du pays nous avons eu pas mal de de températures négatives
8   et même fortement négatives. + Donc pour aujourd'hui c'est le froid qui domine
9   avec encore un ciel clair avec des nuages qui vont arriver dans le nord-est parce
10   que la nouvelle de de la journée et + c'est une nouvelle qui se confirme d'ailleurs
11   parce qu'on le savait mais c'est le changement de temps qui va intervenir c'est-à-
12   dire que maintenant nous allons renouer avec un temps beaucoup plus humide
13   avec beaucoup plus de nuages avec des chutes de neige.

English Translation of Excerpt 1.

1   The news summary from Europe 1 + everywhere all the time
2   So tell us Laurent Cabrol are we going to continue to freeze?
3   Um we're going to be cold in Paris in particular because Paris-Ile de France
4   in the greater Paris suburbs, there the cold is accentuated. It's a little
5   um, um it's it's a little bit relieved I was going to say in the eastern regions where
6   it was a little less cold than yesterday but in Ile de France and in Saulogne, in the
7   more central part of the country we have had quite a few negative temperatures
8   and even very negative. So for today it's the cold that's dominating with
9   again a clear sky with clouds arriving in the northeast because

---

3.   Transcription conventions are provided in the appendices.

10 the news of the day and it's news that is being confirmed moreover because
11 we knew it but it's the change in weather that's going to come that is to say
12 that now we're going to return to much more humid weather
13 with a lot of clouds and snowfall.

The podcast begins with an introduction to the program (1. 1) identifying it as a broadcast that can be listened to anywhere at any time.[4] The host then addresses the weather reporter by name (both first and last) and asks if the cold weather is going to continue (l. 2). The weather reporter answers affirmatively and explains that it will be especially cold in Paris and the surrounding areas (ll. 3–4). He adds that the cold is not quite as bad in some other regions, but in the central part of France there are still some very cold temperatures (ll. 6–8). He predicts that the day's weather will be dominated by cold temperatures and increasing clouds (ll. 8–9) and then announces the weather news of the day (a change in weather), explaining that humidity, clouds, and snow are forecasted (ll. 10–13).

This brief segment, forty-six seconds in length, is an excellent example of the interplay of scripted and non-scripted speech, a feature very common in news and weather broadcasts. The segment is comprised of the weather reporter's mostly scripted speech, meaning that he is using a script for the broadcast. However, the segment does contain elements of non-scripted speech. Some examples of this are the lead-in in line 2 ("alors dites-nous…") and the fillers and repetition in lines 3 and 5 ("euh," "c'est c'est…"). The weather reporter also makes clarifications in lines 5 ("j'allais dire") and 11–12 ("c'est-à-dire"), which is another feature of non-scripted speech.

After the complete weather forecast, which lasts just over one minute, the host reviews the headlines. The basic structure of the show is predictable as it follows a typical news program pattern. It is just under five minutes long and divided into segments of various lengths and topics. There is one main host for all the segments, but some portions of the show include interviews with informants or other external audio segments. In addition, there are several brief breaks in the actual broadcast where commercials are aired. It is safe to say that the format is probably familiar to most listeners no matter what their experience with podcasts might be.

Excerpt 2 is a news segment from the same podcast series, *L'essentiel de l'info*, on the state of the wine industry in France (15 February, 2006).

Excerpt 2.

1 Languedoc Roussillon, Vaucluse, Gironde, Anjou. Les viticulteurs manifestent
2 aujourd'hui un peu partout en France donc vous le voyez pour demander l'aide

---

4. The slogan "partout tout le temps" is used at the beginning of every podcast from Europe 1.

 3   de l'état leurs revenus se sont effondrés au cours des dernières années. Dans le
 4   Roussillon les professionels du vin estiment qu'ils perdent environ mille euros
 5   par hectare. La la faute selon eux à la loi Evin qui interdit la publicité sur les
 6   alcools et la faute à la concurrence des vins étrangers. ils étaient une centaine à
 7   Bordeaux ils ont placardé des affiches remontant à mille neuf cent trente huit
 8   une campagne de l'état français soutenant la viticulture avec ce slogan vin de
 9   France santé gaîté espérance Bernard Farge secrétaire général adjoint du
10   syndicat des Bordeaux et Bordeaux Supérieur regrette cette époque où la
11   France mesurait le rôle essentiel du vin dans son économie et dans son
12   exportation.
13   BF: Nous on souhaite être traités[5] au moins largement aussi bien que
14   l'aérospatiale. L'aérospatiale est un fleuron de de de l'industrie française
15   européenne + et la viticulture est un des fleurons de l'activité économique
16   française. + Et le vin + n'est pas ringard. L'Angleterre considère que c'est une
17   consommation moderne. L'Allemagne euh eum on voit la consommation de vin
18   s'accroître donc ce n'est pas ringard le vin n'est pas ringard. C'est une activité
19   importante pour la France et on doit là qu'on voie. C'est très très très fier lorsque
20   l'on vend les Airbus et lorsque l'on vend un TGV lorque on peut vendre un centre
21   nucléaire à l'étranger euh on est très très fiers mais on est fier de nos produits si
22   on le rapelle et on ne comprend pas que l'état français ne soutient pas cette
23   activité d'homme. Soyons fort sur notre territoire. Ayons l'ambition de ramener
24   à ce produit tout l'être et la noblesse qu'il peut y avoir et on sera forts pour pour
25   partir à l'exportation. Si on est fiers de nos produits à l'intérieur on sera
26   d'autant plus armés pour montrer à nos clients que c'est euh du bon produit.
27   Bernard Farge du syndicat des Bordeaux et des Bordeaux Supérieurs avec
28   Stéphane Place.

English Translation of Excerpt 2.

 1   Languedoc Roussillon, Vaucluse, Gironde, Anjou. Wine producers are protesting
 2   today everywhere in France so you see to ask for help
 3   from the federal government. Their incomes have fallen over recent years. In
 4   Roussillon wine professionals estimate that they are losing around a thousand
 5   euros per hectare. It's the fault according to them of the Evin Law which bans
 6   alcohol advertisements and the fault of competition with foreign wines. They
 7   numbered about a hundred in Bordeaux, they put up posters going back to 1938
 8   a government campaign supporting the wine industry with the slogan Wine of
 9   France health happiness hope. Bernard Farge Secretary General to the union
10   of Bordeaux and Bordeaux Supérieur misses the time when
11   France considered the essential role of wine in its economy and in its

---

5.   The plural marker is used to show the plural use of the pronoun *on*.

12 exports.
13 BF: We wish to be treated at least as well as the aerospace industry
14 The aerospace industry is a jewel of of of French European industry
15 and the wine industry is one of the jewel of French economic activity.
16 + And wine + is not out of date. England considers it to be a
17 modern drink. Germany um um we see the consumption of wine
18 increasing so it is not out of date. Wine is not out of date. It is an important
19 activity for France and we [have to recognize it?]. We are very very very proud
20 when we sell Airbuses and when we sell a TGV when we can sell a nuclear center
21 overseas um we are very very proud but we are proud of our products if
22 we remember it and we don't understand why the French government does not
23 support this human activity. Let's be strong on our land. Let's have ambition to
24 bring back to this product all the entity and nobility that it can have and we will
25 be strong for for exporting it. If we are proud of our products domestically we will
26 be even more ready to show are customers that it's um a good product.

The host immediately draws in his listening audience with a list of four regions, then explains that these are just some of the areas where wine producers are protesting the lack of support from the federal government (ll. 1–3). He explains that the industry is losing money, due largely to the law banning advertisements for alcohol and to the competition with foreign wines (ll. 3–8). Next, he describes the scene in Bordeaux, where protesters displayed posters from 1938 showing a government campaign lauding the value of wine (ll. 7–9). He then introduces Bernard Farge, the secretary general of the wine producers' union in the Bordeaux region (ll. 9–12).

Farge explains that wine producers simply want to be treated at least as well as the aerospace industry, arguing that the two play the same role in the French economy (ll. 13–15). He then announces that wine is not out of style, pointing to two European nations who have high esteem for wine, and then repeats two more times that wine is not outdated (ll. 16–18). He argues that France is proud of selling aerospace technology such as the Airbus[6] and the TGV[7] (a high-speed train), and that it should also be proud of its wine (ll. 19–22). He does not understand the lack of governmental support and calls on all wine producers to remain strong and to bring back the noble qualities to wine (ll. 23–24). According to Farge, this pride is essential to good business and strong exports (ll. 25–26).

For teachers and students, this piece provides a fascinating commentary on both linguistic and cultural levels. The first part of the segment (ll. 1–12) is

---

6. http://www.airbus.com/en/

7. http://www.tgv.com/

almost entirely scripted and contains virtually no features of spontaneous speech. However, during the segment where we hear from Farge, the speech is much more dynamic. He makes his initial plea informally and directly, using the second person plural (l. 13 *nous*) immediately followed by the second person singular (l. 13 *on*). This is a common feature of everyday, spoken French called subject doubling, where *nous* doubles the use of *on* to reinforce its meaning. After this, the speaker continues throughout the interview using *on* as a variant of *nous*, which is another characteristic of everyday, spoken French. He is making his case to the everyday listener, speaking with passion, and the discourse is largely non-scripted. The fillers (*euh*) and repetitions, notably the word *très* in lines 19 and 21, are all common features of non-scripted, spontaneous speech.

This podcast segment is also intriguing on a cultural and lexical level. The secretary general of the Bordeaux wine region, Bernard Farge, who speaks with a meridional French accent, is addressing listeners in a "protest" lexicon. In particular, the repetition of "wine is not outdated" is almost a mantra, repeated three times and meant to bring the wine industry on par with the ultra-modern aerospace industry. In painting an opposition between the wine producers (*nous/on*) and the government, using words that stir emotions and strong feelings ("fier," "noblesse," and "fort"), Farge is attempting to appeal to sympathetic – and patriotic – listeners.

5.2   France Info: *La vie des mots*

La vie des mots ("The Life of Words") is a 2-minute weekly podcast from the French radio station France Info focusing on semantics and etymology of individual words or expressions.[8] Excerpt 3 is a transcript of the first 25 seconds of an episode of *La vie des mots* featuring the word *septembre* (29 August, 2006).

Excerpt 3.

1   **Male speaker:** Podcast France Info +
2   [music – continues until Frédéric starts talking]
3   **Female speaker:** La vie des mots ++++ Frédéric Gersal
4   **FG** Avant la fin de cette semaine nous serons entrés dans le mois de
5   septembre. Septembre. Curieux mot dérivé du latin septeme qui
6   évoque le chiffre sept alors qu'il désigne le neuvième mois de l'année. Pour en
7   comprendre le sens il faut nous plonger dans l'histoire romaine....

---

8.   The name of the program has been changed to *Le mot de la semaine* (The Word of the Week).

English translation of Excerpt 3.

1   **Male speaker:** Podcast France Info +
2   [music – continues until Frédéric starts talking]
3   **Female speaker:** The life of words ++++ Frédéric Gersal
4   FG Before the end of this week, we will have entered into the month of
5   September. September. Curious word derived from the latin *septeme* which
6   evokes the number seven while it designates the ninth month of the year. In order
7   to understand the meaning, we have to delve into roman history…

The program opens with the speaker identifying the broadcast as a podcast from France Info, followed by a short musical interlude (ll. 1–2). Then a woman announces the name of the show, *La vie des mots,* and the name of the host (l. 3). After these twelve seconds of introduction, the host, Frédéric Gersal, begins to explain the historical significance of the featured vocabulary word (l. 4). The broadcast is entirely scripted, with no traces of spontaneous speech such as pauses or false starts.

The language-specific content of this podcast series is relevant for anyone interested in the French language, but the cultural significance is even more intriguing. The mere existence of a series focused on the etymology of words, produced for speakers of French in authentic discourse, is a testimony to France's high regard for the French language, a topic which could be exploited in any French course as a springboard for cultural comparisons.

5.3   *Le Journal en français facile*

The "News in Easy French" is a ten-minute podcast from Radio France Internationale that is specifically designed for those who are less proficient in comprehending spoken French (Excerpt 4). As such, it should be considered an "adapted text" because the speech is slightly slower and the pronunciation clearer than a traditional news broadcast. However, it is included here because the discourse still "approximates authentic form" and uses "appropriate cultural and situational contexts as found in texts used by native speakers" (Vandergrift, 2007 p. 200).

Excerpt 4.

1   (music 3.5 seconds)
2   VR: Merci d'être fidèle à l'écoute de RFI il est neuf heures trente en temps
3   universel onze heures trente à Paris
4   [music continues]

5   (male voice) Valérie Roard
6   VR: Et comme chaque matin c'est l'heure du journal en français facile et
7   l'on commence avec vous Georges Abou par les titres de l'actualité de ce
8   jeudi vingt trois août deux mille sept
9   GA: Et l'actualité ce matin ce sont ces exécutions capitales au Texas et
10   au Japon.
11   VR: Un condamné à mort a été exécuté au Texas + trois au Japon. La
12   méthode utilisée au Japon provoque de nouveau débat sur la peine de mort.

English Translation of Excerpt 4.

1   (music 3.5 seconds)
2   VR: Thank you to our loyal listeners of RFI it is nine thirty in
3   universal time eleven thirty in Paris
4   [music continues]
5   (male voice) Valérie Roard
6   VR: And like each morning it's time for the news in easy French and
7   we begin with you Georges Abou with the headlines on this
8   Thursday the twenty third of August two thousand seven
9   GA: And the news this morning is the capital punishments in Texas and
10   Japan.
11   VR: One on death row was executed in Texas + three in Japan. The
12   method used in Japan provoked once again the debate about the death penalty.

A female voice (Valérie Roard) begins by thanking the loyal listeners of Radio France Internationale and gives the universal time and the time in Paris (ll. 2–3). Then after a brief musical interlude, a male voice introduces her (l. 5). Roard then announces that this is a news report in "easy" French and introduces her co-host (ll. 6–8). Her co-host announces the main headline, and Roard gives the details (ll. 9–12). Roard and Abou go back and forth with the headlines, weather, and sports for just under ten minutes. Unlike the previous segment on the wine industry, where parts of the broadcast were non-scripted, this podcast is entirely scripted in clearly articulated, standard French. It is predictable in its structure and language and could, therefore, be very appealing to language teachers and learners.

The analysis of these sample news archive podcasts has illustrated some typical discourse patterns and possible topics inherent in this type of audio program. Suggestions for implementation of these types of podcasts are offered in the next section.

6.   Podcast discourse and listening comprehension

Numerous possibilities exist for implementation of podcasts in foreign language learning; however, as with any technology, it is essential to consider the pedagogical objectives and to choose materials appropriately. Because the language of authentic podcast discourse is not altered for language learners, choice of the podcast and task design should be done very carefully. When designing learning opportunities with authentic podcasts in French, such as those featured in this chapter, one must certainly take into consideration the level of difficulty of the language (vocabulary, rate of speaking, etc.), but just as important are the familiarity and relevance of the subject matter. The teacher can use almost any authentic text with any level; it is the task that must be designed or adapted so that what the learners are asked to do is appropriate to their level. Task design is absolutely critical when working with authentic texts.

In order to realize the potential of the podcast as a tool for teaching listening, instructors must first provide training in strategies for listening in French, and specifically on how to listen to authentic news discourse in French. Many researchers and practitioners advocate the teaching of listening strategies (Flowerdew & Miller, 2005; Rost, 2002; Vandergrift, 2004; Vandergrift, 2007). The integrated model proposed by Vandergrift (2004, 2007) argues for a process approach, which outlines five stages in a cycle of listening instruction: planning/processing, first verification (monitoring and planning), second verification (monitoring, problem solving, and evaluation), final verification (selective attention and monitoring), and reflection. This approach highlights the importance of developing metacognitive awareness and "real-life" listening skills through "ample practice in listening to realistic texts" (p. 198). The goal is to provide progressively less scaffolding as learners become able to do the process for themselves. Flowerdew and Miller's (2005) "unified" model identifies eight dimensions of the complex process of listening: individualized, cross-cultural, social, affective, contextualized, strategic, intertextual, and critical.

Celce-Murcia and Olshtain (2000) have also proposed an integrated model for listening instruction. Their "discourse perspective" emphasizes the teaching of various bottom-up or data-driven strategies integrated with top-down strategies. Bottom-up strategies might include using "the situational context and/or the preceding and following discourse (co-text) to disambiguate or to decide on the best interpretation" (p. 108). Top-down strategies involve training the learner to establish the topic, or get the gist, of a segment. A unique feature of Celce-Murcia and Olshtain's (2000) discourse perspective is that it advocates engaging learners in the actual transcript analysis, where they study the various features of the discourse by actually studying the text itself. "Access to such transcripts – along with appropriate guidance from the teacher – can make listeners aware of many things (including the fact that spontaneous or live speech is 'messy' much of the time)" (p. 114). They explain that transcript analysis can highlight the function of such items as cue words (i.e. "that is to say"), text patterns and organization, and words used to open or close a topic in conversation (pp. 114–115).

Engaging students in transcript analysis of authentic discourse of news archive podcasts would enhance their awareness of various discourse features, such as those highlighted in the transcripts above, and it would encourage them to delve deeper into the cultural significance and functions of discourse, tying in specifically with the intertextual and critical dimensions of Flowerdew and Miller's (2005) model for listening instruction. Students' analysis of the previously-featured podcast transcripts on word etymologies and the wine industry would be a powerful tool in studying cultural differences by focusing on the significance of language and wine in one's culture. Transcript analysis of the podcast on wine producers could also focus on the finer points of argumentative discourse, where students are asked to find and analyze words or other features of the text that help the speaker make his point. Furthermore, students could listen to the podcast while reading the transcript to scrutinize the intonation and rhythm of spoken French and to determine how these are used to communicate particular messages in this social context.

If the focus is specifically on bottom-up listening strategies, where learners are encouraged to listen more carefully for details rather than the gist, activities such as cloze exercises, where parts of the transcript are blocked out for students to fill in as they listen, work well with authentic podcasts. Other bottom-up type activities could include providing students a list of context-specific vocabulary words and asking them to circle the words they hear in a podcast or to use these words to create a summary of the podcast. Sample exercises of both types are found in the appendices.

The news archive podcast is now commonly available in both *flash* format and full-length reports, as is the case on the websites of France Info and Radio-Canada. As an extension assignment with cultural and linguistic significance, students could consult the "brief" versions of the news podcasts of these websites in order to compare the structure with that of the full-length reports and to highlight any similar or different examples of scripted vs. non-scripted discourse possibly indicating shifts in formality. A similar comparison could be made between the news in *Le journal en français facile,* featuring slightly adapted text, and a regular news podcast intended for native speakers.

6.1   Learner autonomy

After students become familiar with what to expect from news archive podcast discourse, and they have practiced listening strategies in class guided by the instructor, they can then begin to do more independent listening outside of class. Depending on the proficiency level, the transcription of part or all of a podcast such as the *Journal en français facile* could even be done by the students themselves as part of listening training. Guiding students through listening activities enables the instructor to model effective listening strategies and approaches to different discourse patterns. This also helps prepare students not only for more independent listening on their own time, but also for the authorship of their own podcasts (King & Gura, 2007) using software available by free download (Audacity) or on Macintosh computers (Garageband). The software is user-friendly and enables students to collaborate with peers in creative use of the target language. Moreover, this type of expansion activity gives students tactile experience in working with phonology as they listen to their own pronunciation with a critical ear in order to identify areas for improvement (Lord, 2008).

6.2   Access to French-language podcasts

Because podcasts are so easily available on the Internet, teachers can now involve students in accessing digital media in French, teaching them how to find podcasts on their own and to become more autonomous learners. When searching for a French podcast, teachers and students can go directly to iTunes or another podcast directory. An easier option is to go directly to the website of the radio or television station and download the files individually or subscribe to the podcast program. With a course management system such as Blackboard or with a personal web page, the instructor can set up an RSS feed so that the daily or weekly podcast is automatically downloaded, providing students with convenient access to the podcast. The podcast can also be downloaded manually by the instructor, saved in mp3 format and made available on a website for individual download to a computer or handheld device. This is more cumbersome but enables the instructor to hand pick and compile shorter segments of longer podcasts using Garageband or Audacity.

Learner autonomy could also be enhanced by having students search for additional French-language-related resources in cyberspace that have been created for everyday, normal Francophone listeners/viewers. This still relates closely to podcasts but extends beyond it, supplementing podcasts with other language learning resources such as the website of TV5, which features *Merci, professeur,* a 2- or 3-minute clip of a professor explaining a grammar point based on a viewer's question. There is also the Radio-Canada program called *Le français au micro,* the well known French-language-related blog, *Amoureux du français,* or the website of the AOC Bordeaux et Bordeaux Supérieur, to name just a few resources with varied formats. Students could search for these resources, create an inventory, and compare content and format. In this way, they are learning to become more judicious consumers of online information and to explore more of what is available in French beyond the textbook.

7.   Final remarks

The preceding pages have described the widespread availability of podcasts and the array of different types of podcasts. At the time this manuscript was prepared, the technology is still rather new, so the actual number of podcasts appropriate for use in the classroom seems somewhat manageable. However, as with most other technologies, the podcast will undoubtedly find a receptive audience in the language education community thanks to its potential for integrating authentic and current samples of the target language to enable language learning to extend beyond the classroom.

Although the podcast can certainly be used for a traditional type of listening comprehension task focusing on key vocabulary and targeted grammatical structures, this chapter has expanded the types and levels of analysis that are possible, given the affordances of new technologies. In addition to considering the grammatical, sociolinguistic, and pragmatic features of the discourse of podcasts, teachers and students would be well served by (re)examining some of their own beliefs about listening as a so-called skill that can be isolated, practiced, and assessed. Graham (2006), for example, among others, notes that students often perceive listening (framed as a skill that can be isolated for purposes of practice and assessment) as extremely difficult and rather anxiety-laden. Graham also notes that

> [w]ithout a sense that change and improvement are possible, by adopting more appropriate strategies, learners may become demotivated, resigned to being less effective listeners or resorting to more and more 'practice', that is not focused but merely involves the diligent student in longer hours of independent study. (p. 178)

It is certainly possible that the source of students' frustrations might be found in "the speed of delivery of texts, making out individual words in a stream of spoken French, and making sense of any words identified" (Graham, 2006, p. 165); however, it is also possible that teachers and students need to re-think and re-contextualize listening. In other words, since listening can be construed differently depending on its role in different modes of communication (i.e., interpersonal, interpretive, presentational), teachers and students would do well to consider how listening is different when it is viewed as an integral part of one of these modes of communication instead of a skill that can be isolated.

References

Buck, G. (2001). *Assessing listening.* Cambridge: Cambridge University Press.

Celce-Murcia, M. & Olshtain, E. (2000). *Discourse and context in language teaching: A guide for language teachers.* Cambridge: Cambridge University Press.

Fairclough, N. (1995). *Critical discourse analysis: The critical study of language.* New York, NY: Longman.

Flowerdew, J. & Miller, L. (2005). *Second language listening: Theory and practice.* Cambridge: Cambridge University Press.

Graham, S. (2006). Listening comprehension: The learners' perspective. *System, 34,* 165–182.

Hatch, E. (1992). *Discourse and language education.* Cambridge: Cambridge University Press.

Jardin, X. (2005, May 14). Audience with the Podfather. *Wired Magazine.* Available from http://www.wired.com/culture/lifestyle/news/2005/05/67525

King, K. & Gura, M. (2007). *Podcasting for teachers: Using a new technology to revolutionize teaching and learning.* Charlotte, NC: Information Age.

Kinginger, C. (2000). Learning the pragmatics of solidarity in the networked classroom. In J. K. Hall & L. S. Verplaetse. (Eds.), *The Development of Second and Foreign Language Learning Through Classroom Interaction* (pp. 23–46). Mahwah, NJ: Lawrence Erlbaum.

Kramsch, C., A'Ness, F. & Lam, W. (2000). Authenticity and authorship in the computer-mediated acquisition of L2 literacy. *Language Learning & Technology, 4,* 78–104. Available from http://llt.msu.edu/vol4num2/kramsch/

Lord, G. (2008). Podcasting communities and second language pronunciation. *Foreign Language Annals, 41,* 364–379.

Richardson, W. (2006). *Blogs, wikis, podcasts, and other powerful web tools for classrooms.* Thousand Oaks, CA: Corwin Press.

Rost, M. (2002). *Teaching and researching listening.* London: Longman.

Terdiman, D. (2004, Oct. 8). Podcasts: New twist on net audio. *Wired Magazine.* Available from http://www.wired.com/entertainment/music/news/2004/10/65237

Thorne, S. L. & Payne, J. S. (2005). Internet-mediated text and multi-modal expression in foreign language education. CALPER Working Paper Series, No. 5. The Pennsylvania State University, Center for Advanced Language Proficiency, Education and Research.

Van Lier, L. (1996). *Interaction in the language curriculum: Awareness, autonomy and authenticity.* London: Longman.

Vandergrift, L. (2004). Listening to learn or learning to listen? *Annual Review of Applied Linguistics, 24,* 3–25.

Vandergrift, L. (2007). Recent developments in second and foreign language listening comprehension research. *Language Teaching, 40,* 191–210.

Williams, L. (2007, Jan.). French Podcasting. Report for the Commission on Telematics and New Technologies. *National Bulletin of the American Association of Teachers of French, 32,* 3, 31–32. Available from http://www.frenchteachers.org/bulletin/articles/technology/french%20podcasting.pdf

Williams, L. (2008). Terminology for new technologies: A nexus of tradition and modernity. In M.-C. Koop (Ed.), *Le Québec à l'aube du nouveau millénaire: entre tradition et modernité* (pp. 130–138). Presses de l'Université du Québec.

Appendix A
Online resources for finding French-language podcasts

Europe 1 radio network
http://www.europe1.fr

Radio France Internationale
http://www.rfi.fr

France Inter (a Radio France network)
http://www.radiofrance.fr/franceinter/aide/ecou/

French Podclass (free podcast)
http://www.frenchpodclass.com

Podcast Français facile (free podcast)
http://www.podcastfrancaisfacile.com

Radio-Canada
(French-language radio network of the Canadian Broadcasting Corporation)
http://www.radio-canada.ca/

France Info (a Radio France network)
www.france-info.com

Le français au micro (a Radio-Canada podcast about the French language)
http://www.radio-canada.ca/radio/francaisaumicro/

Les amoureux du français (A Cyberpresse blog about the French language)
http://blogues.cyberpresse.ca/amoureuxdufrancais/

Appendix B
Sample Listening Activity 1

Note: Even though a particular podcast on which a lesson is based might not be available, sample tasks have been provided in order to demonstrate the variety of exercises that can be used even with a brief podcast or a segment of a podcast.

Level: 4th Semester French (U.S. University Level)
Topic: Violence à l'école – podcast *d'Europe 1, L'essentiel de l'info* (25/01/06)

Pre-écoute : Questions de discussion

1. Aux Etats-Unis, trouvez-vous que la violence à l'école soit un vrai problème ? Expliquez.
2. Quelles mesures sont prises pour éviter la violence à l'école aux Etats-Unis ?

Ecoutez le podcast et répondez aux questions.

1. Que s'est-il passé ? Servez-vous des mots de vocabulaire (et d'un dictionnaire !) pour reconstituer l'évènement. Renseignez-vous sur le droit de retrait ! Ecrivez une ou deux phrases complètes en utilisant les mots suivants :

    une école   un élève
    un prof   cesser
    un pistolet   la banlieue parisienne
    les cours   tirer
    le droit de retrait

    (http://www.guide-du-travail.com/conditions-de-travail)

2. Les profs ont enfin décidé de faire <u>grève</u> pendant _________ jours. Ils ____________ _____________ aux écoles et ont besoin de ____________________________, _________ _______________ et ____.

3. Comment dit-on *a protest* en français ? (le mot est répété plusieurs fois dans ce segment) ____

Discutez : Quelle est votre réaction personnelle ? Trouvez-vous ces actions efficaces ? Cela arriverait-il aux Etats-Unis ? Pourquoi ou pourquoi pas ?

Appendix C
Sample Listening Activity 2

Activity for 4th Semester French (U.S. University Level)
La météo – podcast *d'Europe 1, L'essentiel de l'info* (10/01/06)

1. Cherchez dans un bon dictionnaire tous les mots que vous ne comprenez pas.
    Ecoutez le premier podcast (la météo). Entourez tous les mots que vous entendez.

brouillard	éclairci	brume	verglas
brumeux	vent	soleil	ensoleillé
nuageux	pluie	givre	givrant
couvert	neige	tempête	épais

2. Ecoutez la météo une deuxième fois.
    → Le 10 janvier il y a beaucoup de **brouillard** en France, mais *dans quelles
       régions* ? Consultez une carte de France avant de répondre.

    - à Paris
    - dans la vallée du _______________________ et du _______________ (fleuves)
    - en Auvergne
    - au _______________ (région)
    - et au _______________ (orientation)

3. Quelles sont les températures (le 10 janvier)…

    … à Paris ? ___________   C ((x2) + 32) = _______________ F
    … à Toulouse ? _______   C ((x2) + 32) = _______________ F
    … à Nice ? ___________   C ((x2) + 32) = _______________ F
    … à Besançon ? _______   C ((x2) + 32) = _______________ F

4. Consultez le site www.meteo.fr. Quel temps fait-il <u>en France</u> aujourd'hui?
    Comparez la météo du 10 janvier avec celle d'aujourd'hui.

5. Quel temps fait-il <u>chez vous</u> aujourd'hui ?

Appendix D
Transcription Conventions (adapted from Hatch, 1992)

[ ]	non-verbal cues, clarification of unclear meaning
( )	inaudible or unclear utterance
(( ))	sounds (e.g., laughter, coughing, etc.)
+	pause of approximately 0–1 second(s)
++	pause of approximately 2–3 seconds
+++	pause of approximately 4 or more seconds
?	rising intonation
.	falling intonation
underlining	emphasis (pitch and/or volume)

PART IV

Blogs

Interactional and discursive features
of English-language weblogs
for language learning and teaching

Rémi A. van Compernolle and Lee B. Abraham

This chapter provides an overview of the nature of authentic (i.e., non-educational) weblogs (blogs) and offers a number a recommendations for using blogs in the English as a second/foreign language (ESL/EFL) curriculum[1] to promote second language literacy. Our discussion centers around blog-writing as social practice as opposed to using blogs to help learners develop formal writing skills. Following a brief overview of a small corpus of diverse blogs, we provide a number of recommendations for integrating blog-reading and blog-writing in the ESL/EFL classroom. We extend Herring's (2007) multifaceted approach to analyzing computer-mediated discourse to the field of second language (L2) learning and teaching, and we discuss ways in which students and teachers can construct, manage, and analyze a corpus of blogs. We also present a number of ways to design learning opportunities in the ESL/EFL classroom around the reading and writing of blogs.

1.   Introduction

The use of the Internet in language learning and teaching is an area of ever-increasing interest. This is because networked communication technologies provide unprecedented access to authentic discourse for developing communicative abilities in the language learners are studying, as well as for facilitating online exchanges and promoting intercultural understanding (Kern, Ware, & Warschauer, 2004; Belz & Thorne, 2006). Online technologies enable language learners to access and interact with a broad range of authentic texts, such as web advertisements, periodicals, electronic discussion fora, and online journals (known as *weblogs* or

---

1.   Although this chapter provides an analysis of English-language blogs, the pedagogical recommendations could be applied to and/or adapted for various other languages.

blogs). Although online authentic texts are increasingly used in language teaching, guidelines based on theoretical and empirical findings to enable their effective integration still require additional research (Bernhardt, 2005; Chapelle, 2003; Chapelle & Liu, 2007; Chun, 2006; Gilmore, 2007; Kern, 2006; Lotherington, 2005). This chapter provides an overview of the nature of authentic (i.e., non-educational) weblogs (i.e., blogs) and offers a number a recommendations for using blogs in the ESL/EFL curriculum to promote second language literacy. We have situated our pedagogical recommendations within the framework of multiliteracies proposed by the New London Group (1996), which provides the flexibility to explore any number of features of blogs in any number of participation structures in the classroom (see Hall, 2001, pp. 50–55).

2.   Blogs in L2 learning and teaching

Integrating blogs into second language curricula has attracted the attention of a number of applied linguists since the early 2000s. Like any CMC tool, blogs can serve a number of functions in the second language classroom. Several writers have recently advocated the use of blogs for promoting critical interpretive reading skills, developing writing abilities, and fostering intercultural understanding among second language learners in formal, structured educational settings (Arena, 2008, Camilleri, Ford, Leja, & Sollas, 2007; Ducate & Lomicka, 2005; Godwin-Jones, 2003; Ward, 2004). Ducate and Lomicka (2005), for instance, speculate that blog-posting can help students "become more proficient at writing in the target language in terms of both content and structure" (p. 419). In addition, blogs may also help to expand the range of discourse options (Kramsch, 1985) available to learners because online micropublishing offers learners "the possibility of writing for readers beyond classmates" (Godwin-Jones, 2003, p. 13).

Several empirically grounded studies of blog use in second language learning have yielded interesting results. In some cases, blog-writing has helped develop learners' rhetorical strategies, such as organizing ideas into cogent discourse and supporting claims by citing outside texts (Bloch, 2007; Bloch & Crosby, 2008). In other cases, researchers have found that blog-writing leads to more varied and appropriate vocabulary use (Ducate & Lomicka, 2008; Fellner & Apple, 2006), and that it can help learners develop their writing with greater formal grammatical accuracy (Murray & Hourigan, 2008). As an additional benefit, students themselves often report that they enjoy reading other (native speaker) blogs and that they feel blog use in the classroom helps them develop their writing abilities in the language they are studying (Ducate & Lomicka, 2008; Pinkman, 2005).

Other researchers have investigated the use of blogs to increase cultural knowledge by using blogs to connect study abroad students with at-home students. In some cases, both study abroad and at-home students appear to develop their intercultural competence as a result of reading and writing blog postings from other students that provide cultural information that may be merely glossed over in typical classroom settings (Elola & Oskoz, 2008). Others have investigated community-building and relationship maintenance via blog-posting. For instance, Hauck and Youngs (2008) found that blog-writing also allowed NNSs to develop "closer relationships with their [NS and more-advanced NNS] learning partners" (p. 103), which suggests that blogs can serve as tools for fostering interpersonal relationships among interactants. However, Petersen, Divitni, and Chabert (2009) report that blog-writing does not always support community-building because some students do not have time outside of class to post messages or to comment on others' blogs.

In the present chapter, we investigate noneducational blogs written by native speakers of American English in order to explore the potential for using this relatively new type of authentic electronic discourse in second language learning contexts. We depart from previous writers inasmuch as our discussion of the pedagogical applications of blogs goes beyond the reading comprehension/writing skills orientation that most previous research has adopted. Instead, we focus primarily on using blogs to raise learners' awareness of the social and cultural practices in which blog authors engage through the written language. We argue that in-class blog corpus analysis grounded in Herring's (2007) faceted classification scheme for computer-mediated discourse can help students to view blog-writing as social activity – that could be extended beyond the classroom – rather than a simple exercise in "writing for writing's sake" that just happens to be mediated by networked technologies.

3.   The data

The data analyzed in this chapter come from a small corpus of freely-accessible blogs. Our goal was not to provide a comprehensive panorama of the world-wide blogosphere, such as done by Susan Herring and her colleagues (e.g., Herring, Scheidt, Kouper, & Wright, 2006), but rather to be selective such that we had at least one example of as many blog genres as possible. Our selection was driven by our concern to provide ESL/EFL teachers and learners with examples of blog interaction and discourse produced in communicative contexts that might be familiar or of general interest to young-adult (e.g., college-age) learners of English. We also decided to incorporate as much variety in terms of topic of discussion and interactional and discursive norms as possible in order to illustrate variation within the blog genre. In this vein, we have selected blogs from two broadly defined categories, which we call "personal" blogs and "commercial" blogs.

Personal blogs are those for which the topic of discussion is not decided or moderated by a for- or not-for-profit commercial sponsor. In other words, a personal blog is one that is authored by an individual who can decide the topic of the blog, post, etc. independently, and who can establish his or her own terms of participation and engagement. In this sense, personal blogs may be thought of as organized and managed from the bottom up, even though the majority of such blogs are hosted by a larger commercial entity (e.g., LiveJournal or Blogger). Personal blogs come in a variety of genres, including diary-like entries and quick updates about one's life, rants about current events (either private or public), poetry and other creative writings, and the like. In fact, many personal blogs include more than one genre of posting, so it is not uncommon to find one that includes postings fitting into several or all of the types mentioned above. This diversity is important to recognize so that teachers and learners of English do not necessarily think of blog discourse as a monolithic style of writing. Instead, the diversity should be embraced by both teachers and students. Incidentally, we believe that this variety presents many opportunities for learners of English who may be interested in reading and/or producing text genres that are not always included in language education (e.g., personal poetry).

Our personal blog data were collected from two sources. First, we selected five personal blogs from the website LiveJournal.com. LiveJournal (LJ) was chosen because it is one of the largest blog-hosting sites available (see work by Susan Herring and her colleagues for additional information). The five blogs represent a wide variety of discussion topics and genres. Second, we chose ten blogs posted on MySpace.com (MS) members' profile pages, five from women and five from men aged 18 to 25 years. We decided to include MS member blogs because of the immense popularity of this social networking site that is free to anyone who wants to create a profile. As such, it is likely that many students are already familiar with the organization of the site and the communicative possibilities provided by it. In addition, we believe that a social networking site like MS might provide learners with more opportunities for joining and creating online communities than would be possible via a site such as LJ.

Commercial blogs are those blogs authored by regular or contracted employees of some commercial entity.[2] The topic is typically decided from the top down,

---

2.   We use the term commercial entity for ease of reference. Blogs sponsored and moderated by not-for-profits groups, such as consumer advocacy groups and political campaigns, can also be included in commercial blog category.

meaning that the commercial entity manages and moderates the blog and its content. On some occasions, commercial blog authors are unidentified, because the blog is simply authored by the entity rather than by an individual. In other cases, commercial blog authors are indentified. This usually occurs when the author's name is of some importance to the topic of the blog itself. Commercial blogs may address topics such as travel advice (usually from a contracted employee of a newspaper who is traveling abroad), popular television shows (typically hosted by the show's website or its network's site), or up-to-the-minute updates of cultural events, such as the 2008 Olympics in Beijing. While there is some variety among commercial blogs, there is virtually no variation within a single blog. That is, in contrast to personal blogs, commercial blog discourse tends to be stable in terms of topic, genre, register, and so forth.

We have selected eight commercial blogs that nicely illustrate the various types of commercial blogs available on the Internet. Five were chosen from the website of the New York Times. These blogs are authored by contracted, syndicated, and free-lance journalists, and they cover topics such as the adventures of a journalist travelling across Europe on 100 Euros per day, the 2008 Beijing Olympic Games, and the like. The remaining commercial blogs used for this chapter are related to the popular television programs *The Bachelorette* (ABC), *Grey's Anatomy* (ABC), and *Law & Order: SVU* (NBC).

4.   Interactional and discursive features of blogs

4.1   Participation framework

Both personal and commercial blogs have very similar in participation frameworks because the technology that mediates them is for all intents and purposes the same. Of course, there are some differences among blog platforms, but a full discussion of these is beyond the scope of this chapter. In general, blogs are moderated by their author(s). This means that, in contrast to a discussion forum, mailing list, or bulletin board system, only the registered author(s) may start discussions on a blog. Thus, the main blog entries are authored by the owner of the blog. Other participants may post comments to these entries if allowed by the author.[3] In addition, participants – including the author – can post rejoinders to comments. As such, the basic participation structure that is allowed by most blog

---

3.   Most blog sites allow authors to choose whether comments are allowed and if comment-posting is open to everyone, friends only, and/or requires moderation and approval by the author before publication.

technology includes three types of messages: (1) author-published blog entries, (2) comments, and (3) rejoinders to comments. Excerpt 1, taken from a personal blog on LJ, illustrates this structure. (Excerpts have been slightly modified for ease of reading. In addition, names have been omitted in order to protect participants' privacy.)

Excerpt 1. Blog entry, comment, and rejoinder from personal blog on LJ

Blog entry:	[BLOG AUTHOR] wrote, @ 2008-04-23 09:40:00

Happy Birthday!
Today is my birthday and I am officially 23 years old! I like the number 23. I mean it is April 23rd, after all. (And me and [NAME] got married on July 23rd.) So being 23 on the 23rd must be good luck or something, right? :) Well anyway, I'm pretty happy about it. This is also my April vacation week, so I have the week off which is nice. And so far today is a beautiful day outside, I do love spring! So hooray for all that! :D

Comment 1:   [USERNAME] 2008-04-23 02:04 pm
Aw, that means it's your golden birthday. Happy Birthday!

Rejoinder 1:   [BLOG AUTHOR] 2008-04-23 03:26 pm
Is that like when you're married and your 50th anniversary is called your golden anniversary or something? When the date of your birthday matches the age you're turning it's your golden birthday? Hehe. :)

Comment 2:   [USERNAME] 2008-04-23 04:30 pm
Happy Birthday hun! *hugs*

Rejoinder 2:   [BLOG AUTHOR] 2008-04-23 06:58 pm
Thanks!! :D *hugs*

In Excerpt 1, the blog's author publishes a blog entry regarding her twenty-third birthday. Two of her friends then post comments wishing her a happy birthday, each of which the author responds to individually. This structure might be the prototypical participation framework for blogging, but it is by no means widespread in the blogosphere. In fact, during our initial exploration of LJ, only 9 of 100 blogs we examined contained any comments at all. This finding is in line with that of Mishne and Glance (2006), who report that out of the over 685,000 blog postings they examined only 15% were commented, averaging only 0.9 comments per posting. However, comments tended to be concentrated among relatively few posts: "the number of comments per post follows a power-law distribution, with a small number of posts containing a high number of comments, and a long tail of posts with few comments" (np). In other words, Mishne and Glance found an unbalanced distribution of comments in their corpus, in that a figure less than 10 weblog postings contained several hundred to over 1,000 comments, while nearly 50,000 postings contained no comments at all.

Commercial blogs, however, appear to be somewhat different. While they potentially have the same participation framework as that of personal blogs, they have higher visibility because they are part of a commercial site when compared to the average personal blog. For example, the eight most recent blog entries as of September 28, 2008 from *The Frugal Traveler* contained 54, 2, 62, 134, 87, 112, 24, and 246 comments, respectively. However, it is rare to see author rejoinders to comments or other participants' rejoinders to comments. In fact, not one example of a rejoinder was found in our corpus of commercial blogs.

4.2   Message length

The length of blog entries, comments, and rejoinders varies greatly within and among the various blogs we analyzed for this study. Generally speaking, however, blog entries tend to be much longer than comments and rejoinders on average. This conclusion was also reached by Mishne and Glance (2006). As a case in point, Table 1 displays relevant information about the five most recent postings of the most active personal blog in the LJ data. On average, blog entries are around 400 words in length, while comments and rejoinder average only 37 words.

Table 1. Blog entry, comment, and rejoinder length in a personal blog

Posting #	No. words in blog entry	Comments/Rejoinders	
		n	No. words (avg)
1	526	4	56 (14)
2	454	2	85 (42.5)
3	89	4	50 (12.5)
4	92	4	234 (58.5)
5	862	12	539 (44.9)
Total	2,023 (avg. = 404.6)	26	964 (37.1)

Three of the five blog entries (1, 2, and 5) were three paragraphs or longer, with detailed commentary of the events of this author's life. Postings 3 and 4, on the other hand, were relatively short updates about events described in previous postings. As for the comments and rejoinders, the data clearly show that these are relatively short. In fact, most were one-sentence reactions to postings or other comments. The lengthier comments to blog entries 4 and 5 dealt with the author's story of her car accident (entry 5) and her follow-up positing reporting that her car was in fact totaled according to the insurance company. These comments were longer because the author's friends asked in-depth questions about the car accident and insurance claim process, and some offered advice. Although based on a small sample of data, this analysis provides some evidence that comment length is related to the topic of the blog entry and/or the function of the comments (e.g., reaction vs. advice-giving or information-seeking).

In contrast to personal blogs, commercial blogs enjoy higher levels of participation on the part of their readership. Not only do commercial blogs tend to receive a greater number of comments, but these comments are also lengthier than those published on personal blogs. Table 2 displays blog entry and comment information from the blog *Grey Matter*, a blog authored by the writers of ABC's television series *Grey's Anatomy*. The blog's theme is centered around upcoming episodes of *Grey's Anatomy* and reactions to previous episodes. The writers for the show provide some behind-the-scenes information and occasionally offer supposedly advance information about the show and its characters.

Table 2. Blog entry and comment length in *Grey Matter* (commercial blog)

Posting #	No. words in blog entry	Comments	
		n	No. words (avg)
1	262	210	21,481 (102.3)
2	1,594	468	50,974 (109)
3	240	116	8,872 (76.5)
4	1,356	996	117,318 (117.8)
5	1,024	286	45,265 (158.3)
Total	4476 (avg. = 895.2)	2,076	243,910 (117.5)

In comparison to the personal blog published on LJ described above, blog entries for *Grey Matter* tend to be somewhat longer, between 240 and 1,594 words (avg. = 895.2). The greater difference, however, is in the length of comments posted by participants, which average 117.5 words each. This average is more than three times that of the comments in the personal blog.

4.3 Personal blog entry genres and discourse

As noted earlier, personal blogs come in a variety of genres, ranging from social commentary and personal diary-like entries to poetry and other types of creative writing. In fact, most of the personal blogs we selected for as examples on LJ and MS include a mix two or more entry genres, rather than keeping with one type throughout all postings. The most common blog entry genres are diary entry and creative writing. Excerpt 2 provides an example of the diary entry genre written by a 22 year-old man on his MS blog.

Excerpt 2. Diary entry from MS blog

long haulin'

havent been as vigilant with the online world as i thought i would be. its been brought to my attention that facebook is actually the thing to have so i thought about getting one of those going, but whats the point? i dont think i maxamize the potential with this as it is.

bonfattos has continued to dog me, so ive been looking for work. as well as doing a little work at the tavern up the road, not a bad gig all things considered but i need something long term. handed in several apps and even have an interview scheduled.... all in good time.

in a very easy-to-please mood recently, deffenitly right now...but im sleepy so that makes sense. why i have been the last few days (maybe week even) im not sure. sort of a mixture of gelling with the outside world as well as continuing to become more content with myself, and the space i take up. its not much but its mine and though no one admits it it can be a struggle to figure out what to do with that space. i know you've got it figured out, but im fine with being in the process, for the long haul.

get er done.

Similar to what might be expected of a traditional (i.e., written) diary entry, this blog author offers information and reflection about his personal life. He writes about his troubles at work, his attempts to apply for other jobs in the hopes of finding long-term employment, and his overall satisfaction with his situation in life. The blog entry is both informative and introspective at the same time. In other words, although blogs are inherently public because they are published on the World Wide Web, many of them appear to be very personal, as if they are really only intended for the poster's own reading or as a means of reflecting on one's own life.

Other diary entry blogs can be more lighthearted in tone and clearly intended for a public readership, as in Excerpt 3, taken from a LJ blog entry. In this excerpt, the author provides an update regarding his taekwondo classes and training. Instead of introspection, however, this particular author provides outward commentary about his classes and instructors. Consequently, the complaint, starting with the author's statement that he has been sick, is intended for a public audience, who is invited to comment on the posting.

Excerpt 3. Diary entry from LJ personal blog

No Pain, No Gain... NOT.

- Sep. 28th, 2008 at 8:49 PM

I've been sick the entire weekend. :(

First of all, I would like to blame taekwondo and training. But the latter being my own decision, I'll just go ahead and rant on taekwondo.

Here's what I don't get about PE131-Taekwondo. WHY? Why must everything be founded on unquestionable respect for your superiors? I'm just so damn sick of having to keep on attending these Taekwondo activities when they are clearly UNORGANIZED, UNPREPARED, and quite frankly, USELESS. In fact, I think these taekwondo classes are actually more detrimental than beneficial to the students.

To be fair, I'll list down some things I like about taekwondo. Well, the coaches are nice, no doubt about that. It's fun because it's engaging, and it's nice exercise. Aaaaaand. That's about it.

Although about 75% of the personal blog entries we collected were diary-type postings, blog authors – most notably young women – often include creative writing postings, such as poetry. In most cases, these entries tend to center around difficult personal issues, for instance, relationships with significant others or family members. Excerpt 4, taken from a young woman's MS blog, is a poem written about the author's recent breakup with her boyfriend although she is apparently now dating someone else. (Verse numbers have been added for ease of reference.)

Excerpt 4. Poetry entry from MS blog

..near to you..

1   He and I had something beautiful
       But so dysfunctional, it couldn't last
       I loved him so but I let him go
       'Cause I knew he'd never love me back

2   Such pain as this
       Shouldn't have to be experienced
       I'm still reeling from the loss,
       Still a little bit delirious

3   Near to you, I am healing
       But it's taking so long
       'Cause though he's gone
       And you are wonderful
       It's hard to move on
       Yet, I'm better near to you.

4   You and I have something different
       And I'm enjoying it cautiously
       I'm battle scarred, I am working oh so hard
       To get back to who I used to be

5   He's disappearing
       Fading suddelly
       I'm so close to being yours
       Won't you stay with me
       Please

6   Near to you, I am healing
       But it's taking so long
       'Cause though he's gone
       And you are wonderful
       It's hard to move on
       Yet, I'm better near to you.

7   I only know that I am
       Better where you are
       I only know that I am
       Better where you are
       I only know that I belong
       Where you are

8   Near to you, I am healing
       But it's taking so long
       Though he's gone
       And you are wonderful
       It's hard to move on

9   Near to you, I am healing
       But it's taking so long
       'Cause though he's gone
       And you are wonderful
       It's hard to move on
       Yet, I'm better near to you.

10   Yet, I'm better near to you.

In many ways, this poetic form of blog-posting is more effective than the more traditional diary entry. We can see the author's struggle between her feelings for her ex-boyfriend and those she has for her new romantic interest. This is especially evident in opposition between "you" (i.e., the new boyfriend), with whom she is better off, and "him" (i.e., the ex), whom she misses and obviously still has feelings for. We can also note the progression from verse 1, which focuses on the ex-boyfriend, to verse 9 and the repetition in 10, where the author concludes that she is better with the new romantic interest. This poetry entry therefore allows the author not only to express her feelings through words (i.e., the information transfer metaphor) but more importantly through the text's genre – poetry, a genre with which most readers are familiar, especially for expressing sadness, struggle, or joy over romantic relationships.

5.   Pedagogical recommendations

The pedagogical recommendations provided below depart from previous L2 blog studies (see literature review above) in that we focus specifically on drawing learners' attention to the social (and by extension sociolinguistic) features of blog interaction. We believe that this type of understanding is a necessary component for the authentic integration of blog writing in L2 curricula. We make our recommendations in three parts. First, we outline a pedagogically oriented application of Herring's (2007) faceted classification scheme for computer-mediated discourse, which is based primarily on Hymes' (1974) SPEAKING model. Second, we provide recommendations for constructing a corpus of blogs for learners to analyze. Third, we describe and enumerate a number of pedagogical tasks aimed at promoting L2 literacy through blog reading and writing. These recommended tasks are situated within the New London Group's (1996) model of a pedagogy of multiliteracies (see also Hall, 2001, pp. 50–55).

5.1   Applying Herring's (2007) faceted classification scheme in the classroom

Susan Herring has developed a faceted classification scheme for the analysis of computer-mediated discourse (see Herring, 2007). In her model, Herring attempts to overcome the inadequacy of other ways of classifying computer-mediated discourse that rely principally on modality (e.g., synchronous vs. asynchronous) or CMC type (e.g., chat, forum, blog) for the analysis of this new type of discourse. Herring calls for a more descriptive framework that takes into account medium factors (e.g., synchronicity, message transmission, message format) and social factors (e.g., participation structure, participants, purpose, topic/theme, tone) in a nonhierarchal way. This classification scheme owes to Hymes' (1974) approach to the ethnography of communication. Hymes' SPEAKING model – an acronym for the social components of communication (i.e., Setting/Scene, Participants, Ends, Act sequence, Key, Instrumentalities, Norms, and Genres) – serves as an etic grid "that draws the researcher's attention to aspects of the speech situation that may assist in interpreting linguistic phenomena of interest" (Herring, 2007, "Conceptual foundations," para. 6).

For teachers interested in using blogs in the L2 classroom, we believe that Herring's (2007) classification scheme can help to draw learners' attention to the social and communicative goals of diverse blogs, without reducing blog discourse to a monolithic or invariable genre. Below, we provide some guiding questions based on selected medium and social factors included in Herring's model.

- Medium factors
  - Source
    - What website is the blog from? What kind of membership is needed to post on this website? Is the blog the main page (e.g., *LiveJournal*, *Blogger*) or is it part of another type of website (e.g., *MySpace*, commercial blogs)? Is the blog "personal" or "commercial"?
  - Private messaging
    - Is the blog public? Private? Friends only? Who can comment?
  - Anonymous messaging
    - Do you have to log in to post a comment on someone's blog? Can anyone comment without identifying himself or herself? How are authors and commentators identified (e.g., real name, screen name)?
  - Message format
    - How to entries appear? In what order? What about comments? Are they on the main page or do you have to click on a "comments" link to a new page?
- Social factors
  - Participation structure
    - Who is posting? How is participation balanced or arranged? How much does/can each participant write? Do blog authors post rejoinders to comments?
  - Participant characteristics
    - Who is the blog author? Age? Gender? What does he or she do? Student, professional, etc.?
  - Purpose
    - Why does this blog exist? Why does the author post anything at all?
  - Topic/Theme
    - Is there a specific topic or theme of the blog? What about each entry?
  - Tone
    - Is the blog serious? Playful? Variable? What about formality?
  - Activity
    - What does the blog author do in each posting? Is it for debate, commentary, etc.? Is this for disseminating information? Writing about personal life? Creative writing? Are there differences within a single blog?
  - Norms
    - Can you find any patterns for participant roles? Language use?

- ○ Code
  - ▪ Can you tell whether the writing is formal or informal? What fonts are used? What about creative uses of graphics (e.g., smileys, capital letters, punctuation)?

The purpose of these questions is to raise learners' and teachers' awareness of the diversity of blog postings in terms of participation structure, technological affordances, discourse, and so forth. At the same time, such a classification enables learners to understand what strategies, norms, and activities blog writers engage in, which helps them to become better blog writers themselves. Blog writing in the L2 classroom should, in our opinion, be construed as an exercise in literacy rather than a simple extension of traditional pen-and-paper written work to an online medium. Consequently, blog authorship requires an understanding of these technological, social, and cultural factors.

5.2 Constructing a blog corpus

One way in which blogs can be successfully integrated into L2 curricula is by constructing a blog corpus for classroom-based analysis. We suggest that students be given primary responsibility for building the corpus, rather than making teachers solely responsible for identifying and collecting samples of blog entries for pedagogical purposes. As such, teachers can ask students to find blogs on various websites (see resources at the end of this chapter) to include in the class's corpus. This can be done as a weekly, semi-weekly, or monthly homework assignment, for example. As learners are finding blogs to include in the corpus, they should be asked to use the classification scheme provided above to code their contributions. In this way, as the corpus is being constructed, students are also responsible for classifying the type of blog entries they find in order to facilitate classroom-based analyses and other types of tasks using the corpus.

Managing the corpus can be an arduous task for the teacher, but there are a number of ways to make this easier. (Our suggestions are based on our own experience constructing the small corpus used for this chapter and the use of blogs and other types of CMC in the classroom.) We suggest that learners copy and paste the blog entries they find into a Word document. At the top of the first page, they should write the name of the website from which the blog comes, the title (if one is given) of the blog (not just the blog entry), and the URL for the blog. For example, an entry for the blog of the first author of this chapter (van Compernolle) would be as follows:

Website:	*LiveJournal.com*
Blog title:	*RAvC @ PSU*
URL:	*http://ravc-psu.livejournal.com/*

Once students have copied and pasted the blog entries and provided the relevant information about their origin, they should classify the blog according to the questions provided above (i.e., Herring's classification scheme). This information should be included in a separate document. Then, the students should send the documents to the teacher, who can review each submission, making sure that the appropriate information is provided. The teacher can then save each blog submission according to the title of the blog and the date that it was collected (for example, RAvC@PSU 01 Feb 2009.doc). The classification information for all blogs can then be compiled into one document that includes the file associated with each entry. Thus, for the RAvC @ PSU blog, the entry in the compiled information document would look like this:

Blog title: *RAvC @ PSU*
Source: *LiveJournal.com*
Date: *01 Feb 2009*
File: *RAvC@PSU 01 Feb 2009.doc*
[Classification information should be given here]

As the academic term continues, the database should be updated and made freely available to students. One way to do this is by using an online course management tool such as Angel or Blackboard. Alternatively, teachers could create a group in Google or use the Google Docs application to store, edit, and access the corpus. Whatever choices teachers make for the management of the corpus, the database (i.e., entries with classification information) and each blog data set (i.e., the actual blog entries collected by students) should be easily accessible and well organized for use both in and outside of the classroom.

5.3   Designing learning opportunities

The New London Group (1996) has developed a theory of pedagogy that encourages teachers to conceptualize tasks to include one or more spheres of learning opportunities: situated practice (i.e., peripheral participation in expert-led tasks), transformed practice (i.e., creating or re-shaping tasks in order to personalize and/or re-contextualize them), overt instruction (i.e., active interventions on the part of a teacher or more capable peer), and critical framing (i.e., taking a reflective step back to consider how and why a particular word, sentence, text, or object was designed and developed). The New London Group's model is particularly attractive for second language pedagogy because of its nonhierarchal view of the spheres of learning opportunities (Hall, 2001, p. 51) and because of its flexibility for integrating multiple types of tasks, including those that incorporate technology and CMC artifacts. It is important to remember that no single task type is associated with a particular sphere of learning opportunities. Instead, most tasks can be conceptualized to include two of more types of learning opportunities at the same time.

As we noted earlier in our discussion of constructing a blog corpus for classroom-based analysis, students should be encouraged to find and classify a variety of blogs available on the Internet. The classification of blogs is a type of situated practice, inasmuch as learners are asked to read and interpret this type of CMC artifact produced by an expert (e.g., a native speaker blog author). At the same time, teachers are encouraged to assist students in classifying and coding the blogs they have found as a type of overt instruction. Ideally, this type of assistance should be as implicit (i.e., nonspecific) as possible in order to promote learner autonomy and agency in the classroom as opposed to teacher-led activity wherein the goal is simply to get the "right answer" (see Aljafreeh & Lantolf, 1994). This requires that teachers be sensitive to the level of assistance needed by learners in order not to under- or over-assist in the completion of a task.

At the same time, we believe that reflection on the language and discourse of blog entries collected for the corpus should also be included as a type of critical framing. For example, teachers and students can take the classification of a particular blog, or several blogs, as a point of departure for analyzing the discourse produced by the author(s). Aspects of blog discourse to consider might include message length, commenting practices, text genre, spelling and other graphical practices, formality/informality, and so forth. Teachers can ask students, for instance, to compare a diary blog and a commercial blog for differences in the level of discourse produced and to relate these discursive practices to the medium and social factors they have identified while classifying each blog. Of course, teachers should also be encouraged to assist learners (i.e., overt instruction) during such analyses in order to draw their attention to discursive features that they may not have identified independently.

For teachers and learners interested in blog writing in the classroom, the corpus analysis tasks can be used as a springboard for students' own blog authorship. We believe that blog writing cannot be construed as a simple exercise in writing (i.e., writing for writing's sake) but as situated and transformed practice, taking into consideration the diverse social, cultural, and discursive purposes and activities engaged in by blog authors in noneducational contexts. As such, teachers should be encouraged to conceptualize blog writing tasks in relation to Herring's (2007) classification scheme. In other words, students should not be simply asked to write a blog entry on topic X, Y, or Z, but to plan their writing according to the specific medium and social factors highlighted above. One way to begin such a task is to ask students to respond to the questions posed for the corpus analysis but in relation to their own purposes for writing a blog: Who is the audience?, What genre is the blog?, What is the topic?, The theme?, The tone?, The code?, etc. In this way, blog writing becomes more than an exercise in writing (broadly, and often ambiguously, defined); it becomes social practice, goal-oriented activity. As a result, learners have the opportunity to shape and recontextualize blog authorship (i.e., transformed practice) in a way personalizes their own CMC artifacts and participation in this relatively new form of social practice.

6.   Conclusion

We conclude our chapter with a final note about assessing student-written blogs in second language learning contexts. As several writers have suggested (Arean, 2008, Camilleri, Ford, Leja, & Sollas, 2007; Ducate & Lomicka, 2005; Godwin-Jones, 2003; Ward, 2004), blogs can be incorporated into classroom pedagogy as a tool for developing writing skills in terms of both formal grammatical and lexical accuracy and quality of content. In many respects we agree with these claims. However, we propose that reducing blog writing to practicing (in the sense of rehearsing) and assessing writing that can be done with pen and paper unnecessarily limits the potential of this new medium for social and cultural activity.[4] We encourage teachers to conceptualize tasks involving blog reading and writing to include one or several spheres of learning opportunities (New London Group, 1996) as a way of taking a step back from the traditional focus of writing instruction, which centers around formal accuracy, to rethink what kinds of social and cultural activities are involved in blog authorship. Consequently, we believe that the focus of tasks involving blogs should be on blog authorship as *social practice* as opposed to a *skill*. If our brief corpus analysis has shown anything, it is that formal accuracy is often of little concern to blog authors in many contexts. Instead, what is important is the expression of ideas, knowledge, emotions, and the like through various text genres – diary entries, expository discourse, and creative writing, for instance. As such, when assessing students' blogs, teachers should, in our opinion, ascribe more importance to the goals and purposes of blog writing – as students' own transformed practice – than to formal accuracy and writing "skills."

There are many websites that offer blog hosting on the Internet. Below, we have provided a number of resources for finding, collecting, and writing blogs.

---

4.   At the same time, we are not suggesting that the authors of the aforementioned studies have suggested that the use of blogs should be limited to "writing practice."

> *Live Journal*:   Free blog-hosting services and easy-to-use interface.
> URL: http://www.livejournal.com/
> *Blogger*:   Google's blog-publishing service. No sign-up required if you already have a Gmail account. URL: http://www.blogger.com/
> *Technorati*:   Blog search engine that is similar to Google or Yahoo!. URL: http://technorati.com/

References

Aljaafreh, A., & Lantolf, J. (1994). Negative feedback as regulation and second language learning in the zone of proximal development. *Modern Language Journal, 78*, 465–483.

Arena, C. (2008). Blogging in the language classroom: It doesn't simply happen. *TESL-EJ, 11, 4*, 1–7. Retrieved May 16, 2008, from http://tesl-ej.org/ej44/a3.pdf

Belz, J. A., & Thorne, S. L. (Eds.). (2006). *Internet-mediated intercultural foreign language education*. Boston, MA: Heinle & Heinle.

Bernhardt, E. (2005). Progress and procrastination in second language reading. *Annual Review of Applied Linguistics, 25*, 133–150.

Bloch, J. (2007). Abdullah's blogging: A generation 1.5 student enters the blogosphere. *Language Learning & Technology, 11*, 128–141. Available from http://llt.msu.edu/ vol11num2/ bloch/default.html

Bloch, J., & Crosby, C. (2008). Blogging and academic writing development. In F. Zhang & B. Barber (Eds.), *Handbook of research on computer-enhanced language acquisition and learning* (pp. 36–47). Hershey, PA: Information Science Reference.

Camilleri, M., Ford, P., Leja, H., & Sollars, V. (2007). *Blogs: Web journals in language education*. Strasbourg: Council of Europe, European Centre for Modern Languages. Available from: http://www.ecml.at/mtp2/publications/D1_Blogs_E_internet.pdf

Campbell, A. P. (2003). Weblogs for use with ESL classes. *TESL Journal, 9*, 2. Retrieved March 1, 2005, from http://iteslj.org/Techniques/Campbell-Weblogs.html

Chapelle, C. (2003). *English language learning and technology*. Amsterdam: John Benjamins.

Chapelle, C.A., & Liu, H. (2007). Theory and research: Investigating authenticity. In J. Egbert & E. Hanson-Smith (Eds.), *CALL environments: Research, practice, and critical issues* (2nd ed.) (pp. 111–130). Alexandria, VA: TESOL.

Chun, D. M. (2006). CALL technologies for L2 reading. In L. Ducate and N. Arnold (Eds.), *Calling on CALL: From theory and research to new directions in foreign language teaching*. CALICO Monograph series volume 5 (pp. 69–98). San Marcos, TX: CALICO.

Ducate, L. C., & Lomicka, L. L. (2005). Exploring the blogosphere: Use of web logs in the foreign language classroom. *Foreign Language Annals, 38*, 410–422.

Ducate, L. C., & Lomicka, L. L. (2008). Adventures in the blogosphere: From blog readers to blog writers. *Computer Assisted Language Learning, 21*, 9–28.

Elola, I., & Oskoz, A. (2008). Blogging: Fostering intercultural competence development in foreign language and study abroad contexts. *Foreign Language Annals, 41*, 421–444.

Gilmore, A. (2007). Authentic materials and authenticity in foreign language learning. *Language Teaching, 40*, 97–118.

Godwin-Jones, R. (2003). Emerging technologies: Blogs and wikis, environments for on-line collaboration. *Language Learning and Technology, 7,* 12–16. Available from http://llt.msu.edu/vol7num2/emerging/

Fellner, T., & Apple, M. (2006). Developing writing fluency and lexical complexity with blogs. *The JALT CALL Journal, 2,* 15–26.

Hall, J. K. (2001). *Methods for teaching foreign languages: Creating a community of learners.* Upper Saddle River, NJ: Prentice Hall.

Hauck, M., & Youngs, B. L. (2008). Telecollaboration in multimodal environments: The impact on task design and learner interaction. *Computer Assisted Language Learning, 21,* 87–124.

Herring, S. C. (2007). A faceted classification scheme for computer-mediated discourse. *Language@Internet, 4,* Article 1. Retrieved April 20, 2007, from http://www.languageatinternet.de/articles/2007/761

Herring, S. C., Scheidt, L. A., Kouper, I., and Wright, E. (2006). A longitudinal content analysis of weblogs: 2003–2004. In M. Tremayne (Ed.), *Blogging, citizenship, and the future of media* (pp. 3–20). London: Routledge.

Hymes, D. (1974). *Foundations in sociolinguistics: An ethnographic approach.* Philadelphia, PA: University of Pennsylvania Press.

Kern, R. (2006). Perspectives on technology in learning and teaching languages. *TESOL Quarterly, 40,* 183–210.

Kern, R., Ware, P. D., & Warschauer, M. (2004). Crossing frontiers: New directions in online pedagogy and research. *Annual Review of Applied Linguistics, 24,* 243–260.

Kramsch, C. (1985). Classroom interaction and discourse options. *Studies in Second Language Acquisition, 7,* 169–183.

Lotherington, H. (2005). Authentic language in digital environments. In J. L. Egbert & G. M. Petrie (Eds.), *CALL research perspectives* (pp. 109–127). Mahwah, NJ: Lawrence Erlbaum.

Mishne, G., & Glance, N. (2006). Leave a reply: An analysis of weblog comments. *3rd Annual Workshop on the Weblogging Ecosystem, 15th International World Wide Web Conference.* Retrieved April 1, 2007, from http://staff.science.uva.nl/~gilad/pubs/ www2006-blogcomments.pdf

Murray, L., & Hourigan, T. (2008). Blogs for specific purposes: Expressivist or socio-cognitivist approach? *ReCALL, 20,* 82–97.

New London Group. (1996). A pedagogy of multiliteracies: Designing social futures. *Harvard Educational Review, 66,* 60–92.

Petersen, S., Divitini, M., & Chabert, G. (2008). Identity, sense of community and connectedness in a community of mobile language learners. *ReCALL, 20,* 361–379.

Pinkman, K. (2005). Using blogs in the foreign language classroom: Encouraging learner independence. *The JALT CALL Journal, 1,* 12–24. Retrieved November 2, 2008, from http://jaltcall.org/journal/articles/1_1_Pinkman.pdf

Ward, J. (2004). Blog assisted language learning (BALL): Push button publishing for the pupils. *TEFL Web Journal, 3,* 1–16.

Second-person pronoun use in French-language blogs

Developing L2 sociopragmatic competence

Kate Douglass

This study explores particular features of the discourse of French-language blogs, both to provide a general understanding of the discourse of these blogs and to provide a model for teachers wishing to perform similar analyses with their students. The chapter begins with an overview of the format of blogs and their development in the francophone world, with a particular focus on France and Canada. Next, using a corpus-driven approach, ten French-language blogs are analyzed in terms of their interactional structure and the use of the second-person address pronouns *tu* and *vous*. The data demonstrate that both interactional structure and second-person address pronoun use patterns are highly complex and not consistently predictable based on blog category or country of origin. The chapter concludes with specific suggestions for accessing and analyzing French-language blogs, both in terms of *tu* and *vous* use and other aspects of language variation.

1. Introduction

In existence since the early- to mid-1990s in the U.S. and just a few years later in France and Canada, blogs, or electronic personal journals, have recently attained increased popularity and more widespread use. It might be more accurate to refer to the phenomenon as an "explosion" since the number of blogs worldwide has more than doubled in the past two years. Sources estimate that there were over 50 million blogs on the Internet in February 2006 (Lomicka Anderson, 2006), and as of July 2008, the blog search engine Technorati was tracking 112.8 million blogs, with over 175,000 new blogs being created every day (Technorati Media, n.d.).

Although the top two languages for blogs continue to be Japanese and English (Sifry, 2007), recent studies reveal the French to be among the most active bloggers in the world. In 2006, more French Internet users visited a blog than British or American users, and they spent more time on their country's most popular blog site, beating out the Americans and the Germans at the same activity (Nussbaum, 2006[1]). Not only do the French read more blogs, but they create more as well. With over sixteen million blogs on the popular French hosting service Skyrock alone (*Blogs: Accueil*, 2008), the percentage of people who have created their own blogs is higher in France than in the U.S. or in any other major European country (Matlack & Faivre d'Arcier, 2005). While they may not be as passionate about blogging as the French, French-speaking Canadians are holding their own in the blogosphere as well. Of those Québecois surveyed in 2007, 26% of adults (and 44% of 18–34 year olds) visited blogs, while 8.3% of adults (and 12% of 18–34 year olds) maintained their own blogs (*NETendances*, 2007).

With such an active and continually growing population of francophone bloggers, it is an ideal time for French instructors to explore this area of the blogosphere and particularly the discourse used within it with the objective of preparing their students to participate in French-language blogs themselves. With such a goal in mind, this chapter investigates selected features of the discourse of French-language blogs and provides a model for teachers to follow as they perform similar analyses with their students. The chapter begins with a general examination of blogs and their format, including a characterization of the three types of blogs that will be analyzed: current events blogs, sports and entertainment blogs, and personal blogs. This description is followed by a brief overview of the development of blogs in the francophone world. Then, variation in terminology is presented through an exploration of the different French translations of the words *blog* and *weblog*, with a particular focus on the use of these terms in francophone Canada and France. The main section of the chapter consists of an examination of the interactional structure of blogs and an analysis of the use of the second-person address pronouns *tu* and *vous*. The chapter concludes with information and suggestions for accessing and analyzing French-language blogs in an effort to encourage learners to expand their discourse options (Kramsch, 1985) beyond the formal learning environment of the classroom. Specific ideas for analyzing language variation (in addition to *tu* and *vous* use) and for preparing students for participation in on-line communities are provided.

2.   Blog format and categories

A *blog*, also known as a *weblog* or *web log* in English or *blogue, bloc-notes, carnet Web*, or *cybercarnet* in French, is a website that consists of regularly updated jour-

---

1.   The article included in Bruce Nussbaum's blog originally appeared in *Newswatch India* (http://www.newswatch.in/), but it can no longer be accessed on that website.

nal-style entries that are usually displayed in reverse chronological order. These entries convey the personal opinion of the blogger on any number of issues and may contain images and/or links to relevant webpages, other blogs, or online audio or video files. Most blogs also include a *comments* function, so that readers can post their reactions to the content of the entry, thus establishing an interaction between reader and writer and often between readers as well, since readers often read and comment not only on the original entry, but also on the comments of other readers. These comments may be displayed in chronological order or reverse chronological order, depending on the blog.

Although there is some debate on the topic, many argue that blogs in their original format were largely link-driven (Blood, 2000; Riley, 2005). Blog entries in this format, the "filter-style weblog," consisted of a link or links to interesting or unusual webpages or news articles accompanied by a brief commentary from the blogger. According to a list maintained by Jesse James Garrett, editor of *Infosift*, there were 23 such weblogs in existence in early 1999 (Blood, 2000; Riley, 2005). With the development of blog building tools like Blogger[2] in the late 1990s, not only did the number of blogs on the web grow exponentially but their focus shifted from "filtering" or "pre-surfing" the web for other users to recording the personal thoughts or even daily activities of the blogger. This "journal-style blog" also contained links, but more often to other blogs, eventually resulting in communities of bloggers who regularly read each other's blogs and shared some of the same interests or opinions. Both types of blogs continue to exist today, but many argue that this "journal-style blog" has largely replaced the original "filter-style weblog" and has become the most popular format among modern bloggers (Blood, 2000; Chaput, 2008).

Regardless of the format (filter-style or journal-style), blogs can be used for a variety of purposes and can address a multitude of topics. Ducate and Lomicka (2005) cite three key purposes of blogs: "individual pursuits, business endeavors, and educational uses" (p. 411). In terms of subject matter, politics and current events remain hot topics, while blogs about music and other forms of entertainment continue to gather attention, especially among younger bloggers. Other blog categories include, for example, travel blogs, sports blogs, legal blogs, corporate blogs, and those maintained by non-profit government or charitable organizations. This chapter will focus on the following three broad categories of blogs: current events blogs, sports and entertainment blogs, and personal blogs. *Current events blogs* are usually housed within the webpages of individual newspapers, news magazines, news channels (television), news stations (radio), or news sites

---

2.   The URL for Blogger is http://www.blogger.com.

(Internet), but they can also be found on those personal blogs in which individuals maintain a commentary on current events. *Sports and entertainment blogs* can be found on the websites of particular television channels, radio stations, newspapers, or news magazines; on sports- or entertainment-related websites; or within the blogs of individuals. This category includes blogs focusing on any area within the broad categories of sports and entertainment, including for example those focusing on individual television shows, films, entertainment personalities, or athletes. Fan sites are therefore included in this category. Finally, *personal blogs* are maintained by individual users who chronicle events in their lives and discuss issues of importance to them personally. Due to their individual nature, the themes addressed in personal blogs can vary widely as they extend beyond the blogger's daily activities to include any topics that interest him/her, from current events and sports and entertainment, as mentioned above, to other topics such as cooking, travel, parenting, technology, etc.

3.   The development of blogs in France and francophone Canada

Shortly after their development in the early- to mid-1990s in the U.S., blogs began to appear in the francophone world as well. While the French may be among the most active bloggers in the world today, it was actually in Canada that French-language blogging got its start. Brigitte Gemme, a 17-year-old from Quebec, is credited with creating the first francophone blog in 1995 (Suply, 2007). The first French blogs appeared in the following year (Brochard, J-C., de Daran, H., Jove, C., Le Borgne, C., & Nguyen, C., 2006; Chautemps, 2007). Over time, the number of blogs in France gradually grew, but they experienced the greatest surge around 2002–2005, with the launching of the French sites Skyrock[3] (originally known as Skyblog) in 2002, and Over-blog.com, the second-most popular French site, in 2004. Meanwhile, in Quebec, blogging was experiencing a similar increase in popularity due to the creation of such sites as MonBlogue.com in 2002.

As francophones began to enter the blogosphere, it soon became necessary to develop the appropriate terminology in French. The current English term *blog* is a synonym for and/or derivation of *weblog*, coined by Jorn Barger in 1997, and later shortened to *blog* (Blood, 2000; Riley, 2005). In Canada, the French version of this

---

3.   Originally created as a blog hosting site, Skyrock now offers not only blog hosting, but also the typical features of social networking sites like MySpace. Skyrock is not only popular in France, but in Quebec, Switzerland, Belgium, Morocco, and other francophone countries or regions. The site is available in other languages as well, including English, Spanish, German, and many others.

term, *blogue*, was proposed in 2000, by the Office québécois de la langue française, in an effort to replace the English terms *blog* and *weblog*. It was preferred over such terms as *blog, weblog, weblogue, journal Web, webjournal, joueb* (from *journal* and *Web*), and *jourel* (from *journal* and *électronique*) (Office québécois de la langue française, n.d.). Meanwhile, in France, although the official term *bloc-notes* and its shortened form *bloc* were recommend in 2005, by the Commission générale de terminologie et de néologie, it is the term *blog*, with its English spelling, that is most frequently used in France today and that appears in the 2006 editions of top French dictionaries. As blog-related terminology continues to grow in English, the search for French equivalents continues as well. A list of 125 related French terms was published as "Les mots de la blogosphère" by the Office québecois de la langue française in December 2006, and Chaput (2008) provides an overview of a number of blog-related terms in English and their equivalents in French.

4.   The second-person address pronouns *tu* and *vous*

Learners of French are generally taught the rules for the second-person address pronouns early in their study of the language, and this may be the only time during their studies that the intricacies of *tu* and *vous* use are explored. Some first-year textbooks are more detailed or explicit in their presentation than others, but students generally learn the following rules: *tu* is to be used among students or young people, between people who know each other well, among family members, with children, and with pets, while *vous* (in its singular form)[4] is to be used between strangers or people who are meeting for the first time or who do not know each other well and with people who are older or in a higher-level position. Some students are also taught to use *vous* if they are unsure of which form of address is appropriate, and others are taught to follow the lead of the native speaker. Students may also learn that the rules for *tu* and *vous* use can vary by region and that *tu* can be more common in Canada and in francophone Africa than in France (e.g., *Motifs*, Jansma & Kassen, 2007).

Tu and *vous* use patterns are not, however, as clearly defined as these simplistic descriptions imply (see Kinginger, 2000, pp. 30–31). They are subject to variation based on a number of factors, including not only region or place, but also age, gender, group membership, and social class, as well as features specific to the particular context, such as the setting, the topic of conversation, the presence of others, and the attitude of the speaker toward the addressee (Gardner-Chloros, 2007; Morford,

---

4.   In this chapter, the word *vous* refers to its singular form/meaning. Any reference to *vous*-plural is made explicitly.

1997; Warren, 2006; Williams & van Compernolle, 2007). These patterns have varied over time (Brown & Gilman, 1960; Maley, 1972; Morford, 1997; Warren, 2006), and they can differ from one family, group, or individual to the next (Gardner-Chloros, 2007). The choice of *tu* or *vous* can demonstrate aspects of an individual's identity and can index politeness, respect, power, solidarity, personal affinity, formality, intimacy, or distance (Brown & Gilman, 1960; Gardner-Chloros, 2007; Morford, 1997; Warren, 2006). The complexity of these patterns, their potential variation, and the multiple implications of the choice of *tu* or *vous* can prove problematic for native speakers, and even more so for non-native speakers learning French.

Since *tu-vous* use patterns vary over time, and since they are dependent on a variety of factors, including the features of a particular context, it is important to analyze these patterns in their evolution, particularly as new contexts for interaction develop. One such developing context is computer-mediated communication, including both synchronous communication environments (i.e., real-time communication environments, such as chat and videoconferencing) and asynchronous communication environments (e.g., e-mail, discussion forums, and blogs). Several studies have revealed an overwhelming preference for *tu* in such electronic contexts. Kinginger (2000), for example, describes the results of a telecollaborative exchange between a class in France and a class in the U.S., involving both e-mail and videoconferencing. In her data, the American students initially used *vous* with their French partners, but with exposure to the use of *tu* by the French students both in e-mail and in the videoconferences and with explicit correction from some of the French students (explaining why *tu* was the appropriate form in this context), the American students gradually came to understand the "pragmatics of solidarity" and switched to consistent *tu* use in their communication with their French peers. In an online communication environment, Williams and van Compernolle (2007) investigated *tu* and *vous* use by native speakers[5] in French-language chat rooms, first by observing the interactions in the chat rooms without participating and then by communicating with chat participants using the *vous* form. Their results revealed a clear preference for *tu* use in the chat rooms, and much like in Kinginger's (2000) data, the researchers' use of *vous* was met either with responses in the *tu* form or with explicit "correction" from the native speakers, who explained that the *vous* form was not appropriate in this context (even though the participants were strangers to each other).

Blogs present an interesting new context for communication as well. With the shift from the filter-style weblog to the journal-style blog and particularly with the

---

5. Although Williams and van Compernolle (2007) had no proof that all the participants were native speakers, there were several co-occurring features of discourse that led them to believe that these non-educational chat rooms were populated primarily or exclusively by native speakers.

addition of the comments function, the opportunities for interaction on blogs have increased, both between the blog owner and his/her readers and among readers. This interaction begins when the blog owner posts an entry or posting on a topic of his/her choice. This entry is directed at the public at large. Then, through the comments function, readers can address the blog owner and respond directly to his/her posting, they can address comments on the topic to the group of readers as a whole, or they can address particular readers of the blog individually. As readers with similar interests and ideas frequent the same blogs, communities of readers develop. As a consequence, the author, readers who "know" each other (in the virtual sense), and readers who are new to the blog can all be found interacting in the comment area for a given blog posting, thus creating interesting dynamics and posing the problem of pronoun use. Should *vous* be used with the blog owner as a sign of respect? Which form should be used among readers? Should *tu* be used among those who already "know" each other and *vous* to address the newcomers? Or should *tu* be used in all interactions due to the electronic communication context? Is the supposedly egalitarian feature of the electronic context a powerful enough factor to outweigh other factors, like the fact that neither the blog owner nor his/her readers have likely ever met? Loïc Le Meur, arguably the most famous French-language blogger, in an interview with Nicolas Sarkozy (who, at the time, was French Minister of the Interior), offered an answer to these questions when he suggested that *tu* is the expected form among bloggers (Le Meur, 2005). The analysis in this chapter takes this statement as its starting point and seeks to explore beyond Le Meur's area of the blogosphere, where this may indeed be a trend, to discover whether this generalization might indeed apply to a wider swath of the francophone blogosphere.

5.   Data collection

The data for this study were collected during June 2008. Ten French-language blogs were selected, five from France and five from francophone Canada. The blogs were selected from the following three categories: personal blogs, current events blogs, and sports and entertainment blogs, as shown in Table 1.

Table 1. Overview of the blogs

	Personal	Current events	Sports & Entertainment
France	Maman-FR	Lambda	Zaho
		Apprendre à enseigner	Nadal
Canada	Maman-CA	Clinton	Garou
		Femmes à l'embauche	Top 10

From each blog, one entry was selected for analysis, based on two criteria: the entry itself had to address one of the three categories listed above, and it had to have at least 20 comments. Table 2 provides more information about each blog, including the name and address of the blog, the title of the blog entry selected for analysis and the date it was posted, the date the blog was accessed for data collection purposes, and a brief summary of the blog entry.

Largely depending on topic or category, finding blogs with a sufficient number of comments to analyze can present a challenge. Personal blogs, for example, rarely have very many comments, if any. In fact, at the end of June 2008, *none* of the personal blogs hosted on the popular Quebec site MonBlogue.com had entries posted in that month with 20 or more comments. Close examination of this site revealed an average of zero to two comments per entry. Similarly, the selected personal blogs listed on the main blog page of the French newspaper site lemonde.fr generally have very few comments or none at all. This phenomenon is most likely due to the sheer number of personal blogs currently in existence. With so many personal blogs available, it is difficult to find any one blog that is visited frequently enough to have a significant number of comments.

In the data collection for this study, the exception to this pattern both for the French data set and the Canadian data set proved to be single mothers, whose blogs received ample and regular comments as readers offered support and gave advice about parenting and other aspects of single parenthood (*Maman-FR, Maman-CA*). Another exception appears to be the personal blogs on Skyrock, which regularly receive thousands of comments per entry, although they are of a unique format. These comments, usually posted by young people, are generally shorter (often one to two lines of text, sometimes as short as one or two words) and are characterized by orthographic variation, non-traditional abbreviations, and slang. They also follow different patterns of interaction as compared to other blogs, as many readers simply post comments to show their appreciation for the blog (e.g., "je kif tro tn blog!"), to request comments on their own blogs (e.g., "passe sur mon blog et lache des com's"), or to participate in a contest (e.g., "j'ai voté").[6] The blog from Skyrock selected for this data set (*Zaho*) has these characteristics as well, although it is not a personal blog but rather a fan blog and thus included in the sports and entertainment category for the purposes of this study.

---

6. These examples demonstrate the type of language commonly found on Skyrock blogs (and others), including non-traditional abbreviations, missing diacritics, and so forth. Throughout the chapter, all examples have been reproduced as they were posted on the blogs, without any corrections. Therefore, *sic* is not used to indicate errors. Since the analysis focuses on *tu* and *vous* forms, translations have not been provided for all excerpts. Instead, *tu*, *vous*, and related forms have been underlined.

Table 2. Additional blog information

Name used to reference the blog	Blog name and address	Entry name and date posted	Date accessed	Topic of entry
Maman-FR	"Le blog de MamanCelib" http://mamancelib.over-blog.com/	"Yes I did it!!!" June 10, 2008	June 12, 2008	A single mother requests suggestions for activities to do in Paris with her young daughter during their vacation
Maman-CA	"Une nouvelle vie, une nouvelle page" http://marieeetheureuse.blogspot.com/	"J'en ai un peu ma claque" June 18, 2008	June 28, 2008	A single mother complains about her ex-husband's reaction to her plans to take their young children on a camping trip
Lambda	"Au fil du Bosphore" http://istanbul.blog.lemonde.fr/	"Un procès Lambda" June 3, 2008	June 9, 2008	The recent ruling to shut down Lambda Istanbul, the only organization for homo-sexuals in Turkey
Apprendre à enseigner	http://www.lemonde.fr/societe/article/2008/06/09/apprendre-a-enseigner-sur-le-tas-ou-a-l-ecole-le-debat-est-relance_1055670_3224.html#ens_id=1050664	"Apprendre à enseigner sur le tas ou à l'école: le débat est relancé" June 9, 2008	June 26, 2008	The recent decision to eliminate the French system of IUFMs, special institutes for the preparation of teacher candidates
Clinton	"À l'Étranger – Etats-Unis" http://blogues.cyberpresse.ca/hetu/	"Clinton : «Yes we can!»" June 7, 2008	June 11, 2008	Hillary Clinton's speech announcing her decision to suspend her campaign for the presidency
Femmes à l'embauche	"Le Big Blogue de Londres" http://blogues.cyberpresse.ca/paquin/	"Priorité aux femmes à l'embauche" June 26, 2008	June 26, 2008	The recent decision which will allow British employers to give preference to women and minorities in hiring

Table 2. (*continued*)

Name used to reference the blog	Blog name and address	Entry name and date posted	Date accessed	Topic of entry
Zaho	"Blog Music de zahoofficiel" http://zahoofficiel.skyrock.com/	"Zaho tunisiano La roue tourne LE CLIP EN EXCLU!!!!" June 12, 2008	June 27, 2008	Zaho, whose music is beginning to gain popularity in France, posts a video clip of a new song
Nadal	http://www.rolandgarros.com/fr_FR/news/articles/2008-06-08/20080608121293841503l.html?promo=hp_toparticles[7]	"Indomptable Nadal!" June 8, 2008	June 27, 2008	Rafael Nadal's victory over Roger Federer in the French Open
Garou	"Garou – Official" http://blog.myspace.com/index.cfm?fuseaction=blog.view&friendID=269244443&blogID=405513446[8]	"Thank You To The Fans / Merci aux fans (Video)" June 13, 2008	June 26, 2008	The Canadian musician Garou posts a video clip thanking his fans for their support
Top 10	"Le blogue de Jozef Siroka" http://blogues.cyberpresse.ca/moncinema/siroka/	"Les Top 10 de l'AFI du cinéma de genre" June 20, 2008	June 28, 2008	A review of and commentary on the American Film Institute's list of the top 10 films in each of 10 different genres

In the past few years, a few new sources of blogs have appeared. One of the blogs in the Canadian data set (*Garou*), for example, is hosted on the popular social networking site MySpace, which has recently added a blog feature. Another new source, not yet officially called a blog, has developed as online news articles add a *comments* or *reactions* feature. Much like on a blog, readers can post comments in response to the original entry or article. The *Nadal* and *Apprendre à enseigner* blogs in the data set belong to this category and should be considered blogs even if they were not listed in the blog area of their respective websites. The *Nadal* blog, for example, was found in the "Articles" category of the Roland Garros website, and the *Apprendre à enseigner* blog was found in the "Société" category of the subscribers' edition of the French newspaper site lemonde.fr.

The data set also includes four blogs posted in the blog area of the most popular newspaper sites of their respective countries: three current events blogs (*Lambda* on blog.lemonde.fr and *Clinton* and *Femmes à l'embauche* on blogues.cyberpresse.ca) and one sports and entertainment blog (*Top 10* on blogues.cyberpresse.ca). These entries were all found on blogs maintained by writers hired by the newspaper sites to post regular entries on a given topic. While these blogs could be considered somewhat permanent, since the bloggers continually post entries within their subject area, it is important to understand that there is some rotation of blogs on such sites. As new issues of importance to the world arise, new blogs are created, and as issues fade from public attention, certain blogs may disappear as well.

Once the 10 blogs in the data set were chosen, 20 comments were selected from each blog for analysis. For most of the blogs, this entailed simply selecting the first 20 comments that were in French. Comments in any other language were disregarded. For three of the blogs, however, the first 20 comments contained few to no instances of *tu* or *vous*-singular. Closer examination of the discussions in these three blogs (*Clinton*, *Apprendre à enseigner*, and *Femmes à l'embauche*) revealed a common pattern. The interaction in all three blogs began with a "warming up period," during which commenters posted comments almost exclusively to the entire group and almost exclusively in the third person, for the first 15 to 30 comments. Then, the commenters began to address one another, but still in the third person. Finally, once they had gotten "warmed up," around comment 31 to 35, they began to address each other using the second-person address pronouns *tu* and *vous*. Due to this interactional pattern, for these three blogs, 20 consecutive comments were selected from later in the discussion (comments 27 to 46 in *Clinton*, comments 21 to 40 in *Apprendre à enseigner*, and comments 28 to 47 in *Femmes à l'embauche*) for the analysis of the use of *tu* and *vous*. The 10 blog entries and the 20 comments selected from each were then archived by the author as text files in order to maintain a permanent record of the data since blogs, like the Internet, are constantly being updated and since their content, or the entire blog, can move or be removed at any time.

6. Data analysis and results

Although the main focus of the analysis will be on the comments, a brief examination of the blog entries that inspired these comments will contribute to the understanding of the interactional structure of the blog as a whole. As explained above, blog entries are posted by the blog owner, who addresses the public at large. Depending on the degree of formality of the entry, we would expect to find second- and/or third-person forms of address, and due to the one-to-many structure of blog entries, any second-person remarks should be made in the *vous*-plural form. Analysis of the blog entries in this data set confirmed these expectations. Exclusive use of the third person was the most common form of address in the blog entries, found in seven of the 10 blogs, while the remaining three blogs (*Maman-FR*, *Zaho*, and *Top 10*) included both third-person and second-person forms in their blog entries, the latter in the *vous*-plural form, as expected. These uses of address forms (i.e., exclusive use of the third person versus use of second- and third-person forms in combination) did not appear to follow any particular pattern based on the country in which the blog originated or the category to which it belonged.

While blog entries are posted in a one-to-many structure (the blog owner addresses the group of readers), comments can be posted in either a one-to-many structure (a reader addresses the group of readers, which can include the blog owner) or a one-to-one/many structure. This final structure has characteristics of both a one-to-one interaction (since a reader can addresses the blog owner or another reader individually) and a one-to-many interaction (since all comments are published on the blog and thus become publicly accessible to all readers). The first feature to be analyzed in the comments was this interactional structure (i.e., who was interacting with whom on the blog). Tables 3 and 4 demonstrate the interactional structure of the blogs by showing the total number of comments by addressee, as analyzed by country (Table 3) and by category (Table 4).

In the analysis of the interaction on the blogs, three types of comments were expected: *commenter to the group* (a reader addresses the entire group of readers, which can include the blog owner), *commenter to the blog owner* (a reader replies directly to the author of the blog entry), and *commenter to another commenter*

Table 3. Total number of comments by addressee (by country)

Name of blog	Commenter to the group	Commenter to the blog owner	Commenter to another commenter	Commenter to the famous person who is the subject of the blog	Blog owner to a commenter	Total no. of addressee changes per blog
FRANCE						
Maman-FR	0	10	0	N/A	10	20
Lambda	18	2	14	N/A	0	34
Apprendre à enseigner	19	0	1	N/A	0	20
Zaho	5	15	0	N/A	0	20
Nadal	19	0	0	9	0	28
Total	61 (50.0%)	27 (22.1%)	15 (12.3%)	9 (7.4%)	10 (8.2%)	122
CANADA						
Maman-CA	0	17	0	N/A	14	31
Clinton	7	0	13	1	0	21
Femmes à l'embauche	13	0	12	N/A	0	25
Garou	0	20	0	N/A	0	20
Top 10	12	5	3	N/A	0	20
Total	32 (27.4%)	42 (35.9%)	28 (23.9%)	1 (0.9%)	14 (12.0%)	117
Grand Total	93 (38.9%)	69 (28.9%)	43 (18.0%)	10 (4.2%)	24 (10.0%)	239

(one reader addresses another reader directly). During the analysis, two additional, yet unexpected, types of comments were found: *blog owner to a commenter* (the blog owner replies directly to a comment from a reader, using the comments feature) and *commenter to the famous person who is the subject of the blog* (a reader directly addresses a famous person who is being discussed in the blog but who is not the blog owner).

For this final comment type (*commenter to the famous person who is the subject of the blog*), it is important to distinguish between fan blogs and other blogs in which readers may address a famous person directly. In fan blogs (e.g., *Zaho* and *Garou*), although the famous person may have some assistance in maintaining the blog, it is understood that s/he will be reading the comments posted on the blog. Zaho and Garou were therefore both considered to be blog owners for

Table 4. Total number of comments by addressee (by category)

Name of blog	Commenter to the group	Commenter to the blog owner	Commenter to another commenter	Commenter to the famous person who is the subject of the blog	Blog owner to a commenter	Total no. of addressee changes per blog
Personal						
Maman-FR	0	10	0	N/A	10	20
Maman-CA	0	17	0	N/A	14	31
Total	**0 (0.0%)**	**27 (52.9%)**	**0 (0.0%)**	**0 (0.0%)**	**24 (47.1%)**	**51**
Current Events						
Lambda	18	2	14	N/A	0	34
Apprendre à enseigner	19	0	1	N/A	0	20
Clinton	7	0	13	1	0	21
Femmes à l'embauche	13	0	12	N/A	0	25
Total	**57 (57.0%)**	**2 (2.0%)**	**40 (40.0%)**	**1 (1.0%)**	**0 (0.0%)**	**100**
Sports/Entertainment						
Zaho	5	15	0	N/A	0	20
Nadal	19	0	0	9	0	28
Garou	0	20	0	N/A	0	20
Top 10	12	5	3	N/A	0	20
Total	**36 (40.9%)**	**40 (45.5%)**	**3 (3.4%)**	**9 (10.2%)**	**0 (0.0%)**	**88**
Grand Total	**93 (38.9%)**	**69 (28.9%)**	**43 (18.0%)**	**10 (4.2%)**	**24 (10.0%)**	**239**

the purpose of this study. On other blogs, although commenters might directly address a famous person who is the topic of conversation but who is not the blog owner, that famous person may never read those comments. For this reason, comments of this type were counted separately and coded as *commenter to the famous person who is the subject of the blog*. This was the case on *Clinton*, when a commenter directly addressed Hillary Clinton even though it did not appear that she was an active participant on the blog (Excerpt 1):

Excerpt 1.

Encore Bravo ! et Merci ! Hillary .
Comme je l'ai dit dans le billet précédent, si <u>vous</u> nous aviez montré ce coté de <u>vous</u> et auriez joue dans ce registre lors de la course à l'investiture, c'est Obama qui aurait prononcé ce discours magistral de réunification, et <u>vous</u> qui seriez la nominée. Mais il y avait Obama … et avez jouez du coté sombre plutôt que de nous monter <u>votre</u> coté lumineux comme <u>vous</u> l'avez fait aujourd'hui !

(posted by dominique34 on June 7, 2008)[7]

It was also the case on *Nadal*, when many commenters addressed Rafael Nadal and Roger Federer directly although neither Nadal nor Federer was the blog owner (Excerpts 2 & 3):

Excerpt 2.

Felicitations Nadal <u>tu</u> es vraiment le roi de la terre battue.

(posted by Cécile M. on June 08, 2008 10:34:29 AM)

Excerpt 3.

GO RODGER à l'année prochaine pour <u>ta</u> victoire!

(posted by Christelle P. on June 08, 2008 10:34:51 AM)

Another issue encountered during the analysis of the interactional structure of the blogs was the frequent occurrence of addressee changes within a given comment. For example, in the following excerpt from a comment on *Maman-CA*, the blog owner, in the space of one comment, addressed a question to mylène and replied to a comment made by touteseule:

Excerpt 4.

@mylène: comment on va appeller notre club?
@touteseule: celui là accepte pas les chiens en laisse. mais pour cette nuit là ça va j'ai quelqu'un. Mais je pars ds une auberge bientôt pour 3 nuits et c'est là que j'ai personne pour garder mon toutou.

(posted by the blog owner on June 19, 2008 9:31 PM)

In the remainder of this comment, the blog owner continued to reply to comments made previously by her readers, resulting in a total of *nine* addressee changes within a single comment. This blog owner signaled each addressee change by using the at sign (@) plus the name of the addressee (e.g., "@mylène").

---

7.   All user names cited in this chapter are pseudonyms.

Other strategies used by participants in this data set to indicate the addressee included inserting the name of the addressee in the remarks (e.g., "je suis d'accord avec vous, david42") as well as preceding remarks with any of the following: the name of the addressee followed by a colon (e.g., "david42:"), *à* plus the name of the addressee (e.g., "à david42"), or *pour* followed by the name of the addressee (e.g., "pour david42").

Since addressee changes may also signal a change of address form (e.g., switching to or from *tu* or *vous*), each addressee change was counted separately. The final column in Tables 3 and 4 demonstrates that the phenomenon of multiple addressee changes was present in five of the 10 blogs analyzed, as *Lambda, Nadal, Maman-CA, Clinton,* and *Femmes à l'embauche* each included greater than 20 addressees in the 20 comments selected for analysis on each blog. *Femmes à l'embauche* provides an example of a blog in which an addressee change resulted in a change of address form. In the excerpted comments below, lemaitre used the third person to address the group and then switched to *tu* to address mounir directly:

Excerpt 5.

Ahhh ces pauvres femmes, ahhhh ces pauvres immigrants, ahhhh ces pauvres aînés…. ahhh ces pauvres hommes blancs entre 20 et 50 ans…. […] Y va toujours avoir des gens qui seront pas contents de leur situation. […] Personnellement j'aime me croire un homme qui respecte ces dames mais no way j'embarque pas dans la discrimination positive ou autre.
@mounir
Merci pour <u>ton</u> dernier paragraphe tout à fait insipide…

(posted by lemaitre on June 26, 2008)

The data in Tables 3 and 4 demonstrate that while the percentage of comments addressed by a *commenter to the group* was slightly higher (38.9%) and while comments by a *commenter to the famous person who is the subject of the blog* were less frequent (4.2%), overall, there was no discernable preference for any one comment type. Table 3 displays similar results based on the analysis by country. In France, although 50.0% of the comments were made by a *commenter to the group*, the remaining comment types were more or less equally popular among the bloggers, with a slight preference for *commenter to the blog owner* and *commenter to another commenter*. In Canada, although there was only one comment made by a *commenter to the famous person who is the subject of the blog*, there was no noticeable preference for any of the remaining comment types.

In Table 4, these same data were analyzed by category, resulting in more striking differences. The personal blogs, for example, contained only two types of comments: *commenter to the blog owner* and *blog owner to a commenter*. Meanwhile, the current events blogs consisted mostly of comments from a *commenter to the group* and those from a *commenter to another commenter*. Finally, the comments on the sports and entertainment blogs addressed a wider range of addressees, with a preference for comments made by a *commenter to the group*, those made by a *commenter to the blog owner*, and those made by a *commenter to the famous person who is the subject of the blog*. These results are to be expected as personal blogs consist mainly of one-to-one/many interactions between the blog owner and individual commenters, as the issues discussed on current events blogs prompt both postings to the group and responses to comments made by individual participants, and as sports and entertainment blogs frequently contain remarks made by fans to a famous person, who may or may not be the blog owner.

After each blog was analyzed for interactional structure, the comments were then analyzed for the use of the second-person address pronouns *tu* and *vous*, resulting in the data shown in Tables 5 and 6.

In the analysis of the use of second-person address forms, as in the analysis of interactional structure, each part of a comment directed at a different addressee was counted separately since a change of addressee can signal a change of address form. Further, the instances of *tu* and *vous* use were counted *per comment* or *per part of a comment*, rather than per individual occurrence of *tu* or *vous* forms. All related forms were counted for *tu* (e.g., *toi, ta, ton, tes, te, t'*, and imperative forms) and for *vous* (e.g., *votre, vos*, and imperative forms), as well as any abbreviations or variations of these forms (e.g., *t* for *tu es*, *tn* for *ton*, etc.). All occurrences of *vous* were *vous*-singular, except in the *commenter to the group* category, where *vous*-plural was sometimes used to address the group of readers.

Table 5 displays the instances of *tu* and *vous* use by addressee and by country. Overall, *tu* was the most frequently used form (68.2%), but that number must be considered alongside an occurrence of *vous* that was not insignificant (31.8%). Both the French and the Canadian data followed this general trend, with 61.9% *tu* use versus 38.1% *vous* use in the French blogs and 72.3% *tu* use versus 27.7% *vous* use in the Canadian blogs. In other words, there was not a great difference in the patterns of *tu* and *vous* use between the two countries when all categories were combined.

Table 6 shows the *tu-vous* data as analyzed by category, and as in the analysis of interactional structure, it was in this second analysis that more differences became apparent. It is not surprising that *tu* was overwhelmingly preferred on the personal blogs (93.3%) since they are typically less formal and since the analysis of their interactional structure revealed a tendency for a one-to-one/many structure.

Table 5. Instances of *tu* (T) and *vous* (V) use by addressee (by country)

Name of blog	Commenter to the group		Commenter to the blog owner		Commenter to another commenter		Commenter to the famous person who is the subject of the blog		Blog owner to a commenter		Total instances of TU and VOUS per blog	
FRANCE	T	V	T	V	T	V	T	V	T	V	T	V
Maman-FR	0	0	7	1	0	0	N/A	N/A	1	1	8 80.0%	2 20.0%
Lambda	0	3	0	1	0	7	N/A	N/A	0	0	0 0.0%	11 100%
Apprendre à enseigner	0	1	0	0	0	1	N/A	N/A	0	0	0 0.0%	2 100%
Zaho	0	0	13	0	0	0	N/A	N/A	0	0	13 100%	0 0.0%
Nadal	0	1	0	0	0	0	5	0	0	0	5 83.3%	1 16.7%
Total	0 0.0%	5 100%	20 90.9%	2 9.1%	0 0.0%	8 100%	5 100%	0 0.0%	1 50.0%	1 50.0%	26 61.9%	16 38.1%
CANADA	T	V	T	V	T	V	T	V	T	V	T	V
Maman-CA	0	0	17	0	0	0	N/A	N/A	3	0	20 100%	0 0.0%
Clinton	0	0	0	0	3	4	0	1	0	0	3 37.5%	5 62.5%
Femmes à l'embauche	0	4	0	0	6	1	N/A	N/A	0	0	6 54.5%	5 45.5%
Garou	0	0	18	1	0	0	N/A	N/A	0	0	18 94.7%	1 5.3%
Top 10	0	1	0	4	0	2	N/A	N/A	0	0	0 0.0%	7 100%
Total	0 0.0%	5 100%	35 87.5%	5 12.5%	9 56.3%	7 43.8%	0 0.0%	1 100%	3 100%	0 0.0%	47 72.3%	18 27.7%
Grand Total	0 0.0%	10 100%	55 88.7%	7 11.3%	9 37.5%	15 62.5%	5 83.3%	1 16.7%	4 80.0%	1 20.0%	73 68.2%	34 31.8%

Table 6. Instances of T and V use by addressee (by category)

Name of blog	Commenter to the group		Commenter to the blog owner		Commenter to another commenter		Commenter to the famous person who is the subject of the blog		Blog owner to a commenter		Total instances of TU and VOUS per blog	
Personal	T	V	T	V	T	V	T	V	T	V	T	V
Maman-FR	0	0	7	1	0	0	N/A	N/A	1	1	8 80.0%	2 20.0%
Maman-CA	0	0	17	0	0	0	N/A	N/A	3	0	20 100%	0 0.0%
Total	**0** 0.0%	**0** 0.0%	**24** 96.0%	**1** 4.0%	**0** 0.0%	**0** 0.0%	**0** 0.0%	**0** 0.0%	**4** 80.0%	**1** 20.0%	**28** 93.3%	**2** 6.7%
Current Events	T	V	T	V	T	V	T	V	T	V	T	V
Lambda	0	3	0	1	0	7	N/A	N/A	0	0	0 0.0%	11 100%
Apprendre à enseigner	0	1	0	0	0	1	N/A	N/A	0	0	0 0.0%	2 100%
Clinton	0	0	0	0	3	4	0	1	0	0	3 37.5%	5 62.5%
Femmes à l'embauche	0	4	0	0	6	1	N/A	N/A	0	0	6 54.5%	5 45.5%
Total	**0** 0.0%	**8** 100%	**0** 0.0%	**1** 100%	**9** 40.9%	**13** 59.1%	**0** 0.0%	**1** 100%	**0** 0.0%	**0** 0.0%	**9** 28.1%	**23** 71.9%

Table 6. (*continued*)

Name of blog	Commenter to the group		Commenter to the blog owner		Commenter to another commenter		Commenter to the famous person who is the subject of the blog		Blog owner to a commenter		Total instances of TU and VOUS per blog	
	T	V	T	V	T	V	T	V	T	V	T	V
Sports & Entertainment												
Zaho	0	0	13	0	0	0	N/A	N/A	0	0	13	0
											100%	0.0%
Nadal	0	1	0	0	0	0	5	0	0	0	5	1
											83.3%	16.7%
Garou	0	0	18	1	0	0	N/A	N/A	0	0	18	1
											94.7%	5.3%
Top 10	0	1	0	4	0	2	N/A	N/A	0	0	0	7
											0.0%	100%
Total	0	2	31	5	0	2	5	0	0	0	36	9
	0.0%	100%	86.1%	13.9%	0.0%	100%	100%	0.0%	0.0%	0.0%	80.0%	20.0%
Grand Total	0	10	55	7	9	15	5	1	4	1	73	34
	0.0%	100%	88.7%	11.3%	37.5%	62.5%	83.3%	16.7%	80.0%	20.0%	68.2%	31.8%

Rather than address their remarks to the group of readers, the blog owners and commenters on these two blogs posted comments and replies for each other individually, using primarily *tu* forms. On the current events blogs, on the other hand, *vous* was preferred by 71.9%. This preference for *vous* could be expected due to the more formal nature of such blogs, but the data in this category were not consistent: on the two French blogs – *Lambda* and *Apprendre à enseigner* – *vous* was used exclusively, while the Canadian bloggers appeared to be more ambivalent regarding the use of *tu* and *vous* on their blogs, with nearly a 50% split between *tu* and *vous* on *Femmes à l'embauche*. Finally, in the sports and entertainment category, *tu* was preferred by 80%, which, it could be argued, is due to the less formal nature of blogs in this category. However, it is important to note that one of the blogs in this category (*Top 10*) did not demonstrate this preference, as it contained *no* instances of *tu* use.

This Canadian blog was one of three blogs in the data set on which there were no occurrences of *tu* forms. Beyond this similarity, however, these three blogs (*Top 10* and the French blogs *Lambda* and *Apprendre à enseigner*) had little in common, particularly in terms of the interactional patterns established on the blogs. On *Top 10*, for example, the majority of the comments were posted to the group, and with only one exception, they were posted in the third person. The remaining comments were addressed to other commenters, primarily using *vous* forms, or to the blog owner. In responding to the blog owner, most commenters again preferred *vous* forms, as shown in the following excerpt from a comment on this blog:

Excerpt 6.

Je suis d'accord avec plusieurs de <u>vos</u> commentaires de "choix douteux" M. [last name of blog owner]. Moi aussi j'ai été outré de constater la présence de LION KING dans la catégorie animation. Ozamu Tezuka doit se retourner dans sa tombe!

(posted by m.bergeron on June 22, 2008)

On the *Apprendre à enseigner* blog, another blog in which there were no occurrences of *tu* use, the interaction was more formal. Almost all of the bloggers posted comments to the group using the third person, no one addressed the blog owner directly, and only one commenter addressed another commenter. This commenter, L.M., chose to use the *vous* form to address Brigitte, another commenter, as shown in Excerpt 7 below:

Excerpt 7.

A Brigitte : ces "formateurs" que <u>vous</u> craignez de récupérer sont <u>vos</u> collègues et le résultat de l'Université, ils ne sont pas l'échec des profs du second degré ou du primaire (les formateurs de terrain) mais de la médiocrité de l'université qui vit dans l'hypocrisie enseignant – chercheur...

(posted by L.M. on June 10, 2008 12:08 AM)

It could be argued that the formality on this blog was due to the relatively new format of online news articles with a *comments* or *reactions* feature, but further investigation of blogs of this type would be required before that conclusion could be drawn.

In *Lambda*, the final example of a blog with no occurrences of *tu* forms, in addition to comments posted to the group, there were a significant number of comments exchanged among commenters (14, as compared to 3 in *Top 10* and one in *Apprendre à enseigner*). *Vous* was the preferred address pronoun, used once to address the blog owner and seven times to address other commenters. As shown in Excerpt 8, commenter marion used *vous* to respond to a previous remark addressed to her by another commenter, A.F.

Excerpt 8.

A.F;
"l'info chopée" vite fait sur Internet???
Non, A.F., j'ai pris le temps de choisir le site, me semble-t-il digne de confiance et de lire.
Maintenant si <u>vous</u> mettez en doute le bien-fondé de ce qui est écrit sur ce sujet sur ce site, à partir d'arguments, je me rangerai à <u>votre</u> avis. [...]
Il serait agréable que tous gardent une honnêteté intellectuelle, lors des échanges.

(posted by marion on June 6, 2009 at 12:51)

In this comment, marion chose to use the *vous* form to defend a URL she had posted on the blog, after which she switched to more indirect discourse to make a remark about the type of interaction she would prefer to see on the blog. In other blogs in the data set, similar conflicts between commenters were either handled in the *tu* form or in the *vous* form, seemingly depending on the personal choice of the blogger.

Personal choice is just one of many factors influencing patterns of *tu* and *vous* use. The country of origin did not appear to have any direct impact on these patterns, and while there were differences based on category, within some categories there were strong deviations from the general patterns. These data demonstrate that the rules for *tu* and *vous* use on blogs are far more complex than Loïc Le Meur or first-year French textbooks might suggest. The number of occurrences of *vous* in the data (over 30%) provides impressive evidence against Le Meur's suggestion that everyone in the blogosphere uses *tu*. Further, the rules for *tu* and *vous* use as they are generally presented in first-year textbooks are far too simple to prepare learners to interact appropriately in this context. Although the data, on *Zaho* for example, did support textbooks' explanation that *tu* is the preferred form "among young people," bloggers in the data set did not consistently use *tu* with "people they knew well" and *vous* with "people they did not know well." While further research by scholars on French-language blogs will contribute to our understanding of the complexity of second-person pronoun use, research *by learners in the classroom* will expand learners' understanding of appropriate *tu* and *vous* use beyond these simplistic rules as they discover first hand the intricacies of these two pronouns as they are used in the context of blogs.

7.   Pedagogical applications

The study described in the previous sections of this chapter presents a model for French instructors wishing to perform such research with their students. The following section provides further suggestions for the implementation of such a project, including variations for different levels of instruction and ideas for expanding the focus of the research. While the blogs in this data set were selected from France and Canada and from three particular categories (personal blogs, current events blogs, and sports and entertainment blogs), instructors and their students need not be limited by this focus. With the assistance of their instructor, for instance, learners could compare their results to those presented here and expand on them by exploring other types of blogs, i.e., blogs from other categories and from other francophone regions.

Depending on the level of proficiency, instructors will want to assist their students in selecting blogs and blog entries, in selecting comments to analyze, and/or in performing the analysis itself. Since locating blogs with sufficient comments to analyze can be one of the most challenging tasks in this type of analysis, instructors should provide a list of suggested blogs or blog hosting sites. In addition to the blog hosting sites explored in this chapter (see Table 2), students and their instructors may want to investigate others, such as those listed in the appendix. Instructors will want to personally investigate each site that they suggest, and they may need to provide guidance for navigating the particular sites (e.g., "choose from the blogs that are listed on the left," "scroll down to … and click on the category …," etc.). It is important to note that on some sites, students will need to click on "Français" to display only those blogs that are in French. For the analysis of *tu* and *vous* use, instructors will also need to instruct students to select blogs that are maintained by a single person (to avoid confusion with *vous*-plural). Each student could be required to select one blog, or students could work in pairs or small groups. More advanced students could be required to examine more than one blog and make comparisons.

Once the students have selected a blog, they will need to select one entry or posting to analyze (or more, for more advanced students). Again, instructors may want to assist their students in this process and/or provide suggestions or tips. For example, entries that are quite recent often have few comments; students may have more luck with entries from earlier that day or from a previous day. In addition, certain categories (such as current events) and sites (such as Skyrock) tend to receive more comments than others. Lower-level students may also need help understanding the layout of a blog, including where the comments are located and how to access them.

After selecting one or more entries, the students will need to select the comments they will analyze. In this chapter, 20 comments were analyzed per blog. This may be an appropriate quantity for intermediate or advanced students, while instructors of lower-level students may prefer to require fewer comments (for example, 10) per blog. Since – as noted above in the analysis in this chapter – some blogs can have a "warming up" period (with no occurrences of *tu* or *vous*-singular) during as many as the first 35 comments, instructors will want to suggest that their students select the most recent comments (or for more advanced students, any consecutive set of comments as long as there is ample use of *tu* and *vous* in that set). Students should be attentive to the dates of postings since comments can be listed in chronological order or reverse chronological order. The blog entry and the comments the students have selected should then be printed.

Instructors may wish to create a table to assist students in their data analysis. It might be advisable to require students to include, in addition to the actual data, information about the blog such as the name of the blog, the name of the blogger, the URL for the blog, the category and country, the title of the entry, and the date it was posted. Lower-level students may require some assistance in determining the category. In the table, advanced students could be required to analyze *tu* and *vous* use by addressee, by category, and by country, as in this chapter. Intermediate students could be required to analyze *tu* and *vous* use by category and by country, but not by addressee (since determining the addressee can be challenging at times), and beginning students could complete a simplified table that perhaps only requires them to identify whether each comment contains *tu*, *vous*, both, or neither. Depending on access to computer labs, instructors may wish to have students perform one or more of the steps in the analysis during class time, and they will find that the project works well when concluded with an in-class discussion of the process and the results, including a tabulation of class results (on large poster board, for example).

This chapter provides a model for the analysis of *tu* and *vous* use in blogs, but instructors may prefer to have their students analyze other aspects of the use of these pronouns or investigate other linguistic and structural features, such as those addressed in the following questions:

1. Do blogs typically display comments in chronological or reverse chronological order?
2. Do blogs typically attract a small group of participants responsible for most of the comments, or are comments posted by many different participants?
3. How could the answer for #2 influence the amount and type of second-person pronouns found in a given blog?
4. Do blogs show any other patterns or features indicating that the discourse is formal/informal or that it is more like written/spoken language (e.g., *on* used as a synonym of *nous*; one or more preferred interrogative structures; the absence or presence of discourse particles that would be found in speech, such as *hein, bon, ben, quoi*)?
5. Are the tokens of *tu* and *vous* all used with definite reference (i.e., a clear, specific addressee), or in some cases is there a higher percentage of indefinite reference (e.g., *tu* or *vous* used as a substitute for the generic French pronoun *on*)? [Although this type of question might seem more appropriate for advanced learners, it may also be quite appropriate for beginning learners whose native language is English (where the pronoun *you* often replaces the generic pronoun *one*) or another language that also uses second-person pronouns for both definite and indefinite reference.]
6. Do different data collection methods influence the results of any analysis? [If students can understand that methodology is indeed crucial and can, in many cases, serve as a highly influential factor in any study, then they will see the importance of considering the difference that might result from an in-depth analysis of a single blog versus a more superficial analysis of a very large number of blogs.]
7. What type of orthographic variation is found in blogs? Is this similar to the amount and types of orthographic variation found in other kinds of computer-mediated communication or in traditional written discourse?

Regardless of the feature selected for analysis, research projects such as the one described in this chapter allow students to access authentic discourse in a new context for communication, assist them in understanding this discourse, and prepare them for participation in such target language communities, enabling interaction beyond the formal learning environment.

References

Blogs: Accueil. (n.d.). Retrieved July 15, 2008, from http://www.skyrock.com/blog/

Blood, R. (2000, September 7). Weblogs: A history and perspective. *Rebecca's Pocket.* Retrieved January 27, 2007, from http://www.rebeccablood.net/ essays/weblog_history.html

Brochard, J-C., de Daran, H., Jove, C., Le Borgne, C., & Nguyen, C. (2006, March). *Les blogs professionnels: Intérêt et limites.* Retrieved September 16, 2008, from Université Henri Poincaré, Service Commun de Documentation Web site: www.scd.uhp-nancy.fr/sante/ Lesblogsprofesionnels.doc

Brown, R., & Gilman, A. (1960). The pronouns of power and solidarity. In T. Sebeok (Ed.), *Style in language* (pp. 253–276). Cambridge, MA: The MIT Press.

Chaput, L. (2008). Bloguez en français s'il vous plaît! *French Review, 81,* 734–749.

Chautemps, M-L. (2007, May 24). Blogs et outils de blogs, caractéristiques et fonctionnalités. Panorama et présentation d'un outil. Paper presented at the Journée GODOC. Retrieved September 16, 2008, from http://www.godoc.u-psud.fr/ IMG/pdf/Blogs-godoc.pdf

Ducate, L. C., & Lomicka, L. L. (2005). Exploring the blogosphere: Use of web logs in the foreign language classroom. *Foreign Language Annals, 38,* 410–421.

Gardner-Chloros, P. (2007). *Tu/vous* choices: An 'act of identity'? In W. Ayres-Bennett & M. C. Jones (Eds.), *The French language and questions of identity* (pp. 106–115: Oxford: Legenda.

Jansma, K., & Kassen, M. A. (2007). *Motifs: An introduction to French* (4th ed.). Boston, MA: Thomson Heinle.

Kinginger, C. (2000). Learning the pragmatics of solidarity in the networked foreign language classroom. In J. K. Hall & L. S. Verplaetse (Eds.), *Second and foreign language learning through classroom interaction* (pp. 23–46). Mahwah, NJ: Erlbaum.

Kramsch, C. (1985). Classroom interaction and discourse options. *Studies in Second Language Acquisition, 7,* 169–183.

Le Meur, L. (2005, December 23). Nicolas Sarkozy, premier podcast vidéo. *Loïc Le Meur Blog.* Retrieved July 18, 2008, from http://loiclemeur.com/france/ 2005/12/nicolas_sarkozy_1. html

Lomicka Anderson, L. (2006, September). The return of the Telematics and New Technologies Commission. *American Association of Teachers of French National Bulletin, 32,* 29.

Maley, C. A. (1972). Historically speaking, *tu* or *vous*? *French Review, 45,* 999–1006.

Matlack, C., & Faivre d'Arcier, C. (2005, July 11). Let them eat cake – and blog about it. *Business Week.* Retrieved January 27, 2007, from http://www.businessweek.com

Morford, J. (1997). Social indexicality in French pronominal address. *Journal of Linguistic Anthropology, 7,* 3–37.

NETendaces 2007. (2008). Retrieved July 15, 2008, from http://www.cefrio.qc.ca/ fr/documents/publications/NETendances-2007--evolution-de-lutilisation-dInternet-au-Quebec-depuis-1999.html

Nussbaum, B. (2006, August 2). The French read blogs more than Americans, Brits and just about everyone. *Business Week: NussbaumOnDesign.* Retrieved July 12, 2008, from http://www. businessweek.com/innovate/NussbaumOnDesign/archives/2006/08/the_french_blog.html

Office québécois de la langue française. (2006). Les mots de la blogosphère. In *Bibliothèque virtuelle: Documents terminologiques et linguistiques.* Available from http://www.oqlf.gouv. qc.ca/ressources/bibliotheque/dictionnaires/ terminologie_blogue/indexfra.html

Office québécois de la langue française. (n.d.). Blogue. In *Bibliothèque virtuelle: Vocabulaire d'Internet*. Available from http://www.oqlf.gouv.qc.ca/ressources/bibliotheque/dictionnaires/Internet/fiches/8370242.html

Riley, D. (2005, March 6). A short history of blogging. *The Blog Herald*. Retrieved July 16, 2008, from http://www.blogherald.com/2005/03/06/a-short-history-of-blogging/

Sifry, D. (2007, April 5). The state of the Live Web, April 2007. Retrieved July 15, 2008, from http://technorati.com/weblog/2007/04/328.html

Suply, L. (2007, October 14). Blogueuse avant l'heure. *Le Figaro*. Retrieved September 16, 2008, from http://www.lefigaro.fr/high-tech/20070720.WWW000000238_blogueuse_avant_ lheure.html

Technorati Media. *Welcome to Technorati*. (n.d.). Retrieved July 15, 2008, from http://technorati.com/about/

Warren, J. (2006). Address pronouns in French: Variation within and outside the workplace. *Australian Review of Applied Linguistics, 29,* 16.1–16.17.

Williams, L., & van Compernolle, R. A. (2007). Second-person pronoun use in on-line French-language chat environments. *French Review, 80,* 804–820.

Appendix

Hosting sites for Francophone blogs

Centerblog   URL: http://www.centerblog.net/
Bloguez   URL: http://www.bloguez.com/
Mabulle   URL: http://www.mabulle.com/

Belgian blog hosting site

Skynet   URL: http://blogs.skynet.be/index.html?new_lang=fr

Swiss blog hosting site

Bleublog   URL: http://bleublog.lematin.ch/

New Caledonian blog hosting site

Blog Nouvelle-Calédonie, Expatrié Nouvelle-Calédonie
URL: http://www.expat-blog.com/fr/annuaire/oceanie/nouvelle-caledonie/

Reunion Island blog hosting site

Blog La Réunion, Expatrié La Réunion
URL: http://www.expat-blog.com/fr/annuaire/afrique/la-reunion/

Blogs in Spanish beyond the classroom

Sociocultural opportunities for second language development

Eduardo Negueruela-Azarola

This chapter explores pedagogical uses of blogs written in Spanish and available in the web as productive digital moments that expand and reorganize the second language (L2) learning experience. Using Sociocultural Theory (SCT) (see Lantolf & Thorne, 2006) as an explanatory framework to understand L2 written and oral communication, I consider the importance of mindful attention for development (see Salomon, 1991) and present two metaphors (expansion and reorganization) for understanding blogs both as a rich locus of communication and conceptualization and as a source of current unique texts for cultural, psychological, and social interpretation outside the classroom but only a digital click away for the L2 learner. A basic sociocultural topic-oriented heuristic for a reflective exploration of the Spanish-language blogosphere is provided so that Spanish teachers have a a sample pedagogical tool to offer to L2 learners. This study promotes meaningful utilization of Spanish-language blogs beyond the L2 classroom by recognizing blogs as a valuable sociocultural human activity.

> "Language makes us human,
> literacy makes us civilized (Olson, 1986),
> and technology makes us powerful.
> Powerful in what ways?"
> Salomon (1991).

1. Introduction

In this chapter, I discuss Spanish-language blogs as pedagogical opportunities for amplification and reorganization (Pea, 1985) of second language (L2) learning beyond the classroom. Although a growing amount of research on blogs and the blogosphere has been produced over the past decade (see Blood, 2000; Blood,

2002; Bolter & Grusin, 1999; Davis & Merchant, 2007; Gurak, Antonijevic, Johnson, Ratliff, & Reyman, n.d.), there is still relatively little research on blogs compared to older types of computer-mediated communication (CMC). Considering this, I first provide a brief introduction to blogs and their rapid growth as part of the phenomenon known as Web 2.0 (O'Reilly, 2007). Next, given that the focus of this chapter is on blogs beyond the Spanish classroom, I provide examples of sites that host blogs written in Spanish. Since the Web is always changing, I have chosen blogs and sites that seem to be relatively stable, even if the very nature of the Web allows for and even promotes a certain degree of instability. Finally, I utilize sociocultural concepts to situate blogs as productive learning tools that have the potential to provide pedagogical affordances for expanding and reorganizing the learning of L2 communicative practices.

Five concepts from sociocultural theory (SCT) – history, mediation, collaboration, social/private, communication/conceptualization – are transformed isomorphically into five pedagogical topics that can promote reflection on social and linguistic aspects of blogs and participation in the Spanish-language blogosphere beyond the formal L2 setting. For each topic, I propose three pedagogical opportunities that blogs offer for promoting mindful attention in our students as they explore blogs on their own: (1) blogs as unique cultural texts; (2) blogs as psychological tools; and (3) blogs as communication. For each opportunity, students can engage in a task with two dimensions: amplification (i.e., a type of expansion) and reorganization (Pea, 1985).

2.   Web 2.0 and blogs in Spanish[1]

The second generation of the World Wide Web, often referred to as Web 2.0, signals a change from the linking of information to the linking of people (Warschauer & Grimes, 2007), from accessing information to participation. Weblogs, or blogs as they are popularly known, are a good example of this shift toward a more social Web. Since their rise in popularity in the late 1990s, websites that foster, integrate, and promote blog writing have grown exponentially. More recently, the proliferation of blogs has lead to the appearance of numerous sites hosting blogs, indexing blogs, publishing information on and about blogs, or providing topic-oriented blog search engines (see the Appendix for sample sites).

The emergence of user-friendly software for creating blog sites, uploading entries, and posting comments quickly and almost effortlessly is in part respon-

---

1.   In Spanish, blogs are occasionally referred to as *bitácoras*, although the borrowed English term *blog* seems to be more widespread.

sible for the rise in popularity of blogs over the past few years. Blogs (like e-mail, chatrooms, online forums, and wikis) are one genre of communication that new technologies have made available for L2 teachers and learners.

A blog is a type of online journal (often) published in reverse chronological order allowing groups and individuals to publish personal experiences, preferences, views on recent events, or any other topic they may wish to write about. Blogs may use texts, photos, videos, and links from other blogs or webpages to portray and create the personal digital universe of the author. Most blogs use primarily written language but, more recently, blogs are increasingly using photos, audio files, and video clips to produce photoblogs (phlogs), audioblogs, and videoblogs (vlogs).

Blogs are now a dynamic source of knowledge conceptualization, information sharing, personal perspectives, and social commentary. According to Warschauer and Grimes (2007), "by mid-2007, the blogging search engine, Technorati,[2] was tracking 85 million blogs around the world" (p. 5). The variety of new blogs and the ease with which new postings can be made have created a universe of bloggers/writers who publish frequently and whose postings are often read by Internet users and other bloggers.

The interconnectedness of blogs can promote folksonomies in which informal, bottom-up classifications are created by users through tagging (vs. taxonomies, in which information is classified a priori by an expert). Folksonomies are dynamic, and other Web users may then use these tags to connect not only to information, but, more importantly, they may also use these tags to connect with other people who are commenting/blogging and people with similar interests. This is one of the ways in which Web 2.0, through tools like blogs, becomes a network of people and not only a network of information.

Although blog topics are initiated by the owner, blogs allow for posting comments and reactions to the main entries, which, in turn, allows readers of the blog to communicate with the author and even with each other. Many blogs are maintained by a single blogger and are updated regularly, in many cases every day or even more frequently. Chesher (2005) notes the existence of two basic types of blogs. The first type includes online personal journals that describe thoughts and experiences of the blogger/author. These blogs allow writers to create a personal record and memory of their experiences. The second type consists of blogs that produce online social commentary in the tradition of newspaper editorials and opinion columns.

As is the case for the Internet as a whole, the blogosphere is still dominated by English-language discourse and virtual spaces; however, there are sites that index Spanish-language blogs (see the Appendix for some examples). It is also possible

---

2. http://www.technorati.com/

to find blogs in Spanish on specific topics through the use of keyword searches on the Google Blog Search site.[3]

In the Spanish-language blogosphere, several major media outlets (mainly television stations and online newspapers) have integrated blog sites into their homepages over the past few years. These blogs are generally maintained by writers and journalists and are updated quite frequently (see the Appendix). Journalists use these blogs to give a personal touch to news, anecdotes from their work, and more direct and candid social and political commentary.

Blogs are especially interesting because of their unique qualities. They allow for personal expression, multidimensionality of images, videos, texts, and hyperlinks. They also foster text hybridity, topic heterogeneity, and chronological memory. As Gurak, Antonijevic, Johnson, Ratliff, and Reyman (n.d.) comment, blogs are a hybrid form because their content "combines musings, memories, jokes, reflections on research, photographs, rants, and essays" (para. 3). They are heterogeneous because they "can be devoted to only one topic, or they can reflect what the author is interested in at any given time" (para. 3). Blogs are by their form and function chronological memory since most "posts to the blog are time-stamped with the most recent post at the top, creating a reverse chronological structure governed by spontaneity and novelty" (para. 3).

Expert bloggers are able to capture not only their personal universes for a public audience using all the multimedia power of the current World Wide Web, but also a personal and anecdotal, yet relevant, message that powerfully communicates with readers in a different, meaningful way. Such writing is difficult – if not impossible – to offer in canonical print journalism (e.g., editorials, opinion columns, and so forth). This new type of written expression can also transform people who write blogs into citizen journalists. Likewise, journalists who write blogs can communicate less formally with the public. Therefore, blogs have become a meaningful, unique genre in late capitalist multimedia-oriented globalized societies (see Miller & Shepperd, n.d., for a sophisticated social analysis on blogs and their relevance today).

3.   Powerful digital technologies and L2 pedagogy

New digital technologies, which create unique electronic discourse moments and texts, have the potential to provide L2 teachers with new opportunities for expanding and reorganizing learning beyond the classroom. Furthermore, the

---

3.   http://blogsearch.google.com/

Internet is an ever-increasing necessity in all aspects of our everyday lives, and educational settings need to address the reality of promoting the development of communicative genres that are part of the competencies needed to function in personal and professional contexts (see Thorne & Black, 2007).

Technology is not a guarantee for better (i.e., more meaningful, interesting, and productive) L2 classrooms. Instead, it may actually hinder L2 development if, as teachers, we are only guided by mindless innovation (Witte, 2007). Even answering the question of effectiveness in integrating technology in and beyond the L2 classroom is not easy (see Zhao, 2003). One may need to distinguish between technology, its pedagogical applications, and other mediating elements such as learners, teachers, and the context of application. As Kern (2006) argues, we need to understand "effectiveness in terms of the specifics of what people do with computers, how they do it, and what it means to them" (p. 187). Recent research has offered insights and guiding principles for understanding and integrating technology in meaningful ways in the L2 classroom (see Kern, 2006; Salaberry, 2001; Thorne, 2003; Warschauer, 1999; among others).

When assessing the potential effects of digital technology in the L2 classroom, two issues must be considered: (1) the quality of new digital technology – in this case CMC through blogs – as a source for potential benefits beyond L2 classroom teaching and learning; (2) our own pedagogical priorities, that is, how new technology matches, expands, or re-shapes our approaches to L2 classroom teaching. For example, the complexity of using blogs in different settings, courses, and proficiency levels is something for teachers and teaching communities to reflect on. The proper integration and use of electronic discourse in the L2 classroom and beyond is not a question of formulas or even general principles. It requires critical, ongoing reflection on the part of L2 teachers and L2 teaching communities (see Johnson, 1999, on "robust reasoning" and the teaching of languages).

One approach for integrating new technologies into the foreign language curriculum would involve modifying traditional tasks through amplification and reorganization (Pea, 1985). First, amplification implies that technology can activate and increase certain abilities necessary for undertaking a particular task. This empowerment may provide better orientation toward the task and greater efficiency in doing it, depending on the case. For instance, in L2 learning, the very nature of blogs has the potential to expand communicative opportunities for students outside the classroom setting. Second, reorganization involves a change in the way a task is carried out through the use of technology. Our capabilities are reshaped to accommodate resources that are made available by technology. In the case of blogs, students' participation through reading, writing, or reacting to blogs in Spanish can provide teachers with a framework for reshaping and reorganizing instructional practices. Likewise, students' analysis of and participation in Spanish-language blogs could help to reorganize the ways in which they communicate in the L2.

The effects of blogs on potential expansion and reorganization of classroom learning can be framed through a specific understanding of teaching and learning languages. Depending on our priorities in the L2 curriculum, that is, how we set our objectives and the pedagogical tasks we value as teachers for promoting L2 development, we will be able to evaluate the effects of using CMC. In this chapter, the analysis and use of Spanish-language blogs is based on a sociocultural understanding of written and oral communication (see Lantolf & Thorne, 2006). From this perspective, L2 teaching and learning are constructed as a sociocultural activity where meaning making and conceptual mediation through engaging in written and oral communication are priorities (see Negueruela, 2008).

4.   Spanish-language blogs in and beyond the classroom

Blogs were not created for the classroom. However, they can easily fit within the curriculum as fluid sources of personal reflection and social commentary. In addition, they are collaborative and interactive, and they can produce social texts with unique personal voices. Blogs allow for the design of a variety of learning tasks connected to writing, reading, the expression of one's opinion, and the fostering of productive learning exchanges (see Godwin-Jones, 2003). In the L2 curriculum, blogs may be utilized in many different ways: for group or individual online reading; for self-expression/free writing in the L2; as an online academic "reaction paper tool" to comment on texts; as collaborative or personal documentation of projects, among other pedagogical uses.

For tasks involving the presentational mode of communication (e.g., writing), blogs are used for a variety of purposes (Barrios, 2003): blogs as diaries or journals that document classroom learning, blogs as research tools to compile information for a specific project or for the whole course, and class blogs for sharing ideas among peers and among students and teachers. As Brooks, Nichols, and Priebe (n.d.) comment, "Weblogging seems like such a potentially rich set of online writing activities because it is relatively low-tech compared to producing hypertext or websites, and it incorporates familiar writing skills like summary, paraphrases and the development of voice" (para. 2).

Thorne and Payne (2005) point out that blogs are productive alternatives to writing tasks such as compositions. As a means for promoting reflection, blogging allows for the creation of a classroom blogosphere where there is a specific audience and a collective process of participation. For teachers, the challenge is "to find means to link informal and recreational writing with formal and academic writing" (Godwin-Jones, 2008, p. 7). Godwin-Jones also notes that "blogs and social networking sites provide new opportunities and incentives for personal writing. This reading-to-write culture requires the use and development of language skills" (p. 7). In the L2 classroom, it is precisely this unique connection between writing and reading that makes blogging a very attractive pedagogical option to be used even outside the classroom. Furthermore, the collaborative nature of blog reading/writing blurs the distinction between social/personal and the public/ private, between communicating and conceptualizing. Such collaboration also highlights the importance of personal history, digital mediation, and interactivity.

There are three basic interrelated pedagogical moves (i.e., possibilities) regarding the use of blogs beyond the L2 classroom as a means for using electronic discourse:

1. A conceptual use: reading, writing, interpreting and publishing blogs in Spanish as complex texts that construct meaning, elaborate topics, and electronic discourse use (word choices, phrases, syntax).
2. A communicative use: interacting with bloggers through commenting or creating a personal or group blog.
3. A community use: sharing with other bloggers in real Spanish blog communities it may be pedagogically fruitful to create a classroom learning community through constructing a classroom blog that links and tags students' preferences while documenting their own learning projects.

Each one of the above three interrelated uses (concept, communication, community) may be explored in several different directions. However, uses of blogs beyond the classroom setting should focus on topics selected by learners. Even in the classroom setting, as Brooks, Nichols, and Priebe (n.d.) highlight, learners seem to enjoy the use of blogs for self-expression and communication with others. Consequently, beyond the L2 classroom, Spanish learners should find blogs that fit their general interest. Using a blog search engine should be fairly easy for students so as to find Spanish-language blogs close to their interest (see Appendix).

All of these are possible complementary options from beginning to advanced levels. The lower the linguistic level of the students, the more time and guidance learners will need with linguistic and cultural issues. Since L2 blogging is a worthwhile activity that should be encouraged through participation in the Spanish-language blogosphere outside the classroom, teachers should make an effort to find blogs that they feel are appropriate for specific instructional contexts.

Personal blogs with everyday language use are a rich source of anecdotes and engaging materials, whereas literary blogs are generally intellectual and academic. Students with a personal passion for literature should be encouraged to read these blogs. However, for those students not too interested in literature or literary topics, these postings may be too distant from their personal preferences. Blogs by journalists are generally suitable for any group of students since they usually deal with current events from a personal point of view. Given the wide variety of available blogs, teachers should be able to design topic-oriented tasks for exploring the blogosphere.

From a pedagogical point of view, and to become genuinely engaged in blogging, learners should be encouraged to create their own personal or group blogs in Spanish. Since blogging is a highly interactive, collaborative activity, learners could embark on creating their own blogs in Spanish. Tasks based on journal writing about oneself and personal sharing are probably the best initial assignments. Also, students should be free to create blogs for personal generic uses, similar to the practice of free writing in the conventional composition class.

Before creating their own blogs, students should find model blogs in Spanish that they may be able to imitate since they are attempting to become part of the Spanish blogosphere. Analyzing existing blogs is a first useful step. Learners should be encouraged to engage in paraphrasing, rephrasing, summarizing, and noticing how personal voices are expressed in Spanish through specific linguistic features. This self-reflection process could also be part of learners' own blogs.

According to Brooks, Nichols, and Priebe (n.d.), group/classroom blogs that are more collaborative in nature also seem to be more conducive to learners' engagement. Since teachers may want to foster participation in the Spanish-language blogosphere, it may be a good idea to create a classroom blog linked to students' personal blogs. This classroom blog may serve as a virtual meeting point or gateway to the Spanish-language blogosphere.

If L2 teachers choose more focused, academic topic-oriented blogs, it is advisable to transform and connect student-initiated topics to the curriculum and pedagogical objectives. The challenge will be to transform blogs from a tool of self-expression – likely the preferred type of blog for students – into a tool-for-thought in academic contexts. This transition from a personal diary to constructing academic blogs is not necessarily the best progression in all L2 courses; however, this is often expected in most academic curricula. In any case, teachers should proceed carefully, since blogs should be a source for personal expression. Balancing postings about oneself with more focused postings about course content should be encouraged. At beginning levels, and especially for new bloggers, self-initiated expression and personal preference should guide blog participation so as to avoid identification of blogging with exclusively academic writing.

Selecting appropriate Spanish-language blogs on the Web for particular Spanish classrooms and learners should depend on specific learning objectives.

Regardless of the learning environment, learners should have as much freedom as possible to participate through reading, writing, and commenting on blogs in Spanish that could foster the creation of their digital selves. As mentioned above, a classroom blog to index all learners' blogs and their preferred blogs written in Spanish may be an ideal tool for encouraging students to participate in the Spanish-language blogosphere beyond the formal L2 learning context. This group blog may also serve as the basis for posting recommendation on blogs in Spanish, initial assignments for exploring blogs, ideas for creating personal blogs, among many other pedagogical options.

5.   Blogs, SCT, and L2 learning

Given that there exists a wide range of blogs available in Spanish as a rich source of unique discourse and commentary on current events, L2 teachers who are part of a rapidly evolving digital society may indeed feel obligated to integrate new digital technologies into instructional practices. Coherent integration of new uses of technology beyond the Spanish classroom requires the ability to reflect – albeit briefly – on one's views of L2 learning. What are our pedagogical priorities? What do we value as learning? Answering these basic questions might encourage L2 teachers to decide what should be counted as learning in order to articulate pedagogical practices and promote learning and participation in the digital semiosphere.

A personal theory of L2 acquisition (SLA) is needed when making decisions involving curriculum, instruction, and assessment. This may be our personal working theory on what we consider to be "good teaching" and "meaningful learning," or it may be based on scholarly insights from the field of SLA (see Mitchell & Myles, 2004, for an overview of SLA theories). We may decide that L2 learning is about basic interactional communication, the explicit or implicit practice of morphosyntax, participation in meaningful communication tasks, or an eclectic combination of these and other ideas. In turn, these ideas tend to reflect the instructional and assessment-related practices that teachers depend on to varying degrees. However, this should not be a unidirectional process. Bottom-up pedagogical ideas emerging from practices that we find effective in the classroom are generally stronger than abstract principles. We tend to adopt this experiential knowledge of what works in the classroom, and then we find matching theoretical insights *ex post facto*. Be that as it may, as reflective practitioners, answering a seemingly simple pedagogical question about L2 acquisition has direct implications for L2 learning in and beyond the classroom.

In the present study, I situate the uses of blogs in the Spanish classroom within a SCT of mind, emerging from the work of Vygotsky (Wieber & Robinson, 2004) applied to the field of L2 teaching and learning (see Lantolf & Thorne, 2006 for a review of SCT principles applied to SLA). From a sociocultural perspective, the development of communicative abilities in a language enables us to construct meaning for the other (i.e., communication) and for the self (i.e., conceptualization). Meaning construction is performed through mediating symbolic tools (see Kozulin, 1998) by historical beings (L2 learners in this case) whose agency is constructed and oriented – but not determined – when participating in collaborative activities that are, at the same time, social and personal.

Consequently, promoting L2 development in learners is fostering the dialectics of communication and conceptualization. That is, L2 meaning creation in written and oral tasks implies using appropriate historical/semiotic tools such as concepts, and conversely, providing appropriate conceptual mediation to learners so that they reflect/participate in meaningful oral and written communicative activity (Negueruela, 2003). The being and becoming of communication and conceptualization – being private in social settings such as the classroom and being social in private settings such as when reading and studying – is the essence of human collaboration and semiotic mediation. Such a dialectic is at the core of a sociocultural understanding of communication.

Participation in CMC is theoretically and pedagogically compatible with a sociocultural understanding of communication. Indeed, the varied nature of blogs in the blogosphere testifies to the importance of human communication as an activity that connects people through the creation of meaning in specific online communities. In Table 1, I demonstrate how five fundamental SCT constructs (history, mediation, collaboration, social/private, and communication/conceptualization) are also fundamental qualities of digital communication through blogs. The application of sociocultural constructs to explain the complexities of digital communication is indexed with the theoretical applicability and practical relevance of SCT principles.

Blogs, as easy-to-use digital tools for creating texts with a specific purpose and for a specific Web audience, make journal writing a valuable sociocultural activity for L2 learning. Learning and development in a Vygotskyan approach is fundamentally about conscious awareness (see Salomon, 1991). Learners need to consciously focus not only on what they do when they are writing or reading blogs, but they must also pay attention to the very nature of the tool they are using for writing, reading, composing, and publishing in Spanish.

Table 1. Concepts from SCT that are inherently present in blogs

Concepts	SCT	Blogs
HISTORY	People are sociocultural beings who are essentially historical. We live with artifacts, cultural activities, and conceptual tools that change, but are historically inherited from our previous social history. Documenting personal history and memory through narratives is a quintessential human activity.	Blogs are essentially historical texts. Their popularity now is partly based on the importance of documenting the personal history of bloggers in specific historical events and circumstances through time-stamped entries.
COLLABORATION	Human beings develop through collaborative activities which in turn lead to the development of personal agency. Participating with others to achieve common goals because of socially and historically situated motives is the basis of collaborative activities.	The intrinsically collaborative nature of blog creation and publishing is indexed by the blogosphere itself, blog-publishing software, multiple author blogs, postings and comments, tagging and folksonomies, blog search engines, and the multimedia dimension of blogs.
MEDIATION	Human beings act in the world through tools and symbols that mediate our activities. Becoming aware of symbolic mediation is critical for human ontogenesis.	The nature and quality of blogs mediate the texts that are finally produced. Becoming aware of the affordances and limitations of blogs as a medium for communication is critical for successful blog creation.
INTERNALIZATION: SOCIAL/PERSONAL	The social and personal coincide in human development in the process of internalization. The distinction between social and psychological activity is nebulous. Once we become social in the process of internalization we are always social, even in private settings.	The social/personal distinction occurs in blog development. Blogs are personal journals published in a social sphere. They are a hybrid genre between personal diaries, opinion columns, and social commentaries.
COMMUNICATION/ CONCEPTUALIZATION	Thinking and speaking are connected in human ontogenesis. Communication is the source of conceptualization, and conceptualization is the source of communication.	Reading to write and writing to read are critical in blogs. Blog writing makes explicit the connection between thinking about ideas and communicating in a unique genre. It is a fundamental interpretative, presentational, and interactive activity.

6.   Isomorphism between SCT and pedagogy

In this final section of the chapter, I propose a pedagogical heuristic for L2 instructors interested in exploring blogs as a sociocultural manifestation of human communication. The five SCT constructs (history, mediation, collaboration, social/private, and communication/conceptualization) explored in the previous section of this chapter can indeed be transformed isomorphically into five pedagogical topics for textual analysis, that is, as topics for learners' exploration beyond the formal L2 setting.

One of the complex issues to resolve in theory-building is how to transition from describing a phenomenon in a theory (i.e., descriptive adequacy) to explaining a phenomenon (i.e., explanatory adequacy). This transition from description to explanation is the basis of much theorizing in the social sciences. Complex descriptions of classrooms are used to explain learning through creating models. But are these models adequate explanations or are they simply describing phenomena? Here, and considering the pedagogical objectives of this chapter, I use the notion of pedagogical isomorphism to show how SCT constructs or concepts are not only descriptively adequate to understand communication and L2 learning and teaching, but also that they are indeed adequate explanations. To make this intellectual move from description to explanation, I use a pedagogical pole by proposing that the explanatory power of SCT constructs derive from their applicability to understanding human practices. Consequently, SCT constructs can be used as reflective topics to promote learning and frame pedagogical practices. To be sure, these constructs are pedagogical isomorphs since they may be used by learners for understanding human communicative activity. As such, pedagogical isomorphism means helping students not only to think about SCT constructs, but also to consider the Spanish-language blogosphere in terms of these five concepts. Isomorphism requires "at least a modicum of structural and functional resemblance" (Salomon, 1991, p. 196). That is, in order to understand and explore blogs in Spanish beyond the L2 classroom, learners can use these SCT constructs as a guide.

These concepts can provide a pedagogical impetus for promoting the use of blogs beyond the formal L2 learning environment if learners find a productive way of applying them to understanding the blogosphere. As such, for each of these five concepts, three pedagogical opportunities are briefly outlined: (1) blogs as cultural texts for reading and interpretation as artifacts that highlight unique features of electronic discourse, topics, and other information; (2) blogs as psychological tools for imitation (in the Vygotskyan sense) or transformation as sources of "intra-action" (Vygotsky, 1978, p. 57) that promote attention to an emerging digital genre that can be imitated, transformed, and internalized by learners; (3) blogs as sources of interaction to promote communication with the Spanish-language blogging community. In each of these opportunities, there are two dimensions (i.e., expansion and reorganization) for understanding blogs as a rich locus for communication, conceptualization, and community sharing (see Table 1).

For instance, if we wish to understand the historical nature of blogs in Spanish as unique texts that expand L2 learning, what evidence do we find in the Spanish-language blogosphere and how can we explain this evidence? Learners may view time stamps in postings as part of the historical nature of blogs as historical artifacts, but topics, which in many cases are linked to current events in the news, can also be considered part of the historical nature of blogs. Students should be asked to find concrete examples that correspond to events in the Spanish-language blogosphere.

As another example, if we wish to explore reorganization as a dimension of learning, what evidence in the Spanish-language blogosphere suggests that blogs as historical texts reorganize human communication? We may wish to explore this option by understanding how reading/writing is reorganized in blog writing. What are the historical writing conventions that are changed in blogs compared to other genres, such as personal diaries? What concrete linguistic, multimedia evidence do we find in the Spanish blogosphere? What about the immediacy of publishing a private text in a foreign language in a public forum?

Table 2 is a pedagogical heuristic for fostering learner autonomy and reflective practices that should help L2 learners frame their reflection on their participation in electronic communication environments outside the L2 formal learning context. This is, of course, only one of the many possible models that could be used. L2 teachers and learners should be able to design their own table with heuristic tools for exploring the Spanish-language blogosphere. Completing the whole table (individually or collaboratively) will allow students to reflect on the nature of blogs; however, students could also work on sections of the table at different times. The table should function as a guide for reading, writing, reacting to, and creating students' own blogs. Instructors should certainly help students to find and formulate appropriate questions and comments. However, instructors should not give too many specific examples of the information students are supposed to produce for the task (i.e., filling in items on the table). Struggling to find these answers is the critical step in this reflection process. The table can be understood in many different ways, and this is precisely the point.

Table 2. A heuristic table for exploring blogs

Exploratory construct for blogs in Spanish	Opportunities	Dimensions	Evidence and rationale in Spanish-language blogs
1. HISTORY – Sociocultural and linguistic conventions unique to the Spanish blogosphere. – Historical and cultural values reflected in the language and discourse of blogs.	Text as cultural artifact	Expansion	
		Reorganization	
	Tools for thinking and imitation	Expansion	
		Reorganization	
	Medium for communicative activity	Expansion	
		Reorganization	
2. COLLABORATION – Specific features of blogs that reveal their collaborative nature: how bloggers anticipate the audience; features of blogs that are inherently collaborative.	Text as cultural artifact	Expansion	
		Reorganization	
	Tools for thinking and imitation	Expansion	
		Reorganization	
	Medium for communicative activity	Expansion	
		Reorganization	
3. MEDIATION – Linguistic affordances and limitations of Spanish. – Multimedia features of blogs that mediate communicative experiences.	Text as cultural artifact	Expansion	
		Reorganization	
	Tools for thinking and imitation	Expansion	
		Reorganization	
	Medium for communicative activity	Expansion	
		Reorganization	
4. SOCIAL/PERSONAL CONNECTION – Characteristics of blogs where the personal/social distinction is blurred, specifically in the Spanish-language blogosphere.	Text as cultural artifact	Expansion	
		Reorganization	
	Tools for thinking and imitation	Expansion	
		Reorganization	
	Medium for communicative activity	Expansion	
		Reorganization	
5. COMMUNICATION/ CONCEPTUALIZATION CONNECTION – Specific uses of language and interpretations of Spanish-language blogs; reflection on features of texts; communicative misunderstandings and understandings on the Web, how blogs manifest communicative challenges.	Text as cultural artifact	Expansion	
		Reorganization	
	Tools for thinking and imitation	Expansion	
		Reorganization	
	Medium for communicative activity	Expansion	
		Reorganization	

L2 learners should be able to find evidence of the sociocultural complexity of blog creation and publishing through 5 concepts, 3 opportunities, and 2 dimensions. The finding of specific evidence in the Spanish-language blogosphere for each of these concepts will not always be easy. It requires not only thinking *about* notions of history, mediation, collaboration, social/private, and communicating/conceptualizing, but more importantly thinking *in terms of* them. This final task is not specifically about developing the L2. Instead, it is designed to promote analysis and understanding of sociocultural aspects of the Spanish-language blogosphere beyond the classroom as genuine opportunities for understanding new forms of human communication.

7.   Conclusion

Blogs, as any cultural manifestation emerging from the digital world, have the potential to become a productive tool for L2 learning in and beyond formal learning environments. As in any other domain, students can benefit from engagement with new digital tools that can mediate and promote communication and knowledge-sharing outside the classroom setting. A coherent integration of blogs in appropriate learning tasks and course projects is a first step to using blogs in the L2 curriculum. It is also critical to develop appropriate forms of assessment that recognize the utilization of blogs by students as valuable learning resources. Insights from research explaining the uses of authentic assessment and authentic texts in the L2 classroom (see Hall, 2001) will help teachers to develop tasks, rubrics, and grading criteria that reward meaningful uses of blogs for L2 learning. A meaningful utilization of Spanish-language blogs can be approached by making sense of the blogosphere through a sociocultural theory. These meaningful uses need to be recognized in formal settings, so that in turn, learners are encouraged to explore the digital universe, as outlined in this chapter or in new ways that may be more appropriate for different learning environments.

FL teachers need to be active and transformative agents beyond their classrooms, not simply passive recipients or mere consumers of technology. Web 2.0 is redefining our conception of knowledge if, as Pea (1985) argues, "'knowing' has become redefined as a verb of access rather than possession" (p. 176). Web tools such as blogging are completely redefining knowing as a verb pertaining not so much to access like in Web 1.0, but to sharing. In this way, knowing and learning together take on a dynamic quality where meaningful participation and learning together entail personal contributions and social relevance through sharing the personal self with the social other and the social self and the personal other. From possessing to accessing and finally to sharing, technology helps to transform not only learning beyond the classroom setting, but also our very own conceptualization of human learning, development, and the mediated self.[4]

References

Barrios, B. (2003). The year of the blog: Weblogs in the writing classroom. *Computers and Composition Online*. Retrieved July 20, 2008, from http://www.bgsu.edu/ cconline/barrios/ blogs/index.html

Blood, R. (2000). Weblogs: A history and perspective. Retrieved July 20, 2008, from http:// www.rebeccablood.net/essays/weblog_history.html

Blood, R. (2002). *The weblog handbook: Practical advice on creating and maintaining your blog.* Cambridge, MA: Perseus.

Bolter, D. J., & Grusin, R. (1999). *Remediation: Understanding new media.* Cambridge, MA: The MIT Press.

Brooks, K., Nichols, C., & Priebe, S. (n.d.). Retrieved July 25, 2008, from http://blog.lib.umn. edu/blogosphere/remediation_genre.html

Chesher, C. (2005, May). Blogs and the crisis of authorship. Paper presented at the Blogtalk Downunder Conference, Sydney, Australia. Retrieved July, 20, 2008, from http://incsub. org/ blogtalk/?page_id=40

Davis, J., & Merchant, G. (2007). Looking from the inside out: Academic blogging as a new literacy. In M. Knobel & C. Lankshear (Eds.), *A new literacies sampler* (pp. 167–197). New York, NY: Peter Lang.

Godwin-Jones, R. (2003). Emerging technologies. Blogs and wikis: Environments for on-line collaboration. *Language Learning & Technology, 7,* 12–16. Available from http://llt.msu. edu/vol7num2/emerging/ default.html

Godwin-Jones, R. (2008). Emerging technologies. Web-writing 2.0: Enabling, documenting, and assessing writing online. *Language Learning & Technology, 12,* 7–13. Available from http://llt.msu.edu/vol12num2/emerging.pdf

Gurak, L. J., Antonijevic, S., Johnson, L., Ratliff, C., & Reyman, J. (Eds.). (n.d.). *Into the Blogosphere: Rhetoric, community, and culture of weblogs.* Available from http://blog.lib.umn. edu/blogosphere/

Hall, J. K. (2001). *Methods for teaching foreign languages: Creating a community of learners in the classroom.* Upper Saddle River, NJ: Prentice Hall.

Johnson, K. (1999). *Understanding language teaching: Reasoning in action.* Boston: Heinle & Heinle.

Kern, R. (2006). Perspectives on technology and learning and teaching languages. *TESOL Quarterly, 40,* 183–210.

---

4. I would like to acknowledge the feedback received on an earlier version of this chapter from Kimberly Buescher. Also, I am thankful to the editors of this volume, Lee Abraham and Lawrence Williams, for all their help, encouragement, and feedback received on this chapter.

Kozulin, A. (1998). *Psychological tools: A sociocultural approach to education.* Cambridge, MA: Harvard University Press.

Lantolf, J. P., & Thorne, S. L. (2006). *Sociocultural theory and the genesis of second language development.* Oxford: Oxford University Press.

Miller, C. R., & Shepperd, D. (n.d.). Blogging as social action: A genre analysis of the weblog. In L. J. Gurak et al. (n.d.), *Into the Blogosphere: Rhetoric, community, and culture of weblogs.* Retrieved July 20, 2008, from http://blog.lib.umn.edu/ blogosphere

Mitchell, F., & Myles, R. (2004). *Second language learning theories* (2nd ed.). London: Arnold.

Negueruela, E. (2003). A sociocultural approach to teaching and researching second languages: Systemic-theoretical instruction and second language development. Unpublished doctoral dissertation, The Pennsylvania State University.

Negueruela, E. (2008). Revolutionary pedagogies: Learning that leads development in the second language classroom. In J. P. Lantolf & M. Poehner (Eds.), *Sociocultural theory and second language teaching* (pp. 189–227). London: Equinox.

O'Reilly, T. (2007). *What is Web 2.0?* Retrieved July 20, 2008, from http://www.oreillynet.com/ pub/a/oreilly/tim/news/2005/09/30/what-is-web-20.html

Pea, S. (1985). Beyond amplification: Using the computer to reorganize mental function. *Educational Psychologist, 20,* 167–182.

Salaberry, R. (2001). The use of technology for second language learning and teaching: A retrospective. *Modern Language Journal, 84,* 537–554.

Salomon, G. (1991). On the cognitive effects of technology. In L. T. Landsmann (Ed.). *Culture, schooling, and psychological development* (pp. 185–204). Norwood, NJ: Ablex.

Thorne, S. (2003). Artifacts and cultures-of-use in intercultural communication. *Language Learning & Technology, 7,* 38–67. Available from http://llt.msu.edu/vol7num2/thorne/

Thorne, S., & Black, R. W. (2007). Language and literacy development in computer-mediated contexts and communities. *Annual Review of Applied Linguistics, 27,* 133–160.

Thorne, S., & Payne, S. (2005). Evolutionary trajectories, Internet-mediated expression, and education. *CALICO Journal, 22,* 371–397.

Vygotsky, L. S. (1978). *Mind in society. The development of higher psychological processes.* Cambridge, MA: Harvard University Press.

Warschauer, M. (1999). *Electronic literacies: Language, culture, and power in online education.* Mahwah, NJ: Erlbaum.

Warschauer, M., & Grimes, D. (2007). Audience, authorship, and artifact: The emergent semiotics of Web 2.0. *Annual Review of Applied Linguistics, 27,* 1–23.

Wieber, R. W., & Robinson, D. K. (Eds.). (2004). *The essential Vygotsky.* Dordrecht: Kluwer Academic.

Witte, J. P. (2007). Why the tail wags the dog: The pernicious influence of product-oriented discourse on the provision of education technology support. *Annual Review of Applied Linguistics, 27,* 203–215.

Zhao, Y. (2003). Recent developments in technology and language learning: A literature review and meta-analysis. *CALICO Journal, 21,* 7–27.

Appendix

1. Websites hosting blogs and information about blogs

    Blog creation sites

        https://www.blogger.com/
        http://www.livejournal.com/
        http://www.xanga.com/
        http://www.diaryland.com/

    Blog search engines and blog tracking sites

        http://www.technorati.com/
        http://www.blogscope.net/
        http://www.blogherald.com/
        http://blogsearch.google.com/
        http://www.blogpulse.com/

2. Blogs in English and Spanish

    Blogs in English

        Blog by Italian political journalist Beppe Grillo
        http://beppegrillo.it/english.php

        Blog on sustainable gardening by Susan Harris
        http://www.sustainablegardeningblog.com/

        Blog on technology
        http://www.engadget.com/

    Blogs in Spanish

        Blog by Argentinean writer Carolina Aguirre
        http://bestiaria.blogspot.com/

        Blog by 95-year-old María Amelia López
        http://amis95.blogspot.com/

        Blog by Cuban writer Yoani Sánchez
        http://www.desdecuba.com/generaciony/

3. Directories of Spanish-language blogs

        http://www.blogs.es/
        http://www.directorio-blogs.com/
        http://www.elboomeran.com/blogs/

4. Spanish-language news media blogs

TVE/RTVE: Spanish public TV blog site
http://blogs.rtve.es/

BBC Blogs in Spanish
http://www.bbc.co.uk/blogs/spanish/

Telecinco: Spanish private TV station blog site
http://www.telecinco.es/blogs/

El País Spanish newspaper blog site
http://www.elpais.com/blogs/

As Spanish sports newspaper blogs
http://www.as.com/blogs/

PART V

Discussion forums

Linguistic and social dimensions
of French-language discussion forums

Géraldine Blattner and Lawrence Williams

This study explores selected linguistic and social dimensions of 20 French-language discussion forums in order to provide teachers and learners of French with an overview of this relatively new type of online communication space. Although the discussion forum is an older type of computer-mediated communication (i.e., compared, for example, to blogs and text messaging), little research has focused on linguistic patterns and tendencies in French-language forums, which seem to vary greatly, depending on any number of factors. As such, this chapter examines the use of second-person pronouns (*tu* and *vous*), the subject pronouns *nous* and *on*, the variable use of the negative particle *ne*, and orthographic variation using a corpus-driven approach. The analyses provided here can serve as models or templates for teachers and/or learners who wish to examine these same linguistic and social dimensions in other forums or compare this type of communication to traditional spoken and/or written discourse, either in or beyond the formal learning context of the classroom.

1.   Introduction

This chapter provides a corpus-driven analysis of selected linguistic and social dimensions of French-language discussion forums. The aim of this research is not to produce potentially generalizable results. Instead, we recognize the great diversity among French-language discussion forums and offer one possible approach for preparing learners to analyze the discourse of forums and to participate in them. Discussion forums have great potential for providing learners with opportunities to use French (or any other language) beyond the formal learning context of the classroom, where sociopragmatic features of communication are often treated superficially or ignored in the curriculum (see Bardovi-Harlig, 2001; Bardovi-Harlig, Hartford, Mahan-Taylor, Morgan, & Reynolds, 1991; Hassal, 2008; Vellenga, 2004). For many students, ideally, becoming an active participant in discussion forums might even lead to life-long participation in a variety of online communities. Thus, our overarching objective is to promote the use of discussion forums as a tool for both language learning and communication as students work progress toward the goals of the (U.S.) Standards for Foreign Language Learning in the 21st Century (Standards for Foreign Language Learning Project, 1999), and specifically the Communities goal (pp. 63–67):

> Standard 5.1: Students use the language both within and beyond the school setting.
>
> Standard 5.2: Students show evidence of becoming life-long learners by using the language for personal enjoyment and enrichment.

Although Standard 5.2 specifically mentions only "personal" enrichment, it also seems reasonable to suggest that life-long learners could also use the language for professional development since the "ability to communicate in other languages … enables [students] to expand their employment opportunities" (p. 63).

1.1   What is a discussion forum?

A discussion forum is actually quite similar to an offline, physical bulletin board where people can leave messages for each other in a central, fixed location. In fact, a predecessor of today's discussion forum was commonly referred to as a Bulletin Board System, or BBS, which eventually faded as e-mail and Newsgroups grew in popularity. Eventually, in the late 1990s, it became possible – and more practical – for messages (i.e., postings) to be housed and organized on a server with a website as the interface. This meant that a subscription was no longer necessary because people could consult a discussion forum's web site at their convenience.

Additional graphological and typographical features have ultimately turned discussion forums into virtual communication environments that can include not only plain text, but also still and animated images as well as video and objects produced with new authoring tools such as Flash®. For all intents and purposes, the forum is a web-based bulletin board with discussion threads organized by themes and/or topics. In most cases, users can reply to any posting, create a new posting, or even begin a new thread. However, some forums only allow operators or moderators to create new threads or topics. The result of so many variables is that no two forums are alike, just like no two offline, physical bulleting boards would ever be identical.

One of the most attractive features of the forum is convenience. People do not have to be connected to the Internet at the same time in order to read each other's messages; however, this means that the time between the posting of a message and a reply to it could take anywhere from 5 seconds to 5 months, or even 5 years. Nonetheless, as the technological affordances have increased and software has become much more user-friendly for creating, maintaining, and using forums with a webpage as an interface, it has become rather easy to evaluate the level of activity by merely consulting a few pieces of information, such as the date and time of the most recent posting and the number of replies to various threads (i.e., series of message with the same subject line). Such information can normally be found on a forum's main page.

1.2   Some comments on terminology

It has already been mentioned above that the discussion forum and the BBS are very similar. In fact, some people still call a forum a BBS because they see it as serving the same purpose, yet being slightly different. Then there are others who like the notion of *board*, from *bulletin board*, so they prefer to use the term *discussion board* to refer to a forum. The fact that Newsgroups – like forums – are organized by topic or theme also lends to the confusion. Even scholarly publications can contain terms that are misleading since there are often many variations of different types of new technologies. Given the ambiguity and confusion surrounding the discussion forum, a basic description might be useful:

> Messages appear on the discussion page immediately after being sent, but they are reviewed and may be removed if they are deemed inappropriate. Messages are posted in order according to the time received, unless they are replies to earlier messages. Replies are positioned with the message to which they relate. The replies are indented and the replies to replies are indented further. For each message there is a header with a subject line by the writer that indicates what the message is about. The date is also given along with the writer's ID, which for most messages is 'anonymous'. Messages range in length from a few lines to a few paragraphs.
> (Morrow, 2006, p. 535)

Although all forums will not have exactly the same features, Morrow's description of the format provides a clear idea of the type of asynchronous communication we refer to in this chapter as the discussion forum. In an effort to reduce the possibility for confusion regarding the terminology related to discussion forums or other types of new technologies, Appendix B provides a list of resources for exploring English and French terminology for new technologies.

1.3   Organization of the chapter

Each main section of this chapter that explores a feature of the structure or discourse of discussion forums is divided into two parts: data analysis and pedagogical applications. Such a format seems appropriate since the features selected for analysis are quite diverse: rules; message/thread structure; the pronouns *tu*, *vous*, *on*, and *nous*; and the variable use of *ne* in verbal negation. Although each feature was chosen specifically for its potential in raising students' awareness of the structure(s) and discourse(s) of discussion forums, there is no single task or pedagogical application that would naturally seem obvious for incorporating all these features.

2.   Discussion forum rules

As is the case with any mode of communication, any genre of text, or any communicative environment, it is nearly impossible to establish a list of features that are always present, always absent, or always stable. Therefore, this section of the chapter provides an overview of the rules that seem to govern actions, behavior(s), and practices in the wide range of forums whose rules were selected for this analysis. Although our corpus of 20 forums is not exhaustive, there are clear indications that it is indeed representative of forums in general. Tables 1 and 2 summarize some of the main features mentioned in each *charte* of our sample of twenty different forums, ten of which are general (i.e., there are multiple categories organized by topics or themes) in nature (Table 1), and ten that have a specific theme or topic (e.g., cooking, wine, the Pyrenees mountain range, and so forth) (Table 2). Each column represents a different forum, and the numbering is the same as the list of forums provided in the Appendix A. It is not important to know the name of each forum here since the main purpose of having the tables is to demonstrate which features or rules are mentioned least and most often. An X indicates the presence of a feature or rule, and readers interested in exploring these forums can find a list of their URLs in Appendix A.

As mentioned above, this table illustrates a certain lack of homogeneity in the rules and regulations that users are supposed to respect. As Hanna & de Nooy (2003) point out, forum participants must be aware of the forum's conventions before being able to participate fully and actively in this type of web-based written communication. Forum users should be aware of and follow the rules that this particular electronic genre requires, and since the rules are important, a few comments are in order regarding the words or phrases used on web sites that allow visitors to identify the rules and consult them.

Table 1. Summary of each *charte* from a sample of multitopic forums

	1	2	3	4	5	6	7	8	9	10
Moderated	X	X	X	X	X	X		X	X	X
Unapproved ads deleted	X	X	X	X	X	X	X		X	
"bon français" "français correct"	X		X		X	X			X	
Punctuation encouraged				X						
Avoid SMS style		X				X				
Politeness encouraged		X	X	X	X	X	X		X	
Offensive remarks deleted	X	X	X	X	X	X	X	X	X	X
Exclusion if rules are not respected	X	X	X		X	X	X			X

First, the terms used to refer to these rules and regulations vary quite a bit. The most common word used in French seems to be *charte*. The terms *avertissement* or *règles* are also common, as are the expressions *netiquette* or *netetiquette*, which are technology-related neologisms likely to provide rules about the language of such web-based discourses that will typically be censored. Second, the information listed under these various names diverges greatly in terms of length and details. Wanner (2008) explains that this heterogeneity is not surprising since discussion forums do not all have moderators. As such, there exists a great deal of variability in the way forums are managed and shaped. For instance, the forum of Radio-Canada specifies that participants should not use any language other than French in their postings, which is an important element to put forward considering the potentially bilingual audience of this website. Multitopic forums such as *lelounge.ca* or *tsr.ch* only provide basic instructions to their members that focus on language use, whereas CommentCaMarche.net has a 45-page detailed presentation of not only the type of communication strategies and behavior(s) to adopt in the discussion threads, but also of many technical aspects regarding the font, posting hyperlinks, the hierarchical organization of messages, and so forth.

The majority – eight out of ten – of the multitopic forums used for this analysis summarize their rules and regulations on an average of two pages or less. The emphasis is directed toward the language that is authorized and in all the *chartes,* specific advice and examples are given regarding the linguistic elements that can not be utilized by the forum users, highlighting the fact that forum interactions are public. The typical forum *charte* states that foul language, racist comments, and aggressive behavior should be avoided and that the users must understand their responsibility in terms of the content of their postings. Many forums – seven of the ten listed in Table 1 – threaten or promise to exclude participants from accessing a specific discussion thread if they do not respect the language-related rules stated on their websites. This is an especially noticeable feature of radio, newspaper, or television websites.

Certain sites (e.g., Affection.org) offer additional pieces of advice to instruct novice users on developing their literacy in an electronic environment, by explaining, for instance, that the use of capital letters usually indicates screaming and/or anger. Moreover, on the *charte* of this particular site, users are advised not to correct other participants' grammatical or orthographic mistakes as it is not a constructive way to extend a discussion, and, in fact, it might abruptly end a thread. Another important convention involves the avoidance of an abundant use of acronyms and other non-traditional truncated forms (e.g., the style of messages sent from mobile phones), unless they are well known and can be recognized and understood by a large audience. Of course such advice is rather vague, so moderation or avoidance would be the best strategy.

There is no age restriction for participation in a discussion forum, which implies that younger users who grew up using technological tools may be familiar with a variety of abbreviations that older generations do not master, because they are *digital immigrants* (Prensky, 2001), who began using networked computers in adulthood. As Wanner (2008) observes, abbreviations are not usual on Internet discussion forums as they typically call for less oral forms of communication in comparison to chatrooms. Asynchronous written exchanges have a tendency to be more formal as these messages are visible to numerous members of online communities. However, Wanner (2008) also notes that some discussion forums are less formal than others, and in those that are less formal, threads resemble more closely oral discourse as participants strive to reach "comfort zones of orality" (p. 125) that often involve the use of graphics and html code.

The topic-specific forums (Table 2) also appear to present great diversity on the page where the specific rules and regulations of each site are listed. The terminology selected by the various webmasters varies greatly, from *charte* to *condition d'utilisation, Avis aux utilisateurs,* or 'frequently asked questions'. All of the specialized forums introduce the regulations that users have to follow in a concise manner. The essential and most important guidelines on language use are comparable to the ones describes above. In other words, participants have to express themselves in a proper way, promoting politeness and the respect

Table 2. Summary of each *charte* in a sample of topic-specific forums

	1	2	3	4	5	6	7	8	9	10
Moderated					X	X	X			
Unapproved ads deleted	X	X			X		X	X	X	X
"un bon usage" "un français correct"	X		X				X	X		X
Punctuation encouraged					X					
Avoid SMS style	X		X		X		X	X		X
Politeness encouraged	X	X	X		X	X	X	X		X
Offensive remarks deleted	X	X	X	X	X	X	X	X	X	X
Exclusion if rules are not respected	X	X	X				X			X

of others. However, topic-specific forums appear usually more flexible in their rules as only three of the forums listed above have a moderator. In addition, five of them specify that not respecting the regulations will results in the exclusion of a user from a specific website.

Depending on the theme of the various forums, other criteria are put forward in the *charte*. The site *doctissimo.com* presents additional legal advisory details as it is a site focusing on health issues. It uses the welcoming page to explain to the future users that the information obtained from the discussion boards should be taken with precaution as often they are incomplete and that the participants should always seek professional medical advice before starting a new treatment that was discussed in the forum. On the site *la passion du vin*, the seven creators of this discussion forum specify that they have no connections to or agreements with any wine producer and that they are simply expressing their opinion on the taste of various products.

2.1   Discussion forum rules: Pedagogical applications

The first task we recommend for students is a closer analysis of Tables 1 and 2, which indicate the frequency of each rule in our sample of *chartes* from both multitopic and topic-specific forums. If students are able to determine which rules are made explicit most often, they will have a better understanding of the relative importance of each rule. The questions provided below offer a starting point for a task that could be designed for a variety of participation structures (whole-class or small-group discussion; individual or small-group written or oral presentation; etc.).

1. Which rules are most frequently stated in this sample of *chartes*?
2. If certain rules are more frequently stated than others, does this necessarily mean that breaking a more frequently stated rule will cause more conflict or confusion in a forum?
3. The rules about "un bon usage" or "un français correct" refer to a linguistic dimension of communication in forums. Which other rules are part of this dimension.
4. Which of the remaining rules could be grouped together as part of the social dimension, and which one(s), if any, could be considered part of a different dimension?
5. Moderation might not seem like a rule, but it has been included since there is a direct link between moderation and the overarching rules, behaviors, and practices of discussion forum participants. What is the moderator's role? What are his/her responsibilities?

The second task we recommend for students is a comparison of the Tables 1 and 2 and rules that the teacher or the students themselves are able to find for English-language forums. Of course, this task could involve finding rules for forums in any language, depending on the cultural-linguistic composition of the students or the curriculum. The rules for bilingual and multilingual forums would certainly broaden the scope of this exploration (see Androutsopoulos, 2007; Climent, Moré, Oliver, Salvatierra, Sànchez, & Taulé, 2007; Su, 2007; Wodak & Wright, 2007).

It is important to encourage students to explore forum rules since not understanding or respecting them can have real-world social consequences, and Hanna and de Nooy (2003) consider it essential for learners to understand forums, as a genre, before becoming active participants in them. In addition, discussion forums can encourage new modes of expressing and interpreting meaning in multiple contexts and media, which are types of competence and performance that today's students need to cultivate (Gonglewski & DuBravac, 2006). In fact, by promoting the development of electronic literacy, language educators also provide learners with opportunities to take advantage of emerging technologies, which can lead to autonomous interaction with native speakers or other speakers/users of the language outside an academic context. As Gonglewski and DuBravac (2006) point out, one goal of foreign language education is to prepare students to participate more actively in global learning communities and use a foreign language in new ways in a "technology-saturated world" (p. 46).

3.   Structural organization of communication in discussion forums

3.1   Analysis of typical thread structure

Although no two forums are alike in every way, there are some patterns that emerge when a large enough corpus is analyzed. In the case of discussion forums, it appears that most of them have been created not as a means for simply disseminating information through a worldwide network, but really as a central location for people with similar interests to exchange ideas and, in most cases, to give advice. This seems especially true of forums related to physical and mental health, relationships, careers, and computers. However, advice-giving is certainly also very prominent in forums centered around games and sports, cinema, automobiles, motorcycles, and travel, even if such forums provide environments that also foster a relatively large amount of opinion-giving and self-promotion (i.e., bragging). Regardless of the type of forum, there is always bound to be some type of advice-giving. As such, Morrow's (2006) analysis of thread structure in an advice-giving forum will be used to demonstrate this feature of forums that students will most likely encounter in any forum they might happen to visit.

According to Morrow (2006), "discussion forum messages can be characterized as being of three general kinds: problem messages, advice messages, and thanks messages" (p. 536), and these different types of messages often occur in the order listed by Morrow: "A problem message initiates the discussion and is usually followed by one or more advice messages" (p. 536). Typically, the person who posted the initial message will thank either one or more specific participants who have provided especially valuable advice or information; however, there are certainly cases when no form of thanks is offered. "Thus, the interaction may consist of many messages, or it may, on the other hand, consist of a problem message and a single advice message. Occasionally there are problem messages that receive no replies" (Morrow, p. 536). Unfortunately, it is impossible to know why there is no up-take (e.g., a reply to the posing of a problem; an answer to a question; or the solution to a dilemma) since such inaction could be explained by disinterest, lack of time, low level of activity in one or more areas of the forum, or any number of other reasons.

3.2   Discussion forum structure: Pedagogical applications

The first task we recommend for students is the analysis of an entire thread in order to test Morrow's (2006) analysis of typical thread structure. Excerpt 3-1[1] was chosen

---

1.   The excerpts analyzed in this chapter are presented as close to the original as possible. They have not been modified, and *sic* has not been used to indicate non-traditional forms, structures, or punctuation.

at random from a corpus of approximately 80,000 words (±700 postings) from four different forums: France 2, the site of a French public television company; Maison facile, a home decorating and repair site; voila.fr, a site based in France with a multitopic forum; and 24heures.ch, a site based in Switzerland with a multitopic forum. As a reminder, analyzing an entire thread means that this will include a series of messages that are linked – in most cases – by having the same topic indicated in the subject line.

The following list of questions could be used to draw students' attention to specific features of the organizational structure of this thread:

1. The discussion thread reproduced below (Excerpt 1) has two participants: MB and NC. How does MB construct the initial posting – without using question marks – so that it is obvious to other participants that advice and information are being solicited and that they would be greatly appreciated?
2. How could the initial posting of this thread be divided into different sections according to the communicative function, intent, or purpose of each part of the message? For example, the last few words of the initial posting include a leave-taking device: "et à Bientôt…". This would be its own section since this is the only part of the message used for indicating that this part of the "conversation" has ended.
3. How well does this three-part discussion thread follow the model proposed by Morrow (2006)? Is there a problem stated, followed by advice (or information or tips), then an expression of thanks?
4. Compare the length of MB's messages and NC's message. Who provides more information? Do they both provide enough information to communicate successfully, in your opinion?
5. How do these two participants use punctuation? Can you find both similarities and differences?
6. How might NC's message be different if this were a face-to-face conversation, an e-mail, or some other type of communication?
7. Now choose a random thread from any French-language forum of your choice. Does that thread also fit in Morrow's model? How well does it fit compared to one or more threads chosen by other students?

Excerpt 1. Discussion thread about decorating bedrooms

Message 1, Excerpt 1.

MB
17/12/2007 21:15:30
[Subject:] Où il y a une Volonté, il y a un Chemin

[Red font used for this posting.]

Je dois entreprendre en début d'Année des travaux de rénovation, si je n'ai pas de mal à trouver des idées Déco pour la cuisine ... le salon/salle à manger et le hall d'entrée ... je cale par contre pour ce qui est des chambres et suis vraiment à court d'inspirations! Je souhaiterais trouver sur le net des sites qui proposent des galeries Photos de manière à me faire une idée précise du résultat obtenus en fonction de diverses tendances – Merci par avance pour vos réponses et à Bientôt ...

Translation of the main text of Message 1
At the beginning of the year I have to begin remodeling. Even though I'm not having any trouble finding decorating ideas for the kitchen, the living room/dining room, and the entryway, I am, however, having trouble with the bedrooms and am really lacking inspiration. I would like to find websites with photo galleries in order to have a real idea of actual results with various themes. Thank you in advance for your replies and see you soon ...

Message 2, Excerpt 1.

NC
19/03/2008 09:16:10
[Subject:] [Nothing appears in «subject» line.]

bonjour..adresses bien utiles.
http://www.cyberbricoleur.com/ ...

http://decobruz.over-blog.com/

Translation of the main text of Message 2
hello..very useful addresses

http://www.cyberbricoleur.com/ ...

http://decobruz.over-blog.com/

Message 3, Excerpt 1.

MB
19/03/2008 10:12:10
[Subject:] Où il y a une Volonté, il y a un Chemin

Franchement Merci NC...je ne connaissais aucun de ces 2 sites et suis très agréablement surpris par la quantité d'idées que l'on peut y trouver – En plus ce message tombe à pic...mes travaux de rénovation commence au mois de Mai...c'est pas de la bonne synchronisation ça ?!

Translation of the main text of Message 3
Really, Thank You NC...I didn't know either of these 2 sites and am very pleasantly surprised by the quantity of ideas that one can find there – Also your message showed up at just the right time...my remodeling work begins in May...that's great timing, isn't it?!

4.   The French pronoun paradigm in discussion forums

Although textbooks and grammar guides often present the French pronoun paradigm as a stable collection of objects that can be memorized, there is a great deal of instability and variation in the paradigm. Fonseca-Greber and Waugh (2003), for example, state rather bluntly that «the standard spoken French taught, for example, in American classrooms is a fiction, based on ideas about how people (should) speak, not on how they actually speak» (p. 226). Their corpus-driven approach demonstrates – using the pronoun paradigm to argue their case – the «wide gulf between spoken and written French, a gulf so wide that some (e.g., Lodge 1993) have begun to talk about possible diglossia in French society – and if not today, then soon» (p. 226).

4.1   Analysis of selected pronouns

The French second-person pronouns *tu* (T) and *vous* (V) present difficulties to learners for a variety of reasons (see Belz & Kinginger, 2002; Kinginger, 2000; Kinginger & Belz, 2005; Liddicoat, 2006), one of which is the number of second-person pronouns in the L1 compared to the number in the L2. However, even if the L1 of a learner of French happens to have the same number of second-person pronouns that are also used in similar ways (e.g., formal vs. informal; singular vs. plural; close vs. distant), their use across languages cannot be memorized as a set of rules and exceptions since the use of these pronouns is determined culturally and socio-situationally. Another difficulty faced by learners of French is the dual role of V, which can be singular or plural. In addition to these – and other – complexities of the French second-person pronouns, they can also be used for either definite or indefinite reference (see Ashby, 1992; Blondeau, 2001; Coveney, 2003; Fonseca-Greber & Waugh, 2003; Jisa & Viguié, 2005; Laberge & Sankoff, 1980; Williams & van Compernolle, 2009). When the second-person pronouns are used with indefinite reference, they can alternate with *on*, which, in turn, can mean either *one* (subject pronoun with indefinite reference) or *we* (subject pronoun with definite reference) in English. Therefore, at some level, these four pronouns are all linked, and they are anything but stable and monolithic. This brief overview cannot capture all the subtleties or types of variation between and among these pronouns. However, students can begin exploring instability and variation in the pronoun paradigm first by understanding that variation exists and then by examining a (small or large) corpus in order to identify, for example, instances of V-singular vs. V-plural; T/V-indefinite vs. T/V-definite; *on*-definite vs. *nous*; and so forth.

Table 3. T and V-singular use

	T	V-singular	Total
24heures.ch	17 (4.8%)	338 (95.2%)	355
voila.fr	107 (74.8%)	36 (25.2%	143
MF	50 (36.8%)	86 (63.2%	136
France 2	31 (17.9%)	142 (82.1%	173
TOTAL	205 (25.4%)	602 (74.6%)	807

Table 4. *Nous* ('we') and *on* ('we') use

	NOUS	ON	Total
24heures.ch	53 (23.1%)	176 (76.9%)	229
voila.fr	17 (14.9%)	97 (85.1%)	114
MF	28 (31.5%)	61 (68.5%)	89
France 2	56 (32.0%)	119 (68.0%)	175
TOTAL	154 (25.4%)	453 (74.6%)	607

4.2 The French pronoun paradigm: Pedagogical applications

The list of questions provided below can guide students as they explore the variety of meanings and references expressed by T, V, *on*, and *nous*. It is always advisable to model the process for students, especially if the variation they will be trying to find is not presented in their textbook or discussed in the classroom.

1. According to the data presented in Table 3, are there any clear (or unclear) patterns of second-person pronoun use in these French-language forums?
2. The data in Table 3 only show whether T or V was used. There is nothing to indicate if these pronouns were used with definite or indefinite reference. What is the difference between definite and indefinite reference? How is the English pronoun *you* used with either definite or indefinite reference?
3. The data in Table 3 do not provide any information about the social identities of these people or their social relationships with or among each other, but this could be very useful information in determining more detailed patterns of second-person pronoun variation. Using data that you collect on your own (or data collected by your instructor), examine one or more discussion threads in order to identify all the postings by a single participant. How does this participant address people he/she obviously already knows or does not know? Does this participant use the same address pronoun with everyone, or does he/she switch?

4. In a study of T and V use in selected French-language public chat rooms (Williams & van Compernolle, 2007), the authors report a rate of T use very close to 100%. How different is this finding from the results presented in Table 3? How might this difference be explained?
5. In Table 4, are there any clear patterns of *nous* and *on* use?
6. If both of these pronouns can mean the same thing, why would one be used instead of the other? Are there any cases like this in English (or another language), where two different words can essentially convey the same meaning?
7. In Table 4, there is nothing to indicate who used which pronoun(s). Using data that you have collected on your own (or data collected by your instructor), examine one or more entire threads and identify all the postings from a single participant. Did this participant use only *on*, only *nous*, or both as an equivalent of the English subject pronoun *we*?
8. How many different grammatical functions can *nous* have in French? (For example, can *nous* be used as a subject, an object of a preposition, an indirect object, and so forth?)
9. How many different grammatical functions can *on* have in French? How is this similar to or different from the case of *nous*?

Although all these questions can be used at the same time, it might be better to divide them into groups of questions so that tasks on variation could be incorporated into the syllabus at times when the textbook or other course materials do not present various pronouns as having variable uses. Students who do not initially understand how to undertake an analysis of variation could be guided through several examples of the substitution test, whereby several tokens of the same pronoun are found in a corpus, and students have to substitute, for example, *nous* for *on*, in order to see if the meaning would change or if it would essentially stay the same. This is one efficient way to demonstrate analysis of variation at its basic level.

5.   Orthographic variation in discussion forums

In spite of the growing amount of research on orthographic variation in French-language computer-mediated communication, most analyses have focused on this phenomenon in synchronous chat (e.g., Anis, 1999; Pierozak, 2003) or mobile phone text messages (e.g., Anis, 2001, 2007; Moise, 2007). Forums may have been ignored because, unlike chat, they are not synchronous, or they may seem less interesting since, unlike mobile phone text messages, there are no tight constraints on the number of characters that can be typed in a single posting. Whatever the reason may be for slighting the study of orthographic variation in forums, there is actually a case

to be made for increasing this area of inquiry since "non-standard" orthography –
especially in French forums – can have serious consequences affecting online communities and relationships in very negative ways. For many cybernauts who own
or participate regularly in French-language forums, traditional spelling seems to be
practically sacred. One reason for this strong affinity with "good" spelling might be
the increased online presence of an organization called the Comité de lutte contre
le language SMS et les fautes volontaires sur Internet[2] (Comité). This group and its
stated mission are explained in the next section, and we then propose a pedagogical
application that will allow students to explore the website of the Comité.

5.1   The fight against orthographic variation on the Internet

As observed in the *chartes* and the various rules discussed above, conventions vary
from site to site. However, an important and widespread stipulation for this genre
of web-based communication is to maintain appropriate spelling and to avoid the
use of obscure acronyms and abbreviations that are often used in text messaging.
It is therefore not surprising that internet-based movements have been formed in
order to reinforce this message. As mentioned above, one of the most visible and
perhaps most influential guardians of standard spelling and language use in cyberspace is the Comité. This group was formed as a grassroots, or e-roots, organization
in 2004, and by late 2008 it had grown to almost 17,000 members, all of whom have
made a commitment to battle orthographic variation. The 17-year-old-founder of
this group originally called it the *Comité anti-SMS*[3] (Anti-SMS Committee), but
during 2006, the Comité changed its name to its current form in order to convey a
less combative image and to clarify the fact that the members only reject the use of
SMS in cyberspace since, for them, such variation is not appropriate.

5.2   Orthographic variation in discussion forums: Pedagogical applications

The concept of not using abbreviations, acronyms/initialisms, and non-traditional spelling is frequently stated in the guidelines of many forums. Consequently,
the use of traditional written French appears to be respected by the majority of
participants, according to a recent study comparing orthographic variation across
three types of French-language CMC: non-moderated chat, moderated chat,
and discussion forums (van Compernolle & Williams, 2007). The results of the

---

2.   2. http://sms.informatiquefrance.com/

3.   The initialism *SMS* stands for *Short-Message Service*, a synonym for *text message*, which is sent
from a mobile phone. In French, a text message is normally referred to as either *un texto* or *un SMS*.

analysis, which focused on a selected French phrases such as *il faut* (it is necessary), *c'est* (that/it is), *il y a* (there is/are), and other forms, showed that standard, traditional spellings are favored in asynchronous discussions (and also in moderated chat). They hypothesize that this trend is linked to the type of interaction and the permanent, archived nature of forums. Contrary to chat rooms, for example, in which immediate replies are *de rigueur*, responses to messages on forums can appear within a few hours or a few days, allowing the contributor sufficient time to create a well-crafted, complete, and coherent message.

In order for students to gain a better understanding of the perspective of those who are against orthographic variation, we recommend a pedagogical application centered around an exploration of the website of the *Comité*. The list of questions provided below will create not only opportunities for students to reflect on orthographic variation in French, but also a way for them to think about their own attitudes toward notions such as *standard, correct,* and *good*. The goal of this task should not be to reinforce a dichotomy of prescriptivism vs. descriptivism. Instead, students should learn how to recognize variation and understand how and when variants are used or not used in order to gain what Hall, Cheng, and Carlson (2006) would call *multiexpertise*. "This view sees language knowledge as provisional, grounded in and emergent from language use in concrete social activity for specific purposes that are tied to specific communities of practice" (p. 235).

1. Go to the site of the Comité *de lutte contre le language SMS et les fautes volontaires sur Internet*, which can be found at the following URL: http://www.

sms.informatiquefrance.com/

2. Find the image on the welcome page. What does this represent? How does this image relate to the name of the organization?
3. Read the text in the box on the middle of the welcome page. What explanation is giving regarding the new name of the site/organization? (This was originally founded as the Comité anti-SMS.)
4. Do you think the organization made a wise choice in changing its name?
5. If you were asked to develop a new name (in English and/or French) for this organization (without using too many elements of the original or current names), what would it be? Which words or phrases would you be sure to include? Which ones would you avoid?
6. What product or service is made available to the public in the Galerie? What purpose does this serve?
7. Now navigate to the Définition page of the website, where you will find an explanation of each part of the name of the organization: comité; de lutte contre; le langage SMS; les fautes volontaires; sur Internet. The final part of the name

of the group was added recently, according to the explanation on this page. Why might this part have been added?

8. Why has this organization chosen to "take on" the entire Internet with their fight against non-traditional spellings? Are all types of online communication the same?

9. For which types of online communication should people observe traditional rules of spelling, grammar, and/or punctuation? For which types should people feel free to use non-traditional forms?

10. Which types of variation in online communication might exist in both English and French?

6.   The variable use of *ne* in discussion forums

As one of the most salient indicators of sociolinguistic variation in French (see Coveney, 1996; Hansen & Malderez, 2004), the negative particle *ne* is often a natural point of departure for any study of shifts between informal and formal discourse. This is, of course, not an absolute way of labeling a sentence or an utterance as simply formal (*ne* + [verb] + [second negative particle]) or informal (Ø + [verb] + [second negative particle]). Instead, registers or levels of formality can be determined by a range of linguistic, paralinguistic, or contextual features during any given communicative event. The primary objective of our analysis and pedagogical application is to expose students to the absence or presence of *ne* in verbal negation since textbooks often do not include information or tasks related to sociolinguistic variation and pragmatic features of discourse (see Bardovi-Harlig, 2001; Hassal, 2008; Vellenga, 2004). Our survey of nearly 25 introductory and intermediate French "programs" (i.e., textbooks, workbooks, and ancillaries) published in the U.S. has revealed that even when the variable use of *ne* is mentioned, reference to it is often relegated to a margin. Nonetheless, there are instances of adequate coverage of this important type of variation, especially in programs that supply authentic discourse in audio or video form.

6.1   Analysis of verbal negation

Table 6 provides a summary of all tokens of verbal negation having either *ne …* *pas* or Ø … pas. The first column in the table indicates the data source, and the second column shows the total number of verbal negations with *ne* present and *ne* absent. The third column displays the number of tokens with *ne* present, and the final column indicates the percentage of tokens with *ne* present. Although every topic except one (Musique in the voila.fr forum) has rates of use of the more formal structure (i.e., with *ne* present) that are greater than 70 percent, there is still a fair amount of variation within each forum and among these forums.

Table 6. Tokens of *pas* in verbal negation

Source	Total *pas*	*ne...pas*	% *ne...pas*
24h/climat	13	12	92.3%
24h/école	95	92	96.8%
24h/parti socialiste	19	18	94.7%
24h/équipe suisse	12	9	75.0%
24h/Kosovo	65	57	87.7%
24h/TV germanophone	25	23	92.0%
24h/capitalisme	122	99	81.1%
24h/Palestine	80	71	88.8%
24h Total	**431**	**381**	**88.4%**
FR2/une affaire criminelle	20	19	95.0%
FR2/métier caissière	28	26	92.9%
FR2/fumer lieux publics	41	37	90.2%
FR2/grande distribution	51	47	92.2%
FR2/infirmiers à domicile	51	49	96.1%
FR2/religions	35	31	88.6%
FR2/RMI	15	15	100.0%
FR2/zyprexa	18	15	83.3%
France 2 Total	**259**	**239**	**92.3%**
VF/animal	25	24	96.0%
VF/sport	16	15	93.8%
VF/informatique	8	7	87.5%
VF/musique	32	17	53.1%
VF/routière	35	30	85.7%
VF/CNIL	18	14	77.8%
VF/bricolage	12	11	91.7%
VF/TVet Vous	18	16	88.9%
voila.fr Total	**164**	**134**	**81.7%**
MF/bébé	36	30	83.3%
MF/fleurs	16	15	93.8%
MF/logement	19	18	94.7%
MF/maison	6	6	100.0%
MF/santé	11	8	72.7%
MF/multimédia	39	29	74.4%
MF/voisinage	51	38	74.5%
MF/intérieur	5	4	80.0%
Maison facile Total	**183**	**149**	**81.4%**
GRAND TOTAL	**1,037**	**903**	**87.1%**

6.2   Verbal negation: Pedagogical applications

If students can find no mention of the variable use of *ne* in their textbook, some initial in-class guidance (or perhaps a worksheet or an online tutorial) will be necessary in order to introduce the concept that *ne* is not always used. Students may indeed be surprised by how infrequently *ne* is used in certain communicative environments (see Fonseca-Greber, 2007; Sankoff & Vincent, 1980; van Compernolle, 2008) if they explore this type of variation beyond this task. Once the students understand that negation exists and how to find data, they should be able to expand their investigation to other types of computer-mediated communication or a range of communicative events where spoken discourse is used (e.g., press conference, news broadcast, scenes in films portraying a variety of contexts, etc.). The list of questions provided below can serve as a starting point for an analysis of the variable use of *ne* that will take students slightly beyond the overview presented in Table 6.

1.   Are there any general patterns that emerge from the final column in Table 6? What does this overview of verbal negation indicate about this sample of discussion forum discourse?
2.   Which of the forums has the greatest range for the use of *ne … pas*?
3.   Choose a group of topics within a single forum on Table 6. Is there any noticeable pattern of the rates of *ne* use? More specifically, is it possible to predict which topics will have higher or lower rates of *ne* based only on the topic when you look at rates of *ne* use in the topics of the other forums?
4.   The results of the overview of *ne* use in Table 6 only indicate very general tendencies. It is impossible to know if one or more participants may have skewed the sample by using *ne* at a disproportionately higher rate than the other people. Using data that you collect on your own (or data collected by your instructor), examine one or more discussion threads in order to identify all the postings by a single participant. Does this person always use *ne*? Does he/she never use *ne*? Does his/her use of *ne* vary?
5.   In the sample of data that you have gathered from a single participant's contributions to the forum, identify the instances – if any – of verbal negation when *ne* has not been used, yet *pas* has been used. Is the subject of the clause/sentence a pronoun or a noun? Is the verb a relatively frequent verb (e.g., a form of *être* or *avoir*)?

Depending on the data that students collect for this task, they may have some difficulty finding a large number of tokens with *ne* absent and *pas* present. However, the analysis of the variable use of *ne* can actually be more straightforward in such cases since the few tokens without *ne* can often be quickly categorized or analyzed according to the following tendencies: (1) *ne* is dropped more often when a pronoun, rather than a noun, is the subject of the clause; (2) likewise, *ne* is often omitted in structures with frequently used verbs (e.g., il faut pas, j'ai pas, je veux pas, ils sont pas, elle est pas, c'est pas, etc.). These are only two of the many factors that affect the variable use of *ne*; however, these factors should be able to explain most of the data that students find.

7.   Conclusion

In order to do the tasks described in the previous sections, students will have to explore one or more forums, unless they are provided with archived discussion forum postings. Since many students will already be familiar with forums in English (or whatever their L1 might be), they should not need too much guidance navigating a website once they have found a forum to explore. It is rather important to use quotation marks in any search engine when using keywords such as *discussion* or *forum* since these two words exist in both for English and French. If students use "forum de discussion" in any major search engine (e.g., Google, Yahoo!), they should have no trouble finding several multitopic forums. In order to find a topic-specific forum, it is almost necessary – and certainly more efficient – to use both "forum de discussion" followed by a common noun (e.g., auto, voyage, informatique, pétanque, etc.) outside the parentheses.

An analysis of the sheer quantity or volume of postings and the timeframe (e.g., very recent, somewhat recent, or distant past) of activity on the forum can provide learners (as potential visitors and/or participants) with valuable information. Quantity and volume are two separate parts of this analysis because forums can have a high number of postings, yet very little text to analyze/read due to low volume in most or all postings. Likewise, an enormous volume of text could be provided in relatively few messages. Moreover, for some types of analysis, it is important to note whether the same or different participants are responsible for all or almost all of the postings, as mentioned in some of the tasks in previous sections of this chapter.

Although students might be tempted to select only high volume sites during their search for French-language discussion forums to explore and analyze, it could be helpful to ask them to use their background knowledge about discussion forums as a genre in order to reflect on the advantages and disadvantages associated with low or high volume and frequent or infrequent activity. For example, the tennis area of the forum Fans de sports[4] has a very low number of main topics

---

4.   http://www.fansdesports.com/discussion/tennis/

(men's tennis and women's tennis), and there are fewer than 5 discussion threads for each of these topics, with a total of fewer than 100 messages in the entire forum. The most recent posting within the *tennis masculin* topics was about Wimbledon 2008 (held every year from the end of June to the beginning of July), and during the past four months there has been no activity. Likewise, the most recent posting in the *tennis féminin* topics was about the Rogers Cup (2008) in Canada (held every year in August), and during the past several months there have been no additional messages. A closer look at the details of each posting reveals that the same five people have posted all the messages on this forum, according to the screen names displayed above the text of each posting.

At first, this might not seem like a forum worth exploring, and it might not be if the only goal were to collect a large corpus and attempt to generalize patterns of interaction, language variation, or the use of punctuation, among other features. However, for the L2 learner, this type of small forum might provide some excellent opportunities for developing relationships with the few people who do participate in this French-language forum. A perusal of the forum's main page with a list of all the sports included in the site indicates that the quantity of postings for all sports have equally sporadic patterns of participation, and there seems to be a small group of somewhat dedicated fans who form the core of each sport's area in the forum. Therefore, students interested in one or more particular sports – or sports in general – might find this site more appealing since they would have a greater chance of one-to-one or one-to-few communication. Conversely, students with little motivation or time to invest in regular and frequent participation may find the relative anonymity of larger and more active forums to be more appealing.

This chapter has focused on linguistic, social, and structural dimensions of forums using a corpus-driven approach in order to provide teachers and students with a model for analyzing any forum, regardless of its topic or theme. If students are given opportunities to engage in the types of analysis outlined in previous sections, they may feel less intimidated once they begin participating in a forum. Likewise, if students gain a better understand of linguistic, social, and structural dimensions of forums, the *foreign* aspect of French-language forums, for example, may fade to the background so that *communication* can become more prominent. Ideally, from our perspective, students would learn various approaches for analyzing the discourse of forums as part of the curriculum in a formal learning context. Then, at any point, they would begin to explore forums beyond the classroom in order to participate in online communities that are of particular interest to them, for either personal or professional reasons.

References

Androutsopoulos, J. (2007). Language choice and code switching in German-based diasporic web forums. In B. Danet & S. Herring (Eds.), *The multilingual Internet: Language, culture, and communication online* (pp. 340–361). Oxford: Oxford University Press.

Anis, J. (1999). Chats et usages graphique. In J. Anis (Ed.), *Internet, communication et langue française* (pp. 71–90). Paris: Hermès Science.

Anis, J. (2001). *Parlez-vous texto?* Guide des nouveaux langages du réseau. Paris: le Cherche Midi.

Anis, J. (2007). Neography: Unconventional spelling in French SMS text messages. In B. Danet & S. Herring (Eds.), *The multilingual Internet: Language, culture, and communication online* (pp. 87–115). Oxford: Oxford University Press.

Ashby, W. (1992). The variable use of *on* versus *tu/vous* for indefinite reference in spoken French. *Journal of French Language Studies, 2,* 135–157.

Bardovi-Harlig, K. (2001). Empirical evidence of the need for instruction in pragmatics. In K. R. Rose & G. Kasper (Eds.), *Pragmatics and language teaching* (pp. 13–22). Cambridge: Cambridge University Press.

Bardovi-Harlig, K., Hartford, B. A. S., Mahan-Taylor, R., Morgan, M. J., & Reynolds, D. W. (1991). Developing pragmatic awareness: Closing the conversation. *ELT Journal, 45,* 4–15.

Belz, J., & Kinginger, C. (2002). The cross-linguistic development of address form use in tele-collaborative language learning: Two case studies. *Canadian Modern Language Review, 59,* 189–214.

Blondeau, H. (2001). Real-time changes in the paradigm of personal pronouns in Montreal French. *Journal of Sociolinguistics, 5,* 453–474.

Climent, C., Moré, J., Oliver, A., Salvatierra, M., Sànchez, I., & Taulé, M. (2007). Enhancing the status of Catalan versus Spanish in online academic forums: Obstacles to machine translation. In B. Danet & S. Herring (Eds.), *The multilingual Internet: Language, culture, and communication online* (pp. 209–230). Oxford: Oxford University Press.

Coveney, A. (1996). *Variability in spoken French: A sociolinguistic study of interrogation and negation.* Exeter, England: Elm Bank.

Coveney, A. (2003). Anything *you* can do *tu* can do better: *Tu* and *vous* as substitutes for indefinite *on* in French. *Journal of Sociolinguistics, 7,* 164–191.

Fonseca-Greber, B. (2007). The emergence of emphatic *ne* in conversational Swiss French. *Journal of French Language Studies, 17,* 249–275.

Fonseca-Greber, B., & Waugh, L. (2003). On the radical difference between the subject personal pronouns in written and spoken European French. In P. Leistyna & C. F. Meyer (Eds.), *Corpus analysis: Language structure and language use* (pp. 225–240). Amsterdam: Rodopi.

Gonglewski, M., & DuBravac, S. (2006). Multiliteracy: Second language literacy in the multimedia environment. In L. Ducate & N. Arnold (Eds.) *Calling on CALL: From theory and research to new directions in foreign language teaching* (pp. 43–68). CALICO Monograph Series Volume 5, San Marcos, TX: CALICO.

Hall, J. K., Cheng, A., & Carlson, M. (2006). Reconceptualizing multicompetence as a theory of language knowledge. *Applied Linguistics, 27,* 220–240.

Hanna, B. E., & de Nooy, J. (2003). A funny thing happened on the way to the forum: electronic discussion and foreign language learning. *Language Learning & Technology, 7,* 71–85. Available from http://llt.msu.edu/vol7num1/hanna/default.html

Hansen, A., & Malderez, I. (2004). Le *ne* de négation en région parisienne: une étude en temps réel. *Langage & Société, 107,* 5–30.

Hassal, T. (2008). Pragmatic performance: What are learners thinking? In E. Alcón Soler & A. Martínez Flor (Eds.), *Investigating pragmatics in foreign language learning, teaching and testing* (pp. 72–93). Clevedon: Multilingual Matters.

Jisa, H., & Viguié, A. (2005). Developmental perspectives on the role of French *on* in written and spoken expository texts. *Journal of Pragmatics, 37,* 125–142.

Kasper, L. (2000). New technologies, new literacies: Focus discipline research and ESL learning communities. *Language Learning & Technology, 4* (2), 105–128. Available from http://llt. msu.edu/vol4num2/kasper/default.html

Kinginger, C. (2000). Learning the pragmatics of solidarity in the networked foreign language classroom. In J. K. Hall & L. S. Verplaetse (Eds.), *Second and foreign language learning through classroom interaction* (pp. 23–46). Mahwah, NJ: Lawrence Erlbaum.

Kinginger, C., & Belz, J. (2005). Sociocultural perspectives on pragmatic development in foreign language learning: Microgenetic and ontogenetic case studies from telecollaboration and study abroad. *Intercultural Pragmatics, 2,* 369–421.

Kol, S., & Schcolnik, M. (2008). Asynchronous forums in EAP: Assessment issues. *Language Learning & Technology, 12,* 49–70. Available from http://llt.msu.edu/vol12num2/abstracts. html

Laberge, S., & Sankoff, G. (1980). Anything *you* can do. In G. Sankoff (Ed.), *The social life of language* (pp. 271–293). Philadelphia: University of Pennsylvania Press.

Liddicoat, A. J. (2006). Learning the culture of interpersonal relationships: Students' understandings of personal address forms in French. *Intercultural Pragmatics, 6,* 55–80.

Moise, R. (2007). Les SMS chez les jeunes: premiers éléments de réflexion, à partir d'un point de vue ethnolinguistique. *Glottopol, 10,* 101-112.

Morrow, P. R. (2006). Telling about problems and giving advice in an Internet discussion forum: Some discourse features. *Discourse Studies, 8,* 531–548.

National Standards for Foreign Language Learning Project. (1999). *Standards for foreign language learning in the 21st century.* Lawrence, KS: Allen Press.

Pierozak, I. (2003). Le français tchaté. Une étude en trois dimensions – sociolinguistique, syntaxique et graphique – d'usages IRC. Unpublished doctoral dissertation, Université d'Aix-Marseille I.

Prensky, M. (2001). Digital natives, digital immigrants: A new way to look at ourselves and our kids. *On the Horizon, 9,* 5. Retrieved May 5, 2008, from http://www.marcprensky.com/ writing/

Romaine, S. (1982). *Socio-historical linguistics: Its status and methodology.* Cambridge: Cambridge University Press.

Sankoff, G., & Vincent, D. (1980). The productive use of *ne* in spoken Montréal French. In G. Sankoff (Ed.), *The social life of language* (pp. 295–310). Philadelphia, PA: University of Pennsylvania Press.

Su, H.-Y. (2007). The multilingual and multiorthographic Taiwan-based Internet: Creative uses of writing systems on college-affiliated BBSs. In B. Danet & S. Herring (Eds.), *The multilingual Internet: Language, culture, and communication online* (pp. 64–86). Oxford: Oxford University Press.

Tai, S.-L. (2005). An exploration of social interaction and vocabulary appropriation among advanced adult ESL learners engage in a threaded discussion forum. Unpublished doctoral dissertation, The Florida State University.

van Compernolle, R. A. (2008). Morphosyntactic and phonological constraints on negative particle variation in French-language chat discourse. *Language Variation and Change, 20*, 317–339.

van Compernolle, R. A., & Williams, L. (2007). De l'oral à l'éléctrnonique: La variation orthographique comme ressource sociostylistique et pragmatique dans le français éléctronique. *Glottopol, 10*, 56–69.

Vellenga, H. (2004). Learning pragmatics from ESL and EFL textbooks: How likely? *TESL-EJ, 8*, 1–18. Available from http://tesl-ej.org/ej48/toc.html

Wanner, A.(2008). Creating comfort zones of orality in online discussion forums. In S. Magnan (Ed.), *Mediating Discourse Online* (pp.125–149). Amsterdam: John Benjamins.

Williams, L., & van Compernolle, R. A. (2007). Second-person pronoun use in on-line French-language chat environments. *French Review, 80*, 804–820.

Williams, L., & van Compernolle, R. A. (2009). *On* versus *tu* and *vous*: Pronouns with indefinite reference in synchronous electronic French discourse. *Language Sciences, 31*, 409–427.

Wodak & Wright, (2007). The European Union in cyberspace: Democratic participation in online multilingual discussion boards. In B. Danet & S. Herring (Eds.), *The multilingual Internet: Language, culture, and communication online* (pp. 385–407). Oxford: Oxford University Press.

Appendix A
URLs for discussion forums and their rules

Multitopic online discussion forums

1. La tribune de Genève (Switzerland)
    Site: http://www.tdg.ch/communaute/forums/forum
    Rules: http://www.tdg.ch/conditions-generales

2. Télévision Suisse Romande (Switzerland)
    Site: http://www.tsrforum.ch/sport/forumslist
    Rules: http://www.tsrforum.ch/tp/1543-regles-forums

3. Affection
    Site: http://www.affection.org/ (Francophone)
    Rules: http://fr.answers.yahoo.com/info/welcome;_ylt=AtSLwcLYDLDKxHwg7c U11QAeAgx.;_ylv=3

4. Yahoo! (France)
    Site: http://fr.answers.yahoo.com/
    Rules: http://fr.docs.yahoo.com/info/utos.html

5. Radio Canada (Quebec)
    Site: http://www.radio-canada.ca/forums/
    Rules: http://agora.radio-canada.ca/ASPforum/doc_netiquette.asp?cat_id=16& forum_id=1014

6. Comment ça marche ? (Francophone)
    Site: http://www.commentcamarche.net/forum/
    Rules: http://www.commentcamarche.net/ccmguide/ccmforum.php3

7. Forum FR (France)
    Site: http://www.forumfr.com/forums.html
    Rules: http://www.forumfr.com/conditions.html

8. Discutons (Francophone)
    Site: http://www.discutons.org/
    Rules: http://www.discutons.org/faq.php

9. France 2 (France)
    Site: http://lesforums.france2.fr/
    Rules: http://forums.france2.fr/charte.php?config=france2.inc

10. Le Lounge (Quebec)
    Site: http://www.lelounge.ca/forum.php
    Rules: http://www.lelounge.ca/register.php

Topic-specific online discussion forums

1. Le Campement
    Site: http://www.lecampement.net/forum.htm
    Rules: http://www.lecampement.net/a-lire-f37/reglement-du-forum-t1.htm

2. La Passion du vin (Francophone)
    Site: http://www.lapassionduvin.com/phorum/
    Rules: http://www.lapassionduvin.com/html/lacharte.php

3. Slappyto (Francophone) - musique
    Site: http://www.slappyto.net/Forum/
    Rules: http://www.slappyto.net/Utilisateurs/Inscription.aspx

4. Autowog (Switzerland) - site suisse sur les voitures (neuve ou d'occasion)
    Site: http://www.autowog.com/ForumFMS.asp
    Rules: http://www.autowog.com/ForumFMS.asp?ActionFMS=info

5. Meilleur du chef (France)
    Site: http://www.meilleurduchef.com/cgi/mdc/forum/fr
    Rules: http://www.meilleurduchef.com/cgi/mdc/l/fr/forum/cond_utilisation.html

6. Doctissimo (France)
    Site: http://forum.doctissimo.fr/
    Rules: http://www.doctissimo.fr/charte_utilisation.htm

7. Volley Zone (Francophone)
    Site: http://www.volley-zone.com/forum/
    Rules: http://www.volley-zone.com/forum/le-reglement-du-forum-vf41.html

8. Lacs des Pyrénées (France)
    Site: http://www.lacsdespyrenees.com/forum/voirforum.php
    Rules: http://www.lacsdespyrenees.com/forum/rubriques/faq.php

9. Maman pour la vie (Quebec)
    Site: http://www.mamanpourlavie.com/forum/
    Rules: http://www.mamanpourlavie.com/forum/tools/attention

10. Maison facile (Francophone)
    Site: http://www.maison-facile.com/forum/
    Rules: http://www.maison-facile.com/forum/070-sujet.asp?id=125

Appendix B
Terminology Resources for English and French

English

1. British Broadcasting Corporation: «jargonbuster»
    http://www.bbc.co.uk/webwise/course/jargon/n.shtml

2. Webopedia: Online computer dictionary for computer and Internet terms and
    definitions
    http://www.webopedia.com/

3. Wikipedia: «List of Internet-related terminology»
    http://en.wikipedia.org/wiki/List_of_Internet-related_terminology

4. Net Lingo: The Internet dictionary
    http://www.netlingo.com/

5. Glossary of Internet and Web jargon
    Part of a tutorial entitled «Research-quality Web Searching»
    University of California at Berkeley's Teaching Library
    http://www.lib.berkeley.edu/TeachingLib/Guides/Internet/Glossary.html

French

1. Vocabulaire d'Internet (English < > French)
   Office québécois de la langue française
   http://www.olf.gouv.qc.ca/ressources/bibliotheque/dictionnaires/Internet/Index/
    index.html

2. France Terme: All terms published in the *Journal officiel* of the French government
   Commission générale de terminologie et de néologie
   http://franceterme.culture.fr/FranceTerme/

3. Wikipédia: «Technologies de l'information et de la communication»
   http://fr.wikipedia.org/wiki/Technologies_de_l%27information_et_de_la_
    communication

4. Inventerm: A dynamic inventory of terminology
   Office québécois de la langue française
   http://www.inventerm.com/

5. Google Terminologique
   http://pages.globetrotter.net/mverge/google/google.htm

The discussion forum as a locus
for developing L2 pragmatic awareness

Kathleen Farrell Whitworth

This chapter analyzes the discourse of two English-language discussion forums with different themes – weight management and dogs – in order to demonstrate how pragmatic functions (e.g., greeting, providing encouragement, requesting information, scolding) can be expressed by a range of linguistic structures. The analysis is theoretically grounded in Lave and Wenger's (1991) view that learning should ideally be socioculturally situated within a Community of Practice (CoP). As such, the concept of the traditional (i.e., offline) CoP is contrasted with the hierarchy, norms, rules, and structures that exist in online communities. This type of contrast is vital to an understanding of online vs. offline social and cultural practices since some of the constructs (e.g., gatekeeping, explicit vs. implicit socialization) are fundamentally different. This chapter thus draws attention to the importance of considering participation and socialization of L2 learners in authentic contexts consistent within recent broad-based theoretical and empirical discussions in SLA (Hall, Cheng, & Carlson, 2006; Kasper, 2001; Kramsch, & Whiteside, 2007; Lafford, 2007; Swain & Deters, 2007). Findings show that CoPs can indeed be created online. Moreover, message boards are effective tools for language teachers and language learners.

1.   Introduction

This chapter analyzes the discourse of two English-language discussion forums with different themes – weight management and dogs – in order to demonstrate how pragmatic functions (e.g., greeting, providing encouragement, requesting information, scolding) can be expressed by a range of linguistic structures. The analysis is theoretically grounded in Lave and Wenger's (1991) view that learning should ideally be socioculturally situated within a Comminity of Practice (CoP). As such, the concept of the traditional (i.e., offline) CoP will be contrasted with the hierarchy, norms, rules, and structures that exist in online communities. This type of contrast is vital to an understanding of online vs. offline social and cultural practices since some of the constructs (e.g., gatekeeping, explicit vs. implicit socialization) are fundamentally different. This chapter thus draws attention to the importance of considering participation and socialization of L2 learners in authentic contexts consistent within recent broad-based theoretical and empirical discussions in SLA (Kasper, 2001; Kramsch, & Whiteside, 2007; Lafford, 2007; Swain & Deters, 2007).

Online communities, for example, are more heavily text-based. The number of contextual cues (Gumperz, 1982) provided by traditional spoken discourse is drastically reduced, and there are often few – or no – gatekeeping devices in place to limit or manage access to communities. The novelty of the discussion forum and the structures and types of discourse found in this communication environment suggest an increase in importance of observation and legitimate peripheral participation (Lave & Wenger, 1991, pp. 29–43) on the part of the L2 learner.

The discussion forums chosen for this analysis have themes with very different foci, but there are also other features that make these two forums quite different. For example, the social organization of the weight management forum[1] is unique in that every new participant begins as a newbie, someone who is either new to the diet program promoted by the company that sponsors the forum site or a user new to the forum. However, participants known as *regulars* (i.e., those who leave messages every day or almost every day) have a higher standing within the social structure of the forum, and achieving status as a *regular* can be extremely frustrating for some. The content of certain discussion threads can quickly become rather aggressive and impolite, which may be a result of never having to confront other users face-to-face and, by extension, no perceived need to maintain positive face in relation to others. This chapter, therefore, analyzes linguistic structures representing specific pragmatic devices and features that cause and resolve social conflict, within a larger analysis of structures representing pragmatic functions that are expected in any communication environment (e.g., greetings, information/confirmation requests).

The main objective of this chapter is to provide a model for students and teachers who wish to explore a discussion forum with a theme of their own choosing. If students are expected to engage in online communication (either as part of a class project or for non-educational purposes), it would be impossible for them to have a heightened awareness of linguistic and pragmatic norms without first having access to the context(s) and discourse(s) they would be expected to produce.

---

1. The Privacy Policy of this site specifically mentions that there is no expectation of privacy for information posted in any public area, including a message board. Even so, no personally identifiable information (e.g., real name, date of birth, surface mailing address, etc.) posted in any public area of the site has been used or quoted for the present study.

This chapter will also contribute to the debate in the professional literature related to the advantages and disadvantages of comparing online CoPs to traditional CoPs. This debate has only begun recently and has been, for the most part, limited to conference papers and panel discussions; however, as more SLA researchers investigate online communities and the concept of *community*, the debate is likely to continue.

2.   Communities of practice

The CoP framework is grounded in the notion that learning is social practice (Lave & Wenger, 1991, p. 4). The authors of this framework describe a CoP in the following way:

> Being alive as human beings means that we are constantly engaged in the pursuit of enterprises of all kinds, from ensuring our physical survival to seeking the most lofty pleasures. As we define these enterprises and engage in their pursuit together, we interact with each other and with the world and we tune our relations with each other and with the world accordingly. In other words, we learn. Over time, this collective learning results in practices that reflect both the pursuit of our enterprises and the attendant social relations. These practices are thus the property of a kind of community created over time by the sustained pursuit of a shared enterprise. It makes sense, therefore, to call these kinds of communities *communities of practice*. (p. 45)

Learning the second language requires access to the social practices ("activities, tasks, functions...") of the host community in which learners find themselves (p. 53). Because the interactions examined here have taken place on line, one could argue that access to these social practices is readily available to those who have Internet access. What tends to be missing with the exchanges is explicit instruction from other message board participants. That is, many times contributors are not specifically told which norms they need to follow or which ones they have flouted. Instead, their messages are simply ignored or attacked. Therefore, some participants choose to lurk (Lueg, 2001) which Lave and Wenger might consider to be "legitimate peripheral participation."

Lave and Wenger (1991) use the terms "legitimate peripheral participation" and "full participation" to suggest that learning is always and everywhere social. The term "legitimate peripheral participation" suggests that:

> ...learners inevitably participate in communities of practitioners and that the mastery of knowledge and skill requires newcomers to move toward full participation in the sociocultural practices of community. 'Legitimate peripheral

> participation' provides a way to speak about the relations between newcomers
> and old-timers, and about activities, identities, artifacts, and communities of
> knowledge and practice. It concerns the process by which newcomers become
> part of a CoP.... (p. 29)

It is legitimate peripheral participation which leads to full participation. The term
"full participation," as opposed to "complete participation", suggests that "full
participation" considers the "diversity of relations involved in varying forms of
community membership" (p. 37). Complete participation would take on a more
teleological form: a collective practice which may have "measurable degrees of
'acquisition' by newcomers" (p. 36).

Moreover, learners' identities are intimately connected to the aforementioned
notions because as Lave and Wenger (1991) suggest:

> ...learning involves the whole person; it implies not only a relation to specific
> activities, but a relation to social communities – it implies becoming a full par-
> ticipant, a member, a kind of person.... Learning thus implies becoming a differ-
> ent person with respect to the possibilities enabled by these systems of relations.
> To ignore this aspect of learning is to overlook the fact that learning involves the
> construction of identities. (p. 53)

That is, as participants learn and engage more, they change and become aware of
opportunities for membership in a particular community. Access to this learning
and to various communities is important for their evolution.

Full participation involves "a great commitment of time, intensified effort, more
and broader responsibilities within the community, and more difficult and risky
tasks, but, more significantly, an increasing sense of identity as a master practitioner" (Lave & Wenger, 1991, p. 111). However, becoming an 'old timer' is not without
personal benefit: old timers are typically revered within their particular CoP. This
"reverence" will be demonstrated in the online community message board forum.

First, though, a discussion of language learning as a social process is presented. This perspective differs from other conceptualizations of language learning since viewing it as a social process presumes that, in order to participate in
language learning, learners need to interact with others. That is, language learning
is not simply a cognitive process.

3. Language learning as a social process

Learners are socialized into a particular linguistic practice via various communities of practice. Therefore, identity, subject positioning, agency and access to
CoPs are essential to understanding the challenges faced by the participants in the

present study. To become a competent user of a given speech community (or message board community) it is imperative to understand how people use language and other symbols to construct their social situation. How learners perform their identities during the activity of language learning contributes to the learning experience at hand. It is not simply a matter of acquiring vocabulary, morphemes and phonology, among other things. Rather, learning how to conduct oneself with language is about performing the identity of, for example, a language learner or of a member of a particular CoP.[2]

Further, learning is not contained in the mind of the individual. That is to say, learners cannot be "reduced to their minds" (Lave & Wenger, 1991, p. 50), and learning is no longer just "the acquisition of knowledge the discourse of dualism effectively segregates even these reductions from the everyday world of engaged participation" (p. 50). Moreover, the learner is not viewed as an individual, but rather as a "person-in-the-world" (p. 52). A social practices view of learning "emphasizes the relational interdependency of agent and world, activity, meaning, cognition, learning, and knowing" (p. 50). This chapter offers an analysis of the social and developmental processes by which learners' participation is (or is not) legitimized (Lave & Wenger), through which they are apprenticed as participants in a given CoP.

Other researchers in the field of SLA have also called for more socially grounded work to be done. Kasper (2001) discusses four different perspectives on L2 pragmatic development. Of interest to the present study are the perspectives which allow for a social consideration of context and of language development. Kasper (2001) states that "sociocultural analyses of peer interaction have contributed important insights into the opportunities for L2 learning afforded by learner-learner collaboration" (p. 517). Thus, message board engagement would, according to this perspective, be a productive way for participants to learn language since the message boards allow for this "learner-learner collaboration." Kasper adds that, from a language socialization perspective, "much of pragmatic socialization is implicit, occurring through the novices' participation in recurrent communicative practices" (p. 520). However, she adds that "in some aspects of pragmatics, explicit socialization is strongly in evidence. Explicit pragmatic socialization reflects metapragmatic awareness of pragmatic practices that are salient and important to the party that invokes the pragmatic norm" (p. 520). Moreover, Kasper adds, "most language socialization occurs implicitly, either through the learners' repeated participation in target discourse practices, or through

---

2. I do not mean to suggest that learning vocabulary, morphology and phonology are not important. I do suggest, however, that they are not the only parts of language learning and communication that need to be researched.

participation *and* various strategies by which the more competent co-participant makes the pragmatic information salient to the learner" (p. 521).

Firth and Wagner (1997) called for SLA research that "requires a significantly enhanced awareness of the contextual and interactional dimensions of language use, an increased 'emic' (i.e., participant-relevant) sensitivity towards fundamental concepts, and the broadening of the traditional SLA data base" (p. 285). Moreover, they believed that some of the core concepts of SLA at that time needed to be reexamined, like the nonnative speaker (NNS), among other things. They considered the NNS to be a "monolithic" (p. 285) element in SLA, one that is "applied and understood in an oversimplified manner, leading to…an analytic mindset that elevates an idealized 'native' speaker above a stereotypicalized 'nonnative,' while viewing the latter as a defective communicator, limited by an underdeveloped communicative competence" (p. 285).

Ten years later, Lafford (2007) called the Firth and Wagner (1997) piece "prominent in the ongoing debate in the field of second language acquisition (SLA)" (p. 735) between researchers who see acquisition of the L2 as primarily a cognitive function and those who see its acquisition as a social process "whereby learners acquire a target language by using the L2 in interactions with speakers of the target language" (p. 735). Though some researchers disagree on the "seminal nature of F&W's (1997) publication" (p. 735), many scholars understand its important place in this ongoing debate between social and cognitive. Lafford also suggests that research done in the domain of computer-mediated communication (CMC) reflects "a mixture of cognitively focused studies … and socially grounded" ones (p. 749). She adds that "(f)uture CMC research informed by both cognitive and social perspectives could use both quantitative and qualitative approaches to study the effect of social factors on specific learner outcomes" (p. 749).

Kramsch and Whiteside (2007) discuss the difference between the notions of language learner and language user first proposed by Firth and Wagner (1997). They explain:

> Firth and Wagner proposed to broaden the notion of language learner to mean someone engaged in the contingent, turn-by-turn negotiation of meaning of conversation practice and who learns the language by using it to solve problems and achieve tasks set by the social setting itself. (p. 911)

Language users are considered "multicompetent, bilingual individuals who use whatever communicative competence is required by the task, the activity or the situation in variable social contexts in real life" (p. 911).

Swain and Deters (2007) state that since Firth and Wagner (1997) there has been a "notable increase" (p. 820) in more socioculturally situated language research. This research also prioritizes "contextual factors…individual agency and multifaceted identities" (p. 820). They add that "the CoP framework emphasizes learning as involving the whole person with a sociocultural history and focuses on 'activity in and with the world' and on the view that 'agent, activity, and the world mutually constitute each other" (Lave & Wenger, 1991, p. 33). Swain and Deters (2007) cite Wenger's (1998) more recent work in which it is stated:

> We not only produce our identities through the practice we engage in, but we also define ourselves through practices we do not engage in. Our identities are constituted not only by what we are but also by what we are not.
> (Wenger, 1998, p. 164, cited in Swain & Deters, 2007, p. 825)

Therefore, lurking (Lueg, 2001) can be seen as a form of practice, allowing participants to situate themselves how they wish, in a non-participatory state of being.

The previous studies all mention the importance of context. Breen (2001) problematizes this notion and offers a schema of "learner contributions to language learning" (Breen, 2001, p. 9 & p. 180). Like Block (2003), Breen critiques standard approaches to research, suggesting that learners are actually "socio-historically situated human beings" (Block, 2003, p. 124). Moreover, the larger society in which the language learning is taking place "are all locations for the articulation and re-working of cultures and the meanings and significances they entail" (Breen, 2001, pp. 177–178). That is, within each overarching context exists another context and within that context are more cultures and meanings with which the learner will become acquainted. Cultures and contexts are thus indivisible.

Breen (2001) also adds that differences among and within contexts are valuable. Each context, diverse in and of itself, provides an opportunity for language learning. As such, different learners can learn different linguistic skills as a result of the various contexts in which they may find themselves. Breen further illustrates this point by stating the following:

> Different contexts are defined differently by participants: what is meaningful and significant to them is likely to be context specific; and how they act in them – including how they interact and what and how they learn through such interaction – is also likely to be context specific. Therefore, the argument concludes, findings from one context, such as those from an experimental task undertaken in a university observation laboratory, should not be generalized to all learning situations. (p. 176)

This consideration of difference is especially important because, unlike first language learning, success in learning a second language is "remarkably variable" (Breen, 2001, p. 2). In short, because the endeavor of second language learning is different, the results of that learning will be different. Moreover, the contexts of second language learning are imbued with issues of power, identities and access, all of which are capable of changing the entire language learning endeavor.

Taken together, these studies show the changes of perspective in SLA research. Instead of focusing solely on acquisition in isolation, researchers in SLA have begun to examine the social context of language learning and use. By looking at the data through the lens of CoP, the present chapter attempts to provide a socially grounded view of participants and of computer-mediated communication.

4.   Review of the literature

Haneda (2006) has recently reviewed several studies, all of which looked at CoP in the classroom. She states that there are strengths and limitations of the CoP theory when applied to L2 classroom research. "By treating the class as a CoP, Toohey (1998) shifts the analytical focus from individual children's mental activities to their participatory opportunities (hence learning) in prevalent classroom practices" (p. 810). Haneda adds that Toohey examines how the children's identities were constructed through the learning processes. That is, English proficient peers can be considered to be old-timers in English and that the symbolic resource is spoken English. "Toohey reveals that, nevertheless, learning was taking place all the time in the Grade 1 class because the children were appropriating the local practices of doing school," and adds that "L2 learning is a part of socialization as a student in a particular sociocultural setting (p. 810)."

Like Toohey's (1998) study of a L2 classroom, Morita (2004) studied Japanese female students' participation in classrooms in a Canadian university. She noted that

> within the apparently homogeneous group of Japanese female graduate students, individual students negotiated their sense of self in significantly different ways; these students also showed considerable intraindividual differences in how they participated in different classes and developed their academic identities; the construction of identity was 'of necessity a mixture of being in and being out,' that is participating actively in one community and participating marginally in another. (pp. 810–811)

Haneda (2006) offers some limitations of a CoP perspective. She states that Lave and Wenger's (1991) version does not examine what a community is and does not distinguish among different types of learning. Additionally, their version "bypasses the issue of power with respect to who can assign certain roles and identities and thus control trajectories that lead (or not) to full participation" (p. 812). Toohey "also makes clear the limited extent to which her target bilingual children were able to exercise agency. Although some of them attempted to resist the classroom's norms and rules, the teacher's authority always prevailed" (812).

In their 2000 article, Hildreth, Kimble, and Wright, focus on knowledge sharing in the business world and the way in which this sharing is done. They introduce the terms *hard knowledge* (knowledge that can be easily articulated and captured), *soft knowledge* (knowledge that is not easily articulated and cannot be readily captured like experience), *work knowledge* which has been internalized, and *tacit knowledge* (like using a word processor).

Into this discussion they bring Lave and Wenger (1991) and their concepts of CoP and legitimate peripheral participation.[3] The authors explain that "Lave and Wenger (1991) use the terms *peripheral* and *full participation* to denote the degree of engagement with and participation in the community but note that peripherality 'must be connected to issues of legitimacy of the social organization and control over resources if it is to gain its full analytical potential'" (p. 29).

Hildreth et al. (2000) explain the difference between teams (a term often used in the business world) and CoPs: teams develop themselves from the "formal hierarchy" imposed upon them (p. 30). In CoPs legitimation comes from participants' participation in the community. They *earn* their status as experts or old timers.

Hildreth, Kimble, and Wright (2000) ask the question, "Can a CoP be virtual?" (p. 31). They explain that "Some aspects of the CoP should translate from the co-located to the virtual world relatively easily, for example, finding a common purpose or at least a shared interest. If the members are doing similar jobs then there will already be a shared domain language and knowledge" (p. 32). They add that, although in Lave and Wenger's (1991) CoP framework the periphery is a social periphery, in a "distributed environment, there will also be a physical and a temporal periphery which will also have certain connotations for the notion of participation" (p. 32).

Based on the case studies in Hildreth et al. (2000), the following conclusions were drawn about virtual CoPs:

> The distributed CoP can evolve from an initial informal contact between its members or from an official grouping which becomes a CoP because of the way the members interact and work together; the co-located CoP may develop links with individuals in other locations who are doing similar work. These people may be members or other CoPs; and the developing CoP may also link up with a similar group, possibly abroad. (p. 33)

---

3.   The term "legitimate peripheral participation" can be analyzed in the following way. Legitimation is concerned with power and authority relations in the group, whereas peripherality considers where a participant situates him/herself in the group.

Overall, the authors found that face-to-face interaction was important for their CoPs. The participants felt that the strong personal relationship carried the group through the periods where they were only e-communicating. By knowing one another, they felt "greater unity and common purpose" (p. 35). The personal relationship also helped members understand who they were communicating with via email. "As members get to know each other, have confidence in each other and trust each other, they gain legitimation in the eyes of each other" (p. 35). The authors add that people "learnt from each other by collaborating, asking for help, solving problems together" (p. 36).

In his 2001 article, Lueg examines how Usenet newsgroups can function as virtual CoP:

> Apart from being a 'regular' information space, Usenet is also a socially constructed space which is shaped by social activity and socially shared 'netiquette' rules that describe how to behave when participating in Usenet discussions. In fact, most newsgroups are the visible results of negotiations among netizens who care about Usenet's structure. (p. 2)

Additionally, newsgroup participants have formed communities. These participants are able to create "shared rules of good conduct … shared humor, insiders and 'outsiders,' shared artifacts, such as web sites where newsgroup-related information is kept and organized, real-world meetings in selected news groups" (p. 2). One phenomenon that tends to occur on message boards and newsgroups is 'lurking.' For Lueg, it is an important part of online communication. "From a communities-of-practice perspective, lurking could be understood as peripheral participation and posting own articles would resemble (visible) participation" (p. 2).

To gain access, to become more visible to the newsgroup community and/or to become an 'old timer,' participants in newsgroups need to contribute their own articles and statements. In this way, they gain "social status" (p. 3). Lueg adds that "writing articles could be viewed as a kind of shared 'practice'" (p. 3). Newsgroups can function as CoPs because there is a shared objective among participants. These participants perhaps want to discover, explore, and/or acquire a richer understanding of a particular phenomenon (e.g., body art, study abroad, language learning). For some, participating in discussion forums or newsgroups can be a type of apprenticeship since they are learning the rules of how to function in the given newsgroup. There is joint knowledge production since members make a decision together and take a course of action together. "That is the outcome of 'joint' knowledge production" (p. 3). The participants also learn by reading others' reports of their own experiences.

Lueg (2000) argues that "the transfer of a concept that is deeply rooted in the lived-in world to the virtual involves conceptual problems, such as the question where learning and doing, two constituents of communities of practice, are to happen in the virtual world" (p. 1). The author states that the purpose of knowledge communities is "knowledge creation and knowledge communication" (p. 1). "The concept of communities of practice has been identified as setting for effective knowledge sharing… [K]nowledge communities are located in the virtual whereas communities of practice are deeply rooted in the lived-in world…" (p. 1).

Lueg (2000) also defines the notion of distributed CoPs as a CoP that is distributed throughout the world, or that is simply not found in one geographical location.

> … the group itself identified themselves as CoP as they match the following definition of such a community: the community has a common set of interests to do something in common, is concerned with motivation, is self-generating, is self-selection, is not necessarily co-located, as has a common set of interests … (p. 3).

Face-to-face interaction is important to advance the evolution of the community itself; however, this face-to-face interaction does not typically happen in virtual communities of practice.

Hildreth, Kimble, and Wright (1998) illustrate how participants in a CoP can participate even if they are not co-located. "Communities of practice provide an excellent forum for knowledge sharing and a vital question is whether the new communications media, which provide new possibilities for collaboration and distributed working, could support the existence of such groups in a distributed environment" (p. 1). Their paper was "the first stage in exploring whether Computer Mediated Communications technologies (CMC) can support distributed international Communities of Practice" (p. 1), and they state that participating in a CoP, particularly online, is important because it is about more than "the transmission of facts and figures, or codified knowledge" (p. 3). Rather, participating in a CoP is about "interaction and communication between individuals in the group as people (who) learn from one another, solve problems together and new knowledge is created" (p. 2). Despite the fact that Lave and Wenger (1991) most likely saw CoP as "co-located non-IT settings" (Hildreth et al., 1998, p. 3), Lave and Wenger (1991) state that "co-presence should not be regarded as essential" (Hildreth et al., p. 3).

Taken together, these studies demonstrate that CoP can develop online, even though participants are not co-located. In the present study, "co-presence" is therefore not regarded as essential either. The importance of this chapter is examining how people gain access to and become more experienced participants in a specific type of online community, the discussion forum, which is very similar to a newsgroup and can also be referred to as a message board, a bulletin board, or an online discussion group.

Gumperz (1982) explains how certain discourse strategies implicate themselves into conversations and discussions. These strategies are often exhibited in message board contexts, as will be shown below. Gumperz whose research focused primarily on spoken discourse, explains that, over time, researchers have become focused on "the analysis of communicative processes involved in human learning, social cooperation and underlying social evolution" (p. 3). Therefore, the language used, produced and learned during message board exchanges generally contributes to human learning and is, in a sense, social cooperation. Message board participants learn linguistic and social appropriateness (pragmatics) from one another. Gumperz understands pragmatics to be "rules of speaking as they apply to speech events…norms for what counts as appropriate speech behavior … [and] the very definitions of such events…vary from culture to culture and context to context" (p. 3). He argues that communication is a "social activity" (p. 1) which requires "the coordinated efforts of two or more individuals" (p. 1). Because communication is viewed in this way, one can argue that message board exchanges are communication since there are typically two or more individuals present reading the exchanges. Gumperz goes on to explain that "speakers who understand each other must conform to common grammatical rules even though the surface forms they employ may differ" (p. 19). He further states that in order to understand the meaning of a conversation, humans "rely on schemata or interpretive frames based on our experience with similar situations as well as on grammatical and lexical knowledge. Such frames enable us to distinguish among permissible options" (p. 21). Message board participants seem to agree on the grammatical and lexical knowledge needed to communicate appropriately. That is, emoticons, chat language (e. g., LOL, *laugh out loud*; DD, *dear daughter*; ROTFL, *rolling on the floor laughing*) and other conventions are employed to show membership in the given message board CoP. Those participants who do not understand such conventions either ask for clarification or are left on their own to figure them out. Previous message board experiences certainly influence the way in which people participate in discussion forum communities. Most importantly, Gumperz (1982) states that "[i]nappropriate usage (in conversational interactions) becomes more than simply a violation of linguistic appropriateness norms. It may lead to misunderstanding of intent. Repeated miscommunications over time seriously affect" one's relationships with others (p. 50). On the message boards studied here, these miscommunications may prevent participants from continuing on the message board. Their contributions may get ignored, or they may be censored by the corporate office (in the case of the weight loss message board). These miscommunications "limit [their] ability to enlist cooperation" (p. 50) and may impact successful participation.

5.   Data analysis[4]

5.1   Weight management message boards

The weight loss company's message boards are divided into topics based on the interests of the weight loss participants. For example, one area is the "general topics board," whereas another is called the newbie board. The boards are also divided by age, profession or vocation (i.e., new moms' message board), and fitness level (i.e., the marathoners' board). Participants can click on a particular tab to see the entire list of the boards. The following discussion examines the marathoners' message board. On this board, one typically finds weight loss participants who are also marathon runners, some of whom are training for upcoming marathons. The experience level of the participants varies greatly: Some people are new to running but have much experience with weight loss community message boards. Others are experienced runners but new to the weight loss community. And, of course, other people are somewhere in between.

The data below were taken from one day at the end of July 2008. The reason for the selection for this particular day is the timing in the marathon year, period when many of the participants were training hard for imminent marathons. First, the general pragmatic functions will be presented. Then, the discourse of one participant in particular, a self-proclaimed "newbie," will be analyzed as she attempts to find solace and support with her running compatriots after a bad run.

The marathon running board appears to have a captain who begins the thread each day. This captain seems to change on a weekly basis, and it is not entirely clear how the captain is selected. It does appear, however, that no other participants will contribute until the captain has posted his message for the day.[5] Participant A, the current week's captain, begins with the standard opening greeting (Excerpt 1):

---

4.   The text of every excerpt has been reproduced as it was found on the Web. Therefore, "sic" is not used.

5.   I draw this conclusion because, after having lurked on the board for several weeks, I noticed that one captain in particular would not post his message until mid-morning. Yet, during previous weeks, the captain would post around 8 a.m., and other posts very quickly followed. It is because of that experience that I make this statement.

Excerpt 1.

This thread is for all of those who love to go the distance. Half, full or ultramarathoners[6] are all welcome; walkers, runners or folks who do a combination of the two. This is the place to discuss our training and nutrition issues that come with going the distance. Most of all, it is a place to share our stories and triumphs. Please join us!

This greeting is used every single day, and it is the message for which all posters seem to wait. Typically, the captain posts this standard message and then immediately posts her own personal message afterwards. On this day, Participant A starts her second message by greeting all of the "new posters from yesterday." She apologizes in advance for being bad with names and asks for patience in that regard. She does not introduce herself to the group, so it is presumed that she is known to the other contributors. At the end of her post (Excerpt 2), she invites her CoP to contribute their thoughts about the chances of her attaining again her PR (personal record):

Excerpt 2.

Hope everyone had a good day and will try to check back later. Oh – mapped out a training plan for the 20K and then some 1/2's in October – hoping to use the marathon plan that I did in the spring, but max out on long runs at 16. Hoping for another pr... Thoughts?

At that point, she signs off and other contributors begin to make themselves known. It is not until one half hour later (and after 4 other posts) that someone (Participant E) acknowledges Participant A's request for thoughts. However, Participant E does not offer thoughts. She simply addresses Participant A directly (Excerpt 3):

Excerpt 3.

Participant A – Hi! I started posting right when you were taking your break so I don't "know" you yet. But, I wanted to send out some hugs. I'm sure you went through a lot with IVF.

It is not known what Participant A's break was for or when it took place. Based on Participant E's introduction, it is clear that these two participants do not have experience communicating with each other. Participant A responds to Participant E (Excerpt 4):

---

6.   Ultramarathoners are those runners who run 50 to 100 mile races.

Excerpt 4.

Thanks Participant E – what's your name – you've probably posted that but of course I missed it!

She also uses self-deprecation when asking for Participant E's name. That is, instead of simply asking for her name again, Participant A claims that not knowing the name is her fault. In this way, she allows Participant E to feel as though she is part of the group.

There is a trend that contributors who have posted for a while and/or who are known to other contributors do not have to identify themselves in the same way that a "newbie" would. For example, Participant B simply states (Excerpt 5):

Excerpt 5.

Morning All. Xtrain day for me. Not sure what I'm doing as it will 98 today here in VA…and storms will be coming in the afternoon. Hope to swim but we will see. Perhaps just abs and lifting tonight. Off to work. Welcome to all the newbies. I'm awful at names too. (morning Participant A).

Compare this to a newbie contribution (Excerpt 6):

Excerpt 6.

Good Morning! One of the newbies from yesterday back again! I just did stretching and lifting yesterday. Going to do 3 this morning. So When it comes to strength training I always shy away from doing alot with my legs because I get worried that my legs will be to sore to run the next day! What do you guys do in order to not have that problem, I know I need to do more. Yesterday I did ball squats and the legs feel fine. Thanx!

Whereas Participant B greets the board, then moves on to her training plan, Participant H, a newbie, explains in great detail what training she did the day before and what her plan is for the current day. Once she gives the explanation of why she does not work her legs too much, she asks the CoP for help with her training program. She thanks ("Thanx!") them in advance for their responses.

Another newbie posts immediately after Participant H. She writes immediately that she is a newbie and explains her training program to the group (Excerpt 7):

Excerpt 7.

Good morning!
I'm a newbie…H from CT…terrible with names, but reading all of yesterday's posts (and today's!) to get the "knack" of who everyone is.

Went out for my morning run today…5am and it was SO gross out! Oddly enough, it was one of my better times…I reversed my usual 6 mile run and took a few minutes off…I've been in a heart-rate slump the last week or so…I haven't been able to get it about 65% max during a workout. But I averaged around 78% today…

Though she never explicitly asks for help, by providing her detailed training program and some of the issues she faces, she has opened the door for comments and suggestions from her CoP.

One final newbie post arrived in the afternoon. Participant U, a newbie, had posted during the previous week, but then never returned, until this particular day. She immediately excuses herself for that gap in communication and then posts her training plan (Excerpt 8):

Excerpt 8.

Hi everyone, I posted on here last week, and haven't been back…oops!
I'm U. from Indianapolis training for my first marathon in November. I'm following the Zero to Marathon in 26 Weeks program.
Today is a rest day for me. I did step aerobics (30min) and running last night (45min).
Hope everyone is having a great day!

In general, it appears that old timers or more experienced users of this message board do not introduce themselves to the group. That is, they greet the group, and then they explain their training schedule for the day. However, newbies are seemingly required to introduce themselves by name. They must claim that they are indeed a newbie, greet everyone, and then explain their running experience, their marathon date and their training schedule. Most often, both groups – newbies and old timers – ask for help and suggestions if they are needed.

Another trend that appears is "marking" one's spot for later. Participant D posts at the very beginning of the strand and simply says, "Marking my spot for later. Quick post. DOR ('day off of running'?) today but may walk some at lunch. Did 5 miles last night." Participant D is not the only person to mark her spot. Participant O posts at 10 a.m., three hours after the thread is started, and states, "Marking my place for later! Waving Hi to all." Marking one's spot may have a pragmatic function on the message board. Because there are so many message boards and so many threads within each one, the weight loss company created a function by which site users may click on their names to find their most recent posts. By doing this, users do not have to search through every page of the message board to find their CoP. Thus, when users mark their spots early on in the day, they can return in the afternoon simply click on their name instead of having to scroll through approximately 15 pages of a message thread.

As mentioned earlier, one contributor in particular, Participant E, a newbie, contributed a post that engendered many reactions, suggestions and advice. In short, she had a very discouraging run during which she felt "heavy" and "overwhelmed" (Excerpt 9).

Excerpt 9.

Soooo I am feeling super discouraged this morning. I just got back from 4 miles and it was just awful. I don't understand how I can feel so good running 10 miles on Saturday and so lousy just trying to go 4 today. I think it is poor nutrition, bad sleep last night, stress at work affecting me. But when I was out there, all I kept thinking about were all of the miles ahead of me between now and October. And what was I thinking that I could go for a full marathon? I felt heavy and overwhelmed…I really want to do a full but now I am feeling unconfident; maybe I really don't have the legs for it. Hopefully this is just one bad day.

After submitting this post, Participant E receives 11 responses, all of which are extremely supportive and attempt to help her understand that "it happens to all of us." Each response is comforting and kind. In fact, one contributor, a self-reported personal trainer, suggests that Participant E ask about the ozone in her area. Participant E's CoP wants her to feel supported and feel like part of the group. A sampling of some of the responses are provided below (Excerpts 10–14):

Excerpt 10.

Participant E don't worry running is like that…one day you have a great run and the next day it may be a lousy run…Don't rule of the marathon yet as the worse part of a marathon is the training. Once you are in the race it is a lot of fun.

Excerpt 11.

As for bad short runs and good long runs – I am the queen of that…Some of it is psychological and is physiological. Your body is still probably recovering from the effort of the long run…Good luck

Excerpt 12.

Participant E: I had 2 awful runs last week..a 7 miler and what ended up being a 5 miler. I am paying a lot more attention to my nutrition this week and I've started taking endurolytes… I think it's (Name X and Name Y) that keep me reminding me that not every run will be a good one. And that's ok!!!

Excerpt 13.

Participant E – Some runs are just bad. It's your body's way of saying hey-something's not quite right, but kudos to you for getting out there even when you didn't have good running karma! But the bad runs sure make you appreciate the runs where you feel like you could fly…The memories of my great runs definately bring a smile to my face.

Excerpt 14.

FYI, for all of us feeling bad on our runs – what is the ozone level in your area? Ours is apparently bad…The symptoms are as follows: (This participant then provides a detailed list of the symptoms of ozone when running).

At the end of the day, Participant E contributes one final post where she thanks everyone for the help and encouragement. She then explains some thoughts that she had during the day while reflecting on her bad run. Once she completes that explanation, she thanks everyone again (Excerpt 15):

Excerpt 15.

THANKS again I can't tell you how much I appreciate this board already.

Participant E was most engaged in message board activity on that particular day. Because of her enthusiasm, it was assumed that she would continue on a regular basis to contribute to the board and to this CoP. When a search of her username was done on the weight loss website, the results indicated that she made only one more contribution on August 31, 2008. On that day, as a self-professed "lurker," she explained that she wanted to share her with her marathon CoP her most recent race experience, a 30K race. She detailed the race, the surroundings, her mileage pace, the weather and the results. She explained that she ran more slowly than she had wanted, but that she was happy with her results. From that post, she received much support and congratulations from her running colleagues. Since August 31, 2008, she had not posted a message; nonetheless, Lueg (2001) explains lurking as a form of participation. When reading the message board, it is clear, for example, that Participant E has learned a lot from reading the marathon board. Therefore, it appears that lurking was a great help to Participant E. Instead of having to focus on what others were writing about her contributions, she could perhaps focus on the content of what was being written, thereby learning as much as she possibly could from her CoP.

Not all boards are as supportive as the marathon board. One board in particular is known for sparking controversy. This particular board is meant to be a resource for those who have questions about the program. Therefore, there is a good mix of newbies and more experienced users. Problems often arise on this board because newbies typically do not identify themselves as such, so, instead of other, more experienced users gently reminding them of the program and website rules, these more experienced people tend to become aggressive and assume that the contributor is purposefully flouting the rules and norms. There are rules about what types of weight loss information can be posted, and these rules are listed on a separate page of the website. Based on a close reading of postings from the past year, it seems reasonable to suggest that few people actually read these rules. Instead, they are instructed about the rules as they post each time. This instruction can get aggressive and abrupt, as in the following exchange (Excerpt 16):

Excerpt 16.

Good morning everyone:
I am back on the X plan after a few months of being on Y and ganing 5 lbs. I realized it was not working for me..
But I have a question..
I wanted to know how many "things" is it for 1/2 cup of cereal that has 60 calories 1 gram of fat and 14 grams of fiber.
I am a bit confused on counting "things" after the fiber count is 4 grams or more..
I would really appreciate the help.
thanks...

The contributor refers to "things," which is a way of asking about "points," the weight management company's way of referring to calorie and fiber count of food. Participants are not allowed to ask for points information nor are others allowed to give feedback on the number of points a food has. So, this participant asks for "things" which is technically not breaking a rule; however, other contributors seem annoyed at this request. The first response to this request is somewhat friendly: "<-------there is a point calculator right over there."[7] The next contributor tries to be a bit friendlier and states, "Not for people without eTools, there's not.

That being said, we can't give out points. We can however tell you that fiber doesn't count past 4 grams." At this point, one contributor becomes very annoyed and suggests that the user carry her paper calculator (slider) with her (Excerpt 17).

Excerpt 17.

What's a thing? You obviously know we can't post points here.
As Gigg said, the points calculator is right there on the left of the screen if you're an onliner or have e-Tools. If you're not either I suggest you carry your slider with you so you can calculate points.

---

7.   The website is open to all, even those who are not registered for the weight loss program. However, the company provides special access to registered users and this special access allows registered users to see and use a points calculator.

It is clear that the contributor above knows exactly what a "thing" is, but refuses to play along. She ends up giving advice (Excerpt 18), but it is not done in the most supportive fashion; she seems to be scolding the original contributor ("I suggest you carry your slider with you…").

Excerpt 18.

No matter what the fiber count is, we can only use 4 as our highest number. So if you ate cereal with 10g of fiber, you will use the number 4 on your slider to calculate your points. 15g = 4 fiber, 4g = 4 fiber, 20g = 4 fiber……..

This person tries to be friendly and explain the points calculation and how to do it. This type of contribution is typically forbidden since it reveals points calculations (Excerpt 19).

Excerpt 19.

Next post: 4 is the maximum grams of fiber used for calculating points. And you can use the word points. You just can't post points values.
Whether an item has 4, 14 or 40 grams of fiber, 4 is the limit. The calculator and slider automatically stop at that point.

This contributor offers her own solution, then explains that one can use the word "points." The problem is posting points values.

As stated earlier, few users read the rules and regulations of the message board, so posting points values happens on a daily basis, and there are just a few experts who monitor this type of rule-breaking.

5.2   Dog ownership

The second message board is one for owners of giant and large breed dogs.[8] In general, the message board participants are extremely supportive of one another. Rarely is there animosity or an unkind message. Typically, this particular website is used by dog owners to share information about their dogs. Some topics cover nutrition and exercise, while others cover personal stories and questions specific to one particular dog and dog owner. Recently, however, a dog owner posted his thoughts about pit bulls who had been rescued from Michael Vick's house during

---

8.   The difference between giant and large breed dogs is a technical distinction established by the American Kennel Club (AKC).

the spring of 2007.[9] Though the incident occurred in 2007, the Vick situation was presented in a National Geographic Channel special in late 2008. The topic is introduced with a thought-provoking question in the subject line: "Topic: Mike Vicks pits....will they ever be safe to have as a family pet?" The contributor then begins the topic by suggesting that she is bored and wants to read what other dog owners think about the Vick situation (Excerpt 20).

Excerpt 20.

I'm bored........you bored? Lets talk about this show I saw.......
So last night I watched the National Geo. show on the Mike Vicks pits.
Although I must say that they have come along way......do you think they will ever safe to have as a family dog?
(untimately, I think they will always have a "tricky trigger" so my answer is no)
Do you think the prospective forever family would try and make a buck by exploiting the fact that they have one of these dogs? (stranger things has brought a buck in the door) Would you trust anyone in your circle of friends or family to have one of these dogs? (not me)

Of note in this original post is that the contributor appears to want other people's thoughts and views on the situation. Instead of asking the questions and waiting for answers, she answers immediately. Although there is nothing against the rules about this tactic, one could wonder if it influences future responses.

The next response is a seemingly emotional one in which the author says that, because the dogs had to go through "temperament testing" they will "be good family pets." The same author states, "...yes, I believe 100% that they can be good family pets...I would trust anyone at all in my family & friends that owned one..." This participant then asks the original contributor, "is it just Vick's American Pits or is the breed in general that you do not trust?" The original contributor never answers that question. At that point in the message thread, there are a few short, condensed answers ("I agree 100%. I would definitely own one!"). The longer, more detailed answers in the thread seem to be less emotional and more based in either fact (what was presented in the media or in the National Geographic program) or in the individual contributor's experiences (Excerpt 21):

Excerpt 21

I would have no problems owning one of his dogs or having a friend or neighbor own one. I saw a show on his dogs as well, although it was on Animal Planet. Out of the 20

---

9. For background on this dog fighting scandal, readers can visit the following URL: http://www.washingtonpost.com/wp-dyn/content/article/2007/07/17/AR2007071701393.html

odd dogs that were taken, only 2 had to be put down........one for its aggression, and one for an illness...one of them is a therapy dog and visits people in hospitals. Many (if not all, can't remember) of the others went to the BadRap organization...These dogs did not go to just anyone. And I believe they all went thru training courses with the new owners.
And a "tricky trigger" for what? Going after other dogs? Since they all went thru temperment testing prior to being released for adoption...... ....they are no more likely than any other dog on the street.

This contributor explains what he understood to be the facts. Then, he asks more questions, all of which seem to be a bit condescending and are never answered by the original contributor.

Another contributor tries to explain that just because the dogs are aggressive does not necessarily mean that they will do damage to someone or something (Excerpt 22).

Excerpt 22.

Keep in mind that some of those dogs never even saw a fight ring. They were too young, or scheduled to be used as bait dogs.
So they are dog agressive...so what. My dobie was dog agressive and just as large and strong and bloody minded as a fighting pit. We didn't take her to off[-]leash parks and took steps to avoid contact with other dogs on even a casual basis. She was a wonderful family dog and I raised my daughter with her only using the same restrictions as with any other dog. She deserved to live out her life in a happy home just as much as Vick's former dogs.

This post is fascinating because most dog owners recognize that dogs are social animals. They are meant to live in packs and behave within the constraints, rules and norms of the pack. Therefore, removing a dog from contact with other dogs seems a bit unnatural. To this message contributor, though, it was normal, safe behavior.[10] Many dog owners who have "dog aggressive" dogs (those that are aggressive only with other dogs) attempt to have the dog work with a dog trainer so that the trainer can teach the dog how to be less "dog ag-gressive." Such behavior is typically not appreciated and should be dealt with immediately. It seems reasonable to suggest that her doberman deserved to live out her life in happiness. However, removing her from contact with other dogs

---

10. Having observed many irresponsible dog owners in the world, I am glad that this particular person understood her dog's limitations and made appropriate accommodations for her dog. Her responsibility is certainly appreciated and respected.

could be considered controversial and even detrimental to the dog's development and socialization.

The rest of the messages support the idea of allowing the dogs to live with new owners and giving them a second chance at a life. Once several posts have been made, the original contributor offers the following response (Excerpt 23) after her message had been accidentally erased:

Excerpt 23.

…first I want to **stress** that I'm also very glad that the dogs were removed from taht situation and not put dowm. With that I'll stop and think more on my next post before I time out again…

The experts in this community demonstrate their expertise by the amount of facts they provide. They also explain the sources of their facts. It is difficult to determine from this exchange if the original contributor, Darlene, is a newbie or a more experienced user. However, although this message board tends to be much more supportive than some of the weight loss company's message boards, there is still some difference of opinion surrounding the Michael Vick controversy. All of the contributors state that they would indeed take in one of these rescued pit bulls. Future research might benefit from an examination of another message board that might have pit bulls as a topic of discussion in order to understand the extent and type of interaction between CoPs.

6.   Implications for foreign/second language curriculum

The previous analysis and examination is important for the classroom in several ways. First, it is quite clear that a CoP can be created and maintained in an online communication environment. For learners who are perhaps timid in person, they can experiment with new linguistic forms online, where the consequences of face-threatening acts are often greatly reduced or simply non-existent.

Second, because message boards are often archived and classified by date, learners can follow and/or read previous posts in chronological order or reverse chronological order. This reading gives them the context they need to contribute appropriately. Additionally, they can examine online language conventions like chat language, greeting and leave-taking styles, and styles of self-presentation. They can read how much personal information other participants provide, which can also contribute to their pragmatic development.

Third, computer-mediated communication can permit further and deeper engagement with the language and its speakers. That is, learners can perhaps meet interlocutors online and develop friendships that might foster the development of both communicative competence and cultural awareness.

Finally, teachers can guide students through the message board posting process. They can draw students' attention to the various linguistic conventions used. This examination can be a spring board to deeper linguistic analysis of the second language.

The two questions provided below serve as a model task that will allow students to reflect on the effect(s) the topic of a discussion forum may have on the discourse produced by its participants. The students' hypotheses can be (partially) confirmed or rejected based on what they find during their own analysis of two or more themes in a single discussion forum or different forums.

Question 1. Which discussion forum themes lend themselves to creating two sides or two groups of people who will have strong, differing opinions one way or the other?

A few examples of such topics might be the following:

a.   Treatment of animals (for or against dog fighting, for and against spaying/neutering, and so forth);
b.   Politics (fiscal conservatives vs. fiscal liberals or those favoring minimal government vs. those who would like a bigger, more involved government);
c.   Use of the instant-replay in sports (e.g., American football and tennis) to settle a disputed call by an official;
d.   Potential benefits vs. potential negative effects of certain immunizations; and
e.   PC vs. Mac.

Students could easily create their own list of such topics and then investigate how much of the discourse is related to insulting people with the opposite opinion vs. debating the topic with arguments supported by facts. Discourse analysis at this basic level will allow students to begin understanding that while examining the vocabulary and syntax of postings is certainly important, an analysis of the pragmatic functions of postings will reveal much more about the nature of the discourse beyond the traditional text comprehension type of task.

While Question 1 focuses on discussion forums with potentially adversarial discourse, Question 2 (below) asks students to anticipate topics or themes that could be much less divisive.

Question 2. Which discussion forum themes do not lend themselves to creating two opposing groups with strong, differing opinions about a topic?

A few examples of such topics might be the following:

a.   Baking and cooking (family traditions, recipes, techniques);
b.   Travel (finding good and/or reasonable transportation, lodging, and food; recommendations based on personal experience);
c.   Tips for using computers (connecting peripherals; recovering data from a hard disk; troubleshooting); and
d.   Personal wellness (weight/stress management; meditation; stop-smoking aids).

Students who have already worked on preparing the list for (1) will notice that although there are many topics that could be included in this list, it is not always easy to anticipate which topics might create two opposing sides with starkly different views. For example, although sharing stories of family traditions and recipes might not typically encourage diametrically opposed groups, some people may have rather strong opinions, for example, either for or against the use of sea salt vs. table salt in certain contexts. Therefore, the goal of this task is to have students explore and analyze one or more discussion threads on a topic from the lists in (1) and (2) in order to determine if there is more of a focus on debate of the topic or – as was the case in the weight management forum – a substantial portion of the discourse dedicated to training newbies and creating a supportive environment that attempts to include all members in the CoP.

Although this task focuses on analysis of the discourse, students will inevitably discover many other features (navigational, linguistic, and social) of the discussion forums they choose to explore. As such, they will most likely have a distinct advantage over the unprepared student who might discover a forum and begin participating immediately without taking any time to consider the expected amount and type of content in postings and structures of participation.

7.   Conclusion

CoPs can be created online. The weight loss message board is often a place of instruction in the ways of rules and norms. It is often used as a place of support, suggestions and ideas. Sometimes, users become upset with or annoyed at other users. Overall, though, it is a useful CoP. It is important to become familiar with the message board rules and regulations in order to avoid attacks, insults or reprimands. The dog owner forum tends to focus on support and help. It is often very hard to find messages with animosity or insults. There seem to be few rules (other than no foul language and no advertising of dogs or dog products) and most contributors are respectful and kind.

Forums can be an effective tool for language teachers and language learners. Learners can read and observe various pragmatic conventions used on message boards and become more comfortable with their second language. Teachers can guide their students to certain message boards, allowing their students to be more independent and assertive in their language learning. It is important, though, that both teachers and learners observe the posted message board rules.

References

Block, D. (2003). *The social turn in second language acquisition*. Washington, DC: Georgetown University Press.

Breen, M. (Ed.). (2001). *Learner contributions to language learning*. London: Longman.

Firth, A., & Wagner, J. (1997). On discourse, communication, and (some) fundamental concepts in SLA research. *Modern Language Journal, 81*, 285–300.

Gumperz, J. J. (1982). *Discourse strategies*. Cambridge: Cambridge University Press.

Hall, J. K., Cheng, A., & Carlson, M. (2006). Reconceptualizing multicompetence as a theory of language knowledge. *Applied Linguistics, 27*, 220-240.

Haneda, M. (2006). Classrooms as communities of practice: A reevaluation. *TESOL Quarterly, 40*, 807–817.

Hildreth, P., Kimble, C., & Wright, P. (1998). Computer mediated communications and international communities of practice. *Proceedings of Ethicomp '98*, Erasmus University, The Netherlands, 275–286.

Hildreth, P., Kimble, C., & Wright, P. (2000). Communities of practice in the distributed international environment. *Journal of Knowledge Management, 4*, 27–38.

Kasper, G. (2001). Four perspectives on L2 pragmatic development. *Applied Linguistics, 22*, 502–530.

Kramsch, C., & Whiteside, A. (2007). Three fundamental concepts in second language acquisition and their relevance in multilingual contexts. *Modern Language Journal, 91*, 907–922.

Lafford, B. A. (2007). Second language acquisition reconceptualized? The impact of Firth and Wagner (1997). *Modern Language Journal, 91*, 735–756.

Lave, J., & Wenger, E. (1991). *Situated learning: Legitimate peripheral participation*. Cambridge: Cambridge University Press.

Lueg, C. (2000). Where is the action in virtual communities of practice? *Proceedings of the workshop 'Communication and Cooperation in Knowledge Communities at the German Conference on Computer-Supported Cooperative Work Conference (D-CSCW)*, Munich, Germany. Retrieved July 22, 2008, from http://www staff.it.uts.edu.au/~lueg/abstracts/comm_dcscw00.html

Lueg, C. (2001, September). Newsgroups as virtual communities of practice. Position paper presented for the workshop *Actions and identities in virtual communities of practice*. 7th European Conference on Computer Supported Cooperative Work (ECSW 2001), Bonn,

Germany. Retrieved July 22, 2008, from http://www-staff.it.uts.edu.au/~lueg/abstracts/cop_ecscw01.html

Morita, N. (2004). Negotiating participation and identity in second language academic communities. *TESOL Quarterly, 38,* 573-603.

Swain, M., & Deters, P. (2007). "New" mainstream SLA theory: Expanded and enriched. *Modern Language Journal, 91,* 820–836.

Toohey, K. (1998). "Breaking them up, taking them away": ESL students in Grade 1. *TESOL Quarterly, 32,* 61-84.

Wenger, E. (1998). *Communities of practice: Learning, meaning, and identity.* Cambridge: Cambridge University Press.

The discussion forum as a component of a technology-enhanced Integrated Performance Assessment

Lee B. Abraham and Lawrence Williams

This chapter explores the use of online discussion forums as a component of an Integrated Performance Assessment (IPA) (Adair-Hauck, Glisan, Koda, Swender, & Sandrock, 2006; Glisan, Uribe, & Adair-Hauck, 2007) within a (foreign) language curriculum. First, we examine the linguistic, discursive, and interactional versatility of discussion forums. Next, we describe the background of the IPA and highlight the advantages of integrating discussion forums into a proposed Technology-Enhanced Performance Assessment (TIPA). This chapter presents two models for incorporating the discussion forum into a TIPA as either the interpretive or the interpersonal mode of communication for a theme-based unit on ecology and the environment. An analysis of the discourse in these models also illustrates the linguistic affordances that this online communication environment offers for signaling participants' stance and attitudes through the use of pronouns, verb tense, aspect, and mood. As such, an interpersonal task in a TIPA could expand discourse options (Kramsch, 1985) beyond those that are typically available to students. The TIPA offers a framework that would allow students to participate in these online environments for academic, professional, or personal reasons. Recommendations for integrating a TIPA with offline collaborative tasks are also presented.

1.   Introduction

This chapter expands the model of the Integrated Performance Assessment (IPA) (Adair-Hauck, Glisan, Koda, Swender, & Sandrock, 2006; Glisan, Uribe, & Adair-Hauck, 2007) by including the discussion forum as one of the main components of this alternative to the traditional chapter or unit test (Adair-Hauck et al., p. 360; Glisan et al., p. 42). The discussion forum is an ideal candidate for incorporation into the IPA since the asynchronous nature of this type of online communication and the organization and archiving of messages can allow participants to exploit it immediately as the interpretive mode of communication or, over time, as the interpersonal mode (National Standards for Foreign Language Education Project, 1999, pp. 36–37). Such versatility offers any number of possibilities for incorporating the discussion forum into the existing IPA model as a means for integrating new technologies, literacies, and discourses into the foreign language curriculum, which could foster and facilitate what Van Deusen-Scholl, Frei, and Dixon (2005) refer to as "spiraled interaction" (p. 674).

> In technologically enhanced instruction, spiraled interaction – the dynamic interplay of (a) in-class activities that in part focus on meaning, (b) focus on form as an integral part of scaffolded learning sequences, and (c) online collaborations that have as their primary goal student-constructed representations of knowledge – must become more accepted practice so that research findings in turn can substantiate the incorporation of technology-mediated pedagogy into curricula that firmly reflect insights from SLA (p. 674).

In the same way that instructional tasks – both those that rely on new technologies and those that do not – can form a spiral, then an assessment project such as the IPA should be flexible enough to incorporate a component involving one or more types of computer-mediated communication (CMC).

1.1   Research questions

This chapter is guided by some of the overarching questions that have been posed in the literature as new technologies have gained increased presence across the educational landscape. The first three questions are from Salaberry's (2001) list of "concern[s] about the pedagogical effectiveness of different technologies" (p. 51). The fourth question is taken from Meredith's (1983) "problems to overcome" (p. 429, also mentioned in Salaberry, p. 52)

1. "What technical attributes specific to the new technologies can be profitably exploited for pedagogical purposes? (e.g., coding options specific to each medium)" (Salaberry, p. 51).
2. "How can new technologies be successfully integrated into the curriculum? (e.g., interaction 'with' the computer versus interaction 'around' the computer" (Salaberry, p. 51).
3. "Do new technologies provide for an efficient use of human and material resources? (e.g., use of blackboard vs. overhead projector vs. PowerPoint for presentations)" (Salaberry, p. 51).

4. Will the potential constraints (Meredith, p. 429) promote or discourage the inclusion of the discussion forum in the existing model of the IPA?

1.2   Background

A number of studies have examined linguistic features of discussion forums.[1] Yates (1996) compared the use of modal auxiliaries in asynchronous CMC, spoken, and written corpora. The distribution of modal auxiliaries in asynchronous CMC was similar to that of speech and greater than in writing.[2] Asynchronous CMC also had a greater use of first and second person pronouns than spoken or written discourse. Sotillo and Wang-Gempp (2004) investigated the linguistic and rhetorical characteristics of four online political discussion forums. Similar to Yates, Sotillo and Wang-Gempp observed that first person ("I") and second person singular ("you") were used to a greater extent than first person plural ("we") and third person plural pronouns ("they"). Montero-Fleta, Montesinos-López, Pérez-Sabater, and Turney (2009) examined the presence of spoken features of English, Spanish, and Catalan discourse in political and sports discussion forums. Overall, English-language forum posts consisted of more oral language features than either Catalan or Spanish. English-language political and sports forums had very brief messages, greater dependency on previous messages, and little topic coherence (i.e., greater off-topic posts) than their corresponding Spanish and Catalan forums. Patterns in these English-language forums suggested that "participants are tending to use the asynchronous forum as a synchronous chat" (p. 777).[3]

Other research has focused on the discussion forum in the context of bilingual and multilingual online communities. Androutsopoulos (2007) investigated language choice and code-switching in discussion boards on Web sites specifically designed for migrants from Iran, India, and Greece living in Germany. He identified several factors to account for the use of the home language (Persian, Hindi, Punjabi, Bengali, Greek) or German on the discussion board postings. German seemed to predominate but users often switched to the home language to engage

---

1. See Blattner and Williams (this volume) for an overview of terminology and functionality of discussion forums.

2. Obligation and Necessity: must, need, should, ought; Ability and Possibility: can, could; Epistemic Possibility: may, might; Volition and Prediction: will, shall; Hypothetical: would, should (Yates, p. 42).

3. See Herring (1999) for a detailed discussion of the typical features of synchronous and asynchronous CMC.

in playful language, express greetings, wishes, and to mitigate face-threatening acts. Androutsopoulos suggested that "… factors such as strength of the home language in the repertoire of a user population, the nature of users' relationships, and the discourse genres they engage in are also decisive for the frequency and function of bilingual talk on the Internet" (p. 358). Wodak and Wright (2007) explored the use of languages in a European Union discussion forum. English was the predominant language of the postings, although users contributed posts in other languages, especially when a thread was initiated in a language other than English. Discussion forum participants use a number of rhetorical devices (e.g., rhetorical questions, comparisons, irony) and pragmatic features of argumentation and persuasion (e.g., mitigation, forms of address, praise). "Negotiations and comprises are achieved. There is dialogue. Reference from one posting to another is achieved by connecting issues seen as relevant and related to the everyday experiences and knowledge of the discussants: issues of language policies and a Europe of all regions" (p. 402).

Studies have investigated the use of discussion forums in second language (L2) learning and teaching applying different theories and principles of second of language acquisition.[4] Lamy and Goodfellow (1999) analyzed discussion boards of learners of French and identified three types of exchanges: (1) monologue-type exchange, (2) social conversation, and (3) reflective conversation. They propose that language learning in online environments will best occur when learners engage in reflective conversations with their peers, that is sustained over time, and in which they pay attention to form, and negotiate meaning. Sotillo (2000) found that students who engaged in asynchronous CMC paid more attention to form and that students' discourse was "lengthy and syntactically more complex than that available in synchronous discussions" (p. 104). Other research has demonstrated that discussion forums provided opportunities for learners not only to focus on grammatical forms but also raised their intercultural awareness (Basharina, 2009; Hanna & de Nooy, 2003; Liaw, 2006; Sengupta, 2001; Ware & O'Dowd, 2008).

The findings of a relatively small number of studies investigating the relationship between participation in asynchronous and synchronous CMC, face-to-face discussions, and transferability to L2 oral performance are inconclusive. Abrams (2003) found that asynchronous CMC in German was less effective than synchronous or face-to-face interaction for preparing learners for oral discussions about

---

4. Although a detailed discussion of recent research in synchronous and asynchronous CMC in L2 learning is beyond the scope of this chapter, see Chun (2008) for a comprehensive review. For studies of the use of asynchronous CMC for L2 teacher education, see Arnold & Ducate (2006) and Lord & Lomicka (2007).

topics previously discussed online. The syntactically more complex sentences in asynchronous than in synchronous CMC reported in Hirotani (2009) match those of Sotillo (2000). Learners who produced syntactically more complex discourse in asynchronous CMC also produced syntactically more complex sentences in their oral performance in Japanese (Hirotani, p. 429).

Other research has shown that discussion forums support L2 learners' critical thinking (Weasenforth, Biesenbach-Lucas, & Meloni, 2002) and the development of academic registers (Davis & Thiede, 2000; Montero, Watts, & García-Carbonell, 2007; Van Deusen-Scholl, Frei, & Dixon, 2005).

Taken together, findings of the studies summarized in this section indicate that discussion forums are discursively and interactionally versatile communication environments. Participants can incorporate all the same rhetorical, pragmatic, syntactic, and grammatical devices that are used in both spoken and written discourse, and at the same time, this CMC environment can be shaped as more or less synchronous or asynchronous. Sociolinguistic features of the language can also be used to adjust register or level of formality among topics or within a single thread. Such flexibility of all these features has allowed us to adapt the discussion forum as a component in two different models of the Technology-Enhanced IPA (TIPA). Teachers who decide to use the discussion forum – for the TIPA or other tasks – will almost immediately begin to see many new participation structures and task types that this versatile tool can accommodate for the purposes of both language teaching/learning and communication.

1.3   Organization of the chapter

The next section of this chapter provides an overview of the IPA and possibilities for transforming the original model into a TIPA. The discussion forum is then situated within the TIPA as a component of either the Interpretive Task or the Interpersonal Task. The conclusion provides suggestions for adjusting the TIPA for use in a variety of contexts.

2.   Why use the IPA?

A major advantage of the IPA – all parts of which are centered around a theme – is the use of tasks that are centered around modes of communication (i.e., interpersonal, interpretive, and presentational) instead of the so-called "four skills" (i.e., listening, speaking, reading, writing), which have often been conceptualized as components that can be isolated for curricular, instructional, and assessment-related purposes. According to the National Standards for Foreign Language Education Project (Standards Project) (1999):

> It is obvious in working with the content standards that they encompass much more than the separate skills format outlined in the proficiency guidelines. Teachers will recognize the influence of the guidelines within the standards, particularly in the area of communication. However, in keeping with the attempt to create broadly conceived standards, communication is organized around a framework of interpersonal, interpretive, and presentational modes…rather than carved into separate skill areas of listening, speaking, reading, and writing (pp. 14–15).

Any perspective with the four skills as components that can be isolated risks placing the primary focus on language systems and linguistic resources – not communication. Such a perspective is undesirable because a language-centric view does not capture the other dimensions of communication, namely the social identities of the participants and the sociocultural contexts in which communicative activity occurs. Emphasizing *communication* might encourage or remind students, teachers, and research alike to (re)frame and (re)imagine the goals of foreign/second *language* learning and teaching in the following way, as stated by Hall (2001):

> [W]hen individuals engage in a communicative activity, they bring with them their own sets of linguistic resources. These resources come with meanings developed from their past uses in other sociocultural contexts. In addition, individuals bring with them their various social identities. Together, individuals work with the meanings embedded in the linguistic resources and their social identities to negotiate their goals and work toward the mutual accomplishment of a particular communicative activity (pp. 6–7).

2.1 Core features of the IPA

This section of the chapter provides an overview of four areas of focus in recent research on language assessment: "(1) the design of performance-based and authentic tests, (2) sharing of performance criteria and exemplars with students before the assessment, (3) the role of feedback in assessment to improve learner performance, and (4) the use of assessment information to improve instruction and learning…" (Adair-Hauck et al., 2006, p. 361; see also Poehner & Lantolf, 2005; Lynch, 2001; McNamara, 2001).

In their discussion on reconceptualizing assessment practices, Adair-Hauck et al. (2006, pp. 361–363) note the following:

> In performance-based assessments, learners use their repertoire of knowledge and skills to create a product or a response, either individually or collaboratively

> (Liskin-Gasparro, 1996). Typically, learners respond to prompts (complex questions or situations) or tasks and there is more than one correct response. (p. 361)

This description illustrates two features of an IPA that are not normally associated with a traditional test. First, the participation structure can be either individual or collaborative in an IPA. Second, students engage in tasks developed to encourage creativity and imagination since there is not only one possible correct response.

Authenticity is also mentioned in this section of the discussion on reconceptualizing assessment practices. Adair-Hauck et al. (2006), citing Wiggins (1998, pp. 23–24), consider an assessment tool to be authentic if, among other things, it allows for an evaluation of "the learner's knowledge and abilities in real-world situations, or those that occur outside of the classroom context" (Adair-Hauck et al., p. 361). Relatedly, an authentic assessment "replicates or simulates the contexts in which adults are 'tested' in the workplace, in civil life, and in personal life; these contexts involve situations that have particular constraints, purposes, and audiences... " (Adair-Hauck et al., p. 361). These features related to authenticity are indeed primary considerations for anyone developing or selecting an assessment tool or a scoring rubric; however, it is also important to remember that teachers and students do not always approach or frame assessments in the same way (see Coughlan & Duff, 1994).

> The basic problem for language testing is that tests are, by their very nature, artificial contexts for language use. As Spolsky points out, a test-taker is always being asked primarily to display knowledge and skills, and therefore test interaction follows different rules from nontest interaction, and can never be totally authentic as an example of nontest behaviour (Spolsky, 1985). In fact, for assessment to be valid and reliable it is necessary that assessees understand and abide by the norms governing test-taker behaviour, as well as those governing the surface discourse event used for the test.   (Spence-Brown, 2001, p. 464)

These cautionary remarks by Spence-Brown stem from her study (similar to an IPA) of a "teaching and assessment activity based around interviewing native speakers [of Japanese] outside the classroom, which was designed to optimize authenticity" (p. 463). The analysis of Spence-Brown's case studies demonstrated that even when a project is clearly explained to students and specifically includes an opportunity to engage in authentic communication, "the students' own framing of the task was much more influential in determining specifically what occurred" (pp. 467–468).

In addition to other features that characterize authentic assessments, Adair-Hauck et al. mention the following: "Of additional assistance to learners in demystifying performance expectations is seeing exemplars or models of the performance expected, together with the rubrics" (p. 362). From our perspective, the

Internet greatly expands the range of available exemplars and models of authentic, beyond-the-classroom communication. The key here is to share exemplars and criteria with students *prior to* the assessment.

In a traditional model of assessment, feedback might be limited to a score and a general comment (e.g., "This is very good work!"). However, in more recent models, assessment often has greater potential for improving instruction.

> Further support for connecting instruction and assessment is offered through the concept of "dynamic assessment," used in recent research to refer to the type of assessment in which the test examiner (i.e., the teacher) intervenes in order to help the test taker improve test performance, in similar ways to how the teacher guides learners in their individual zones of proximal development (ZPDs) in the classroom (Poehner & Lantolf, 2003; Vygotsky, 1978).
>
> (Adair-Hauck, 2006, pp. 362–363)

As a framework in which instruction and assessment are not viewed as mutually exclusive, but rather "dialectically integrated as a single activity that seeks to understand development by actively promoting it" (Poehner, 2007, p. 323), dynamic assessment (DA) holds great potential for the IPA, which highlights ongoing feedback during the interrelated tasks as one of its core features.

Although the IPA seems well suited for use within the theoretical framework of DA, some teachers may have concerns when considering a model involving instruction and assessment as a single activity. The first of these is related to the practical matter of classroom management:

> For instance, a major challenge to implementing DA concerns the feasibility of dialogic interaction when classroom teachers may see dozens or even hundreds of learners.... This approach entails mediating the group as its members cooperatively engage in activities. Individual learners no doubt experience their own difficulties and can be expected to contribute differently, but mediating the group not only moves the group's ZPD forward but also promotes the development of individuals (see Poehner & Lantolf, 2005, for further discussion).
>
> (Poehner, 2007, p. 338; see also Poehner, 2009)

Referring specifically to asynchronous CMC, Poehner (personal communication, Mar. 10, 2009) observes the following:

> [T]here might be an advantage to offering mediation through something such as an online discussion forum, where the mediation would be simultaneously available to all learners. It might not be directly relevant to some of them (i.e., they might not need it or it might not be explicit enough for them to respond to), but it does offer the possibility that the mediation might benefit a subset of the learners rather than one at a time.

Given that instruction and assessment are viewed as a unified activity in the DA framework, its implementation may also face some resistance from parents, students, teachers, or administrators who are either against change in general or in cases that would involve a substantial re-framing and re-formulation of policies and paradigms, especially if additional time and energy were required for training. Nonetheless, even for schools or teachers who do not wish to make an abrupt change of the entire curriculum, there is always the possibility of incorporating DA into one or more of the tasks in the IPA on a pilot basis. Poehner (personal communication, Mar. 10, 2009) explains that

> improving performance during assessment is a common byproduct of DA but is not the goal. DA proceeds from the premise that a person's independent performance (as is usual in assessment) is important because it reveals the development that has occurred up to the present point in time, but that this is insufficient for fully understanding individuals' abilities. Through interaction in which mediation is offered to help individuals extend their performance beyond what they can do independently, one gains insights into abilities that have not yet fully developed but are still forming. So, in this sense, DA attempts to provide a broader and more nuanced diagnosis. However, at the same time, the mediation that is offered during DA can impact their development. That is, the mediation essentially performs an instructional function, targeting abilities that haven't quite developed yet, and helping them along. This is the basis for the idea that the [zone of proximal development] compels us to think about teaching and assessment as an integrated activity.

Further discussion of DA is beyond the scope of this chapter; however, readers should consult Poehner (2008) for a comprehensive guide to DA, including recommendations for implementing its principles in L2 classrooms. A related resource is *Dynamic Assessment: A teacher's guide* (Lantolf & Poehner, 2007), a DVD-ROM (including video, video texts, examples, and analyses of case studies) available from the Center for Advanced Language Proficiency Education and Research[5] (CALPER) at The Pennsylvania State University.

2.2   Modes of communication

The first mode of communication identified in the Standards Project (1999) is the interpersonal mode, which is "characterized by active negotiation of meaning among individuals. Participants observe and [evaluate] one another to see how their meanings and intentions are being communicated. Adjustments and

---

5.   http://calper.la.psu.edu/dyna_assess.php

clarifications can be made accordingly" (p. 36). The Standards Project lists three aspects of cultural knowledge associated with this mode (p. 37):

1. "Knowledge of cultural perspectives governing interactions between individuals of different ages, statuses, backgrounds"
2. "Ability to recognize that languages use different practices to communicate"
3. "Ability to recognize that cultures use different patterns of interaction"

The second mode of communication in the Standards Project (1999) is the interpretive mode: "The Interpretive Mode is focused on the appropriate cultural interpretation of meanings that occur in written and spoken form where there is no recourse to the active negotiation of meaning with the writer or the speaker" (p. 36). Consequently, and unfortunately, communicative activity associated with this mode has often been perceived as simply reading or listening in a one-way, almost passive, manner. Instead, as Kern (2000) explains, "reading [like listening and viewing] is not simply an act of absorbing information, but a communicative act that involves creating discourse from text" (p. 107). The Standards Project lists several aspects of cultural knowledge associated with this mode (p. 37):

1. "Knowledge of how cultural perspectives are embedded in products (literary and artistic)
2. "Knowledge of how meaning is encoded in products"
3. "Ability to analyze content, compare it to information available in own language and assess linguistic and cultural differences"
4. "Ability to analyze and compare content in one culture to interpret U.S. culture"

It is clear from these aspects of cultural knowledge associated with the interpretive mode of communication that listening, reading, and viewing involve processes that are not passive, but instead quite dynamic.

The third mode of communication outlined in the Standards Project (1999) is the presentational mode, which "refers to the creation of messages in a manner that facilitates interpretation by members of the other culture where no direct opportunity for the active negotiation of meaning between members of the two cultures exists" (p. 38). For the presentational mode of communication, it is once again important to understand that although there is no direct or simultaneous negotiation of meaning involved in the types of communicative activity normally associated with, for example, giving a presentation or writing a report, the presentational mode does indeed involve dynamic processes. "If reading involves creating discourse from texts, writing involves designing texts to create a potentiality for that realized discourse. Like reading, writing involves the use of Available Designs … as resources in a dialogic negotiation between internal and external representations of meaning" (Kern, 2000, p. 171; see also New London Group, 1996). The Standards Project lists three aspects of cultural knowledge associated with this mode (p. 37):

1. "Knowledge of cultural perspectives governing interactions between a speaker and his/her audience and a writer and his/her reader"
2. "Ability to present crosscultural information based on background of the audience"
3. "Ability to recognize that cultures use different patterns of interaction"

3.   Two models for the Technology-Enhanced IPA (TIPA)

In this section, we present two models for using the discussion forum as a component of the TIPA. Our aim is not to suggest that a technology-enhanced version of the IPA is somehow better or more appropriate for all educational contexts. Instead, we explore some of the affordances that new technologies offer to the IPA as a way of expanding the original model. For the purposes of this chapter, the exact instructions for tasks are less important than the possibilities we share regarding the flexibility of the discussion forum to facilitate the Interpretive Task or the Interpersonal Task. Likewise, although we provide models for tasks with two different modes of communication, we view the discussion forum as primarily suitable for the interpersonal mode of communication, even if it can also be used to varying degrees for interpretive (or possibly even presentational) communication.

Why is the discussion forum so flexible? The answer to this is quite simple. This new type of online communication environment has some features of each mode of communication. However, this should not actually be too surprising since many types of communicative events and contexts involve some interpretation, some presentation, and some interpersonal interaction. Consider, for example, the fax machine, which can be used to send unsolicited advertisements, legal contracts, birthday greetings, and so forth. Prior to sending a fax, it is necessary to engage in the presentational mode of communication (using a written form, in this case). Then, the receiver will use the interpretive mode of communication. At what point does this exchange become interpersonal? It all depends on what the interlocutors do. The technology itself does not determine how they will use the fax machine. The participants decide how they will frame the communicative activity, which might actually only involve – at some point – the interpersonal mode for one of the participants while the other one no longer has interest in exchanging faxes (e.g., to negotiate meaning, edit the same document, request additional information, etc.), for whatever reason. The same holds for e-mail, the discussion forum (see Montero-Fleta, Montesinos-López, Pérez-Sabater, & Turney, 2009), voice mail, and many types of communication. Thus, analogously to the position taken by Garcia and Jacobs (1999) that synchronous chat is actually quasi-synchronous, an argument can easily be made that, depending on the participants' framing of the communicative activity, asynchronous forums are quasi-asynchronous within a perspective that views synchronicity on a continuum. Such a view that recognizes the fluidity of synchronicity allows great flexibility for the use of the discussion forum as part of the TIPA.

The type of discussion forum we recommend for the Interpretive Task is a relatively recent variation of this type of online communication environment. This newer type of forum shares many features of a blog, yet it retains the essential features of a forum, namely its ability for interaction and its topic-centric nature. This new type of forum (elaborated below in Section 3.1), has as its point of departure a relatively long text, usually in the form of an article. In fact, this type of forum structure has now become commonplace on the websites of most news outlets (e.g., *Los Angeles Times*, *Le Monde*, *El País*), which allow readers to post comments and opinions about news articles and the issues mentioned in the articles. Essentially, the author of the article – in the online version of the newspaper/media outlet – publishes his or her piece as the initial turn of the thread. In the older, more standard type of forum (see Section 3.2), the initial posting can also be quite long, but the discussion thread can usually be initiated by anyone.

Both forum types are nonetheless similar regarding the presence of a topic or theme. Although news outlets publish articles on many topics every day, there is never a guarantee that a specific topic will appear in any of these articles. However, a common feature on media outlet websites is a navigational tool in the left or right margin (or below the story, in the case of *El País*) indicating to readers which other articles might interest them based on the way in which maintainers of the website have linked articles with similar topics. The dynamic nature of the website allows readers to access articles (which have become like forums on these sites) that are linked thematically instead of both spatially and thematically.

3.1   The discussion forum for the Interpretive Task

The forum we have chosen as an example of the type that could be used for the Interpretive Task is part of a website housed on a server in Argentina: Eco Portal.[6] In Spanish, *eco* is an abbreviated form of the adjective *ecológico(-ca)*, which is a

---

6.   http://www.ecoportal.net/

part of the full name of the site: *el directorio ecológico y natural.* In the main area of this site, several articles on environmental issues are featured, and links to recent articles are also displayed. Readers who click on a link to any story will notice the phrase *Comente este artículo,* which indicates that readers can post comments about the article. As mentioned above, this feature is one that is now available on many news and media websites of all sizes, and the amount of participation varies from site to site, for any number of reasons. The Eco Portal site, for example, receives over 350,000 hits (i.e., visits) per month, and over 100,000 people have subscribed to the weekly newsletter distributed by e-mail. However, there is little – if any – noticeable interaction among visitors via the Comment function of the articles. The apparently low quantity of comments may also have something to do with the fact that at least one new article seems to be published every day, and as new articles appear, older articles within the main area of the welcome page are moved to the archives of the site, where each article is just one of a large number of links to older articles. Nonetheless, this can still be considered a forum that simply has an article about the environment as the first posting of a new discussion thread. This combination of large amounts of information, yet little activity, makes Eco Portal an excellent site for introducing a Spanish-language forum to students as part of the Interpretive Task.

This discussion forum – or any other one like it – is ideal for this type of task because the forum is actually embedded within the larger context of a website, which creates – to some extent – the linguistic and thematic support structure for this communication space. In many ways, using this type of material as the source for the Interpretive Task could provide a distinct advantage over an offline source such as a photocopied article that is distributed to the class or even a documentary on DVD, yet we are certainly not criticizing the use of photocopies or DVDs because the affordances or constraints of an offline or online media may be more appropriate for a particular task. Since the Eco Portal forum is one component among many on this website, students would also have access to the *glosario ambiental* [glossary of terms related to environmental issues], *enlaces* [links], and information about various advertising campaigns designed to make the public more aware of environmental issues. All these sources provide different types of information in different formats, and they could easily be used by students while they work on an Interpretive Task based on this forum.

Depending on students' level of familiarity with this topic, an initial task (or part of a task) including the text in the navigation areas of the website and, possibly, one of the articles could involve the Comparisons goals, specifically Standard 4.1. "Students demonstrate understanding of the nature of language through comparisons of the language studied and their own" (Standards Project, 1999, p. 58). We recommend a task that requires students to distinguish between true and false cognates taken from different areas of the main page or elsewhere in the site as a way to force students to begin exploring the site by looking for these cognates used in context. This is somewhat different from simply asking students to identify words they do not know or recognize; in such a task, students would risk skipping too many false cognates. If students are given a list of all – or most – potential false cognates, they are required to check each word, but more importantly, they have an opportunity to realize that not all words that appear to be cognates are necessarily true cognates.

If students are already online, they could work on a more global task that would require them to find and compare the official environment-related website of a particular government (e.g., Argentina, Uruguay, Chile, the U.S., Canada, European Union) or non-governmental organization, for example, in order to find information in texts about an item or product, such as water, milk, camels, bicycles, tungsten, gold, and so forth. This task would require students to work toward a goal of one of the Cultures standards, specifically Standard 2.2: "Students demonstrate an understanding of the relationship between the products and perspectives of the cultures studied" (Standards Project, 1999, p. 51). For this part of a task, students could compare, for example, views on water conservation found on the Eco Portal forum to those that have been made available on the website of any government that the student would like to investigate.

This section has provided only a few ideas for using a discussion forum to facilitate the interpretive mode of communication. Regardless of the actual task designed for students, it is perhaps most important to remember three main recommendations for the use of the IPA (or the TIPA). First, the tasks are interrelated, designed around a common theme so that these three tasks fit together as a single project. Second, useful feedback is an essential component throughout every step of the process. Third, in addition to the Communication standards, part of the task should touch at least one other goal elaborated in the Standards Project (1999).

3.2   The discussion forum for the Interpersonal Task

The type of forum we recommend for the interpersonal mode of communication as part of the TIPA is a more traditional discussion forum that allows participants to begin new threads[7] (i.e., strands with the same information in the "subject" line of the posting). This is slightly different from the Eco Portal forum, in which

---

7.   In this forum, like others, participants simply click on the link *nuevo tema* in order to create a posting with a new subject line, which would constitute a new thread.

an article posted by the website's owners or maintainers serves as the first thread of every conversational thread or strand. The sample forum for the Interpersonal Task is *Cambio climático y energía*, which is one area of a site (i.e., a microsite or minisite) on climate change and energy[8] within the Debate Europe[9] section of the European Union's web portal.[10] Like Eco Portal, this Debate Europe forum is embedded within a webpage with navigational tools and links to content such as F.A.Q. [Frequently Asked Questions or *Preguntas frecuentes*]; *Buscar* [Search]; *Perfil* [Profile], which allows users to create a profile; and so forth.

Excerpts EU1 through EU4 (below) are the first four postings of the thread "hidrogeno es el presente y futuro" [hydrogen is the present and the future] from December 2008. In these excerpts, conjugated verbs have been marked in italics, and first-person verbs have also been underlined. No grammatical or typographical errors have been corrected, neither has punctuation been altered. These excerpts have not been translated because the limited analysis presented below does not involve a typical reading comprehension task.

These four postings show different ways of presenting ideas that can either be one's own or those of others, and all four messages have conjugated verbs that follow this general pattern. Second-person pronouns are noticeably absent. In Excerpt EU1, it is clear from the beginning of the message that MSM is posting a strong personal belief or opinion. This is seen in the use of *Creo firmemente que …* [I firmly believe that …]. The use of a verb of belief/opinion establishes the statements that follow as part of MSM's own plan and recommendations regarding climate change and energy conservation. The use of first-person singular is then extended to first-person plural in the second paragraph of the posting. This can have the effect of including the reader/interpreter and the writer/presenter of the message in the same cause, or this can at least suggest to the reader that he or she can be part of this movement promoting the use of hydrogen. An inventory of all the conjugated verbs reveals that, apart from a few first-person forms, the author uses primarily the third person (singular and plural). Since most of these third-person verbs are in the conditional, the reader might also interpret this to include hypothetical or idealistic statements. An overview of pronouns and verbs (mood, tense, aspect) is often a useful way to begin looking at discourse in any communication environment because these features can provide important insights into agency, identity, perspective, social indexicality, stance, and so forth (Dafouz, Núñez, & Sancho, 2004; D'Ambrosio, 2004; Davidson, 1996; Garnham, Oakhill, Ehrlich, & Carreiras, 1995;

---

8. http://europa.eu/debateeurope/climate-change/index_es.htm

9. http://europa.eu/debateeurope/index_es.htm

10. http://europa.eu/index_es.htm

Mejías-Bikandi, 2009; Mühlhäusler & Harré, 1990; Palmer, 1986; Reilly, Zamora, & McGivern, 2005; Thibault, 2004; Tolchinsky & Rosado, 2005).

Excerpt EU1. Posting from MSM, EU Climate forum.

Publicado: Mar Ago 12, 2008 4:58 pm
Título del mensaje: hidrogeno es el presente y futuro

Creo firmemente que los Europeos *podrian* tener un estandar comun de estaciones de hidrogeno y que *deberian* de pensar en tenerlas instaladas ya por todas las autovias, autopistas haciendo un proyecto comun y unico de abastecimiento para vehiculos de transporte, turismos, furgonetas, buses, camiones.

Y todo *seria* tan facil como dar empleo a los parados europeos que *engrosan* nuestras filas del paro, *deberian* aparte dar ayudas a la industria automobilistica y forzar ya el diseño, comercializacion en masa y puesta en circulacion de coches de hidrogeno. Cuanto mas euros *dediquemos* en ese sentido todos juntos a ese proyecto, antes *terminaremos* con las dudas y problemas.

Potenciar mucho mas el sector eolico y solar.

BLINDAR esas empresas ante compras o opas del extranjero.

AUTOCARAVANS de hidrogeno ya!!!

In Excerpt EU2, there is a clear difference regarding the type and placement of the only first-person verb form in this message, compared to EU2. The majority of the message, until the last line, present facts in the third person, and verbs are either in a past form of the indicative to explain what has been done or a form of the future, indicating what will be done. Almost the entire message is very factual since the writer's goal seems only to make readers aware of the progress being made on various projects. In other words, this provides a good model for students who are preparing a rather neutral message with little or no personal opinions or beliefs stated directly. In this message, for example, only one verb is in the conditional, which is often used to give advice, as is done here.

Excerpt EU2. Posting from PCA, EU Climate forum.

Publicado: Mar Ago 12, 2008 10:21 pm
Título del mensaje: [No message title provided.]

La Universidad de Florida Atlantic *ha puesto en marcha* un projecto de turbinas marinas para sacar hidrogeno, electricidad y calor-vapor … .

esto *se puede instalar* en todo la Costa Atlantica desde Bilbao (con corrientes y oleaje masivo de 20 metros de altura) hasta La Linea , toda la costa Atlantica *es* una fuente de energia con turbinas de todo tipo descomunal, la fabricacion de estas turbinas y montaje de tendido electrico, partes y servicio *va a ser* un negocio de muy alto volumen, ya de turbinas de viento *hay* problemas de suministro de piezas de precision, y el cable electrico submarino y terrestre a redes *esta siendo acaparado* por 3 empresas, pues ya *ven* que para 2014 *habra* una demanda muy grande y el pais que este dentro se beneficiara, el que no *se quedara* sin ninguna parte del negocio, los politicos *deberian* ver la importancia de entrenamiento y fabricacion de piezas, ahora!

ademas la distribucion de hydrogeno, que ahora *acaparan* con experiancia Islandia y Canada con Ballard FuelCells (que ahora *han comprado* G. M. y Mercedes Benz), tambien *va a necesitar* entrenamiento masivo.

los avances de la Universidad Complutense y U. Politecnica con fuel-cells en Madrid *son* importantisimos, <u>esperemos</u> que *reciban* todo lo necesario para avanzar con rapidez.

Excerpt EU3. Posting from MDS, EU Climate forum.

Publicado: Jue Oct 23, 2008 5:34 pm
Título del mensaje: [*No message title provided.*]

Tal vez, el hidrogeno no *sea* una solución viable para el medio ambiente.

<u>*Invito*</u> a que investiguen el consumo de energía bajo los métodos actuales de obtención de hidrogeno.

Es decir, validar el impacto ecológico y ambiental de la producción de grandes cantidades de hidrogeno bajo los métodos actuales, ya que este *seria* mayor al impacto generado por el uso y producción de hidrocarburos.

Si todos los transportes y maquinas que *utilizan* destilados del petróleo *cambiaran* y *utilizaran* hidrogeno, el efecto ambiental *seria* igual o mayor.

Esto sin considerar las plantas generadoras de energía eléctrica basadas en subproductos petrolíferos o carbón.

Por favor si les *es* posible comprobar quien y como *se obtendría* las masivas cantidades de hidrogeno que *se requerirían* para sustituir al petróleo y lo más importante si estos metodos realmente *reducirian* la contaminación y efectos negativos ambientales.

The posting from GA, reproduced as Excerpt EU4, is the last message in this thread, and it is the first one to provide a comment/reaction linked directly to a previous posting. It seems that the first four messages in this thread were intended to provide information on the topic in general, as if remaining for some time in the presentational mode of communication; however, once this fourth message is posted, the forum begins to take shape as a more interactive online discussion in the interpersonal mode of communication, a true exchange of ideas and opinions. As mentioned above, the lack of second-person pronouns seems almost strange. However, this thread is very short, yet the students should be asked to identify at least one way in which there is some type of contact (either direct or indirect) between two or more of the participants. Two possible answers are the following: (1) the use of the same subject line; and (2) selecting the option to quote a previously posted message. These two affordances of this new type of communication tool effectively allow participants to create a relationship between their messages even when they do not use direct forms of address, such as second-person pronouns. Of course this is more visually obvious on line, where the forum participant would see the quoted message with a different color of background and text to make it stand out from the newer posting. In Excerpt EU4, the fact that there was a quoted message above the text of this posting is indicated in brackets, which does not create the same visual effect that students might be able recognize immediately.

Excerpt EU4. Posting from GA

Publicado: Mie Dic 03, 2008 9:46 pm
Título del mensaje: Re: hidrogeno es el presente y futuro

[Posting from MSM, Excerpt EU1, is quoted here.]
Es una buena idea, en general. Sin embargo, <u>*entiendo*</u> que la "carbon footprint" del proceso de la fabricación *es* enorme. Quizás con la ayuda de tecnología, esta industria *puede* alcanzar su potencial máximo, sin dañar el planeta!.

Such a thread with a relatively low amount of activity would be ideal for learners to engage in discussion since it seems that most participants have chosen to read the postings, yet not comment on or react to them. The ratio of reading/posting is available for all the threads of this forum on the main page. In fact, most threads in this forum appear to have a relatively large amount of *Lecturas* (no. of times viewed) compared to *Respuestas* (no. of postings). A comment from a student might reactivate the interpersonal dimension of this communicative activity. The frequency of postings is important information as students decide if they want to participate in a slow, medium-paced, or busy forum, based on the task and their academic, personal, or professional goals.

Further analysis of these features is beyond the scope of this chapter, and such an overview may be all that some teachers would ask students to undertake, but this will depend on any number of curricular and institutional factors. Readers interested in developing the analysis of pronouns and verbs in more detail should consult the references listed above, which focus primarily on Spanish. For teachers of other languages, it should not be difficult to find published research on pronouns and verbs; likewise, there are many excellent guides to discourse analysis (e.g., Brown & Yule, 1983; Johnstone, 2008).

3.3   Additional comments about the IPA/TIPA

Although we have proposed incorporating CMC into the IPA, there are certain aspects related to using the discussion forum that might not fit within the existing model of the IPA. This does not cause us great concern since the introduction of any type of CMC for any of the tasks would necessarily require some adjustments to the existing model that relies on traditional spoken and written communication. For instance, the IPA advocates *spontaneous* interaction during the Interpersonal Task as opposed to *rehearsed* communication for the Presentational Task. Since there is no specific expectation of spontaneity for discussion forum participants, the communicative event would be different from one involving face-to-face interpersonal communication.

However, this is not problematic from our perspective since our ideal model of the IPA is not one that would posit the use of only a single mode of communication for each task, even if one is given some preference. We favor a model more closely aligned with the one proposed by Kern (2000), in which modes of communication overlap instead of being "typically discrete and sequential, rather than recursive..." (p. 131). Kern explains that reading and writing assignments are often given as homework in order to reserve class meetings for oral tasks, which can lead to the perception that they are somehow more important than reading- and writing-related tasks. "Were reading and writing to be more frequently brought into the mainstream of classroom activity, made to be more collaborative as well as individual activities, more integrated with speaking and with one another, they would perhaps not seem so difficult" (p. 131). Within a framework of communicative language teaching (CLT) (Savignon 1983, 1997, 2001, 2002), no particular skill or mode of communication enjoys a privileged status. "CLT is not concerned exclusively with face-to-face oral communication. The principles of CLT apply equally to reading and writing activities that involve readers and writers engaged in the interpretation, expression, and negotiation of meaning" (Savignon, 2007, p. 213). Consequently, for the TIPA, there could be two options. First, the discussion forum in the TIPA could simply replace the small-group discussion that is often used for the IPA. The second option would include using both a discussion forum and small-group discussion (ideally with spiraling, as mentioned above, between the two types of communication). For either option, we recommend combining the interpretive and interpersonal modes in the first task in order to give students an opportunity to engage in spontaneous communication, either between the whole class and the teacher or within small groups of students. This would make the degree of synchronicity or spontaneity of the discussion forum-based Interpersonal Task irrelevant. Since the tasks are interrelated, students would then choose how to incorporate ideas and information from the Interpersonal Task into the Presentational Task, which could be any type of oral presentation or written essay.

Another potential advantage of the discussion forum as a component of the TIPA is the fact that the interaction is archived and available for the entire class to read. We imagine several different ways to structure the Interpersonal Task. First, following the existing model of the IPA, groups of two or more students could exchange ideas and engage in discussion (via an online forum) as a continuation of the first phase. However, each student could, instead, identify an appropriate (i.e., related to the topic of the TIPA) online forum and engage in an exchange of ideas and opinions with (native or non-native) speakers of the L2 beyond-the-classroom setting.

> CLT does not require small group or pair work; group tasks have been found helpful in many contexts as a way or providing increased opportunity and motivation for communication. However, classroom group or pair work should not be considered an essential feature and may well be inappropriate in some contexts.
> (Savignon, 2007, p. 213)

Regardless of the specific task and its participation structure, the interpersonal communication would be archived for use during the TIPA or at a later point in time since post-task analysis of discourse can promote language learning (Kinginger, 1998; see also Salaberry, 2000, p. 35).

Given the possibility – even likelihood – that at least some students will frame any assessment differently than was intended by the teacher (see above discussion of the study by Spence-Brown, 2001), we also recommend a post-TIPA inquiry of students' perceptions of the tasks. Such an investigation could be achieved either through a survey, interviews with students, or any kind of written summary or reflective essay based on a series of questions provided by the teacher. In the same way that the existing model of the IPA includes a feedback loop between each phase, an analysis of students' framing of the TIPA might allow the teacher to make improvements prior to using it for a later unit or during a subsequent semester or year.

4.   Conclusion

In addition to promoting participation in a variety of communities (Standards Project, 1999, pp. 63–67) beyond the context of the classroom, for academic, personal, or professional enrichment, we see the forum as an excellent means for students to develop a knowledge base that includes a wide range of topics, given the vast array of theme-based forums in so many different languages (see Research

Question 2). The goals related to the Connections standards (Standards Project, pp. 53–36) advocate interdisciplinarity, and students who can communicate in Spanish have opportunities to "acquire information and recognize the distinctive viewpoints that are available only through the Spanish language and its many cultures" (Spanish-specific section of the Standards Project, p. 450).

In order to be useful and effective as part of a TIPA, the discussion forum must be able to accomplish everything that would be expected of a traditional type of communication environment (e.g., face-to-face discussion in class as interpersonal communication or written text as interpretive communication for the IPA) (see Research Question 2). It is especially the case for interpersonal communication that the discussion forum offers greater access to a wider variety of interlocutors, and, by extension, this has the potential for expanding discourse options (Kramsch, 1985) beyond those typically associated with the formal learning environment (see Research Question 1). This does not necessarily imply that the discourse of the classroom is always contextually (i.e., sociopragmatically) impoverished. Kasper and Rose (2002), for example, argue that "[d]ifferent classroom arrangements and their implementation in activities, both teacher-fronted and student-centered, have the potential to provide acquisitionally relevant pragmatic input" (p. 217). Instead of focusing on the constraints of the traditional IPA, we prefer to emphasize the real and potential affordances of the TIPA (see Research Question 1 above).

Since we have already addressed the first two research questions enumerated at the beginning of this chapter, we now turn to Research Questions 3 and 4. These both relate more to the material and physical affordances and constraints than to curricular and pedagogical issues, even though all such issues are – at some level – inextricably linked. If the main advantage of the discussion forum, like other types of CMC, can provide access to a great number of people with whom learners could interact, then it seems clear that CMC is much more efficient (see Research Question 3) than traveling the region or country where each potential interlocutor lives, which does not minimize the enormous potential for learning while traveling and living in places where the L2 is an official or widely used language. Although it would be necessary for students to have an Internet connection at home or school in order to use the discussion forum for the TIPA, this constraint seems to be less and less of an issue with each passing year (see Research Question 4). Whereas it is certainly still true that many households do not have an Internet connection, there seem to be increased efforts in many countries to provide at least a limited number of computers with Internet connections at schools and libraries in addition to the numerous wireless networks that have been installed in many rural parts of various countries where Internet access would not otherwise be possible.

We have proposed an expansion of the IPA as a way to redesign the curriculum by incorporating new and ever-changing communication environments, with a specific focus on the discussion forum. The treatment of the IPA and the TIPA in this chapter is by no means exhaustive. We therefore encourage readers interested in additional sample tasks, assessment rubrics, and other information related to the implementation of the IPA to consult Adair-Hauck et al. (2006) and Glisan, Uribe, and Adair-Hauck (2007). Another important resource is the Integrated Performance Assessment manual (Glisan et al. 2003), published by the American Council on the Teaching of Foreign Languages[11] (ACTFL). Teachers can also find instructional and assessment materials for the use of the IPA for Content-Based Instruction (CBI) in the online manual by Tedick and Cammarata[12] (n.d.) on the website of the Center for Advanced Research on Language Acquisition (CARLA).

References

Abrams, Z. I. (2003). The effect of synchronous and asynchronous CMC on oral performance in German. *Modern Language Journal, 87,* 157–167.

Adair-Hauck, B., Glisan, E., Koda, K., Swender, E., & Sandrock, P. (2006). The Integrated Performance Assessment (IPA): Connecting assessment to instruction and learning. *Foreign Language Annals, 39,* 359–382.

Androutsopoulos, J. (2007). Language choice and code switching in German-based diasporic web forums. In B. Danet & S. Herring (Eds.), *The multilingual Internet: Language, culture, and communication online* (pp. 340–361). Oxford: Oxford University Press.

Arnold, N., & Ducate, L. (2006). Future foreign language teachers' social and cognitive collaboration in an online environment. *Language Learning & Technology 10,* 42–66. Available from http://llt.msu.edu/vol10num1/arnoldducate/

Basharina, O. (2009). Student agency and language-learning processes and outcomes in international online environments. *CALICO Journal, 26,* 390–412.

Brown, G., & Yule, G. (1983). *Discourse analysis.* Cambridge: Cambridge University Press.

Chun, D. M. (2008). Computer-mediated discourse in instructed environments. In S. S. Magnan (Ed.), *Mediating discourse online* (pp. 15–45). Amsterdam: John Benjamins.

Coughlan, P., & Duff, P. A. (1994). Same task, different activities: Analysis of a SLA task from an activity theory perspective. In J. P. Lantolf & G. Appel (Eds.), *Vygotskian approaches to second language research* (pp. 173–194). Norwood, NJ: Ablex.

Dafouz, E., Núñez, B., & Sancho, C. (2007). Analysing stance in a CLIL university context: Non-native speaker use of personal pronouns and modal verbs. *International Journal of Bilingual Education and Bilingualism, 10,* 647–662.

---

11. http://www.actfl.org/

12. http://www.carla.umn.edu/cobaltt/modules/assessment/ipa/index.html

D'Ambrosio, H. D. (2004). Pragmática, sociolingüística y pedagogía de los pronombres de tratamiento en lengua española [The pragmatics, sociolinguistics and pedagogy of Spanish pronouns of address]. *Estudios de Lingüística Aplicada, 22*, 37–52.

Davidson, B. (1996). 'Pragmatic weight' and Spanish subject pronouns: The pragmatic and discourse uses of *tú* and *yo* in spoken Madrid Spanish. *Journal of Pragmatics, 26*, 543–565.

Davis, B., & Thiede, R. (2000). Writing into change: Style shifting in asynchronous electronic discourse. In M. Warschauer & R. Kern (Eds.), *Network-based language teaching: Concepts and practice* (pp. 87–120). Cambridge: Cambridge University Press.

Garcia, A., & Jacobs, J. (1999). The eyes of the beholder: Understanding the turn-taking system in quasi-synchronous computer-mediated communication. *Research on Language and Social Interaction, 32*, 337–367.

Garnham, A., Oakhill, J., Ehrlich, M.-F., & Carreiras, M. (1995). Representations and processes in the interpretation of pronouns: New evidence from Spanish and French. *Journal of Memory and Language, 34*, 41–62.

Glisan, E., Adair-Hauck, B., Koda, K., Sandrock, S. P., & Swender, E. (2003). *ACTFL Integrated Performance Assessment*. Yonkers, NY: ACTFL.

Glisan, E., Uribe, D., & Adair-Hauck, B. (2007). Research on Integrated Performance Assessment at the post-secondary level: Student performance across the modes of communication. *Canadian Modern Language Review, 64*, 39–68.

Hall, J. K. (2001). *Methods for teaching foreign languages: Creating a community of learners in the classroom*. Upper Saddle River, NJ: Prentice Hall.

Hanna, B., & de Nooy, J. (2003). A funny thing happened to me on the way to the forum: Electronic discussion and foreign language learning. *Language Learning & Technology, 7*, 71–85. Available from http://llt.msu.edu/vol7num1/hanna/

Herring, S. (1999). Interactional coherence in CMC. *Journal of Computer-Mediated Communication, 4, 4*, n.p. Retrieved September 1, 1999, from http://jcmc.indiana.edu/ vol4/issue4/ herring.html

Hirotani, M. (2009). Synchronous versus asynchronous CMC and transfer to Japanese oral performance. *CALICO Journal, 26*, 413–438.

Johnstone, B. (2008). *Discourse analysis* (2nd ed.). Oxford: Blackwell.

Kasper, G., & Rose, K. R. (2002). *Pragmatic development in a second language*. Malden, MA: Wiley-Blackwell.

Kern, R. (2000). *Literacy and language teaching*. Oxford, England: Oxford University Press.

Kinginger, C. (1998). Videoconferencing as access to spoken French. *Modern Language Journal, 82*, 502–513.

Kramsch, C. J. (1985). Classroom interaction and discourse options. *Studies in Second Language Acquisition, 7*, 169–183.

Lamy, M.-N., & Goodfellow, R. (1999). Reflective conversation in the virtual language classroom. *Language Learning & Technology 2*, 43–61. Available from http://llt.msu.edu/ vol2num2/article2/

Lantolf, J., & Poehner, M. (2007). Dynamic Assessment: A teacher's guide [DVD]. State College, PA: Center for Advanced Language Proficiency Education and Research, The Pennsylvania State University.

Liaw, M. (2006). E-learning and the development of intercultural competence. *Language Learning & Technology, 10*, 49–64. Available from http://llt.msu.edu/vol10num3/liaw/default.html

Lord, G., & Lomicka, L. (2007). Foreign language teacher preparation and asynchronous CMC: Promoting reflective teaching. *Journal of Technology and Teacher Education, 15*, 513–532.

Lynch, B. (2001). Rethinking assessment from a critical perspective. *Language Testing, 18,* 351–372.

McNamara, T. (2001). Language assessment as social practice: Challenges for research. *Language Testing, 18,* 333–349.

Mejías-Bikandi, E. (2009). Conditional sentences and mood in Spanish. *Journal of Pragmatics, 41,* 163–172.

Meredith, R. (1983). Materials and equipment: The new generation. *Modern Language Journal, 67,* 424–430.

Montero, B., Watts, F., & García-Carbonell, A. (2007). Discussion forum interactions: Text and context. *System, 35,* 566–582.

Montero-Fleta, B., Montesinos-López, A., Pérez-Sabater, C., & Turney, E. (2009). Computer mediated communication and informalization of discourse: The influence of culture and subject matter. *Journal of Pragmatics, 41,* 770–779.

Mühlhäusler, P., & Harré, R. (1990). *Pronouns and people: The linguistic construction of social and personal identity.* Oxford, England: Blackwell.

National Standards for Foreign Language Learning Project. (1999). *Standards for foreign language learning in the 21st century.* Lawrence, KS: Allen Press.

New London Group. (1996). A pedagogy of multiliteracies: Designing social futures. *Harvard Educational Review, 66,* 60–92.

Palmer, F. R. (1986). *Mood and modality.* Cambridge: Cambridge University Press.

Poehner, M. E. (2007). Beyond the test: L2 Dynamic Assessment and the transcendence of mediated learning. *Modern Language Journal, 91,* 323–340.

Poehner, M. E. (2008). *Dynamic assessment: A Vygotskian approach to understanding and promoting L2 development.* Norwell, MA: Springer.

Poehner, M. E. (2009). Group Dynamic Assessment: Mediation for the L2 classroom. *TESOL Quarterly, 43,* 471–491.

Poehner, M. E., & Lantolf, J. P. (2005). Dynamic assessment in the language classroom. *Language Teaching Research, 9,* 233–265.

Reilly, J., Zamora, A., & McGivern, R. F. (2005). Acquiring perspective in English: The development of stance. *Journal of Pragmatics, 37,* 185–208.

Salaberry, M. R. (2000). Pedagogical design of computer mediated communication tasks: Learning objectives and technological capabilities. *Modern Language Journal, 84,* 28–37.

Salaberry, M. R. (2001). The use of technology for second language learning and teaching: A retrospective. *Modern Language Journal, 85,* 39–56.

Savignon, S. J. (1983). *Communicative competence: Theory and classroom practice.* Reading, MA: Addison-Wesley.

Savignon, S. J. (1997). *Communicative competence: Theory and classroom practice* (2nd ed.). New York, NY: McGraw-Hill.

Savignon, S. J. (2001). Communicative language teaching for the twenty-first century. In M. Celce-Murcia (Ed.), *Teaching English as a second or foreign language* (pp. 13–28). Boston, MA: Heinle & Heinle.

Savignon, S. J. (2002). (Ed.). *Interpreting communicative language teaching: Contexts and concerns in teacher education.* New Haven, CT: Yale University Press.

Savignon, S. J. (2007). Beyond communicative language teaching: What's ahead? *Journal of Pragmatics, 39,* 207–220.

Sengupta, S. (2001). Exchanging ideas with peers in network-based classrooms: An aid or a pain? *Language Learning & Technology, 5,* 103–134. Available from http://llt.msu.edu/vol5num1/sengupta/

Sotillo, S. M. (2000) Discourse functions and syntactic complexity in synchronous and asynchronous communication. *Language Learning & Technology, 4,* 82–119. Available from http://llt.msu.edu/vol4num1/sotillo/

Sotillo, S. M., & Wang-Gempp, J. (2004). Using corpus linguistics to investigate class, ideology, and discursive practices in online political discussions. In U. Connor & T. A. Upton (Eds.), *Applied corpus linguistics: A multidimensional perspective* (pp. 91–122). Amsterdam: Rodopi.

Spence-Brown, R. (2001). The eye of the beholder: Authenticity in an embedded assessment task. *Language Testing, 18,* 463–481.

Thibault, P. (2004). *Agency and consciousness in discourse: Self-Other dynamics as a complex system.* London: Continuum.

Tolchinsky, L., & Rosado, E. (2005). The effect of literacy, text type, and modality on the use of grammatical means for agency alternation in Spanish. *Journal of Pragmatics, 37,* 209–237.

Van Deusen-Scholl, N., Frei, C., & Dixon, E. (2005). Co-constructing learning: The dynamic nature of foreign language pedagogy in a CMC environment. *CALICO Journal, 22,* 657–678.

Ware, P., & O'Dowd, R. (2008). Peer feedback on language form in telecollaboration. *Language Learning & Technology, 12,* 43–63. Available from http://llt.msu.edu/ vol12num1/wareodowd/

Weasenforth, D., Biesenbach-Lucas, S., & Meloni, C. (2002). Realizing constructivist objectives through collaborative technologies: Threaded discussions. *Language Learning & Technology, 6,* 58–86. Available from http://llt.msu.edu/vol6num3/weasenforth/

Wiggins, G. (1998). *Educative assessment.* San Francisco, CA: Jossey-Bass.

Wodak, R., & Wright, S. (2007). The European Union in cyberspace: Democratic participation in online multilingual discussion boards. In B. Danet & S. Herring (Eds.), *The multilingual Internet: Language, culture, and communication online* (pp. 385–407). Oxford: Oxford University Press.

Yates, S. J. (1996). Oral and written linguistic aspects of computer conferencing: A corpus based study. In S. C. Herring (Ed.), *Computer-mediated communication: Linguistic, social, and cross-cultural perspectives* (pp. 29–46). Amsterdam: John Benjamins.

Index

In the series *Language Learning & Language Teaching* the following titles have been published thus far or are scheduled for publication:

29 **VERSPOOR, Marjolijn H., Kees de BOT and Wander LOWIE (eds.):** A Dynamic Approach to Second Language Development. Methods and techniques. *Expected January 2011*

28 **PORTE, Graeme Keith:** Appraising Research in Second Language Learning. A practical approach to critical analysis of quantitative research. **Second edition.** 2010. xxv, 307 pp.

27 **BLOM, Elma and Sharon UNSWORTH (eds.):** Experimental Methods in Language Acquisition Research. vii, 292 pp. *Expected October 2010*

26 **MARTÍNEZ-FLOR, Alicia and Esther USÓ-JUAN (eds.):** Speech Act Performance. Theoretical, empirical and methodological issues. 2010. xiv, 277 pp.

25 **ABRAHAM, Lee B. and Lawrence WILLIAMS (eds.):** Electronic Discourse in Language Learning and Language Teaching. 2009. x, 346 pp.

24 **MEARA, Paul:** Connected Words. Word associations and second language vocabulary acquisition. 2009. xvii, 174 pp.

23 **PHILP, Jenefer, Rhonda OLIVER and Alison MACKEY (eds.):** Second Language Acquisition and the Younger Learner. Child's play? 2008. viii, 334 pp.

22 **EAST, Martin:** Dictionary Use in Foreign Language Writing Exams. Impact and implications. 2008. xiii, 228 pp.

21 **AYOUN, Dalila (ed.):** Studies in French Applied Linguistics. 2008. xiii, 400 pp.

20 **DALTON-PUFFER, Christiane:** Discourse in *Content and Language Integrated Learning* (CLIL) Classrooms. 2007. xii, 330 pp.

19 **RANDALL, Mick:** Memory, Psychology and Second Language Learning. 2007. x, 220 pp.

18 **LYSTER, Roy:** Learning and Teaching Languages Through Content. A counterbalanced approach. 2007. xii, 173 pp.

17 **BOHN, Ocke-Schwen and Murray J. MUNRO (eds.):** Language Experience in Second Language Speech Learning. In honor of James Emil Flege. 2007. xvii, 406 pp.

16 **AYOUN, Dalila (ed.):** French Applied Linguistics. 2007. xvi, 560 pp.

15 **CUMMING, Alister (ed.):** Goals for Academic Writing. ESL students and their instructors. 2006. xii, 204 pp.

14 **HUBBARD, Philip and Mike LEVY (eds.):** Teacher Education in CALL. 2006. xii, 354 pp.

13 **NORRIS, John M. and Lourdes ORTEGA (eds.):** Synthesizing Research on Language Learning and Teaching. 2006. xiv, 350 pp.

12 **CHALHOUB-DEVILLE, Micheline, Carol A. CHAPELLE and Patricia A. DUFF (eds.):** Inference and Generalizability in Applied Linguistics. Multiple perspectives. 2006. vi, 248 pp.

11 **ELLIS, Rod (ed.):** Planning and Task Performance in a Second Language. 2005. viii, 313 pp.

10 **BOGAARDS, Paul and Batia LAUFER (eds.):** Vocabulary in a Second Language. Selection, acquisition, and testing. 2004. xiv, 234 pp.

9 **SCHMITT, Norbert (ed.):** Formulaic Sequences. Acquisition, processing and use. 2004. x, 304 pp.

8 **JORDAN, Geoff:** Theory Construction in Second Language Acquisition. 2004. xviii, 295 pp.

7 **CHAPELLE, Carol A.:** English Language Learning and Technology. Lectures on applied linguistics in the age of information and communication technology. 2003. xvi, 213 pp.

6 **GRANGER, Sylviane, Joseph HUNG and Stephanie PETCH-TYSON (eds.):** Computer Learner Corpora, Second Language Acquisition and Foreign Language Teaching. 2002. x, 246 pp.

5 **GASS, Susan M., Kathleen BARDOVI-HARLIG, Sally Sieloff MAGNAN and Joel WALZ (eds.):** Pedagogical Norms for Second and Foreign Language Learning and Teaching. Studies in honour of Albert Valdman. 2002. vi, 305 pp.

4 **TRAPPES-LOMAX, Hugh and Gibson FERGUSON (eds.):** Language in Language Teacher Education. 2002. vi, 258 pp.

3 (1st) **PORTE, Graeme Keith:** Appraising Research in Second Language Learning. A practical approach to critical analysis of quantitative research. 2002. xx, 268 pp.

2 **ROBINSON, Peter (ed.):** Individual Differences and Instructed Language Learning. 2002. xii, 387 pp.

1 **CHUN, Dorothy M.:** Discourse Intonation in L2. From theory and research to practice. 2002. xviii, 285 pp. (incl. CD-rom).